Remembering
Strawberry Fields

A Memoir

Mary E. Matury Gibson

Remembering Strawberry Fields: A Memoir

Published by Wheatmark®
1760 East River Road, Suite 145
Tucson, Arizona 85718 USA
www.wheatmark.com

ISBN: 978-1-62787-181-5
LCCN: 2014953987

For Tommy,
my old pal of yesterday.
I will always love you.

Contents

Preface   vii

1   Sherman Acres   1
2   The Last Child   7
3   The Many Lives and Tales of the Last Child   11
4   The Mystery of Antonia   27
5   School Days in a Land Divided   37
6   Carmella Leaves Home   56
7   Junior High Blues   75
8   Lucy   108
9   The End of Dreams for the Dream Girl   127
10 He Came on a Horse Named Midnight   141
11 1963: The Year That Everything Changed   183
12 Letting Go of Jimmy   235
13 Today I Met the Boy I'm Going to Marry   243
14 Seeing Christ in the Faces of Others   269
15 The Graduate Nurse   283
16 Big-City Woman   308
17 Storm Clouds Gathering   332
18 The Heart Won't Lie   349

Contents

19   Illness: The Great Equalizer   378

20   No Longer Young and No Longer Beautiful   400

21   Still Looking for Jimmy   420

A Note from the Author   *429*

Preface

EVERYONE THINKS THAT HIS or her past life story is something other people will want to know. The promise of a good tale must, however, lie in the telling of it. For the most part, I have loved the recalling of my past life. What I didn't realize when I started was that I would find out so many things about myself that I didn't know—and some I would rather not know. The problem with bringing my past life back to my conscious mind is that I can see things so clearly; I just can't change any of it. Dwelling on what might have been is totally unproductive as well as damaging to the psyche.

"So you are writing a book?" Ann Marie asked. She has been my friend for many years. "I don't know how you do that. I would need to have written notes to myself over the years. I simply do not remember anything."

No notes, Ann Marie. It's all from memory. It is my interpretation of the events. They are my memories, my life.

My painful memories have been so repressed that I truly haven't thought about them since I left Strawberry Fields. One of these memories includes a little song I sang so long ago. I can't recall where I learned it or who might have written it. The song was recorded by

Jimmie Rodgers, a singer from the thirties and forties. It reminds me
of home. It helps me remember:

> Old pal, I'm so blue since you left me
> Life's been a burden today
> I'm wondering, old pal, if you miss me
> Please come back again to stay
> Does your memory stray to yesterday
> Picture two hearts better light and gay
> Please come back for I still love you
> My old pal of yesterday.

⋟1⋞

Sherman Acres

LONG BEFORE THE BEATLES sang about it, and long before Tom T. Hall wrote of it in his song, I knew Strawberry Fields. It was the farm where I grew up. It wasn't called that back then, but that was what everyone in the area knew it to be. It's right there in the northwest part of Henderson County. Just take that big highway down to Sherman Acres Road; some say that highway runs all the way to the Gulf of Mexico. Turn right, take it until it comes to the bend, and just go right around it. Look into those trees on the right about a mile from that bend. The farm sits way back there on that hill. The driveway is long. It goes down and then up again. You can see the house and a few outbuildings. There's a big pole barn to the right on the hill. All of those fields you just passed used to be Strawberry Fields.

We used to grow the best strawberries in all of Henderson County. My father was known back then as the Strawberry King. But it was my mother who taught him all about farming. She had grown up in the country in her native Italy, while my father had grown up in a little village in Sicily, one so small that it isn't even on the map. It's there right by Catania, the buried city. I'm not sure how they met. I think their families knew one another at some time in their lives.

In Sicily, if you left your village to find a mate, it was thought there must be something wrong with you. Second and third cousins would marry quite often. I have relatives with the same last name on both sides of the family.

My father told me that he was a street kid from about the age of ten. His father was a mean man, he said, and they fought often. This is why he left home at such a young age. He described his mother as an eccentric who pretty much did as she pleased. He told me she went to the market one day and came back home with a small boy that she raised as her own. She adopted him but did not change his name; he kept his original family name. About fifteen years ago, I found out that if the child's name didn't change, then the adoptive family would receive money from the Italian government to help care for him. My father loved the boy, called Miguel, who was a year his junior. He told me that the boy looked up to him and followed him everywhere.

After my father left home, he earned money by guarding pigpens at night in the stockyards, which were near a large shipping port. After a few years of watching the ships, he decided that those ships could take him to the land of the free and the home of the brave—America. So one night before his eighteenth birthday, he became a stowaway, hiding in the galley at the bottom of one of the ships.

The cook knew he was there but didn't tell anyone; he just left some food out for him each night. When the ship docked at Ellis Island, the authorities sent my father right back to Sicily. He was handed over to the police. Since he was homeless, the Italian authorities sent him directly into the Italian army and right into World War I. He was captured and taken prisoner. He spent thirteen long months in a German prison camp, until President Woodrow Wilson sent in American troops and the war ended. Thank God for good old President Wilson. If it hadn't been for him, we never would have existed. I wouldn't be here to tell this story.

My father made a career of the army until he was almost thirty-five. He achieved the rank of cavalier before going back to his little village in Sicily. Things must have been better between him and his father, because he moved back into his family's home.

My eccentric grandmother was so excited that she chose a bride for him. She gave a large garden party at their villa so they could meet. My father was upset that she had done this. He told her he would stay in his room, look down into the garden, and observe his mother's choice. If he didn't like what he saw, he would not join the party. He didn't like the girl because she was very dark with dark hair. I have never understood this, because my father, the dashing young soldier, was very dark, with dark, curly hair. He had dark, snappy, bright eyes that didn't miss anything. He didn't attend the party, and my grandmother was furious.

It was the custom in those days for people to go out in the evening and hang around the town square. They dressed in their finest clothes to enjoy the evening air, which was more tolerable than the hot afternoon sun. That part of the day was for rest. There was dancing and music, and street vendors sold food and beverages around the small central park. People strolled and visited, playing cards and singing songs.

On one particular evening, shortly after his mother's unsuccessful matchmaking attempt, my father and some of his brothers and friends went into the town square. That was where my father spotted a beautiful young girl with long, light-brown hair, which was fastened into a bun at the nape of her neck. He always said that this was the perfect hairstyle for a woman. She had beautiful fair skin, and her eyes were a clear sea green. When my father asked one of his friends who she was, he was amazed to discover that she was someone he had known since childhood but had never paid any attention to. He hadn't seen her since she was about four years old and had no idea she had grown into such a beauty. That night in the piazza, however, he knew he would marry my mother.

My grandfather on my mother's side was deceased, so my father went to see my grandmother Rosa and asked for her daughter's hand in marriage. A dowry was agreed upon, and they were married. My mother must have liked my father too, or she would not have agreed to the match. It's amazing that such marriages lasted, because it was almost like marrying a complete stranger. A large portrait of my eccentric grandmother and my mother hangs in the entrance hall of my home. A gold necklace her mother-in-law gave to her that day hangs around my mother's neck. It is a medallion of the Blessed Mother, the patron saint of all women.

Soon after the wedding, my father set off again for America, the land of opportunity, in hopes of finding work and a home for his new bride. My parents wanted to raise their children in a land that would offer them a better life than they had in Italy. That was how everyone in Europe felt in the late 1920s.

My pa headed for America with his uncle, his aunt, their four kids, other cousins, and some friends. When he left for America, three of his brothers immigrated to Australia, chasing their own dreams of a better world. It was many years before I met my Australian cousins, who look like my siblings and me but speak with a thick accent.

I had the pleasure of getting to know my father's cousin Mike, who made the journey with him and the others.

"I was scared to death when I came here with your father. He talked me into it," Mike told me many years ago. "I was only fifteen years old. All I had were the clothes on my back. I was afraid I would die on that ship coming over. Look at me now! I have a fine home, good children, and a successful restaurant business. I met and married my wife when she was only fifteen. I was just eighteen. We built all of this together. Only in America could anyone like me do this. I never went to school in my life."

My mother came to America, all by herself, to join my father almost a year later. She was so young—only nineteen—and very seasick the entire journey. She told me once that it was the happiest day of her life when she saw the Statue of Liberty. She knew that she would soon be on land again at Ellis Island. After leaving Ellis Island, my father had settled in a city by a big lake in the Midwest where lots of Italian immigrants lived. When my mother joined him in North End, they moved into an apartment on the big highway.

The landlady, a kind American woman, taught my mother English, how to ride the bus, and where to shop. "I don't speak Italian, and you don't speak English, but we'll get used to each other and live in harmony," Esther told my mother.

Having never been to school, my father worked every job he could find. It was the height of the Great Depression, and there were few good-paying jobs. At night he swept floors at a hot dog shop, and during the day he sold ice cream from a cart. He worked as a barber, cutting hair in the early evening. You didn't need a license or any training in those days; another barber simply showed you what to do.

The babies began to come. First, in January, came Enzo; Carmella arrived in December of that same year. We always said that Enzo started the year and Carmella finished it. Four years later it was Sammy (Santo was his given name); two and a half years after that, it was Marco. He was more than eleven pounds! I think he almost did my mother in. Births in those days happened at home. No one went to the hospital or even to a doctor. A midwife was secured to do the job. She was found by the best method of communication there is: word of mouth.

Everything was going fine until Sammy got hit by a car. He was okay, but it scared my mother. She hated the city! She had been a farm girl in Sicily, and she longed to return to that life. It was quiet and steady and brought her much comfort. My father knew she wanted the country life.

My father knew it was time to start looking for his American dream. He bought a car and drove it up and down the alley until he learned to operate it properly. In the 1930s there were no driving schools—at least none my father could afford. He tried to teach my mother, but she was too afraid of it. She never learned to drive.

One Sunday afternoon my father loaded everyone into the car for a drive into the country. They did it every Sunday, both for pleasure and for house hunting. Accustomed to driving and feeling more adventurous, he turned onto Sherman Acres Road. He went past the schoolhouse and around the bend. There was that little farm up on that hill with its long driveway. It was for sale! The price was right, and he had the money. They all knew it would be our home.

John Fairmont was an unusual man who drank a lot. He owned the place and was happy to sell it to my father for cash money. Fifteen thousand dollars was a lot of money in the early days after the Great Depression. My father had saved it by working all of those jobs since coming to America. He was in his late forties and realizing his great American dream of owning his own land and home. He knew his wife would be happy there. The children loved the open spaces to play, never worrying about cars or buses. Pa had been in America only twelve years. In his mind he had all the riches of a wealthy man.

≋2≋

The Last Child

M Y SISTER ANTONIA WAS born about a year after the move to the little farm. I came two and a half years later. My mother was sick a lot after I was born. Unlike the others, I was not a pretty baby. Everyone wondered if it was worth all the pain and illness my mother suffered from that birth. I had been born with lots of black hair, but instead of falling out, as most babies' hair does after birth, it started to grow in a very light-brown blonde shade. I looked like an old woman who forgot to dye her hair.

I recall standing in someone's living room, in front of my mother, as she sat in a dark-green wing chair in obvious pain. There was something hanging from her mouth. I heard her say to another woman in the room, "This is how they are keeping my throat from closing up." It was a string. The doctor had made my mother swallow a string in order to keep her throat open!

"Don't let the baby near her!" a voice rang out sternly. I never got close to my mother again—not physically close, anyway. From the way everyone talked, I felt that I was the cause of all her pain and infirmity. I didn't know how I had caused it, but from what I could understand of the talk that went on around me, it was my fault.

Because my mother was always sick, I was sent away to live in another household, with people I didn't know. I asked for my mother every day and asked when I could go back home. "I'm your mother now," said the gray-haired lady that cared for me. She told me to call her Mama. If I didn't, she would not answer me. I called her Mama, but I knew she wasn't my mother, even though she had a thick Italian accent. I stopped eating, and I stopped talking. After some time had passed, what seemed to me like years, the woman finally said, "It's no use. Let's just take her back home."

I was seated in the backseat of a high-roofed, rat-colored car. I was between two older girls. There was a man driving the car, and that woman who wanted me to call her Mama sat next to him in the front. Those girls must have been their daughters.

I was wearing a pair of light-blue corduroy bib overalls with flowers embroidered on them and a white blouse. It was a gray day outside, as if it was about to rain. I recognized the long driveway of Strawberry Fields Farm as the car went slowly down it and then up again. When the car came to a stop, a girl of about sixteen pulled the door open and started calling me by name. "Come on now. Get out," she was saying. "Look, I have candy for you. You're home now."

I leaned forward and looked around. I saw other children. I thought I knew them to be my brothers and sisters. I finally got out and went to my sister Carmella, who gave me the candy sucker. I didn't go to my mother. I thought she didn't want me; after all, she'd tried to give me away.

Soon my mother fell ill again. I was sent away to yet another family I didn't know. A woman with an Italian accent in that house said she was my godmother and that she would take care of me. There were no children in the house and the adults all ignored me. I slept in a crib for the first time. I was never a good sleeper. When those people came in to check on me, I was always awake. The woman took care of me, but she was cold and unfriendly, and she never spoke to me unless it was to order me to do something. "Go to bed," she would say. "Eat your dinner," or "Wash your hands."

One day I spilled milk all over myself. The lady got mad at me.

"These are the last clean clothes I have for you. Go outside and play!" she said after she helped me into my last pair of clean overalls. I was happy to go, because I thought I'd seen my father pass by the big front window in his car earlier that morning. I opened the big door of the brown brick building that was now my home and went out into the sunlight. I walked down the steps and onto the sidewalk. I went along the street for a little more than two blocks. Then I saw it. I knew right away that the black Dodge car belonged to my father. I ran back to the house. I told the woman I wanted to go home with my father. "But where is he?" she wanted to know.

"Come, I'll show you," I said. So she packed my clothes into a big brown paper bag, and we left the house. I took her down the street to where my father's car was parked. He was nowhere in sight.

"Are you sure it is his car?" she asked. I knew that car well. I had ridden in it many times. When my parents went out at night to visit friends, they would first come to our room and make sure we were all asleep. At least four of us slept in the same bed. I was always awake. My father would bundle me into a blanket and put me in the backseat, and I went along for the ride. I could never remember where we went or how I came to be back in my bed in the morning.

"Yes, this is my pa's car," I insisted. She opened the back door, put me inside with my bag of clothes, and left me there. No one locked car doors then. But what kind of person would leave a three-year-old child unattended in a car she wasn't even sure was the right one? It would be child endangerment today and carry a hefty jail sentence.

My father was shocked to find me there when he returned. He took me back to the house where the woman lived. "Why was she in the car?" he asked.

"She wants to go home, so take her. I'm too tired to care for her anyway," she replied.

So my father took me by the hand, and we went back to his car. We headed down the big highway toward Strawberry Fields Farm. As we crossed over the big steel bridge, he said, "I'll never leave you there again."

I was finally home again to stay. My mother's health slowly improved. A doctor had found a way to get her throat to stay open. He put some tubes made out of rubber down her throat. These tubes were called boogies. He did this every week for several weeks, putting down a larger tube each week until her throat was dilated to a normal size, so she could eat. She gained weight, and the string was gone from her mouth. She would get these treatments on and off throughout her life. I still couldn't bring myself to go too near her, because I thought I would make her sick again and get sent away forever.

My sister Carmella cared for me. She bathed and dressed me every day. She combed my long hair and sang to me. We listened to the radio together. She loved those broadcasts of serial stories—*Portia Faces Life, Young Dr. Malone*, and *Stella Dallas*. We liked country music and sang along with all of the great hits of the 1940s. I can remember all of the words to those songs. Hank Williams's voice filled the kitchen. I could hear Gene Autry, the singing cowboy. How I loved the radio: it was my only connection with the outside world.

The Many Lives and Tales of the Last Child

ALL TOO MANY TIMES in my life, I have come very close to dying. Recalling those times, it's amazing to me now that I am still alive. But you can't question God's divine plan. It was thought that I was a good tale-teller when I was a small child, but the truth is that the tales I told were real and not at all made up. Since I slept so little, I knew that all these events had really happened. I didn't dream them or make them up out of my head. Small children are very perceptive and aware of what goes on around them. Back then, children were supposed to be seen and not heard. They were largely ignored by adults.

When I was about nine months old and back with the family, my sister Carmella was supposed to be watching me. I was in the large black buggy with the white lace cover on it. I knew I was in there because there were people looking through that lace into the buggy. They were my sister's friends. They were laughing and talking, and their voices sounded farther and farther away as I started to drift off to sleep. When she thought I was asleep, Carmella went off to play with them.

The sky grew dark, and the wind began to blow. Everyone ran for cover when the rain started to fall. In the hillside just below our front yard, there was a cave made of stone. John Fairmont told my father the Indians built it more than one hundred years ago. Mr. Fairmont could never resist putting his name on everything he built. His name was all over the house and in each of the outbuildings on the farm. Since he had inscribed his signature on the wall in the stone of that cave, we knew it was built by him. It was, however, quite an amazing place. The temperature in it was the same all year round. It was a great place for my mother to store her canning and other fruits and vegetables. Shelves were built into the walls, and bins that held the fresh produce. Years later it was the perfect spot for Carmella to hide love letters from her boyfriends. As the rain began to drench the earth, all the children ran for the cave. They huddled there while the wind blew louder and the rain came down in sheets that looked like waterfalls.

My mother came screaming from the house, calling out for all her children. She went right to the cave and found them huddled inside. She let out a sigh of relief at the sight of them, but in a split second, she knew some were missing. "Where is the baby?" she cried out. "Where is Marco?"

My sister Carmella let out a loud scream when she realized she had left me in the buggy at the top of the driveway. My mother, frail and ill, started running toward the long driveway and saw the buggy being swept down it by the wind. The fast-falling rain had begun to swell the creek that ran at the bottom of the hill under the drive, turning the racing water black. She ran as fast as she could, with the strength one seems to possess in such a crisis, and caught the buggy before it went over into the creek.

After rescuing me, she looked up and saw Marco coming from the pasture with Stella, our milking cow. They were both drenched from the rain but unharmed. Everyone was safe but very wet. From then on, the fun-loving Carmella kept a closer eye on my sister Antonia and me.

But in spite of my sister's efforts to keep me safe, the brushes with death kept coming. The next near-death experience happened when I was about four or five. I remember it clearly. We were all in the downstairs summer kitchen, which was really in the basement of our house. Hunting season was upon us, and my brother Enzo had purchased his first rifle. Carmella and Antonia were sitting at the kitchen table. My mother was cooking something on the stove. The other boys were standing around Enzo; they were facing one of the kitchen windows. I was standing under that window with my back against the wall.

"Enzo!" my mother called. "Please put away that gun. The little one is standing right there, and I'm afraid she will get hurt."

"Oh, Ma, the gun is not loaded," replied Enzo. Just as I turned to lean against the wall with my left side, a loud bang rang out from that double-barreled shotgun. I felt the breeze from the bullet as it flew by me and into the wall, leaving a large hole only inches from my chest. The sound of it burned in my ears for what seemed like a very long time. I couldn't move. I heard my mother screaming from somewhere far off. No one moved as the smell of gunpowder filled the air around me. My mother fell to her knees in front of me; grabbing me by both shoulders, she began to shake me.

"Stop it, Ma! She is not even hurt. The bullet missed her," Enzo said firmly. Everyone became calm again and went on with what they were doing. Enzo and the boys took the gun outside. I don't think they realized I was in shock until sometime later, when I started to cry. In my child's mind, I thought their lack of reaction meant that no one cared. Since that day, I have hated guns and the sound of them firing.

I'm not sure what age I was when, late one fall, I was playing at our neighbors' house with their two boys, Tommy and Tad, and my sister Antonia. We were in some type of shed when a big black widow spider came crawling across the floor. The other kids jumped to get out of its way, but I just stood there as it came partway up my leg and then went back down and away from us. I think I was too young at the time to be frightened. I like to think that maybe I knew not to react, so the spider would leave.

Shortly after my encounter with the shotgun, I overheard Marco talking to Mama late one night. I could tell by his voice that he was upset. "Mama, I just came from the Meadows place. You won't believe what has happened. Steven got a new gun, and he tried to hide it from his little sister, so he put it under his bed. Early this morning after he left for school, his sister went into his room and found the gun under the bed. When she tried to pull it out, it got tangled in the fringe of the spread, and it discharged, hitting her in the chest and killing her instantly."

"Oh, Marco, no! I tell you boys those guns are no good in the house," my mother replied, and she started to cry. I listened to them discuss funeral arrangement for the little girl, who was just my age. I never met her, but Steven came to Strawberry Fields to see Marco often. When he returned to our place after that awful day, I saw a wounded and broken boy. His hands shook all the time, and he had a sad and vacant look in his eyes. He never recovered from that tragedy. I believe he hanged himself in the barn on their farm some years later. The whole incident was kept very quiet.

Time was always playing tricks on me, but I think I was about seven or eight on one hot day in late summer when yet another brush with death occurred. Enzo was tearing down the old corn crib and building a new one. He wanted to get it finished before harvest time.

I was wearing a summer dress that my mother made for me out of the sacks that feed for the animals came in. They came in different colors and patterns. When Mr. Ferguson delivered feed in his truck, we would jump into the back and pick out what we wanted. He wouldn't get too grouchy if we didn't make him move a bunch of those sacks to get to the ones we liked. This was where most of our clothes came from. My mother could sew anything. She even made us bathing suits out of those feed sacks once.

It must have been a Sunday, because I had shoes and stockings on as well as that dress. Most likely I had been to church with my father.

I was standing about twenty feet from the corn crib that Enzo was tearing down. The thing was infested with field mice. Enzo had his handgun with him in its holster. His fascination with weapons was never-ending. By the time I came to see what was going on, he had already shot and killed about one hundred and twenty-five of those mice. I was watching Enzo on top of the crib, ripping boards off the roof and tossing them to the ground. My hands were behind my back as I gazed up. I was aware of something on top of my feet, so I slowly dropped my head to look at them. I was stunned to see a scaly, six-foot-long snake crawling across my Mary Jane shoes. I could feel its cool, clammy body right through my little white stockings. I couldn't speak or utter a sound. I didn't move either.

"My God in heaven, don't move!" called Enzo from the roof. The snake took its time making that journey over me. As soon as its tail passed over my left shoe, a shot rang out. The snake spun around and was dead. There were six sets of rattles on its tail, lined up two by two, to equal one dozen. The snake measured exactly six feet. Rattlesnakes weren't known to be found in the area, so people came from all over the community to see it. Enzo showed it off whenever he could. He took the rattles off and kept them for a very long time. Once again, everyone was more interested in the snake than in whether I was hurt or traumatized by the whole incident.

Another incident happened when we had all gone to New Moon Lake to swim. I'm not sure how old I was, but I couldn't swim. We went with Carmella in her car. She wanted to be with her friends, and the only way she could do that was to take Marco, Sammy, Antonia, and me along. I remember standing on the pier, looking at the water. A high school boy knocked me right into the water as he ran past me. Carmella started screaming, and Marco jumped in after me. By the time Marco got me out, Carmella had beaten the boy so badly that he had bruises everywhere. She was always beating up boys. She thought she was so tough, but the real reason she could beat them was that they all liked her, because she was so beautiful. The other reason Carmella could get away with it was that most boys were taught, from the time they were very small, that it was a sin to hit a girl, ever. Other than having swallowed a little too much smelly lake water, I was perfectly fine.

As a small child, I never talked much. Most people thought I was retarded and could not speak. The real reason was that I had nothing to say. Everyone else talked so much around me that I didn't feel the need to say anything. My mother thought I had a wild imagination, because when I was about three years old, I told her what sounded like a fantastic tale. I did most of my talking when there were fewer people around. I had just rejoined the family on the farm after living with strangers. There was construction going on at our house. My father was having an addition built to accommodate his growing family. A work crew of about five black men came to our farm every day to do the construction. They were all very nice, and I liked being around where they were working. They sang beautiful gospel songs all day long as they worked. It sounded so beautiful to me that I couldn't tell it from what I heard on the radio. "What a Friend We Have in Jesus," "How Great Thou Art," and "The Old Rugged Cross" rang out across the land from sunup until sundown every day. I loved their wonderful voices. I used to sit on a pile of bricks in the morning light and listen for hours without moving. I can still hear them in my head, those songs of long ago.

At the end of the day, one of the men didn't leave to go home like the rest of them. I watched him every day in the evening light as he climbed the side of our house and went into the attic, through a window that had no glass. He would see me standing there in the yard, looking up at him. He put a finger to his lips and shook his head from side to side. I knew it meant that I was to say nothing of his presence. Some time passed before I told my mother that there was a black man in our attic.

One morning I was sitting at the kitchen table; my brothers and sisters had gone to school, and my father was away at work. I was pushing an egg around on my plate with a piece of toast. I never could eat much. As a matter of fact, I ate little or nothing at all, most of the time.

"There is one of those black men up in our attic," I said, pointing upward.

"I think you make a dream," my mother replied in her broken English. It was what we kids called "Italish," meaning English and Italian spoken at the same time. She knew I didn't sleep well at night, and she thought that I walked in my sleep. More than once she had found me wandering through the house many hours after the lights went out. Unless the moon and stars were out, there was complete darkness on the farm when the lights were turned off. I used to find it soothing to walk in the dark. On these occasions when she found me, she would lead me back to bed without saying a word.

"No, he is there. You can go and look," I told her, getting up from the table. She did not go to the attic, and she continued to insist it was a dream. I knew he was no dream; he was a real, live man.

After many mornings of my telling her this while I played with my food, she decided that the two of us would go up there and look. "Come, we go and look, so you know it is not so." She took a large flashlight from the kitchen drawer, and we climbed the stairs. In the upstairs pantry, there was an opening to the attic. We went up the little ladder. I followed my mother as she shone that light in front of us.

"See, there is no one here," she said, and her light landed on the face of the black man. His eyes went wild and white as my mother screamed and cried out with terror in her native tongue. She always went back to pure Italian when she was upset. The man bolted for the open window without its glass and scampered down the side of the house. He was gone.

I could hear my mother and father talking late into the night after we had all gone to bed. I could tell by her voice and the straight Italian that she was still very upset. In spite of all his loud yelling, strict rules, and strangeness, my father could be a reasonable man. He talked with the foreman the next day, and the man was allowed to stay on and help finish our house. When the boss of the crew told my father how badly the man needed the job and how he had no way to get back and forth from the job site, he understood. Pa had struggled himself when he first came to America.

For such a young person, I already had lots of bad habits. My eating and sleep patterns did not improve with time. They may have even gotten worse. Listening to adult conversation was high on my list of forbidden activities. My sister Antonia and I listened in whenever we could. Being close in age, we played together for most of the day.

One early spring morning, my father did not return home after his night shift at the steel mill in North End. Small farming didn't always pay the bills, so he worked many hours away from home to keep us all fed. It was almost noon when my mother sent Enzo to look for him. Enzo didn't return to the farm until later that afternoon. It was dark and gray outside by then. A spring rain had fallen and turned all the freshly plowed fields into black pools of water. "Mama, I have bad news for you," Enzo said with a sad look on his young face. "Pa has been in a bad accident on the highway, coming home early this morning. He is in bad shape in the hospital. Pa's new car was demolished, and the men that hit him were going the wrong way on the highway. The police believe they were drinking, but all three are dead. I have borrowed Jenson's car. I will take you there." Enzo had a pickup truck at that time, but it had only one seat.

I could hear my mother crying and screaming while she bathed in the big cast-iron tub in our basement. She dressed in a clean house-dress. She wound her ankle-length dark hair into a bun at the nape of her neck. Her hair had turned black when the family moved to the farm; I heard my father say it many times. It must have happened because of the well water that had so much iron and sulfur in it.

My father was in the hospital for what seemed to me a very long time, but it was probably only a few weeks. My mother cried all the time. She would beg my brother Enzo to go there and try to reason with him, as he was giving the doctors and hospital staff a very hard time. He was worried about his family and the farm, and he wanted to come home. He didn't want to do any of the things they were telling him he had to do in order to get well.

There was no such thing as health insurance at that time. It may have existed, but no one in Henderson County had it. Whenever anyone was sick in the hospital, all of the people in the community would give as much money as they could until the bill was paid.

When she wasn't at the hospital with my father, my mother was in the fields, working the land. Everyone who was able was out there picking strawberries, hoeing, and weeding all day—everyone except me. I wandered the farm all that summer on bare feet, with little or no supervision. Occasionally someone would remember to bathe me and change my clothes.

Early one summer morning, a strange-looking station wagon came down our long driveway. Two men in white coats got out, went to the back door, and opened it. From the back of that car, they pulled out my father, on a stretcher with wheels. All of us were standing by, watching. Although Pa was bandaged all over, I knew him. I stood by with bare feet, watching as the two men maneuvered the cart with wheels. Then one of my brothers yelled out, "Pa has a hole in his neck!" My siblings scattered and started running in all different directions across the yard and fields.

I followed those men up the steps and into the house. I wasn't afraid. I was fascinated by the way my pa looked with all of that stuff on him. I learned that the hole in his neck was called a tracheotomy. When he put his finger over it, my father could talk. I stayed by him almost the whole day, watching my mother feed him and change bandages. I would hand her things as she worked—tape, scissors, water. I watched her as she fed him his lunch. "I could do that," I said. I couldn't have been more than five years old at the time.

"You can feed you father?" Mother asked. I nodded, and she gave me the spoon that she had been using to feed him soup. It took a lot of time because of his condition, but I managed to get it all into him. My mother was so pleased that she let me do this every day, three times.

"Mama, I think this one will turn out to be a nurse. Look how she helps you care for me," my father told my mother about a week or so into his convalescence. I knew my mother was overwhelmed with caring for him and trying to manage the farm.

Walking first with a set of crutches and then with the aid of two canes, my father began to recover. But I noticed there was tension in the air around our house. I wasn't sure what it was, but it felt like something bad was going to happen.

No one paid much attention to Antonia or me. In the summer months, we did whatever we wanted, all day. Enzo had graduated from high school and was working in the same plant as my father. They worked different shifts, and they were not in the same department. One day Enzo came home with a woman named Nina. I thought Nina was very beautiful. She had long brown hair and grayish-green eyes that sparkled. She seemed shy and quiet. She leaned over to Enzo and asked, "Why is everyone yelling so loudly? Why are they all so mad?"

"That's just the way they are. You will just have to get used to it," I heard Enzo tell her. It did seem to me that something had happened to upset everyone. It was true that everyone in our house yelled all the time, but I knew when something was really wrong.

Soon after dinner, Antonia and I were sent outside to play. We were told not to come back into the house until we were called. Instead of playing, we went and sat in one of the windows to the downstairs kitchen. I don't think anyone realized we could hear every word that was being said. My parents seemed to be very mad at both Enzo and Nina. I heard Enzo say he had to marry her and that she would be coming to live with us. I wondered how this would work, as there didn't seem to be enough room for all of us, let alone another person.

Where would she sleep? My parents had moved to a room upstairs after my father's accident. Enzo now had his own room downstairs next to ours, and all the rest of us still slept in the same bed.

A few weeks later, everyone left the farm dressed in their very best, with the exception of Antonia and me; we stayed home with our father. I understood that Enzo and Nina were to be married that evening at Nina's church in downtown Henderson.

For one week before the wedding, Enzo had worked nonstop to install a toilet in our upstairs bathroom. We only had an outhouse; in wintertime we all used a slop bucket in the coal shed in the basement. He didn't want his bride to have to go in any outhouse. I thought the toilet was the greatest thing I had ever seen in my entire little life. My parents still made us use the outhouse during good weather. They thought that the toilet would wear out if it was flushed too much.

After Enzo and Nina moved into his bedroom, I continued my eavesdropping. I heard everything they said and did every night. I knew when they argued, and I knew when they made love. I knew all of their plans for the future. I knew there would be a baby coming soon. I didn't mean to hear all of this, but after all I was awake all night. It was hard not to listen to what was going on around me.

Another school year started that fall, but again I didn't go. They said I wasn't ready for school, so I was home all day, alone and bored. I think that was when I started to live mostly in my own head. I had daydreams about things I wanted to do and places I thought I might like to go, although I knew they didn't exist. To me the only place was Strawberry Fields Farm. I didn't know of any other.

My sister Carmella didn't graduate from high school when Enzo did, although they were in the same class. She didn't have enough credits. The principal of the school came to the farm to talk to her and my parents. He wanted to help her finish high school, but she refused. "I already have a job," she said.

My parents were very disappointed, but Carmella was determined to have a job and her own money. She wanted to buy her own car. My father had given his old car to all of my older siblings, but Carmella drove it most of the time. She was old enough to drive, but Sammy and Marco drove that car too, even though they were nowhere near the legal age to drive. In the country, kids were always able to bend the rules, because they had to help out on the family farm, and driving was a necessity.

Sammy and Marco had been driving since they were very small. I remember Marco taking the black car out one day and accidentally knocking off the front bumper. He was afraid my father would be so mad that he would beat him. Marco hid in the barn for three days. He didn't even come in for mealtimes. I think Carmella must have been sneaking him food at night.

Whenever my father caught sight of him, he would call out, "Marco, come, I not hurt you!" I don't know what made Marco finally come inside. It might have been the fact that when Carmella drove the old Dodge-a-Dee, as we liked to call it, she had more crashes than anyone.

Once, Antonia and I were in the backseat when Carmella was driving. As she went around a corner, she noticed a spider crawling on her shoulder. She screamed and took both hands from the steering wheel to swat at the spider, and the car crashed into some bushes. She wasn't going fast, and we weren't hurt.

In those days cars had no seat belts, and safety rules for the inside of the car didn't exist. There were no such things as turn signals. You stuck your arm straight out the window for a left turn, and you bent it up at the elbow for a right turn.

The problem was that Carmella did stuff like this all the time. One day she was going to Mr. Greesidinger's Gas Station and General Store. As she was pulling into the place, she saw some friends of hers. Taking both hands off the wheel, she started to wave and call out to them, and she crashed into several gas pumps. Again, no one was injured, but she had to pay for the damages done to those gas pumps.

My mother and Nina didn't get on well. Two women in the same house, with very different ways of doing things, was a recipe for disaster. Nina was young and had no experience with farm life. She couldn't do anything right, as far as my mother was concerned. Most of the time, before cooking and eating food, you had to kill it first. One bright, sunny day, my mother was showing Nina how to catch a chicken, strangle it, break its neck, chop its head off, and remove all the feathers before cooking. Nina caught the chicken all right, but she couldn't strangle it. Instead she held it down on a bench, under the oak tree, and chopped off its head. Blood spurted out everywhere, and she couldn't bring herself to hold on to the chicken. She let go, and the chicken jumped off the bench. It ran around the yard, leaving a massive trail of blood. It finally succumbed, but it made for very tough eating at dinnertime, and it made a bloody mess of the front yard, like someone had been killed. Nina cried a lot over those first few months of their marriage. At night I could hear her telling Enzo that she couldn't stand it on the farm. She wanted to leave and go home. He would calm her down, they would make love again, and everything would be fine in the morning.

I remember the night the baby came. It was late, so we were all in bed, but no one slept. We were all waiting for Enzo to call from the hospital with the news of what kind of baby it was. Everyone wanted a boy but me. When the telephone finally rang sometime after midnight, we all ran for it. Buddy was born two days after Enzo's birthday on that cold January night. The baby was beautiful! I loved him very much, even if he wasn't the girl I wanted. I stayed by his cradle all day. I watched him while my mother tended to the farm work and the animals. Nina had gone back to work. She and Enzo were saving every penny they could in order to build their own house.

Whenever Nina bathed little Buddy, my mother supervised, but it was more like she stood there and criticized. I sat at the table and watched too as Nina put out all the things she needed for the bath. Little Buddy lay there on his back, kicking his chubby legs in the air. She removed his diaper and started to wash him, and he suddenly spurted urine right into her face. All she could do was scream, "Oh no, help!" My mother reached over and put a diaper over him. Then she finished the bath while Nina went to clean herself.

Sammy and Marco got their own room upstairs. It was just off the dining room. It only had a bed in it, but it got them out of the bed with us girls. It didn't help to curb my nocturnal wandering. I still did it almost every night. Since my parents' room was now upstairs, my mother no longer found me doing it. I guess it didn't occur to anyone that my poor sleeping patterns might have been due to all the coffee I drank as a child.

My mother made the best cappuccino in the world, along with tasty biscotti. That was what we had for breakfast every morning. She made the coffee in a saucepan on the stove. The grounds went into the pan with the water, and she brought it to a boil and then let it sit until the grounds settled to the bottom of the pan. She would beat an egg and add cream at the same time to that strained coffee, along with sugar, vanilla, and sometimes cinnamon. People will pay top dollar for it at a coffee shop today, but this is what we had because we were poor.

One day about the middle of summer, I was at the breakfast table in the summer kitchen in the basement, with my mother and little Buddy. I started to tell her another fantastic tale. This one was about a man under the bed in our room. Once again, she tried to tell me that it was my imagination. "He is there right now, Mama. I saw him."

"No, I think you dream this," she replied.

"Sometimes I see him in the closet, smoking a cigarette," I said, without looking up from the coffee and biscotti I was eating.

"The door, it is lock at night, so how he get in here?" my mother asked, trying to prove me wrong; I knew, because no one ever locked the door.

"He comes in through the window, and he leaves that way too," I answered her.

Since I was always awake, I knew for certain that I was not dreaming. Antonia, on the other hand, slept like the dead. She never woke until morning, and she always went promptly to sleep each night. She slept like this the whole time I shared a room with her. Carmella was awake on most of those nights I saw the man. Sometimes she went into the closet with him. Other times she stayed in bed and slept or pretended to sleep. The bed would move when he got under it. I could hear him breathing. He sometimes sat on the floor by the bed and stroked her hair as she pretended to sleep. At other times the light from his cigarette shone brightly in the closet as he raised it to his lips and brought it back down again. I lay awake watching the orange glow move silently in the dark closet that had no door.

When little Buddy went down for his morning nap, my mother went to the wringer washer in the room next to the kitchen. Our bedroom was just off that room, to the left. I walked into the room and toward my mother, who was running a load of clothes through the wringer, and I stopped in front of the door of our bedroom and pointed inside the room. The loud humming of the washer filled the room. My mother left the big machine and came to where I was standing. She was looking at me, and then her eyes followed my arm to where I was pointing, in time for her to see the man's legs and feet as he pulled himself through the open window of our bedroom. Mama yelled at him in Italian, but he got to his feet and ran away as fast as he could. I knew by the look on her face that she recognized him as he scurried from the backyard and over the fence into the open field, never stopping or looking back.

My mother never told my father about that man, I was certain. She began lobbying him for a room for Antonia and me upstairs, leaving Carmella to have her own room in the basement. "The girls, they are growing, Pa. The one bed, it too small for them all. The room is also unable to fit another bed," she pleaded. She was always good at getting what she wanted out of my father, although she would tell us that he was the head of the household and made all the decisions. A few months later, they purchased another bed. Antonia and I were moved upstairs, to the smallest room in the house, which measured only ten feet by ten feet and had no closet. We would share the tiny space for the next seven years.

I knew my mother was very mad at Carmella. I would sometimes overhear them arguing, and I was sure it was about the man in the closet. My parents seemed to be very strict with Carmella, but somehow it only served to make her want to be more wild and do all of the things they said she shouldn't. She was very social, and she loved dances. She always wanted to go to the Gleaners Hall for the dances held there every Friday night. I think she was happy to have her own room. She began buying nice things to decorate it. I don't know if that man ever visited her again.

The man in the closet left an everlasting impression on me. For many years I had dreams of a man in my bedroom. He would always smoke. I would see the orange glow from the tip of his cigarette, and I would wake in a cold sweat,certain he had been there. The faint scent of smoke, I was sure, lingered in the air around me. Other times, I thought I was awake and he was standing over me next to my bed, so I pretended to be asleep. The bed sometimes moved. I knew he was trying to see if I was awake. It was only after I woke that I realized it was once again a dream. I could never go back to sleep after one of those vivid dreams. The man with the cigarette would visit me in my dreams for the rest of my life.

≥4≤

The Mystery of Antonia

I'M NOT SURE WHEN it started or why, but Antonia began to change. When I was three, four, five, and even six, we played together every day. For the most part, we were pretty much unsupervised. We ran wild most of the summer, without shoes, wearing the same dresses for days at a time.

The place we played all through summer was in the woods just off our backyard. The trees were very unusual. The branches, with their thick, tightly packed leaves, reached the ground and seemed to root there, making a very private space under the greenery, creating a kind of house. I loved mine! I would stay there all day and sometimes all night. The ground under there was packed hard and stayed dry, even in rain. We made furniture out of old wooden crates and boxes. I took a blanket and put it in my house under the trees. It was ragged and torn. Mama had intended it for rags to wash the floor. My quiet sanctuary brought me a sense of peace that couldn't be found inside our house, with all its activity and loud voices, none of which was ever for me. I was pretty much invisible to all and of no consequence to anyone.

We buried treasure in our hideouts in the woods—a cup, old spoons, a piece of silk from an old dress of my mother's, and an old love letter from one of Carmella's boyfriends who had gone away to the army. The letter started with "Dearest darling Carmella." This would send us into laughing fits. I cannot recall ever hearing the full contents of any of those letters Marco and Antonia found. They would read them often. I couldn't read, and I wouldn't learn how for many years. We all took delight in hearing Marco read them aloud.

We didn't have many toys. People who were as poor as we were didn't waste money on such things. Left on our own all day, we made up our entertainment from what we could find lying around, both outdoors and indoors. There was an abandoned outbuilding just in front of the woods. Boxes of old clothes were stored in that little building with the wooden floor. The boxes had come from some people in the city who sent them to my mother after some woman died. They contained her clothes and shoes. The people thought my mother could use them because we were so poor. Super-stition about wearing clothes that belonged to the dead was part of Italian culture, however, so my parents had stored them rather than offend the well-meaning folk who had given them to us. So we played dress-up in them. We didn't know we weren't supposed to wear them. Antonia and I had never seen a dead person, so we had no fear of them.

Antonia had her own tree, right next to mine, with her own furniture and buried treasure. We visited and played side by side in those early years. When my mother called us to come in the house for mealtimes or bedtime, she would always call only Antonia. I did everything I could think of to get her to call my name as well, but nothing worked. I wouldn't come when she called, so she would just send Antonia or Marco to find me. I tried staying out in the woods all night, but my mother never came to get me, so I went inside. I asked her once why she never called me to the house like the rest of my brothers and sisters. "When I call Antonia, it means you too," she said.

"But Mama, you named me Evalina after the song because you liked it. Carmella told me so," I said, trying to understand.

"Yes, this is true, and I still like the name," she replied. In my child's mind, I felt that since she once wanted to give me away, that was why she never called me by name. Even after Antonia left home, she still called her name when she wanted me. After I refused to answer her many times, she would make an attempt to correct this habit. But in her old age she just went back to calling for Antonia.

Marco was five years older than Antonia and seven years older than me. He loved to use the excuse of having to watch us for my mother so he could stay home from school. I think he was bored at school because he was already so smart. On those days, when he got away with it, he would make us cakes. He liked to cook, and he did it all from scratch. He was good at measuring out the flour, sugar, egg, and milk. His cakes looked like works of art. Cooking was just one of his many talents.

He would build little toys for us out of scraps of wood and other materials he found lying around. He loved going to the junkyard. He would get old buggy wheels and old bikes and make carts for us out of them, and he would rebuild bikes, making them look almost as good as new. When he was twelve, Marco built his own gasoline-powered motorcar that could go about twenty miles an hour. It was beautiful, with a navy-blue and silver exterior. He was the envy of every boy in the neighborhood. But jealousy and hard feelings led him to abandon the little car, so he would still have his friends. The little roadster rusted away in the rain, waiting for Marco to return.

For Marco, lying was a pastime, like some people played checkers. He lied about his age so he could get a driver's license and go to work. Then he got interested in flying airplanes and lied about his age so he could take lessons. He abandoned the little car and us to go flying whenever he could. There was a little airport in New Moon Lake, about ten miles from Strawberry Fields. In order to have money to go flying, he had to work. I don't know how he got through school, because he missed so much when he was working at the bowling alley, setting up pins every night and watching us during the day. Bowling pins back then didn't reset automatically, as they do today. All lanes were boy-powered. Marco spent all of his money and his spare time learning to fly.

Antonia never displayed any of her strange behavior around Marco. I'm not sure when it started, because it was subtle at first. She would get mad at me, and I didn't know why. She never would tell me. Other times we would play just fine. Then she would leave, go into the house, and tell our mother some wildly untrue story about something I was supposed to have done. When I came into the house, Mother would be mad at me and punish me for something I didn't do or even know about.

Other times Antonia could go for days without speaking to me. She would come to me days or sometimes weeks later and start playing and talking as if nothing had happened. When we were getting along well, she would start to tell me a story about how I wasn't really one of them—I was adopted. I believed her, because the story sounded so true. After all, I had lived in all those different households. "Look in the mirror," she would say. "Just look. You can see how different you are from us. You can see that you don't belong." She kept up this mean talk until I went crying to my mother, who would assure me that I wasn't adopted.

"Now go and play," Mama would say. Antonia was never reprimanded for these episodes. Sometimes my mother even laughed at her stories of how I came to live in our family.

"You belonged to another family from a far-off land," Antonia would say. "They couldn't care for you, so they dumped you here with us. You're just lucky we let you stay here, so don't get too comfortable, because we might send you on your way if you don't do everything I tell you." The story struck fear in my heart. I lay awake at night, wondering when I would be sent away.

"We found you in the woods, living with the animals, and we took you in, but you really don't belong here, living with people." This was another story that I could almost believe. I think I even wanted to believe it. I liked the idea of having been raised by a red fox and a family of raccoons.

When she went to school, the gap between us got even wider. Antonia was very bright; learning came easy to her. Just like Carmella, she was beautiful. She didn't look exactly like Carmella, though; she had some unique features of her own. She was small but well-built and sturdy. Her skin was a light olive, in contrast to Carmella, who was several shades darker. Antonia's hair was the color of a copper-bottom pot that had been left on the stove too long. The reddish-black color complemented her sparkling black eyes. She drew lots of attention wherever she went. When she wore her red velvet dress with the white collar and her hair fell down her back in a cascade of wiry curls, people found it hard to resist her.

On one special occasion, all three of us were dressed and seated in someone's house. I was too young to know where we were or why. Carmella, with her long curly hair that was black as coal, dark skin, and sparkling black eyes, was dressed in a forest-green velvet dress with a white collar. I was dressed in a blue velvet dress with a white collar. My hair was light dishwater-colored, soft and wavy, my skin a very light olive. I was skinny, with eyes of drab brown. Antonia was in her striking red velvet. The people at the celebration would come up and say how beautiful my sisters were, and then they would look at me and want to know, "What happened to this one? You must have run out of good materials when you got to her." I don't think people realized that I understood what they said, even if I didn't respond.

Antonia was everyone's favorite in the family. Enzo was very taken with her. Before little Buddy was born, he carried her around everywhere he went. Enzo behaved as if he hated Carmella. He treated her cruelly most of the time. They argued loudly and violently whenever they were in the same room. I never understood why they couldn't get along; they were so close in age.

I was no one's favorite. I was special to none of the members of the family. I still feared being sent away, so I was very quiet when the whole family was together, with everyone talking and yelling at once. I kept all of this inside me and never spoke of it to anyone.

As she got older, Antonia's behavior toward others began to

change. I used to think it was only me she hated and liked to torment. She started to get mad at her closest friends. She told stories about them that I knew weren't true. Rosemary was her best friend from the first grade until they went to junior high. Lorenzo was also one of her constant companions until seventh grade. Antonia broke ties with Tommy from next door even earlier than junior high. Unlike me, the others did not make up with her after these episodes. They moved on and got new friends, so she moved on as well.

I was the only one in our house that thought her behavior was wrong. Everyone supported everything she did without question. Many years later, my daughter Sarah-Jane wanted to know, "Who was the oldest of your brothers and sisters, Mom?" She was shocked to learn that Antonia was only a little over two years older than me. "I thought she was the oldest, from the way you all talked about her."

Antonia's stories and drawings delighted the whole family. In school every teacher she ever had thought she was some kind of miracle. Most of them didn't know what to do with such a gifted child, so they did nothing.

One of the unique things about Antonia was her perfect handwriting. When she wrote anything, it looked like it had come from a typewriter instead of being handwritten. Antonia could write equally well with both hands. She did it with ease, and no one could tell which hand she had used.

In Italy anyone left-handed was thought to be possessed by the devil. My father refused to let his children use their left hands. My brothers and sisters were all forced to write and do everything right-handed. By the time I came along, my father had mellowed a lot. It was clear very early that I was left-handed. He must have been tired of changing all the other children, so he just decided it would be all right if I was left-handed. Being a lefty would prove to be a problem for me all my life. It wasn't the devil that got me; it was people who were right-handed and couldn't accept someone who was so unlike them.

Antonia did not seem to take to music. Carmella always sang

with the radio and would do anything to get to go to dances. When my father decided that Marco should learn to play the accordion, Antonia didn't seem interested in hearing the music. Carmella, on the other hand, was very upset that Pa didn't offer her lessons. When Mrs. Monarch came to the farm to give Marco his lesson, Carmella watched intently. Then she would beg Marco to let her play his accordion. She was as good, if not better, at playing it. She would play the piano and organ all her life, never having had a single lesson.

When I could no longer tolerate her treatment of me, I stopped begging Antonia to play with me. I started to live in my own head. I made up friends for myself that were half animal and half human. They were very real to me. I talked to them all the time. I somehow knew not to talk out loud to them, for fear someone would hear. I only talked to them inside my head. They lived with me under my tree in the woods next to our backyard. I spent every waking hour I could with them. I would go there in winter too, cutting a path through the snow to my special place under that tree. Even in winter, snow never fell in my special place. These friends became more real to me every day, and the world became less important. I lived in a place I didn't understand or like. I withdrew from it.

Somewhere in my mind, I knew it was a way to avoid hurt from Antonia's rejection of me. I knew talking to eagles and other birds that were half human wasn't normal, although it made me feel better. In my mind the half man, half eagle would fly me around at night and bring me back home before dawn could be seen on the horizon. He told me stories of his people and his homeland. The half wolf, half lady sang beautiful songs to me. They lived in my house under the tree and kept it warm, neat, and safe for me. I kept these made-up people to myself and never spoke of them to anyone.

Mama received a letter from her nephew. He was coming for a visit, and he wanted to stay in America. Months passed, and he didn't arrive. Then another letter came, explaining that he had been detained in New York on business. He would come to Strawberry Fields soon. "He is a well-educated man, and I'm sure he is quite busy," she said every time we questioned her about his uncertain arrival date.

I don't know how old I was, but I remember looking up at a very tall, dark man who was accompanied by a tall, thin woman. They spoke Italian to Mama. He introduced the woman as his wife. They had married in New York. Although he only spoke Italian, I understood that the woman had followed him to America and was quite distraught when he wouldn't marry her. I was never sure what had occurred to make him change his mind.

The visit took place during the time when I was still listening to adult conversations without anyone suspecting that I could understand what was being said. I still didn't talk much, so I could see why adults thought I didn't comprehend. My cousin, I understood, wanted to start a restaurant here in the United States. He wanted help from my parents and my brother Enzo, who was about his age. No one had much money in those days. Enzo and Nina were still building their house in Henderson. Somehow my cousin Nuncio talked Enzo into lending him money. The sum was two hundred dollars, which was quite a lot in the early fifties.

I always felt a little sorry for Nuncio, because he seemed to be struggling to please and impress everyone while keeping a whining wife happy. Antonia took such a dislike to him that it scared me. Although some thought him handsome, he was a rather imposing figure, with his height and dark, wavy hair. His eyes were the same green as Mama's, but they were very sharp and intense, giving him a sinister appearance.

The visit lasted a month. Nuncio and the woman returned to New York. "See, I told you he was a crook!" Antonia said. "He stole Enzo's money, and now he's gone off to spend it." Mama assured Antonia that Nuncio was a good man and that all would be fine. Lots of time passed before we heard from him. The letter had little substance and revealed nothing about how he was doing with the starting of the restaurant. A letter came to Strawberry Fields about once a year. They had a child, a little boy named after his father. Nuncio's letters spoke of his wife's battle with mental illness. She spent lots of time in the hospital.

Enzo came to the farm one day, very excited. "Go get Mama from the field!" he ordered me. I ran down the hill and told her to come right away. "Look, Mama," he said, pulling an envelope from his pocket. "It's from Nuncio! He has written to say he's sorry the restaurant venture didn't work out. He sent me a check for the two hundred dollars!" I could see Mama's relief.

Cousin Nuncio didn't have a happy life. I learned he had spent some time in prison for an illegal business venture. They settled in England, where he died of a heart attack a short time later. He was Mama's only nephew. His loss pained her very much. His son remains a very well-known politician in the state of New York, where he lives with his family and his mother.

Every Christmas my father told us a story about cows in Italy that talked at midnight on Christmas Eve. We had cows. I was sure they too would be able to talk that night. On Christmas Eve I lay awake long after the lights were off. I listened for the rhythmic breathing as my family slept. I got out of bed, put on my shoes, and somehow found my coat hanging on a hook by the door. Without making any noise, I opened the door and went out into the night. The moon was bright as I made my way down the snowy path to the barn. It was dark in there. We had no heat or electric light outside the house. I went to Stella's stall. I knew which one was hers. Her body gave off enough heat to keep us both warm. I'm not sure how long I was there. I wasn't afraid when I heard Stella speak: "Behold, on this night a child is born in Bethlehem to a virgin and shall call His name Emmanuel."

I woke the next morning to bright sunlight. I was in our bed. I had no idea how I had gotten there from the barn. I was so happy that I had heard Stella talk! I spoke of this to no one. Later that morning we sat at the table with the contents of our stockings in front of us. It was the usual orange, nuts, and a few pieces of candy. I didn't tell Antonia about our cow talking on Christmas Eve. It was my secret, and it made me feel good. I knew then that I would need her approval, and everyone else's, a lot less. If I was special enough for God to make Stella talk on Christmas Eve, then I must be all right.

⇒5⇐

School Days in a Land Divided

Eᴺᴢᴏ ᴀɴᴅ Nɪɴᴀ ᴛᴏᴏᴋ little Buddy and moved into their new house on a quiet street at the edge of Henderson. A new baby was due soon. Enzo was proud of the house he had built. I didn't understand, because I knew Nina had driven just as many nails into it as he had. I used to go with them and watch little Buddy while they worked. I didn't know why men got credit for everything, when women who worked just as hard got no praise for their efforts.

It didn't occur to anyone that I took literally the things they said to me. I was excited about the baby. I kept asking him when she would arrive. Enzo said that if the baby was a girl, he would drown her in the creek, like he did the puppies when our dog had too many. "I don't want any girl babies!" he said. "All they do is cry. If it is a girl, she is going into the creek." This was another thing for me to worry about and to keep me awake all night. Enzo was always good at tormenting me. He never could bother Antonia. She only laughed when he said these things that made me cry.

Shortly after the move, Enzo came to Strawberry Fields alone. He followed Mama around the kitchen as she worked. He was complaining loudly about Nina. "She can't cook anything, and she can't iron my shirts the way you do. I'll just have to start bringing them here, so you

37

can do them for me," he said, pacing back and forth. "I don't know why she's so lazy, and she just won't learn to do anything for me."

Mama was a gentle woman most of the time, unless you got her really mad; then she was a force to be reckoned with. She was in her usual housedress with the big apron over it, a red rag tied around her head. She walked calmly over to the pantry and got out the broom. She held it firmly like a bat and began to hit Enzo across the seat of his pants with it. She started to yell at him in Italian. "You no good man, you! You marry your wife, did you not? You go home, and if you no like what she cook, you teach her better. If you no like how she iron your shirt, you iron yourself or show her how. If you no can do this, you keepa you mouth shut!" she yelled while chasing him about the kitchen, smacking him hard with the broom. Enzo never complained about Nina to Mama again. He stopped wearing his fancy shirts and pants. Instead, he donned a T-shirt and a pair of overalls every day. No one argued with Mama when she got her broom. We didn't like it when she came after us with it.

Since Enzo and his family moved, life sure was different for me without little Buddy to look after. I knew it was all about to change again soon. My mother told me I was going to start school. I wasn't sure I wanted to go, after being home all this time, talking to my friends in my head. They had become important to me and more real than ever.

It's hard to believe how children were treated. People didn't take their kids to school on the first day. They just put you on the bus with everyone else. You had to find your own way. Antonia didn't sit with me that first day or acknowledge that I was her little sister. We would be in the same room. The little schoolhouse in Sherman Acres only had two classrooms, a basement with a stage, and two bathrooms. There was a bathroom for the girls on the far side of the stage and one for the boys near the furnace room. The boys' bathroom was always hot, and the girls' bathroom was always cold. Each classroom had four grades. We filed in and took seats by row and by grade. There were eleven kids in my class. There was no such thing as registering your kid. You registered yourself. No adult was there to tell you that everything would be all right and get you acquainted with the school system. In my day, there was no kindergarten or preschool in rural America.

We all had to stand, one by one, and give our names to the teacher. When it was my turn, I stood and gave my name. "So you're one of those people, are you?" said Mrs. Trent; it was a question that I knew didn't require an answer. "Well, I hope you're as smart as your brothers and sisters." I sat down without a word.

Behind me the next child got to his feet and gave his name. "What did you say your name was?" asked Mrs. Trent, coming to stand next to him.

"It's Teddy Roosevelt," he repeated.

"How about you go stand outside until you're ready to tell me your real name," said Mrs. Trent, displeased with the student. Teddy left the room. I knew Teddy Roosevelt. I felt bad for him.

Over in the fourth-grade row, Madeline Roosevelt got to her feet. "Mrs. Trent, if you please, that's his name. He's my little brother."

"Well, you should have told me sooner, young lady. You can go out there and stand with him until I call you both back in. Who would name their child Teddy Roosevelt in the first place?" she demanded. No one dared answer. I didn't know teachers could be so mean. Maddy was one of Antonia's friends. She would bring Teddy with her when she came to play. I liked Teddy; he was always nice to me. I felt bad for both of them. Antonia sat looking straight ahead, without blinking an eye.

Jimmy Loveless was almost identical to Teddy in size and manner. They were both very small for their age. They acted loud and tough. Neither was a good student. They wreaked havoc in the classroom whenever they could. From that day on, they were like bookends. Wherever you found one, you would find the other.

There was a heavy girl named Margaret and a strange one named Elizabeth. They were both smart and poor. Mrs. Trent was nice to them but didn't pay them a lot of attention.

Betty Sue and Christine formed an instant friendship and sat next to each other the whole time we were at Sherman Grade School. Each was smart, rich, and the apple of the teacher's eye. They got to do everything, like pass out papers, give out chalk, and help others who were having problems.

Big Mike Zabowski—he was big even then—sat in the back row. He lived right on the corner of Sherman Acres Road. He always had a silly grin on his face, and he laughed all the time. Everything was funny to him. He was smart but poor, so Mrs. Trent ignored him.

Waldo lived right next to the school, on a large farm. All he could talk about was farming. Although he was far from being smart, Mrs. Trent gave him lots of attention because he was the son of a big land-owner, and they were rich. Over eighty years earlier, his family had donated the very land where Sherman Acres School stood.

Faith Jones wandered around the room, talking to everyone. She was mentally retarded, as they called it back then. She was sweet to everyone, and she was very easy to redirect. "What's your name?" she would ask every time she saw you. It didn't matter if you had just told her fifteen minutes ago.

Graham Wilson was the trustee's son. No one bothered him, not even Mrs. Trent. He was very good-looking. I liked him. I guess he was as shy as I was. He seemed to be very confident. He was nice to me, even though he was in love with Christine from the first day of school.

Scotty Brooks barely spoke above a whisper. "If you can't talk louder than that, I can't hear you," Mrs. Trent said. She ignored him for the rest of the time we were in her class.

I soon learned that if you were smart, Mrs. Trent liked you; she would talk to you, even try to help you. If you were smart and came from a family with money, that was even better in her eyes. If you were not a bright star, she was mean and cruel to you. I knew I was in trouble that first day. I knew I wasn't smart. I was poor and foreign.

The only things Mrs. Trent taught us were the alphabet and our numbers. There was a little adding and subtraction. If you didn't know how to take it from there and figure things out, you were doomed to be a failure. If you could read well, she called on you and praised you. If you couldn't get it, she would stand you in front of the class and make fun of you. She told your classmates to make fun of you too.

Scotty Brooks, Faith Jones, Teddy Roosevelt, Jimmy Loveless, and I were the dumb ones. We were the laughingstock of the class. I was a justice seeker even back then. I could see the unfair treatment of my classmates and myself but could do nothing to change it.

The county nurses came to the school to give us shots and eye exams. After my exam, I was given a letter to take home to my parents. I had failed the exam. We went into the city to see an eye doctor. "You know, this child has a serious eye problem. She should have had glasses soon after her first year. I don't know if we can correct the damage done already," the doctor said sternly to my mother. As if it wasn't bad enough that I was ugly, now I was ugly with glasses too. Mama was embarrassed; she hadn't known I couldn't see.

The glasses did nothing to improve my vision or my looks. I still had lots of trouble in school. My mother took me back to the eye doctor. He put a patch over my right eye and told Mama to keep it on for two weeks and then bring me back to see him. I couldn't see at all with that patch over my right eye. Everything was one big blur of different colors. I kept falling down and getting hurt. I had big bruises everywhere. I couldn't read my letters.

We went back to the eye doctor. "She no can see at all now," my mother told him.

"I know that," the doctor said. "She can only see out of her right eye. I put that patch over it so the left eye would get stronger." It didn't work. I wore that patch over my right eye for a year. I knew that if I was going to survive, I needed to see. When seeing something was vital, like a car or the bus coming, I would lift the patch and look with both eyes. My left eye still doesn't see. If I cover the right one, everything will go blurry, just as it did when I was a child.

Since I couldn't see, I couldn't learn to read well. But I could hear just fine. I loved listening while others read and talked of all the things they were learning in school. I learned so much by just hearing what went on around me. When promotion to the next grade came along, I passed.

That November, Eisenhower was elected president. Everyone in Henderson County was wearing buttons that read "I like Ike." My pa was a diehard Democrat since Woodrow Wilson had saved him from the prison camp in World War I. Pa and Mama voted for Adlai Stevenson. The voting age then was twenty-one. No one else in the family was old enough to vote. Decades later I would have the pleasure of meeting Mr. Stevenson personally, and I wished all over again that he had been elected president. I guess Eisenhower made an okay president, but he was sick a lot. The one thing he did that had a direct effect on my life would happen many years later. When I went to the big city to go to nursing school, I had to take all of those expressways. Thanks to Ike, we have many wonderful roads running all through the land, north and south, east and west.

There was a problem with the polio shots the county was giving us at school. Children started dying like flies on a cold day. Sammy was leaving for the army, and he made Mama promise she wouldn't let us get vaccinated. We never received the shots. We never got polio, although all summer long we played in the mud and swam in the creek that ran through Strawberry Fields Farm.

Polio did hit our family the following spring, but it was Marco who got it. I will never forget his grave illness. He cried out in pain and yelled in the night. The doctor came to the farm to look at him. "Well, in twenty-four hours, we'll know. If he makes it through, he will be all right." That was the longest day ever at Strawberry Fields. No one slept; everyone stood watch. Marco made it through the night. His legs and arms slowly started to move again. In two weeks' time, he was back on his feet. He was very weak, but he was going to make it.

Second grade was no better than first grade for me. I still had problems seeing and reading. I didn't know right from left. Mrs. Trent was appalled when she learned of this. "I don't know how you can be so stupid. You're left-handed, so which way is left?" asked Mrs. Trent. I got it wrong again.

She made me stand in front of the class with my arm outstretched, pointing left. I had to keep pointing and saying, "Left, left, left," for the rest of the day. When my arm started to drift downward, she would come by and slap it back up in the air. I was glad Antonia was no longer in the same room with me. She would have gone home and told our parents. I would have gotten punished for not being good at school.

It was in the second grade that I began to notice how different we were from everyone in Sherman Acres. Not only did Mrs. Trent refer to us as "those people," so did everyone in the area. I knew we were different. I could see it now. All of the other children had fair skin and blond, light-brown, or red hair. None resembled us in the least. I spent a lot of time looking at myself in the mirror. I was hoping I would change and look like everyone else. The more I looked in the mirror, the more I saw those differences.

Our social standing in the neighborhood was a big problem. Society in our area was very structured, and there were unwritten rules that were never allowed to change or be broken. Sherman Acres was made up of small farms like ours. In order to build a house there, you needed to own at least five acres of land. Small farmers were considered the poorest people around. Surrounding these small farms were big landowners who had thousands and thousands of acres of farmland. These farmers would either farm the land themselves or contract it out to big food companies that would do all of the hiring, firing, and farming. Whether the farms were company-run or farmer-run, the landowners were very rich. They didn't like any of us small-farm people. We weren't allowed to associate with them. All social events were done separately. There were small-farmer events and big-landowner ones.

Sherman Acres lies between two small towns: New Moon Lake to the north and Henderson to the south. In those towns there were rich people who were lawyers, doctors, and businessmen. They associated with the big landowners. There were poor people too—factory workers, teachers, secretaries, store clerks, and waitresses. These were the people with whom small farmers could associate.

The churches in the area were pretty much the same. We were Catholics, and there were only two churches we could attend. We belonged to Christ the King Church in New Moon Lake. Saint John the Baptist was in Henderson; it was a new church, built to replace the old one. It was right across the street from Enzo's new home. All the rest of the churches were non-Catholic, and there were a ton of them all over Henderson and New Moon.

Since we didn't go to Catholic school, we had to attend religious education classes once a week. It was the only time we were in social contact with big landowners. A few of them belonged to our church and, like my parents, sent their children to public school.

I was lost in the social norms of the area. I didn't fit in anywhere. Reality started to slip further away. When I went to those friends of mine I had in my head, it became harder to leave them and live in the real world, which had become so painful. I was ugly and stupid, and everyone made fun of me. I did my daydreaming even in school. When I went to that place in my head, I couldn't hear anything or anyone. Letters were going home to my parents. My mother sent Carmella to school to talk to Mrs. Trent and explain to her that I was already behind in school. She wanted to know what could be done so that I could pass to the next grade. It was the custom for the eldest girl child to help look after younger siblings. My mother's English made her reluctant to talk to people outside the family. It was Carmella's job to help her with these things.

"Well, we will see how she does on the testing. If it is satisfactory, I will consider her promotion," Mrs. Trent said.

My brothers and sisters approached all social matters very differently than I did. They were all very friendly and outgoing. Enzo had been popular in school and married a popular girl. Carmella was beautiful and had many friends and a ton of boyfriends. She dressed in the latest style and went to all of the dances, no matter what groups sponsored them. Sammy and Marco worked hard to fit in. They saved their money and bought good clothes. They mixed well in any group. Sammy was a big football star; although he was small, he was fast. Football made him an acceptable friend to his classmates.

Spring came early that year. Enzo and Nina had a baby girl they named Susie. She was very cute. She looked just like Buddy when he was born. I was very relieved when Enzo didn't drown her in the creek. On the rare nights when I slept, I no longer dreamed of puppies and baby girls in sacks floating in that creek. Enzo could be so cruel! It always scared me. I couldn't wait until school was out, so I could go to his house and play with the new baby.

I really looked forward to spring each year, when something very special happened at Strawberry Fields Farm. In early March, Mama sent away for fertilized eggs that she would place in a contraption called a brooder house. It did look sort of like a house. Behind the big coal furnace was the warmest place. The brooder house was able to maintain a constant temperature of ninety-eight degrees back there, until the eggs became baby chicks. It was like a miracle to watch this happen every year. Seeing the shells of those eggs crack open and little yellow chicks come out gave me hope and comfort. The brooder was removed, and the baby chicks lived behind the furnace until they were big and strong enough to survive out of doors. They would grow to lay lots of eggs and become many chicken dinners in winter.

There was talk at school of getting out early due to planting season. It sometimes took precedence over school. During this time there were new kids at school whose parents had come north in order to find work. These people were called "wetbacks." I didn't know why. I kept looking at their backs to see if they were wet, but they were always dry. They spoke another language. It was close to my parents' Italian. Someone said it was Spanish. A little boy joined our second-grade class. He was very dark and didn't speak a word of English. I didn't know how he was going to be able to do anything in school. One day while Mrs. Trent was talking to us, he went up to her and said something. No one knew what it meant. "*Dónde está el baño?*" he said.

"I can't help you. I don't know what you are saying," Mrs. Trent answered, quite irritated. The child came to my desk and said it again. I guess since I was dark with dark hair, he thought I could understand him.

"Teacher, he wants to know where the bathroom is," I said.

"Now how would you know that, Evaleene? You're too stupid to know anything else. Isn't that true?" asked Mrs. Trent very loudly. The whole class laughed. She never could say my name and always called me Evaleene, drawing out the last syllable. I always hated being called a name that wasn't mine.

"Because what he is saying sounds a lot like Italian, and *baño* means 'bathroom,'" I said. I was never brave or talkative, but I felt sorry for the boy. I was sure I knew what he wanted.

"Oh, well…okay, then," Mrs. Trent stammered. "Teddy, you take him to the bathroom. Thank you, Evaleene, for your help." I believe that these were the only kind words Mrs. Trent ever spoke to Teddy and me in the three years she was our teacher. Those wetback children would come and go from our school without any warning. They never stayed more than a few weeks, and they never returned. We would see new ones every season.

Teachers ruled the school. Parents never questioned their wisdom or authority, and heaven help the student brave enough to try. When testing time came, Mrs. Trent was shocked to find that I tested at the third-grade, fifth-month level. She knew I couldn't cheat, because even with my glasses, I still couldn't see well. We sat in every other seat for a test. I always sat right up front. "I don't know what to say, Evaleene. You are a mystery to me. I guess you pass to the next grade," she said, pushing up her glasses and rubbing her tired eyes.

I was excited when I got home and told Mama, "I'm going into the third grade." She was relieved, although she said nothing. I could tell.

That summer, it was very hot. I stayed outdoors almost all the time. Some ladies formed the Play Mate Club for all girls in the area. It was at a different girl's house every other week. One of those girls had a swimming pool, and that's when Mama made us those bathing suits out of feed sacks. We loved them and thought they were great. I knew that other girls made fun of us behind our backs. It wasn't long before Antonia started her usual trick of pitting one person against another. All the girls began to argue. No one got along after the first few weeks of meetings. The club broke up before it was our turn to have a meeting. I didn't care much for the club anyway. I was happy to spend the summer under my tree in the woods, with my made-up friends.

My other favorite thing to do that summer was riding the neighbor's horse. His name was Captain Tony. He was big, old, and gray. He couldn't even trot. He could only walk around the fields and meadows, but he took us wherever we wanted to go. I loved that horse. All of my brothers and sisters had ridden him at some time in their lives. I was glad it was my time to have him. We rode bareback on Captain Tony all summer long.

Third grade was no better than second grade and first grade. It might have been a little worse. Mrs. Jones decided to take Faith out of school for good. The school had no programs for a child like her. The other children were mean to her. Mrs. Trent wasn't kind to her either and didn't have time for her. I felt bad for Faith. I wondered what she would do all day at home, with just her mother and no playmates. She didn't live far from Strawberry Fields.

Crazy Elizabeth lived next door to Faith. She was one of my few friends. Everyone said she was crazy, even though she was very smart in school. I played with her throughout most of my school days. I had no clue, until I was well into my adult years, that she was being abused by her father and her two older brothers. It put all of those years of strange behavior into perspective. I went to Elizabeth's house, and we walked together over to the Joneses' to visit Faith. She was her usual self, so glad to see us, as if we were new to her all over again. Faith was always happy and seldom complained or cried about anything. "How are you? It is so good to see you. What's your name?" One solid hour of Faith repeating herself over and over again was all we were able to stand. After that visit, I figured her mother had made the right decision for her. Mrs. Jones treated her much better than anyone at school.

Teddy Roosevelt and Jimmy Loveless were inseparable. They did everything together, including getting into trouble. Some of the things they did scared me. They got punished for some of the most trivial things, yet when they did things I thought were horrifying, no one seemed to care. One of those things was called "choking." They would hold their breath and put their hands around their necks until their faces turned black from lack of oxygen, and then they would pass out and lie there on the floor until they regained consciousness. Mrs. Trent never said a thing to them and made no attempt to stop them. Sometimes they would be out for over an hour before fully responding again. She would go right on with the lesson plan, as if nothing were wrong.

Another boy who was in second grade liked to drop his pants and show all the girls his penis. He would come up to you, shake it at you, and laugh. Some of the girls liked it! They would join in the fun, dancing around and laughing. I was horrified and confused by it and the lack of concern by our two teachers. There was no response from Mrs. Trent or the principal. But God help a kid who dropped or spilled something or got caught chewing gum. Mrs. Trent would go into overdrive on them. Punishment for these crimes was high. The yardstick came out, or even the big wooden paddle. Scotty Brooks still could not bring himself to talk above a whisper. He peed his pants whenever Mrs. Trent yelled at him, which was almost every day.

Betty Sue and Christine were the darlings of the class and could do no wrong. They played together every day, excluding everyone except Graham Wilson, Waldo, and the boy in the second grade who was always showing them his penis.

Margaret was smart and well-behaved, but she was fat, so Mrs. Trent left her alone. She kept to herself most of the time, reading books and writing things down on paper. I went to her house a few times to play. She was treated so badly by her whole family that I couldn't stand it. They made fun of her and called her terrible names that I can't even repeat. It was worse than the treatment I got from my siblings. I lost interest in trying to be her friend. I would come to regret this later in life.

Waldo was probably retarded or slow, but since he was the son of a big landowner, he was passed from grade to grade. It was felt that you didn't need much of an education if all you were going to do was farm anyway.

At the end of the summer, Enzo and Nina had another baby. They named him Joey. He was very dark, with lots of black hair. He was a big boy, but I learned to handle him just fine. Enzo and Nina often argued. Nina cried a lot. One day I heard her say that she was only twenty-one and had three children, only a little more than a year apart. She and Enzo would holler and scream at each other all the time. I did my best to help care for the children when Nina would lock herself in the bathroom and cry for hours. I changed and fed the babies. "I never should have gotten married," I heard her say to one of her sisters. "It isn't how I thought it would be. I'm so unhappy!" She had three sisters, and each was more miserable than the next. She had a brother, but he seemed to be happy all the time.

Halloween was a big deal in Sherman Acres. We kids talked about it for weeks before and made plans for the three-day celebration. We always made it last as long as we could. It is nothing today like it was back then. There was no adult supervision for trick-or-treating. No one worried about razor blades or poison candy. The stuff we got was mostly homemade or homegrown. We would get apples, pears, and the occasional orange. Our neighbors made homemade fudge and taffy. We got popcorn balls and candied or caramel apples. Some of the rich landowners would give out candy bars—Hershey, Baby Ruth, or Butterfinger. Pennies were given out, and we hoped to get lots of them. Homes were few and far between. Trick-or-treating took three days in order to reach all the places where we might get good treats.

The tricks were planned way in advance. Some of them were the same each year, like the annual turning over of Mrs. Horton's outhouse. Marco and his friends loved doing it. They thought it was funny. This particular year Mrs. Horton thought she was better prepared for them. She tied her dogs to the outhouse. She had several large, mean animals that were known to attack. They were loud; their howling could be heard for miles. Since we were in the country, there were no streetlights, and few places had outdoor lighting. When the boys began to sneak up to the outhouse to do the job, the dogs howled loudly. They started running after the boys, pulling the outhouse and its contents along with it. The dogs ran after Marco and his friends for more than a mile until the dogs became entangled in some bushes at the bend in the road, where they were found still entwined the following morning, outhouse and all, by a farmer on his way to a nearby cornfield. Neither Mrs. Horton nor her dogs ever caught the boys.

The darkness offered great cover for other pranks that the older kids liked to play on us younger folk. If there was no moon in the black-as-pitch night, we would all walk down the road arm in arm, so no one would fall or get lost. The older boys would always walk way ahead of us. They would take along a length of dark-colored twine and string it across the road, holding it taut on either side. We, of course, couldn't see it. We would trip and fall, bursting our bags and scattering our candy all over the road. The big boys would steal it and run away, leaving a bunch of crying children in their wake.

Big changes came to Sherman Acres School the following year. The principal, who had been there for forty years, passed away. Now that he was gone, things began to change for the better, most people said. The seventh and eighth grades were moved to a different school. Since there would be only six grades now, three grades would be in each room. My fourth-grade class would be with Mr. Randle. I was excited to have him as a teacher, as Antonia talked about him at the dinner table every night, telling us that he was a great teacher. Antonia would be going to another school. She would be riding a different bus, which came an hour before the one that took us to Sherman Acres School.

It could be said that Mr. Randle was exactly like Mrs. Trent, only he was a man. He didn't like kids who weren't smart, and he didn't teach much. He spent a lot of time in the basement of the school. His face was always red, his nose ran a lot, and his speech was sometimes hard to understand. There were days he couldn't come to school at all. I remember that he smelled of cologne and wine.

I knew the smell of wine, because my father made it every autumn from grapes we grew on our farm. I used to like wine when I was very little. I would go to the wine cellar and listen to the grapes fermenting. The sound and the smell were enchanting to me. I would lie under one of the wooden barrels, turn the spout to a nice steady drip, and drink all the wine I wanted. My pa's homemade was the best in the land. But after smelling it on Mr. Randle, I lost my taste for it altogether.

Things were no different in "the big room," as we called it. Mrs. Trent's room was known as "the little room." Once again, Teddy Roosevelt got tossed out because he said he was Teddy Roosevelt. This time he went out without an argument. There was no big sister Maddy to try to set things right for him. She had moved on to the junior high with Antonia. He liked getting put outside. He knew the teacher would figure it out sooner or later, and he would be allowed back in.

One day at the beginning of the school year, Mr. Randle

announced that anyone who didn't know his or her multiplication tables would be put back into the third grade. I told my parents at the dinner table that night. My mother sent Carmella to school to talk to Mr. Randle and plead my case, to say that I was too old to be in the fourth grade, let alone to be put back. The whole class was talking loudly the next day while Carmella met with Mr. Randle at the front of the room. I watched intently, but I couldn't hear a word. After she left, Mr. Randle came and sat down at the desk in front of me. "I didn't say you would be the only one going back to the third grade. It would be everyone. No one in this class knows those tables. I was only talking about math, not the whole class moving back."

"Well, I guess I didn't understand what you meant," I said.

"I guess you didn't," he replied with a mean stare.

I was more scared than ever. When we went home for the weekend, I sat in the basement, at the table by the washing machine, and wrote out all my times tables until I had them memorized. I wrote them over and over again until my fingers ached. Although Mr. Randle was impressed that I had done this so well, he wasn't happy. I was still having problems in fourth grade. There were new subjects I knew nothing about and didn't understand. When I read my geography book, I didn't know what any of those words meant.

Carmella was going steady with a boy named Norman Schultz. They had been dating on and off for the last year. He wasn't rich or good-looking like many of Carmella's other boyfriends, but he was nice, and he fit in well with our family. He was kind and made my brothers behave much better. "Don't talk to your little sister like that, you guys. Use some manners, won't you?" He brought a certain order to our house that had been missing. The best thing about him was that he always helped me with my homework, even when he was tired and just wanted to visit with Carmella. Norman Schultz helped me with my geography, and I managed to get a passing grade. But everything made me cry. I cried every time I didn't understand my homework. I had never been a crier; I didn't put up a fuss about anything. Something strange was beginning to happen to me. I didn't understand it, and I couldn't stop it, either.

That fall I was turning ten. Carmella and Norman got me a present and a cake. It was the best birthday of my entire young life. In our family, no one got gifts or a cake for their birthday. There just wasn't money for such things. When I opened the big, nicely wrapped box, it contained a brown herringbone pleated skirt and a yellow sweater I had admired at the general store in New Moon Lake. It was only the second time I had clothes that were not made from the feed sacks containing animal food. The first outfit I had was a gray poodle skirt and a pink sweater with a poodle on it. I wore it until it fell apart. "Oh, thank you, Norman and Carmella!" I said, jumping up and down.

"You better go try it on, make sure it fits," said Carmella. I went to my parents' bedroom, where there was a full-length mirror on the wardrobe closet. When I turned to look at myself, I couldn't believe what I saw. I knew my body was changing. It had started in the third grade, when I noticed black hair starting to grow between my legs. I ignored it. I just didn't look at it. In the mirror I saw that I had breasts. That sweater was showing them off. Even Antonia didn't have breasts like these yet. I looked more like Carmella from the waist up. Those breasts had been hurting me for some time.

"Mama!" I called. "Could you come here?" When she entered the room, I turned around. "Look."

"Looka whata?" she asked in her broken English.

"Look at these," I said, pointing to my chest. "I think I need one of those bra things like Carmella wears." Mama took a tape measure from her dresser drawer. She rarely went shopping. My father bought all the groceries and whatever else she told him to buy. I wasn't sure how he was going to buy me a bra, but he came home from work the next day with one that actually fit me. He had gotten one for Antonia too. I guess it was so she wouldn't feel bad because I needed something that she didn't need yet. Besides my body starting to change and the crying all the time, other strange things were happening. I wasn't visiting my imaginary friends so much anymore. They were still there in my head. I could bring them to reality, but it wasn't as satisfying.

A few weeks later, my father came home from work with a television set. Everyone in the house was so excited, yelling and talking at once. We were the last family in Sherman Acres to get one. All of our neighbors had them. The whole family would sometimes go to one of the neighbors' houses and watch their television. My father would take them some wine and produce from the gardens in exchange for letting us watch their TV. I couldn't recall the last time we did it. I could hardly wait to get on the bus in the morning so I could talk to everyone about the TV shows. Everyone watched the same ones: *I Love Lucy*, *Amos and Andy*, *Fibber Magee and Molly*, and *Father Knows Best*. These shows were all the kids talked about on the bus ride. Now that we finally had a TV, I could join in the conversation!

Television was my first glimpse into what I thought was the real world. I loved it! I was fascinated. I learned so much from watching it. It was a look into the way other people lived. They dressed in fine clothes and spoke to each other politely. I loved all the shows. I would watch it nonstop if I didn't get caught. No one was home when I got off the bus. If it was winter, my mother was feeding the animals or cooking in the kitchen. If it was warm weather, she would be working in the fields. I had the house and the TV all to myself until my father came home from work. Pa only liked westerns, *Dragnet*, and *The Lawrence Welk Show*. Mama only liked *Lawrence Welk*. The TV was in the living room. I would sometimes watch it from the dining room, where no one could see me hiding on the stairs that led to the basement. I did it even when I was supposed to be in bed.

I still didn't sleep well, but Antonia continued to sleep like a log. She didn't seem to be fazed by the TV. She rarely watched it. I would slip out of bed in the middle of the night, turn the set on at low volume, and watch the late movie. I would stay up until the test pattern came on. We only got three channels, and even they were fuzzy.

One cold early morning in January, I awoke with a severe pain in my lower abdomen. I knew what it was almost immediately. It hadn't been that long since Antonia started her period. Carmella told her all about it and taught her what to do when it came. "Mama never told me a thing. I thought I was dying when I got mine, so I wanted you to be prepared and know what it's all about." She told Antonia in detail why a woman gets her period every month. I listened outside the bedroom door, so I would know what to do when the time came.

I got out of bed, went to the bathroom, and found the box of Kotex on the top shelf of the closet. "Mama, I need some of those things. It's time," I said when I came down for breakfast. I didn't need to say another word. She knew what I was talking about, but she had a sad look as she added the item to Pa's shopping list. We were never allowed to say "Kotex." It was always "those things." I think Mama was disappointed that I had started so young. Antonia was twelve when hers came. Carmella was seventeen. I was only ten! I was taller than Mama, Carmella, and Antonia. They were all less than five feet. I was five feet and two inches.

Sammy, Marco, Carmella, and Antonia all made fun of the way I looked. "She's so tall and awkward-looking," they all said. "Let's hope she doesn't grow anymore." I didn't grow much more, only about a half inch. I became very depressed. I was ugly; I had glasses, big breasts, and a period too. It was the name-calling that was the worst—Long Tall Sally, Beanpole, Ichabod Crane. I didn't realize that they did this because they were all short people. It wouldn't do for the youngest to be taller than all of them. I was terrified that I would grow and keep growing until I was too big to fit in the house. It was another worry to keep me awake.

≫6≪

Carmella Leaves Home

CARMELLA TOLD MY MOTHER that she was engaged to Norman Schultz. They were going to get married in the spring. I was so glad. I liked Norman a lot. It would be nice to have him at Strawberry Fields Farm. I would have help with my homework every night. My siblings would have to be nicer to me, because Norman always insisted on it. He would take us places with him and Carmella. When I found out about the engagement, I was awake and listening again to stuff I wasn't supposed to hear. "I knew it would happen," I heard Mama say. "You are not smart, Carmella. You lucky this guy, he marry you. Man doesn't want to marry bad girl."

"Well, it isn't for a while yet, so no one will know," Carmella said.

Things became very busy that spring. We were always going places in Carmella's car, to get stuff for the wedding or to make plans at her friends' houses. June seemed like a long way off to me. I was happy. I had never been to so many places. I didn't know there were so many stores. The department stores we went to had air conditioning, and it was the first time I felt it. I thought it was wonderful, but it was often too cold for me. Since the heat never bothered me, cool air chilled me very quickly. In those days no one spent more than a few minutes in any one store. I had no idea there were so many places to go, and there were so many people everywhere we went.

Sammy was still in the army. He was going to be sent to somewhere far away called Japan. I didn't care. I thought it was a good trade—Sammy gone, and Norman here instead. He was so nice to Antonia and me. He always took us to the movies and roller skating. Carmella had discovered roller skating after she started working as a waitress at a diner on the big highway. When she bought her own car, she started going everywhere. She found the roller rink on New Moon Lake, and Norman Schultz. He was younger than she was, by about four years. He was in the same class as Sammy, but I don't think he finished high school, although he was smart. He could skate like a professional. People would stop skating just to watch him move around the floor with Carmella in a waltz, a foxtrot, or even a jitterbug.

Carmella liked skating so much because it helped to correct her only flaw. Her legs had been bowed since birth. Roller skating helped to straighten and strengthen them. She would sometimes take Antonia and me with her. I wasn't crazy about skating. I always fell a lot, but it got me off the farm for a few hours. I got to visit with Wanda, Norman's younger sister, who was six months younger than me, but she was a year ahead of me in school. She went to the Catholic school at Christ the King Church. Skating was the only time we got to see each other. I always thought she was so pretty. She had freckles on her face, and her hair was blonde.

I didn't learn that I was to be in the wedding until a powder-blue dress arrived in the mail from the Bellas Hess catalog. Antonia and I had been playing in the creek. We were covered with mud when Mama called us to come into the house. It was one of those rare times when Antonia played with me without displaying any strange behavior. We had spent the afternoon in the creek, wading, laughing, and making mud pies. There was no talk of my being adopted. For the first time since I could remember, Antonia didn't run home and tell Mama I had done some terrible things to her. Reluctantly we came out of the creek and walked up the hill to the house.

I had to be put in the big cast-iron tub and washed with Mama's homemade lye soap in order to get clean enough to try on my dress. It fit me just fine. I loved it so much that I had a hard time taking it off. We had to go shopping for an under-slip and shoes. I realized then that Antonia didn't get a dress and that she wasn't going to be in the wedding. Mama bought her a white dress with big pink cabbage roses all over it. She looked beautiful. When we were standing next to each other, I noticed for the first time that I looked much older.

June 9 seemed to me some time far away in the future, but it probably was only a month away. I loved that blue dress so much that I begged Mama every day to let me wear it. She always said no, of course; it was for the wedding. Marco was graduating from high school. I wanted to wear my new dress. I began to scream and cry. "You no go at all to the graduation if you cry. You will stay at home with Nina and the babies," said Mama. Antonia and I stayed home with Nina and the three babies. I really didn't mind, because I liked to play with them. The blue dress hung on a hook in the basement kitchen all those days before the wedding.

It was bright and sunny outdoors on the wedding day. We all rose very early. We had to pick the strawberries and get them to the local grocery store early. We finished around eight. Carmella was up. I cannot remember a day before or since then when she was ever that quiet. She looked scared and said little. She was the same the night before, at the church for the rehearsal. There was no fancy dinner after the practice; people didn't do that back then. We all just went home and went to bed, even Carmella, who always had somewhere to go and someone to meet. I was sure that Enzo and Marco had taken Norman out for a few too many beers that night.

We all got cleaned up and dressed in record time. Carmella looked like a bride from a magazine ad. She was so pretty in a full-skirted, tea-length white lace and organza wedding dress with long lace sleeves. On her head she wore a crown of iridescent pearls; they reflected rainbow colors in the morning sun. The crown had a short veil that came to her fingertips. She wore lacy high-heeled shoes.

Mama was in the traditional black dress that she wore for everything important—weddings, funerals, or to visit the sick. Nina had cut and set my hair in pin curls the night before. She came to the farm early that morning to comb it out. She was wearing her yellow organdy halter dress with the full skirt. It had been her own wedding dress five years ago. Antonia wore the white dress with the pink cabbage roses. Pa was in his only suit and tie; the suit was black. Marco had on a tuxedo with a white jacket. Enzo wore his only suit as well.

We all gathered outside. Pa assigned everyone a seat in the cars. I rode in the backseat of my father's car with Carmella, while Mama rode up in the front. Antonia rode with Marco in his car. Enzo, Nina, and the three babies went in their own car.

We arrived at the church at nine-thirty. I was starving! In those days we were not allowed to eat anything after midnight before receiving Holy Communion. The bridesmaids had arrived. Dee-Dee Schultz was Norman's cousin, and Shirley White was Carmella's best friend. Gloria Winooski was Marco's girlfriend. She was the maid of honor. He was breaking up with her because he was going to join the army. She was a sweet and loving person who was kind to everyone. I can't say that Marco treated her very well.

The girls were all wearing the same powder-blue strapless dress with a tiny bolero jacket. The dresses were full and also tea-length, made of lace and organza. They wore white heels and we all had pink flowers in our hair. Mine were on a headband that kept digging into my head.

Marco went to the front of the church, to a room just off of the altar, to join the other groomsmen and Norman. Norman's brother Melvin was the best man, and his best friend, Roger Wilkes, was a groomsman. They all wore the same tuxedo, with a pink carnation in the lapel of the white jacket.

Christ the King Church was crowded with relatives, friends, and neighbors of both families. My parents' Italian friends came from the city. Norman had a large family with many aunts and uncles. He had another older brother and sister. There were many farm families in attendance, big landowners as well as small-farm people.

I was the first one down the aisle when the music started to play. Holding my bouquet of pink camellias, I walked slowly, as I had been taught the night before. I can still recall how beautiful those flowers smelled. Every time I see pink camellias, they remind me of Carmella.

My sister was truly a vision in white as she came to the altar with Pa. In those days the Mass was a full hour long, and even longer if it was a High Mass. Weddings were always High Masses. We had to kneel a lot more then. The whole bridal party stayed at the altar the entire time the Mass was being said.

Ever so discreetly, I began munching on my flowers as I knelt and tried to listen to what was going on. Suddenly I heard a loud thump, and I turned to see Cousin Dee-Dee hit the floor hard as she fainted away from lack of food and water. Although it was only ten in the morning, the church with no air conditioning was already sweltering hot. Marco and the other boys ran to her aid and had her on her feet. She sat for the rest of the Mass.

A large crowd threw rice as we descended the church steps. Well-wishes rang out as we fled for the parking lot and the cars that would take us to Fienberg Studios for pictures. I was squeezed into Marco's decorated car along with Shirley, Dee-Dee, and Roger Wilkes. I didn't mind, because I got to sit on Roger's lap. He was a wonderful guy who always played with me. He was like a big kid. He would swing me into the air, laugh, and talk like a boy. He even danced with me at the reception that night. Norman and Carmella were in the backseat of Melvin's car ahead of us, with Gloria. There was a sign on the heavily decorated car that said JUST MARRIED. Tin cans and old shoes were tied to the back bumper. Marco and Melvin blew the cars' horns, and we made a lot of noise as we rode around New Moon Lake several times.

Mrs. Fienberg took all the pictures that day, just as she did at my own wedding many years later. She did pictures for all of my family and relatives. I regret never going back to collect them when the Fienbergs closed their studio some five decades after Carmella's wedding day. They sent a notice to each of their customers, telling them of the closing and giving them the choice of negatives and pictures they had archived over many years.

It was traditional then to hold a wedding breakfast at the house of the bride. My parents rushed home to prepare the meal. In attendance were the entire wedding party and the priest from our church. Mama was in a tizzy as she ran around the upstairs kitchen table, serving everyone. She made what she knew best to cook: spaghetti, meatballs, and fried chicken with the trimmings.

Later that afternoon, Carmella wanted to ride around some more and blow the horn in celebration. After the bridal party left, Mama, Mrs. Schultz, and a few of Norman's aunts stayed at Strawberry Fields to help prepare for the reception. They all assembled in the downstairs kitchen. They made many egg-salad and ham-salad sandwiches—over two hundred and fifty.

I was not allowed to go on the second round of car rides. I was made to stay at home in the downstairs kitchen while the women worked. I had taken my dress off, and it hung there from a hook on the jack post. I was supposed to take a nap on the couch. With a single white sheet over me, I lay there in my white slip and stocking feet, unable to sleep. The day had grown very hot, without a cloud in the sky. It was the year of the seventeen-year locust. The sound of their mating call filled the thick, hot air that came in through the open windows. There were millions and millions of those katydids, as we called them, because that was what their cry sounded like to us: "Katydid! Katydid!" They chanted all day and night. The ground outside was covered in the brown shells of the dead insects, as they died soon after mating. When you walked across the yard, they made a crunching noise under your feet.

The reception was held at the Henderson County fairgrounds, in the Fine Arts Pavilion. The grounds were alive with people. It was a place where lots of sales went on when there wasn't a fair. Livestock and farm goods and equipment were auctioned off all day and well into the evening.

The pavilion had three wings, and it was so big that you could drive several semi-trucks into it at once. I sat at a long, white table with Norman, Carmella, and the rest of the bridal party, eating those sandwiches. I drank a lot of pop that night; it was something we rarely had at home. A band was playing music, and everyone danced, having a good time. I ran around playing with Wanda. There were lots of those sandwiches left over. Some sailors came walking through the Fine Arts Pavilion as the reception was coming to an end. When Mama spotted the sailors, she turned to Mrs. Schultz and asked, "Would it be all right with you if we give the leftover sandwiches to those boys?"

"What a great idea! Since we have so much stuff we need to take back home, it would help us too," Mrs. Schultz replied. The sailors stayed and ate. They danced and had a good time until the band stopped playing at midnight. I can't remember coming home. I must have fallen asleep in the backseat of Pa's car.

I was pretty happy. I started to sleep a little better, although I wouldn't have if I had known how drastically everything was about to change. A few weeks after the wedding, Norman and Carmella went away on a honeymoon. I didn't know what that was, but they were gone for a few weeks. Marco left for the army. The house at Strawberry Fields Farm became unbearably quiet. Antonia was not talking to me. She didn't come anywhere near me. I roamed the fields and wooded areas alone. It was so lonely without Norman and Carmella. I could barely pull any of my imaginary friends up into my head for company. There was no more skating or movies, no trips to the store to buy things for the wedding. It was over. The TV was all I had. I watched it continuously. Mama would find me there and make me turn it off and go outdoors. Life had come to a complete standstill.

Norman and Carmella did not return to Strawberry Fields after they came home from their trip. The day Carmella came to visit us, Mama cried. Carmella was wearing one of those big blouses like Nina wore when she was expecting another baby. In the few weeks she was gone, her stomach had ballooned to twice its size. "What will people think when they see you?" Mama wanted to know.

"I'll tell them it happened while we were away," Carmella answered, making Mama cry even more.

The summer dragged on, long and hot. One late August morning, I woke up with a terrible pain in my lower stomach. I had another one of those periods. They were starting to come quite regularly. The pain that morning was different, much more intense. I cried and paced the floor upstairs, from the living room through the dining room, into the kitchen, the bathroom, and back. I bent forward and held my stomach, crying harder and louder. Antonia watched me for some time and then went outside. I was surprised when she returned with Mama, who had been in the field with Pa, getting in the last of the summer vegetables and fruits.

"Whata wrong?" she asked in her broken English.

"It's pain, Mama, bad pain. I can't take it much longer," I cried.

"You go to bed, and you lay down," Mama said. I did as I was told. She came into our room a few minutes later with some water and two aspirin tablets. She placed a hot-water bottle on my abdomen and told me to go to sleep. I slept for two days, getting up only to use the bathroom and eat a few bites. I couldn't eat much. I only weighed about fifty pounds. The following month when I got my period, the pain wasn't quite as bad. When I limped to the bathroom, bent over once again, Antonia followed. She gave me another aspirin out of the medicine cabinet. I stayed in bed until the afternoon.

In October Carmella gave birth to a baby girl they called Katie. It seemed to me that the baby took a long time coming, but not long enough for Mama. She wasn't happy that Carmella had little Katie so soon after the wedding. The baby cried all the time. Carmella said she had the colic. She would drive her around in the car for hours to get her to go to sleep. The baby never cried when Mama held her. I watched Katie a lot for my sister. I walked the floor, holding her. I could never stand to hear a baby cry. I never let any of the babies cry. I did everything I could to get them to stop. I held them, rocked them, and gave them trinkets. My life seemed to be filled with caring for babies. If I wasn't at Carmella's with Katie, I was at Enzo's with their three little ones. It seemed like I got old overnight. I didn't play anymore; television was my best friend.

My breasts got bigger and my monthly periods more painful. Pa brought home a bigger bra for me. Antonia still wore her first one. I was ugly, with even bigger breasts and a regular period. My hair had changed to a golden-brown color that glistened in the sunlight. I started to grow lots of hair all over my body. It was on my arms, legs, and underarms. I complained to Mama about it. She had Pa take his barber's razor and shave it off my underarms. I hated all the hair on my legs. I went into the bathroom late at night and took out the razor and the sharp blade my father used to shave his beard. I shaved all the hair on my legs. Before the week was out, it had grown back darker and more bristly. I had to keep shaving every week, then every other day. Pa came home with a new razor and gave me his old one. "You no touch this one," he said in his broken tongue. No razor was safe from me, not even the ones Pa locked in a steel box. I knew where he kept the key. I started shaving every day. I couldn't stop.

I was beginning to accept my new body a little when men began to look at me in a way that made me feel strange. The man that married one of the girls that lived next door was always watching me. He had pale skin and piercing blue eyes. He slicked back his thin black hair straight from his face, giving him an eerie look. He would approach me on the road to my friend's house. His car slowed, and he would stare at me. "Hello. Where are you going?" he would ask. If I ignored him, he would keep driving his car next to me until I got to where I was going. Then I learned that if I turned and started walking across one of the fields, he would drive off. He did nothing more, but it became clear to me in adulthood what he might have been doing as he sat behind the wheel of his car and drove by me slowly. He did it for sixty years. It was never reported that he hurt anyone, but no one talked of such things back then. He was so creepy that I actually got cold and shivered just thinking about those piercing blue eyes.

There was talk at the dinner table that Mama was going back to the old country. She hadn't returned since coming to America. She longed to see her homeland again. One cold November day, I came home from school to an empty house. "Where is Mama?" I asked Antonia when she got off her bus.

"She went into North End with Pa this morning, after you got on your bus. She told me she was going before I left this morning," she said. It was dark outside by the time they arrived home. I was shocked when Mama walked into the house. I almost didn't know her. She had been to the beauty shop and had all her hair cut off. It was really black and cut in a short, curly bob. The only hairstyle I had ever known my mother to have was a bun at the nape of her neck.

"Where is your hair?" I asked.

"It is in the bag," she answered, placing her things on the couch in the downstairs kitchen. I opened the bag to see. I felt sick and closed it again. "I have new dresses too, see?" She held up two very stylish dresses, one of which still hangs here in my closet after fifty-five years. It's black chiffon, with pink embroidered flowers on the skirt. Once, my daughter Jenna-Lisa wore it to a wedding she attended with her husband. Wearing the dress, she reminded me so much of Mama.

Many bags were brought in from the car. "What is all of this, Mama?" I asked, hoping some of it might be for me. I had a birthday the month before, but no one remembered it.

"It is things I take with me back to old country to give to my family," she said. After looking through a few of her bags filled with dish towels and other household items, I lost interest and went upstairs to the TV.

When Mama left for Italy, I had no idea she would be gone so long. The plan was for Norman and Carmella to come and stay at

Strawberry Fields. They had their own little three-room apartment in a building near Norman's parents' house. It had been transformed from an old chicken coop. Carmella had no intention of ever returning to the farm or watching us. She was twenty-five years old, with a family of her own. We would have to fend for ourselves until Mama returned.

Italians were known for many strange things—couches in the kitchen, an upstairs kitchen and a downstairs kitchen in the home, and never flying on airplanes. Mama took the train to New York City, where she would catch a boat bound for Europe. Since she never left the farm, I wasn't sure how she would manage alone. Pa assured me that she had come here alone at age nineteen, and that at forty-six she was capable of doing as she wished.

If I thought life was hard before Mama left, it was harder when she was gone. She didn't call home, because it cost too much. She wrote very little English and only wrote one or two letters to Pa, who couldn't read English or Italian. I wondered how he did all the shopping. I would later come to know all about charming store clerks who were always glad to help you spend money. They were always surprised to learn that Pa could count money, even if he only knew how to read a few words. Pa's cooking was not as good as Mama's, either. I ate very little of hers and less of his. Thanksgiving at Strawberry Fields remained very quiet. Enzo and Nina were spending the holiday at the Pullmans', Nina's parents. Norman and Carmella took Katie to the Schultzes' to show her off to all the relatives. Pa cooked a turkey that was so tough and tasteless that even the dog left his portion in his bowl next to the furnace.

When Pa was at work, I came home to a cold, empty house. It took a while to get the fire going well enough in the big coal furnace to heat the whole house. I shoveled coal and sat as close to the furnace as I could get without catching myself on fire. I sat shivering all alone and listening to the sounds of an empty house. It creaked and moaned in the blowing winter wind. Those hours alone passed like an eternity. Antonia chose not to come home right after school. She went to her friends' houses, or she rode the school bus into Henderson. Nina or Enzo drove her home. It never crossed anyone's mind that I was entirely on my own.

Casting for the Christmas play was held at school as soon as we returned from the short Thanksgiving break. I wanted a good part. I had been watching movies and shows on TV. I just knew I could be a good actress if I had a chance to prove it. Even in fifth grade, I still couldn't read very well. Mr. Randle didn't assign parts for the play he picked. He read the whole thing to us first, and then he asked who would like to play the part of this character or that one. I held out as my classmates chose their parts. I was the only girl left without a part when casting came for the main character. Mr. Randle had to give me the part!

Betty Sue and Christine were really mad at me. They had been mad at me since the first grade, when Betty Sue's mother allowed her to have a grown-up dinner party, with dancing. It was held at their house, which was very luxurious when compared to others. Christine got the fever when it hit Henderson County that year. She was out of school for over a month. Janie, Graham Wilson's older sister, called me on the phone to ask if I would attend Betty Sue's party with Graham. "He is too shy to ask you himself, so I'm calling for him," she explained. I loved Graham, with his blond hair and beautiful blue eyes. I didn't hesitate to say yes, even if I was his second choice.

Carmella washed and curled my long hair into banana curls that fell in long ringlets down my back. Mama made me a white satin dress with white roses on the neckline and a belt at the waist. I remember telling her how I needed a new dress for something special at school. She believed me and made me that beautiful dress. I think she was a little shocked when she learned it wasn't required for any special event. I was glad I had the dress to wear to the fancy party. Mama sure could fashion a pretty rose. I wore clean white socks and white shoes.

I was proud to be looking as good as the other girls, even if I was the ugly one in my family.

We had hamburgers and French fries at a dinner table set with fancy dishes and glasses in the dining room of Betty Sue's home. We got to drink Coca-Cola, too! These were foods I had never tasted in my life. I had only heard about them from others at school. I never had anything so fine. Graham and I sat next to each other. I don't recall what he said to me, but we laughed and talked through the whole meal. We went into the recreation room, played games, and danced. Graham and I danced every dance together. He chose me when we played games. It was the most fun time of my whole life, even if Graham was in love with Christine.

Betty Sue was with Waldo. I'm sure she chose him because his family was the richest in the whole area. It wouldn't do to be with someone who wasn't wealthy. Waldo couldn't dance, and he kept falling off the chairs when we played musical chairs. I thought there was nothing nice or attractive about him. He was just a clumsy farm boy.

"How do you think you are going to be able to do that part, when you can't even read?" Betty Sue demanded during recess that afternoon.

"I can too read! I'll do just fine," I said. Later, when we started to read our lines, I stumbled painfully.

Mr. Randle said nothing during the rehearsal, but he came to me after class. "Evaleene, would you like to exchange parts with one of the other girls? Maybe a simpler part would be better for you," he suggested.

"No, Mr. Randle," I said. "I just need to practice those lines. I'll get it, I'm sure."

"Well, if you don't, you will have to give up that part to one of the other girls," he said as he walked away.

That night I knew what I had to do in order to keep my part in the Christmas play. I stayed up all night, reading and memorizing lines. It was better the next day at practice, but it still wasn't as good as Betty Sue would have done it. I went home more determined than ever not to lose my part to her. Pa was working the afternoon shift in the factory. Antonia hadn't returned home from school. I was sure she was in town again. I made coffee and got some biscotti from the freezer. I ate a few and drank almost a whole pot of coffee. I was up until after midnight, going over and over those lines. The next day it went pretty well, and it was even better the following day. I started to add expression to the lines, as if saying them, not just reading them from a page. I watched so much TV that I knew how those Hollywood actresses did it.

No one at school commented on the way I seemed to fit into that part of the spoiled girl child at Christmas. I played that part so naturally that I began to think I really was that girl. I walked across the stage, tossing my hair and saying my lines with emphasis, one hand on my hip. I said my lines with perfect diction: "Because I'm a poor child, everyone will want to give me a gift this Christmas. Why, I'm even invited to City Hall to meet the mayor." Mr. Randle said nothing.

The night of the play, I wore the beautiful powder-blue dress I had worn for Carmella's wedding. She and Norman took Antonia and me to the play. Pa had to work. The basement of the school was completely filled with parents and family members. I was so determined to do well that I probably overacted my part. I was the only one who didn't miss a cue or a line. The audience's reaction surprised me. They laughed at a lot of my lines. I knew better than to react. After each act, they gave a standing ovation, with applause and cheers. My family said nothing of my acting ability on the way home. Mr. Randle said nothing either. Although they disappointed me, I was so pleased with my own performance that it didn't seem to matter. I knew not to expect a whole lot from people. Since I was ugly and stupid, I had come to accept whatever anyone said to me or about me.

Christmas vacation started the very next day. We were only in school for a few hours. Everyone was excited about the holidays. I didn't know why we had to be there, since there was no teaching or learning going on. The buses were loaded at noon. I went home to an empty house. Although no one said it, I felt sure that all had enjoyed the play. I just wished I had a little feedback from my teachers and my friends, or even a family member.

The next day Pa brought home a tree and set it up in the living room. I did my best to decorate it, although I wasn't good at such things. Antonia was very artistic, but she never came near any of our Christmas trees. It had always been Carmella, Sammy, and Marco dressing the tree in past years. Even Enzo used to help decorate it. He taught the others how to go to the homes of our neighbors, steal bulbs and lights off of their trees, and bring them home for ours. Most of the ornaments on our tree were things we made. Marco was the best at making them, but I loved the bright-colored red and green ones that my siblings stole from others. I knew it was wrong, and I didn't like that part. Since they had all left home, the tree I decorated looked sad.

It was a sad Christmas. Enzo was with his family and Carmella with hers. Sammy was still in Japan. Marco was in the army in Kentucky. He wouldn't spend any money to come home. He saved it all, because he said he had a plan to get himself out of poverty. I had no plan; I lived from day to day, just hoping to survive. I had little faith that Mama would return. She had been gone for more than a month, with no word of her coming back. I found a heating vent in the upstairs kitchen. Wrapped in a blanket, huddled near it was where I spent the whole of my vacation. I was locked in fantasies of becoming a great actress in the movies or on television. I rocked back and forth, dreaming of better days. Pa took his vacation from the factory. He commandeered the TV for the two weeks of vacation. It was too cold in the living room for me anyway. It was the farthest from the furnace.

Antonia found her own heating vent in the dining room. She

spent her vacation reading romance magazines that Carmella had brought to Strawberry Fields for Mama. That was the one thing Carmella and Mama had in common: they both loved those stories. Carmella bought at least five of them a week. When she was done with them, she passed them on to Mama. Now Antonia sat reading *True Story*, *Modern Romance*, and *Real Romance* magazines. Since Pa didn't read, supervising our reading material never crossed his mind.

At the end of January, Enzo and Nina had another baby. It took me by surprise. I had no idea she was expecting; no one had told us. Carmella knew. "Of course I knew! She didn't say anything to me either, but I'm not stupid, you know. I have eyes." I was glad I didn't know. I didn't have to endure any stories about drowning girl babies in the creek. Sally was a lovely baby with big gray-green eyes and golden-brown hair. She was sweet, and unlike Katie, she hardly cried.

We struggled through a cold January and February. I had a hole in the bottom of my shoe that kept getting bigger. Pa kept trying to patch it, hoping a new pair could wait until warmer weather. My clothes were getting too small for me. The feed-sack dresses did nothing to keep out the cold air.

It wasn't until the middle of March that I saw my mother again. I came home from school to find her in the kitchen, cooking something. She smiled and laughed and said she was glad to see me. Having nothing as nice as that to say, I told her how awful the last four months had been, how I had spent most of them alone. "You had no right to go off and leave us all alone. You never wrote or called! I wasn't even sure you were coming back," I yelled.

"But Antonia—" she started to say.

"She isn't here, and she hasn't been. She only comes home to sleep. Do you see her here now? Besides, she never talks to me anyway," I told her.

"But Carmella, she was staying here, no?" Mama offered.

"No, Mama, she wasn't. She has her own life and her own family," I said. I was even ruder to her when all I got from her trip abroad was an Italian headscarf. "But you took those people so many nice things and all my old clothes. All I get is this scarf? I'm going to my room." Disappointed, I stormed up the steps. I left one very stunned Italian mother with her mouth gaping open.

"But you don't understand. Those people are very poor over there, and we have much," she said. I kept on walking up the steps. I didn't go down to dinner that night when she called for Antonia, who had returned with Enzo. She went down, but I stayed in our room. I left for school the next morning without a word. I had been looking after myself for so long that I thought I didn't need her.

Spring finally came, bringing a new problem for me. Besides the bad cramps every month, big breasts, and hair growing all over me, I developed a pain in my chest. It was right in the center, just above my stomach. It wasn't there all the time, but it came and went without warning. I complained about it a lot. It kept me from eating what little food I usually ate.

The doctor in New Moon had me jumping up and down for a whole minute. He listened to my heart. "I don't think it's her heart, Mrs. Rosario. It sounds fine," he said.

"So what you think is this pain?" asked Mama.

"I'm not sure exactly, but I don't think it is anything to worry about." He gave my mother a chart with different things written on it in columns. They said "pain after eating," "pain before eating," "pain at rest," and "pain with activity." He said, "Use this to keep track of it. You can just put a mark under the one that fits."

Mama kept the chart, but it was no help to Dr. Hemming. After three months of tracking the pain, the hash marks were all over it. "She get the pain no matter what she do," Mama said.

"I see. Maybe she is just making it up, like those bad cramps she keeps having every month." He turned to me and said, "Just wait until you have a baby, young lady. Then you will really know what pain is." I looked away and said nothing.

After another three months, Mama and I returned to see Dr. Hemming. The pain was coming more frequently. "Just don't feed her any of that spicy Italian food. Give her bland stuff like oatmeal,

scrambled eggs, applesauce, and baked chicken—nothing fried." I
didn't eat that food any better than Mama's Italian food. I suffered all
summer with pain.

Two new girls joined us at Sherman Acres School in the fifth
grade. Juanita I knew already, because her family went to our church.
Carmella worked in her parents' restaurant next to their house on the
big highway. Juanita was smart, and she formed an instant friendship
with Crazy Elizabeth. Many years later I learned that they shared the
same type of devastating mental illness. They had experienced a lot of
the same type of trauma growing up. The illness would claim Juanita's
life when she reached her thirties. She died in a mental hospital from
a massive heart attack.

She came from the Catholic school in New Moon Lake. The
reason for the transfer was unclear. I later thought it was because of
her sister Joan, who was the same age as Antonia. Joan looked and
acted much older. She had a steady boyfriend who was in his twenties.
An older man pursuing a younger girl wasn't an unusual thing back
then; no one thought it a form of child abuse. Joan was planning on
quitting school at sixteen, when it was legal, to marry Douglas James.

Julia Marshall moved into Sherman Acres with her family that
year. Like me, she was dumb and couldn't learn. It was the label the
school gave you if you didn't perform the way you were supposed to
at your grade level. Julia was odd, but she wasn't dumb. She seemed
to be interested in lots of things, but they just weren't what a fifth-
grader was supposed to like. She read the papers, always interested
in real-life murder mysteries. She especially liked the story of the
Lindbergh baby kidnapping. She read all about it, and she kept the
articles. Although it happened many years ago, the story was retold in
many papers whenever a baby was reported missing

She came to school all bruised up. I think she was being beaten,
but I was never sure. They were quiet people who didn't mix with
anyone in the neighborhood. She had several younger brothers and
sisters. She alone took care of them. We were paired up a lot. In some
respects it was nice to have another girl who was dumb, instead of

just boys. There were always more boys at school than girls. We didn't know it then, but something called the Vietnam War would come along and change that forever. So many of the boys I grew up with never returned to Sherman Acres after the war. Some would be killed, some went missing, and some just didn't want to be found.

≈7≈

Junior High Blues

MORE BIG CHANGES HIT the school system that fall. The sixth grade moved to the Prairie Farm School. Sixth-graders became junior high students. I was excited because our class would be even larger. Not only were the children from Sherman Acres going there but also the sixth grade from Snake Creek to the south and Oak Creek School in Henderson. They combined the seventh and eighth grades of these schools when Antonia's class moved there.

I grew so much and had a woman's figure. Mama took Antonia and me to Freedom Falls to shop for clothes. Antonia was entering high school at Henderson High. She needed a lot more things than I did. She was still smaller, so we couldn't share things. I got a lot of things from Carmella when she didn't like them anymore, which happened pretty often. I got two new skirts and two new blouses.

Things from Carmella came as payment for babysitting Katie. She still worked as a waitress, because she always wanted her own money. She went roller-skating at least three times a week. She had a pair of professional skates that cost a bundle. Whenever Norman was at work, she went out with friends much younger than she was. "You make it too easy for her not to stay at home and take care of her baby," Mama complained, but she didn't stop me from going to

Carmella's. The lure of new clothes and a chance to get away from Strawberry Fields carried more weight with me than anything Mama said. When I was there, I got to eat anything I wanted, not that I ate much. I had the whole TV to myself after I put Katie to bed. It was like having my own place.

I treated Mama very badly whenever I could get away with it. I said such hateful things to her. "I can't wait to leave here forever and never see you again," I told her. "I don't ever want to be like you or live the way you do. Your life is awful. You had a bunch of kids, and all you do is work day and night." I said these things to her whenever I felt I wasn't getting any attention or when I thought I was treated unfairly. I lived to regret saying those things. I didn't know they would come true one day.

Sammy and Marco returned home from the army. Sammy spent four years there, and Marco was still finishing his two-year stint. He was closer and came home more often. Having them home brought me no joy. They constantly made fun of the way I looked. Even Enzo did it.

"Oh, Enzo, don't say such hurtful things to your sister! Why, I think she will be the prettiest one of all your family," Mrs. Pullman said. She was Enzo's mother-in-law. The Pullmans were lovely, gentle people who lived in a great house outside Henderson, on a street that ended in the country. I liked going there with Enzo, Nina, and the children. I was treated as one of their own when we went for picnics and other family gatherings. It was a reward for babysitting the children.

The carnival came to Henderson late that summer. I loved the shows they brought. It was the only time I saw people from other towns and states. I dreamed of leaving with them when they moved on to new places. I wanted to see the snake woman and the two-headed baby, the bearded lady and someone they called a half man, half woman. I was now old enough to view such entertainment. I was twelve and looked much older. On Labor Day, after the picnic at the Pullmans', Enzo gave me a dollar. The rest of my babysitting money went to Mama to buy socks, underwear, and school supplies. I cashed in the dollar for ten dimes. Everything at the carnival cost a dime. Eisenhower was still president, and everything was cheap.

It was early afternoon. I paid my dime and entered the big top to see the sideshow. I was the only one in there. It was dark! Only a single bare bulb hung from a wire to light the big, dark-brown canvas tent. It smelled of sawdust and sweat. I walked to the first curtain and entered slowly. I saw the two-headed baby lying in a crib, surrounded by a locked fence. The body was small, with tiny hands and feet; the heads were big, one somewhat larger than the other. I searched the floor for an electrical cord somewhere, thinking it some sort of electronic thing. The baby made small, gentle movements with his hands and feet. "Baby Johnny," the sign hanging on the fence said. He was dressed in a tank top and short pants. "Have you seen enough?" one of the heads said as the eyes opened wide and looked into my face. I bolted from the tent, running fast. I didn't want to see behind the next two curtains! I remembered how Marco came out vomiting after he saw the half man, half woman when he was my age. I thought those people were faking until I became an adult and moved to the big city to become a nurse. Not only were they real, but sideshows were their only means of making a living for themselves and their families.

While junior high was a looming mystery for me, Antonia started high school right away that summer. She wanted to be a majorette with the high school marching band. She had to enroll before the school year actually started. She took baton-twirling lessons two days a week. She was fitted with white boots and a red and white costume. It was made of a shiny material with a very short skirt and a red crinoline under it. I loved it! I wanted to do it when I went to high school.

Boys came around Antonia by the score that summer, but she only had eyes for one of them. His name was Warren Kenneth. I didn't know why he had two first names. People like Warren were known in the area as "river rats." His family farm was down by the Wanatau River, which was right on the border between Henderson and Judson counties. His father was a big landowner. To say that Warren was a spoiled child was putting it mildly. He had an older sister and a dead older brother. He was precious to his entire family. Sissy was married with children, but she did everything for him. He was the apple of his mama's and daddy's eyes since his brother was killed accidentally while he was in the army.

Warren always wore black clothes: black jeans and shirt, black leather jacket, white socks, and black shoes. He combed his hair into a pompadour, and his blue-green eyes gave him a look of distinction. He was a "hood," which was short for "hoodlum." He ran with a fast set known as the bad boys of Henderson County. They were all rich and drove fast cars. Those boys smoked, drank, and got into fights. They were known to get girls pregnant. I liked most of them, although they paid little attention to me.

I thought that since Antonia was dating, she would get less attention from the boys in the family. I couldn't have been more wrong. Sammy, Marco, and even Enzo seemed impressed with her choice of boyfriend. She got more positive attention. The boys made sure she had money and nice clothes. They all came around to talk to Warren when he came to Strawberry Fields. "Hey, buddy, how are you?" they would ask, giving him a slap on the back.

Mama was the only one who seemed to worry about Antonia's dating. "Evalina, you go with them when they go out. You make sure nothing happen to her," Mama said. She made me go on dates with them when Warren picked up Antonia in his car.

Antonia cried and screamed, "Why does she have to come with us? Can't I even have my own boyfriend without her tagging along?" But Mama was firm, and Pa backed her up. I was indifferent to the whole matter. I didn't dislike going with them, but it wasn't much fun. If we went to the movies, I never saw the two of them once we were inside. They came for me after the show. I didn't see why Mama insisted that I go with them. I had no idea what I was supposed to make sure didn't happen.

When school started, I rode the early bus to Prairie Farm School Junior High. It was crowded with high school kids. They were mostly those older boys. Driving to school was only permitted if you had a job in the afternoon. Those bad boys didn't have to work, so they piled onto the bus. Lamont Wolf and Billy Hearts were early riders. "Hi, cutie pie, what's your name?" asked Billy that first morning. He was so good-looking, and he was talking to me! He looked just like one of the Everly Brothers I had seen on TV.

"I'm Evalina," I answered. I couldn't bring myself to look up at him. He reached down and gently picked me up out of my seat. Then he sat down, holding me on his lap. He began to stroke my hair.

"Now, isn't this nice? We both have a seat on the bus," he said. I could only nod my head in agreement. "Here, baby, look what I got for you." He held out a Tootsie Roll.

"Thanks," I said, barely above a whisper.

When Lamont Wolf boarded the bus, he greeted everyone with a smile and a warm hello. He talked to us junior high kids and made us feel important. He wasn't handsome, but his presence filled the entire bus. He was tall with blond hair, and he wore black horn-rimmed glasses. He had bad acne, but it didn't seem to bother him. After school, if Lamont made it on the bus before Billy, then I sat in his lap. The junior high got out ahead of the high school kids.

"You got the cutie pie?" Billy asked.

"Yep, I got her," Lamont answered. I knew they were doing it just to get a seat on the bus, but I liked the attention; it was my little secret. Antonia didn't ride the bus anymore. Warren picked her up for school every day and drove her home. If she had been on the bus, I wouldn't have been noticed. The bad boys might have been bad, but they were nice to a little nothing like me.

Junior high was not at all what I had expected. The school was no bigger than Sherman Acres School. There were two classrooms upstairs and a basement below, where the sixth grade was located.

There were twenty-eight of us packed into a small room with a folding door for a wall on one side. There was so little room that desks had to be pushed together before we could get in and out. Boys and girls had to sit side by side.

Confidence left me when the teacher got up and introduced herself as Mrs. Conway. "Some of you might have had my sister, Mrs. Trent, as your teacher." I knew right away that they were sisters, because their teaching style was the same: it was nonexistent.

Teddy Roosevelt got sent outside again. You would think that by now, someone would have sent a list of children transferring from other schools. Teddy said he didn't mind, but I knew it hurt him. There were lots of new kids. I met Grace Cain for the first time. She was at the piano in the room adjacent to our classroom. She was banging out a country song. I started to sing it with her. She smiled at me and did the harmony part. "Why, Evaleene, you can sing a little, can't you?" she said in a deep southern accent. She and her family had come north from Georgia. Her daddy was a hired man on one of the big farms near Prairie Farm School. A hired man would run a farm for a gentleman farmer. Grace was pretty in a southern, homespun way. She had black hair cut short and brown eyes, with lots of freckles on her face. I liked the freckles and wished I had them. I liked the way she talked, holding on to the last syllable of every word. I didn't mind it so much when she called me Evaleene.

"I just like that song," I answered shyly.

"Well, here, do you know this one?" She began to play and sing. "I want to drink my java from an old tin can and see the moon go sailing by. I want to hear the call of the whippoorwill and hear the coyotes cry." I joined her. It was so much fun.

"Evaleene, I believe you need to come by the house and meet my brother Layton and sing with us. He plays the guitar," she said.

"I'd love to come! I'll ask my mother, if it's all right with yours," I replied. I had a friend who was popular. I was so excited.

Grace made friends with everyone, but it was clear that her very best friend was Ada May Louis. They did everything together. Ada

May was the daughter of our mailman. Mr. Louis was a kind man. He admired my father very much. "I just can't get over how your dad came here and started a whole new life. He is quite the man, your father," Mr. Louis said. Whenever they met up in Henderson, Mr. Louis would buy Pa a cup of coffee and a doughnut, or a drink. Pa gave him some of his homemade wine. Mr. Louis farmed on some big landowner's place a few miles from Sherman Acres.

Our class blended together as a group. It didn't seem to be as divided as Sherman Acres School. I met Susan Ball and Kay Baily, whose fathers drove the school bus. Shirley Martin and Sharon Laity both came from Oak Creek School in Henderson. Shirley was poor and unkempt. Her single mother was, according to most in town, a prostitute. Sharon Laity's mother was a prostitute, even though she was married and took good care of her family.

The boys outnumbered the girls. Bobby Ray was very quiet and nice. He played the guitar, and his younger sister Janet sang. Grace told me that they were only allowed to play at their church. William Keene was handsome and friendly to everyone.

The boys and girls sometimes played together at lunch. We played a game I hadn't heard of until junior high. It was called Winkem. Chairs were placed in a circle. The boys stood behind them, and the girls sat in the chairs. There would be one empty chair and one boy standing behind it. That boy would then wink at a girl sitting in one of the chairs in the circle. She would have to run and sit in the empty chair in front of the winking boy before she was tagged by the boy standing behind her chair. After a while we would switch and play with the boys sitting. I never really understood who won or lost this game, but it was great fun.

I got to go to Grace's after school. We were there alone with her big brother and little sister. Mrs. Cain worked at the phone company and wouldn't be home until after nine o'clock. I couldn't stop looking at Layton Cain; he was so beautiful. He looked just like Grace, but for some reason, he was more attractive. He had the same dark hair, but it was curly. Those dark brown eyes seemed to have a twinkle.

He had a dimple in his chin and the same freckled face as Grace. His shoulders were very broad. His voice was the real attraction. He sang like an angel and played the guitar. Grace and I joined him. He paid me little attention. I noticed that he treated Grace a lot better than my brothers treated me.

"So you're Antonia's little sister, are you?" he asked, but he didn't wait for a reply. "She's real nice. It's too bad she and Warren are such an item around school." Like Warren, Layton was a senior, and he was probably the ringleader of the bad boys of Henderson County. He had a fast car and a job. School was just something he had to do for his mother, who insisted that he stay until graduation.

Later that evening, fast sports cars began to arrive. Many young men piled out of them. They took out instruments and began to play the latest rock-and-roll music. I was in heaven. I didn't want to go home. Harland Hicks was Layton's best friend. He was big, very good-looking, and rich. He had a big personality and talked to everyone, even me. "Well, howdy there, little one. It's good to see you. I think you sing real nice, honey." I couldn't believe he was actually talking to me. I was too shy to answer. I just smiled at him as my face turned crimson. He just kept looking at me. I had to say something. I could only mumble a thank-you.

Among them was a guy named Lyle North, whom I heard Antonia talk about sometimes. Lamont and Billy were there. They said nice things to me and called me their little cutie pie. The boy who caught my eye was a quiet boy named Bobby Blaze. He wasn't as good-looking, but there was something about the way he looked at me that held me captive to his light brown eyes. He sang beautifully and played well. When he spoke to me, I couldn't understand what he was saying; he had a very heavy southern accent. I just smiled. Bobby never took his eyes off me. I was not supposed to be there with all those older boys. If Mama knew, she would be upset. I was only twelve. I justified it by telling myself that Grace was here, and she was a year younger.

I started to daydream about Bobby Blaze and me. In my dreams, we would dance together and kiss. We sang sweetly to each other as he played his guitar. These fantasies started to become real to me, just like when I used to be with my imaginary friends in my head. Imaginary Bobby and I had such wonderful conversations, telling each other beautiful things.

Although things were a little better for me, I still had lots of trouble in school. Mrs. Conway was no help. I was still ugly and getting a bigger-sized bra every year. I had cramps every month, and that pain in my chest seemed to be coming more often. I still felt lost and isolated from everyone. Antonia spent all her time with Warren. She came to bed long after I did, and she never spoke to me. She went out with Warren every Friday, Saturday, and Sunday. He was there early in the morning to drive her to school, and he brought her home. His daddy had submitted a written request to the trustee's office so Warren could drive to school every day, even though he didn't hold a job.

It seemed that his family enabled him to be bad. Warren was always getting into trouble for fighting and driving too fast. He had been in trouble with the police several times. Antonia defended him, saying, "They're just out to cause trouble for him. He doesn't do anything wrong. Those cops have it in for him." I didn't think it was true. No type of punishment ever came from Mr. and Mrs. Kenneth. They would go to the police and settle it with money.

Warren would take his pocketknife and cut things into his skin. He would draw pictures and carve his name all over his arms and upper body. He did a new carving almost every day. I don't remember why, but I started doing it too. I carved my name into my forearm. It looked awful, but Mama said nothing. It bothered me, but for some reason I couldn't stop. Whenever it healed over, I did it again. I showed it to Mrs. Conway one day at school. She took me into her office and cleaned and bandaged it. "I think it is going to be fine. The body has such a marvelous way of healing itself. We will keep an eye on it together and watch it heal," she said. I was so surprised that she didn't yell at me or threaten to send a note home to my parents. I stopped doing it after that meeting with her.

After school was out, the pain in my chest came every day. I was having more trouble eating. The doctor decided I would need hospital tests. Mama bought me two new pairs of pajamas. I didn't know that she and Pa would leave me in the pediatric ward! Those pajamas were just a little too sheer. My big breasts could be seen under them. When my roommate's father came to visit, he stood at the foot of my bed, staring at me. "How old are you?" he asked.

"Twelve," I said. I pulled my sheet up to my neck, closed my eyes, and pretended to sleep. He didn't leave. I could feel his eye still on me.

His daughter started yelling as she lay in the bed across from mine, with her leg in traction. "Daddy, Daddy, come read to me!"

The following day I had a bunch of X-rays. I was in a hospital gown, lying on a table, with male doctors poking me, asking questions. "How old are you?" they asked every day.

"I'm the same age I was yesterday, twelve," I answered.

"Well, you just look a lot older," the doctor who came to see me every day said.

Marco came once during that week I spent in the hospital at North End. He brought me two bananas and an orange. He was on his way to work and only stayed for a few minutes. "Where are Pa and Mama?" I wanted to know. "When can I go home?"

"They're just busy at home. They'll come when the doctor says you can leave." He left.

A few days later, the family doctor finally appeared. "There's nothing seriously wrong with you. I'm going to send you home," he said, and without missing a step, he walked right back out. At the end of the day, Pa arrived. I was never so glad to see Strawberry Fields as I was that day.

All I wanted to do the next day was go to my friend's house, ride her bike, and play all day. I didn't have a bike. We were too poor. When

I got to the road, the Creeper was in his car, driving slowly,. That's what we called him then. I saw him from a distance. I cut into an open field that would take me fairly close to my destination. He drove off.

There was construction on Sherman Acres Road. It was being made wider to accommodate larger farm equipment. There were lots of men working. They all stopped to watch me as I walked along. Since I had survived being away from home by myself in the hospital with all those men, I thought I could handle road workers. I smiled and waved at the one who seemed unable to stop staring at me. He dropped his shovel and started to come after me. I ran as fast as I could, all the way to my friend's back door. It was a comfort to know I could outrun these men.

Mama took me back to the doctor for the results of the tests. "All she has is a spastic esophagus, Mrs. Rosario," Dr. Hemming said.

"Oh, no!" Mama cried. "Will she need to have the tubes put down her throat?"

"No, no, it isn't that bad. We'll give her some medication. She will do just fine." I took the green liquid medicine three times a day before eating, and it helped ease the pain.

When school started in September, I became more outgoing. Over the summer I had discovered *American Bandstand* on TV. I learned to dance by watching it. Antonia liked it too. She would sometimes dance with me. I loved *Bandstand*, the kids on it, and all the latest fashions. I raced home after school to watch it.

I got clothes from Carmella that were the latest styles: her old Fiaco skirt and a bulky white knit sweater that was all the rage. Everyone wore white bucks and saddle shoes, thanks to Pat Boone. I got a pair of each. I'd never had more than one pair of shoes a year in my entire life. I was a teenager with all of the latest clothes.

Grace Cain wasn't pleased that I'd become so vocal over the summer. "I believe I liked you better when you were quiet and reserved," she said.

"Well, I had quite a summer, and I've started to learn to stand up for myself," I replied.

At home I grew even more difficult for Mama. "In three years I'll be able to quit school and do whatever I want," I said, walking around the downstairs kitchen with one of Sammy's cigarettes in my hand like I was really smoking it. I liked seeing my mother go into fits. She didn't know how to control me. Talking to Pa was out. His remedy for bad behavior was a heavy fist. Since negative attention was all I got, I strived for it. Some attention was better than no attention.

"You come to no good if you quit school, you silly girl. Smoking, it is only for the bad girls!" she yelled. The thing wasn't even lit; I was just being a brat. I tormented her for the first part of seventh grade. Mama never seemed to notice Antonia reeking of cigarette smoke. She said it was because Warren smoked. Antonia's behavior had grown so strange that I couldn't comprehend it. One night we happened to be getting ready for bed at the same time, which happened rarely. I sat on the bed, watching her as she hung her clothes on a chair next to the dresser. The sight of her back astonished me. She had large black and blue marks. When she turned, I saw other strange marks on her chest, just below her neck. The small oval marks almost formed a chain around it. Suddenly she looked into the mirror and saw me looking at her with an expression of dread in my eyes.

"Antonia, what happened to you?" I asked softly.

"Just shut up! Don't ask questions about things you wouldn't understand. You're too young to know," she answered. After pulling an old T-shirt of Pa's over her head, she climbed into our bed. She always slept in the corner, facing the wall. I knew she still sucked her thumb. I think she might have been a thumb-sucker until she was well into her twenties. It was a mystery how she managed to have perfect teeth.

I slept on the outside, next to the door. I turned out the light. In a few minutes, Antonia was fast asleep, with the soft, rhythmic breathing of someone in dreamland. I lay on my right side, with my arm dangling off the bed. I listened to the entire house as it went quiet. There were many things I didn't understand. I was rolling them over in my head. I started with the state of Antonia's body and her strange behavior. I thought about the way grown men looked at me. I was sure it wasn't right. My mind came to rest on the Creeper driving by very slowly in his car. "Where are you going, little girl?" I could hear him say as I turned into the open field, and he faded away. I saw that high-roofed, rat-colored car in our driveway. I was inside of it. I knew my mother had tried to give me away. I knew it. I knew it.

"Antonia. Antonia!" It was Mama's voice, far off. "Please get up. You will be late for the school." I sat up, and then I realized I had been asleep. Antonia slipped out the bottom of the bed, collected her clean clothes, and left the room. I stayed in bed for another fifteen minutes. I was hoping Mama would call my name too.

Layton Cain thought Grace and I were good enough at singing to try out for the all-schools show. I decided to do a sweet song called "My Angel Baby." It was my favorite. I practiced it daily. I can't recall what Grace sang. We practiced at her house with Layton. I took the bus home with Grace on a Friday when we only had a half day. Layton and Harland Hicks were there; we practiced all afternoon. About four o'clock, Layton realized he had to go to work. He and Grace were supposed to drive me home. "I can't do it," he said. "I'll be late." He turned to Harland. "You could run her home for me, couldn't you, Harland?"

"Sure, buddy, no problem," he said as he stood up. My God, he was a big guy and so handsome. "Come on, little one. You get to ride in the fastest wheels in Henderson County."

I was so excited when I climbed into the Corvette as he held the door open. I didn't stop to think what others might say about my being out with a bad boy. The radio blasted "Johnny B. Goode" as we pulled out of the drive at a speed that would have made a race-car driver tremble. It was winter; the roads were covered in ice. The car swerved this way and that on those country roads between the Cain house and Strawberry Fields.

"Did you have fun, honey?" Harland asked as we squealed to a stop at the top of the driveway at our farm.

"Yes, Harland," I said, smiling at him. "Thank you for driving me home. I can let myself out."

"Nonsense, I open the door for all my girls." He came around and helped me out of the low-riding car. We said another good-bye, and I went into the house as he pulled away, squealing the tires loudly.

When I entered the basement kitchen, Antonia was looking out the window. I didn't know she was home. She always sat in the car with Warren after school, until Mama made me go tell her to come in. "What were you doing in that car with Harland Hicks? Have you lost your mind?"

"No, he just gave me a ride home from Grace's," I said. She made a little sound in her throat and walked away.

That night at dinner, Antonia announced to Marco, Sammy, and everyone else at the table, "Your stupid, ugly little sister got in Harland Hicks's car with him. He gave her a ride home from the Cains' today." All went silent. Marco and Sammy stared at me. Then Sammy brought his fist down on the table so hard that all the plates jumped into the air. I jumped too.

"What in the hell has gotten into you, that you would do something so stupid?" he demanded. "I never want to hear of you getting in a car with any of those guys! Do you understand?"

I didn't, but I nodded anyway. Antonia looked very pleased. I trembled in fear of a slap. Mama said nothing. She only looked at me with sad eyes. Pa often deferred discipline of me to Marco and Sammy. I didn't understand. Harland was always so kind to me. I wished I had brothers like him or Layton.

The all-schools show was a big deal for the whole community. Children from all surrounding schools could participate. Kids took their act to tryouts at Henderson High. Mr. Blackstone assigned each act a spot in the show. If the community liked the performance and it received good reviews in the local paper, the kids were asked to perform at other community functions.

The gym at Henderson High School was packed! I remember standing on the big stage in a pink dress with a full skirt and a bow that tied in the back. Antonia had borrowed it for me. I felt like an angel in it as I sang, "It's just like heaven being here with you. You're like an angel, too good to be true...Because I love you, I love you, I do, angel baby, my angel baby." I was nervous, and I couldn't remember a thing that happened after I came off the stage. But I had to take a second bow. Layton and the boys said I did just fine. Bobby Blaze was in the wings, smoking a cigarette and watching me with his beautiful light-brown eyes.

No one in my family said anything about my performance. Marco, Sammy, Antonia, and Warren attended. Pa was at work. Mama never went to anything at school. The following evening, Sammy left the local paper lying on the kitchen table. I looked for my own review. "'My Angel Baby' sung sweetly by Evaleene Rosario. She sounded promising."

The following week we performed the show for local dignitaries. Layton Cain had to work, so he asked a friend of his to play for Grace and me.

Richard Lively lived on the big highway with his two brothers and a sister. His mother had deserted the family after her last child was born; Richard's father had discovered her in a cornfield behind their place with another man. Mr. Lively then married a woman with six children of her own. It just didn't work out. He left the family and went to live in a town downstate. Richard took care of his younger siblings. He was religious, a Baptist, and he didn't like that I was a Catholic. If he could have convinced me to change my religion, our relationship would have been very different. He wasn't too tall, with straight blond hair and brown eyes. No one seemed to mind that he came for me in his car and took me to his home to practice. The children loved to hear us. Richard changed the key I sang in. He had me sing notes I didn't even know I could hit. "See, a little practice, a little effort, and you sound great! I'm going to fix dinner for us. I'd be pleased if you stayed. It isn't much, just plain food," he said.

"Thank you, Richard, I'll stay," I said. I went to their home frequently throughout my school years. Although Richard was five years older, we respected and loved each other.

Richard's sister Sarah told me many years later, "You know, you're the reason I became a nurse. If it hadn't been for you, I would be nothing today. I had no mother, and you were my role model." It amazed me to learn that I was her idol.

Spring always brought hope and a feeling of a new beginning. That spring, however, something went terribly wrong. It was a warm March. The grass was green already. Tension fell over Strawberry Fields Farm. Mama and Antonia argued all the time. I paid little attention. I had fantasies of Bobby Blaze in my head. When I daydreamed, I could shut out everything. When I heard Sammy yelling at Antonia, I listened. He never yelled at her. "Come on, let's take a ride in my car and talk," he said to her when he saw me.

Bobby didn't go to school, so I knew he had to be about twenty. I read in a movie star magazine that Jerry Lee Lewis, who was twenty-two, had married his thirteen-year-old cousin. I didn't want marriage, but dating sounded fun. Going dancing with Bobby was a fantasy that played in my head like a forty-five record.

I went to a few dances with my town friends. Every girl in the seventh grade was at the big dance in Henderson when Jim Lange and His Dance Party came to town. He had a local TV show of the same name on Saturdays. He was a disc jockey too. His station was broadcasting from the dance that night in late February. I was the only one who wanted to go on the radio and ask Jim to play a song for someone special. Everyone cheered loudly when it was my turn to talk to Jim on WYTM radio. I requested "My Angel Baby" for Bobby. All the girls screamed. The boys didn't dance; they were watching the girls. I loved dancing, even if it was just us girls. We wore our full skirts with lots of crinolines, bobby socks, and white bucks. We tried to outdo each other with our jitterbug moves, because the boys watched us.

On a warm day in mid-March, I came home to a very quiet house.

No one spoke to me. Mama was standing over the stove, cooking. She was crying. I went up to our room to change and watch *Bandstand* on TV. I loved it and watched it almost every day. Antonia didn't watch it anymore. I used the front door as my partner, holding on to the doorknob while I danced to rock-and-roll music.

I remembered that day I watched Frankie Lymon and the Teenagers performing one of their latest hits. Frankie jumped off the stage and started dancing with a white girl on the show. Suddenly the TV went black, and then the test pattern came on. The set started emitting that beeping sound. I thought I had broken the TV! I was scared my pa would kill me. I ran to our room and stayed there the whole evening. Later when I was sneaking through the dark dining room, I heard the late news. Faye Heflin was reporting that the station had pulled the plug on *Bandstand* because Frankie Lymon danced on the nationwide TV show with a white girl. He said that if it ever happened again, the FCC would remove the program from the air forever. Confused and afraid, I went back to my bed. I didn't know what was so wrong about Frankie dancing with that girl. Every day when I turned on the TV, I feared *Bandstand* would be gone. That March day was no exception.

"Turn off TV, and go to your room!" Mama yelled from the basement kitchen. She never yelled at me. I took my homework and sat on the bed, trying to concentrate.

An hour later I could hear everyone assembling for dinner. I heard Pa, Sammy, and Marco yelling loudly. Antonia wasn't home. No one called me for dinner. Mama cried, talking in a shrill voice. "I knew it was going to happen. I knew it," she wailed. With our little room right over the downstairs kitchen, it was easy to see and hear everything from the heating vent by removing its cover. I learned that Pa planned to go to our church in New Moon Lake and talk to the priest about Antonia and Warren getting married. They were to meet him at the priest's home in an hour. Everyone ate while Mama cried. "I knew she was doing it with that boy. I could see it in her eyes and on her face every day."

"Oh, shut up, Mama!" Sammy yelled. "Evalina will hear you. She has the ears of a dog, you know." They took the rest of their meal in silence, with the exception of Mama's sobbing. I wondered how Mama could tell by looking into Antonia's face that she was letting Warren do things to her. I vowed never to do things with a boy, for fear that everyone would know just by looking at me. The problem was that I still didn't know what things.

I heard Pa when he came back from Christ the King Church. He was yelling and swearing loudly. He called Father Norton, our pastor, a communist. Back then, that was the worst thing you could call a person. Communism was the top fear in the country. Being a commie was worse than being a murderer. "He no marry them!" said Pa. "He say she is too young, not ready to be wife and mother. Do you believe it? He want us to send her away to have the baby and give it away to someone else to raise. This is criminal. It is communism, I tell you!" he yelled, banging his fist on the table. Pa ranted on about communists and said he would stop giving money to the church. "No one gives away his own flesh and blood, no one. Do you hear me? That is what it means to be family!" As I listened, I had to agree with the priest. I knew he was right. Antonia was too selfish to have a baby. I was the one who watched babies. It was expected, understood. I was never asked. I never saw Antonia so much as change a diaper or give a baby a bottle. I knew how soundly she slept. I was fearful she wouldn't hear a baby's cry.

Antonia did not return home that night so very many years ago. Except for the time I slept in that crib when Mama tried to give me away, it was the first time in my life that I had a bed to myself. I didn't sleep. I lay awake, listening to my parents talk about their Antonia, how she had been the shining star of the family. A silence, like no other I had ever known, fell on the house at Strawberry Fields.

Daylight came with the profound quiet of a house in mourning. I heard Mama on the stairs, calling for Antonia. When I came to the top of the stairs, she sat down on the bottom step. She cried, letting out loud sobs of grief. I left her there and got ready for school. She didn't speak when I left. I knew she would never call my name for school in the morning. I became the invisible child in the smallest room upstairs.

I looked forward to school as my escape from the devastation at home. I thought of it as a refuge, a place where I could forget about what happened to Antonia. Somehow I knew she was never coming home again. School proved no place to hide my troubles. I messed up a math assignment at the end of the week. Mr. Sellers wasn't happy with me. "I'm sorry, Mr. Sellers. I just can't get this. I might need some help."

"There is no amount of help that will save you. I can see you'll end up just like your sister, pregnant and a dropout before your second year in high school!" he ranted in front of the whole class. "Just look at her, class, and let this be a lesson to all you girls. Don't end up like this one."

I was so humiliated! At the end of the day, I got on the bus with my head down. I went straight to my room when I got home. There would be no *Bandstand* for me. I must have drifted off to sleep, but I sat up with a start when Sammy banged on my door. (I locked it now that I was alone.) "Open up now!" he demanded. I unlocked the door, and he burst in. "Do you know where they are?"

"What, Sammy?" I asked, totally in the dark as to what he wanted.

"Those magazines she was always reading. Come on, you know the ones," he said. I got off the bed and onto my knees. I pulled them out from under the bed.

"Get out of the way," said Sammy as he dropped to his knees and began to pull them out.

"Those are mine, Sammy," I said when he took a stack of movie star magazines. "I want to keep them."

"I will not allow you to read any such trash. If I catch you with any of it, I will beat the hell out of you! Is that clear?" he yelled. I just nodded my head. "Now help me get these to the basement. They're going into the furnace!" It was the end of March and too warm out for a fire. He loaded every magazine into the furnace and lit it.

I never read one of those romances, but I was pretty sure they were not the cause of Antonia's getting pregnant. I didn't understand why it was all her fault. I didn't know anything about sex, but I was sure that Warren had something to do with it. No one seemed mad at him. They weren't blaming him for this situation they called a real-life tragedy. I heard Mama say to Carmella that it was always the woman's responsibility to keep herself pure until she married. "Men," she said, "have no control, and it is up to the woman to be smart and save herself for the right man."

Sammy had taken my movie stars away from me. I'd kept them so I could see pictures of my favorite actor, Sal Mineo. I had loved him since the first time I saw him on TV. It was the first time I became aware that there were other people who actually looked like us. Sal was dark, with dark hair and eyes. He looked like he could be a member of our family, and he was a famous actor! Well, I still had that letter hidden in my dresser, the one I'd received when I joined his fan club. I went to Carmella's almost every week to babysit Katie. Carmella had a ton of those magazines. I would have to read them there. Mama loved those romance ones. I didn't know how Sammy would tell her that she couldn't have them.

Pa came home from work one evening a few weeks after Antonia left. He knocked on my bedroom door. "Hey!" he yelled. "You open the door!" I was sure I was in trouble. When I opened the door, he handed me a box the size of a shoebox. "Here, you use this to get yourself up in the morning for the school. Mama, she's a no feel good anymore. We are going to let her sleep. If I here and you want to eat, I cook for you. Okay?"

"Okay, Pa," I said and closed the door. I was expecting an eight-day wind-up clock. When I opened the box, it was an RCA clock radio. It cost three dollars and ninety-five cents. That radio was the best thing I ever had in my life. I listened to all my favorite disc jockeys all night! The clock gave a pleasant buzz in the morning to wake me, but I was usually awake anyway. The sad thing I came to realize was that Mama never had to call my name for school.

I became the loneliest girl in the world. No one at school talked to me. Grace Cain no longer asked me to her home. Shirley Martin was my only friend, other than Julia Marshall, who still looked as if she was beaten every day. Shirley had no other friends. Some of the boys giggled and laughed when they walked by me. Teddy Roosevelt and Jimmy Loveless said nothing. Bobby Ray was silent. Scotty Brooks sat next to me on the bus and dared anyone, by the look on his face, to say something to me. I don't know what he could have done. He never talked above a whisper.

Mama cried every day. She went to the doctor on a regular basis. I worried that she might be getting sick. Would she try to give me away again? She cooked low-fat meals and ate much less. She spent all her time on the brooder house behind the furnace with those eggs. She tended the baby chickens when they hatched. She looked after the farm animals and the dogs. She never looked at me. I was invisible to her.

I wished I were invisible to Sammy and Marco, who watched my every move. "Hey, where are you? Get down here right now!" yelled Sammy. I came out of my room and stood at the top of the stairs. "You're not pulling that nonsense like Antonia. You'll get down here and have dinner with your family! You're not hiding in your room, planning I don't know what kind of bad behavior." I had no idea what he meant. I sat at the table, taking little food. I moved it around on my plate. My hands always shook when I had to be there with Sammy and Marco.

"Why the hell are you shaking like that?" asked Marco.

"I don't know. No reason," I answered.

"Well, knock it off," demanded Sammy. I asked to be excused. I had homework. I left the room. I shook all the time. I was so anxious and worried about everything. I wasn't doing well in school. I had very few friends, no one I could talk to about things.

Coffee helped my nerves. I drank even more of it. Mama drank a lot too. She made a fresh saucepan of strong coffee every night after dinner. I would go to the downstairs kitchen after everyone was in bed, reheat the powerful brew, and drink several cups.

Sleeping in that small room alone brought back dreams of the man with the cigarette. He would stand beside the bed at night while I pretended to sleep. I was sure I could smell his smoke and hear him breathing. Sometimes the bed would move slightly, causing me to stop breathing. It was hard for me to start breathing again. I gasped for air. When I woke in a cold sweat, I realized it was a dream. I could not go back to sleep.

Antonia married Warren on a Friday the second week of April. No one in the family attended the ceremony at the Kenneth family home. I remember seeing a black-and-white photo of Warren and Antonia, taken after the wedding. Antonia was just fifteen years old. She was wearing a straight white dress with black threads running through it and short black velvet sleeves and collar. Black velvet buttons ran down one side. She wore flat black shoes and had a corsage of white roses pinned to her shoulder. Her hair hung in ringlets. She looked so small, with no sign of the pregnancy. She didn't smile, and Warren had a scowl on his face. The caption, if there had been one, should have read, "Child bride."

In late July Antonia returned to Strawberry Fields for the first time. I almost didn't recognize her. She was wearing one of those maternity tops and a pair of pants that were too tight. She was more than twice her normal size. She had a puffy face and pudgy arms and legs. Mama and Pa were actually glad to see her. I think she was glad to be home, where she was the center of attention once again. The baby was due in October. I hoped that the child would arrive on my birthday.

She and Warren lived in a three-room apartment in downtown Henderson, in an old house across from the library. When I went into town with Pa, I visited Antonia. I could only stay for a few minutes. Each time, I found her asleep, and it was difficult to wake her. I learned that she suffered from a condition called toxemia. It sounded bad to me. Because of it, and her small size and extreme weight gain, our family doctor worried how he would deliver the baby.

I wondered why the Kenneth's decided at that time to deny Warren their support. He was able to finish high school, while Antonia wasn't allowed back after that fateful announcement of pregnancy. After graduation, he had to get a job and take care of his family. It didn't take an adult to figure out that a seventeen-year-old boy and a fifteen-year-old girl weren't prepared for life. The only job Warren found was at a vacuum cleaner repair company in North End.

Things between Mama and me became less volatile. I stopped tormenting her to gain attention. There was no point, now that Antonia was gone. Mama went about her work, ignoring me and my growing need for adult guidance and advice. I lived in my own head, with dreams of Bobby Blaze.

More attention than I wanted came from Marco and Sammy. They watched my every move. I wasn't allowed anywhere other than Carmella's or Enzo's. I went to Sunday Mass in late August with Pa. After Mass, we had our large noon meal. I was wearing a white sailor dress, tight-fitting, with a red and blue stripe around the big collar. It was another hand-me-down from Carmella. After the meal, I wanted to go to my room to listen to the radio and daydream. I left the table and started for the stairs. Sammy watched me. When he thought I couldn't hear, he said to Marco, "Christ, she looks like a dime-store whore in everything she wears. I guess we'll have to keep a closer eye on her."

Marco, always more reasonable, responded, "Come on, Sammy, it isn't that bad." I locked my door and played the radio softly. I could hear the conversation at the table. It was all about politics and current events happening in the news. I had my own opinions on this stuff but knew better than to express them at the table. I wasn't allowed to say anything during a meal, unlike Antonia, who spoke freely about everything, good or bad.

I heard the phone ring, and I sat up. I was disappointed when Mama called out, "Sammy, it is for you!" I went back to my dreaming. I was in a half sleep as voices began to fill the upstairs kitchen. I stayed in my bed. They were male voices. Sammy's friends, I thought. I didn't like any of the guys he hung around with, because they looked at me the way I hated. Some of them tried to talk to me, even reached out to touch me in all the wrong places if I was alone. I avoided them.

There was a loud bang on my door, and Sammy yelled, "Hey, get out here, will you?" As I stepped from my room, I was surprised to see the upstairs kitchen filled with the bad boys of Henderson County. I didn't stop to think how I looked. I was still in that white sailor dress that flattered my figure a little too well, although I weighed seventy-five pounds. My feet were bare. I hadn't combed my golden-brown hair, which hung down past my waist in long, loose waves. Every eye was upon me as I entered the kitchen.

Harland Hicks and Layton Cain started tuning their guitars to Sammy's, while Bobby Blaze stared at me. I must have looked wild, like some untamed animal. It seemed to appeal to older men. "Hey, Bobby, you playin' with us or what?" asked Layton. It was some time before he tuned his guitar. I sat just inside the kitchen door and listened to the music. Sammy only fooled around with the guitar. He didn't play well, but the others were quite skilled. They played and sang songs for almost an hour. Sammy left the room. After about ten minutes, I got nervous. I went to look for him. He was in the downstairs kitchen, heading for the door. "Where are you going, Sammy?" I asked. "The boys are still here playing."

"They're here to see you, idiot," he replied. "I got to go. Marco left for work already. Pa and Mama are in the field. Don't do anything stupid, like get into a car with them." He left. I returned to the upstairs kitchen and sat, listening to Layton sing "Oh Donna" and a few other songs. He sang like an angel.

"I think I'll go out and have a smoke," Layton said. "You coming, Harland?"

"Yep, sure," Harland replied, looking a little confused as he followed Layton. I sat in my chair with my legs crossed and my head down; my hair fell to my lap. Bobby was still staring at me. He set his guitar down and pulled his chair closer to mine. Reaching forward, he took my foot in his hand. His hand was warm, and my foot was very cold. My feet could be cold even in ninety-degree weather; it didn't matter.

"No shoes, little girl?" Bobby asked in his deep southern accent.

"Oh, I'm sorry! I'll go put them on," I replied as I tried to stand.

"No, it's okay," he said softly, putting a hand on my shoulder and keeping me there. "I like you this way, with no shoes. It excites me." My head was down again. I was staring at my hands in my lap. Bobby lifted my chin and gently pushed my hair from my face. "Do you know what it means to get a man excited, little girl?"

I shook my head, softly said, "No," and dropped my eyes.

"How old are you, honey?" he asked, trying to get me to look into his eyes.

"Thirteen. I'll be fourteen in October," I said, trying hard to keep from looking at him. My face felt hot. My eyes were burning.

"Where I come from, down in Mississippi, girls your age are getting married and having babies. Most don't own shoes," he said, getting to his feet.

The other boys came back into the kitchen and started to pack up their gear. Bobby was still staring at me. "You about ready to pack up and go, Bobby?" asked Layton. Bobby started packing in his guitar.

I went out on the porch and watched them put their gear into the cars. They lit cigarettes and took cans of beer from the trunk of Layton's car. I could hear what Layton said to Bobby. They weren't that far away. "Christ, Bobby! I told you she's too young. She comes over to play with my little sister, for God's sake." Bobby mumbled something I couldn't hear. "Yeah, I know what she looks like, but damn it all, man! This ain't Mississippi, you know."

Harland walked over to his pretty red Corvette and opened the door. He looked up at me standing on the porch. "Bye, angel baby!" he said, smiling. He had called me that since the all-schools show.

"Good-bye, Harland," I said, watching him.

"You be sweet, now. Promise your old buddy Harland," he said.

"I will, Harland. I promise," I replied, not knowing what I was promising. With tires squealing and gravel flying, they left in a cloud of late afternoon dust. I felt a profound sense of relief as the sound of their engines faded away and the dust settled. I realized that dreaming about Bobby was more satisfying than actually being with him. I was too shy and unwise to the ways of grown men.

I saw Bobby Blaze once after that hot August day. He and his band came to Christ the King Church to play for a teen dance. He was over me by then. I felt a little more self-confident. I didn't want to have babies or marry. I liked wearing shoes, if only once in a while.

Big news came to Henderson that school year. The new school building was finished ahead of schedule. It would combine the old Sherman Acres School, Snake Creek School, Oak Creek School, and Prairie Farm School into one big school with eight grades. It would be called Prairie Farm School, with no separate junior high.

It was sad to see Sherman Acres School standing empty. The Gleaners Hall across the big yard had fallen into disrepair. Dances hadn't been held there since Carmella's teen years. I felt strangely sad when Waldo's family reclaimed the land and tore down the buildings. A part of me knew that history was being destroyed. I understood that life was changing. I no longer had to have Mr. Sellers as a teacher! I had Mr. Perry instead. He was the principal at the junior high, but he had lost the job to Mr. Forecastle, who had more education.

Beginning the year in a new school gave everyone a lift. New classes were offered. The boys had shop, and the girls had home economics. We actually had a modern kitchen in which to prepare meals. It was decided that for one week, we would change places with the boys. They came to the home economics room to cook. We went into the wood shop and built magazine racks.

Shirley Martin didn't return to school. Her mother moved the family down south, where she hoped to find work. I missed her at first. She was my only friend. I went to her house once. It was a deplorable place, with little furniture and no heat. Her mother lay on the sofa while her older sister, who had three kids of her own, did the cooking. No one cleaned the place. It was the first time I had Waldorf salad. It was all they had to eat. I liked it. My family was poor, but Shirley's had nothing. It was the first time I realized there were families much poorer than mine.

After school, I went straight to my room. When I opened the door, I saw new clothes: two skirts, two sweaters and a blouse, a bra in a bigger size, and new underpants with all the days of the week written on them. I started bouncing up and down when I saw a black bucket handbag. Every girl at school had one or wanted one. Mama seemed glad that I was happy. We talked about every piece—how it looked, how I could mix and match them to make several different outfits. I didn't know Mama knew so much about fashion.

The steel strike ended, and there was money for clothes. All the steelworkers in North End and the nation were on strike for over a year. It was the largest strike in history. Workers held out for a large raise. The strike crippled the US trade market. We were fortunate to have the farm and its produce to see us through. While the strike was on, Sammy went to work for a chemical company, and he never returned to the mill. Marco, forever the penny saver, took odd jobs repairing machinery around Henderson. He wasn't affected by the strike. He saved all his money. I think even today he still has his First Communion money. He went back to the mill at higher wages.

In mid-October Carmella and Mama came to school. I was dismissed at noon. "Where are we going, Mama?" I asked as I climbed into the backseat of Carmella's car. I had never been taken out of school; it felt strange.

"Antonia, she have the baby," Mama said. "We go to hospital to visit her. It is boy, big boy, nine pounds and seven ounces. He is already twenty-two inches long. I hope she is going to be okay. She is so small to have such a big baby." I didn't know why Mama was so concerned about Antonia. Mama wasn't even five feet tall. When she came to America, she hadn't weighed even ninety pounds. She gave birth to six babies, some weighing more than eleven pounds. She had four at home with only a midwife. Antonia and I were born in the hospital.

Dean Martin Kenneth was the most beautiful baby I ever saw. He had dark olive skin and big dark eyes that would be black like Antonia's. He had a full head of curly black hair. I felt happy for Antonia.

I wasn't prepared for what I saw when we entered Antonia's hospital room. She was lying with all sorts of tubes in her. Her face was incredibly swollen! Her eyes appeared as two slits. Her hair was cut short and plastered against her head from sweat. Her pudgy arms and legs had long, reddish-purple marks running up and down them. They looked painful. A bag hung from the bed with urine dripping into it. Her stomach was just as big as when the baby was in it. All I did was stare. If this was what being in love with a man did to you, and this was how you ended up after you had a baby, I was sure I wanted no part of it. Mama had a sad look in her eyes as she and Carmella helped Antonia sit up in a chair and eat lunch. It was the first time Antonia had been out of bed since the birth five days earlier. Our family doctor came into the room.

"Well, I did my best to deliver that baby," he said. "She had a lot of damage to the perineal area. She tore, even with the episiotomy. She'll be here about three weeks, I think. I told you she was too small to be having a baby. Her body's too immature." I wondered what he expected Mama to do. She had no control over Antonia before she married Warren. "Babies having babies," he said and left. I could tell Mama was embarrassed. I liked Dr. Hemming even less. Marco and Sammy had nothing to fear. I would never let a man do this to me. It took months to get that image out of my mind, of Antonia in that hospital bed looking like a used-up, middle-aged woman. But I never could get it out of my heart.

I tried harder than ever to do well in school. Teachers still treated me like I had half a brain. We had a class in current events. We were supposed to read a paper called *My Weekly Reader*. I still had trouble reading, but I watched the news on TV every day. I listened to conversations that went on at the dinner table. Mr. Perry asked the class if we understood what was going on in South Africa. "Who can tell me what the conflict is all about?" he asked. "It's in your *Weekly Reader.* Did anyone read it?" Since no one raised a hand, I raised mine. Mr. Perry looked all around the room before he called on me. There were no other hands in the air.

"Yes, Evaleene," he said, with the look of someone who was sure I didn't know what I was talking about. He gave a deep sigh.

"I believe the problem is that the black people—the Negro people, that is—of South Africa want more rights and more freedom. The whites don't want to give it to them," I said with confidence.

Mr. Perry came and stood next to my desk; he stared down at me for what seemed an immense amount of time. "Well, yes, that's correct, but those black people aren't capable of handling more rights and freedoms."

"Why not?" I retorted. "They handled it just fine before the white man went there." Instead of calling for a discussion or offering more information, Mr. Perry did the prudent and manly thing: he just walked away. He went on with other articles from the *Weekly Reader.*

The winter was cold that year. We had a lot of snow. Since the school board didn't want the floors to be ruined, they made us stay in for lunch and recess. Grace Cain and Ada May Louis decided to give everyone in the seventh and eighth grades dancing lessons, even the boys. They were big *Bandstand* watchers. They convinced the principal that they were the best dancers and could teach everyone. Some of the girls brought records to school. We all practiced in the gym. The boys didn't like it, but some were actually pretty good. William Keene was my partner and a great dancer.

On New Year's Eve, Ada May had a party for the whole class at her house. It was a real, grown-up party. The boys were dressed in suits and ties and the girls in beautiful dresses. Ada May was in love with that boy who used to show his penis. They'd met when we were at Prairie Farm Junior High. I was sure that he was the reason she wanted to have the party.

There were many Christmas lights on a big tree in the picture window. Snow was falling outside, and it looked just like a winter wonderland as we danced. We changed partners every song, so all got a chance to dance. Other than Betty Sue's first-grade party, it was the most enchanting evening I could remember. Russell Greer told me I looked like the snow princess as we danced. I was wearing a dress borrowed from Carmella. It was a white A-line dress with a white fur collar, three-quarter-length sleeves, and white fur cuffs. The collar was a scooped style that ended in a V shape in the back, with a white bow hanging from it. I wore Carmella's black high heels with rhinestones. My hair hung in long waves past my waist. I danced every dance that night of the snow dance party.

Grace and Ada May convinced school officials to let us have dances. We had three dances that spring semester. The first was on Valentine's Day, and then there was one each in March and April. The first two dances went well. Not only did the seventh- and eighth-grade kids come, but most of the parents came and danced too.

The dance in April was the biggest and the last before graduation. I was in charge of refreshments and decorations. The gym looked great decked in many-colored tissue-paper flowers. We had doughnuts, apple cider, milk, tea, and coffee from the local IGA store in Henderson.

Carmella was supposed to get me a dress in payment for babysitting. She refused to do it, saying, "I just don't have the money, and besides you haven't been babysitting enough." I was devastated. I had no dress for the last dance of the year.

When I came home from school, Antonia was visiting Mama with Dean. "I brought you something," she said. "It's in that bag on the couch." I opened the bag. "Well, go try it on for size." I couldn't move. "What's wrong with you?" she demanded.

"Antonia, it's your wedding dress. I can't wear this!" I said, starting to cry.

"Sure you can," she said. "It's a cinch I'm never wearing it again." It was true; she was twice the size she had been when she married Warren. "Go try it on."

The dress was well made and expensive. The Kenneths never bought anything cheap. When I came back into the room, she and Mama looked at me. I knew what I looked like in the dress. Sammy's words rang in my head. The dress really flattered my ever-growing bust line. My waist was tiny, and I had no hips. The words "dime-store whore" kept repeating in my head like a record skipping. I wasn't sure just what that meant, but I knew it was something bad. I took a deep breath, held my head high, and walked slowly around the downstairs kitchen.

"It looks real nice on you," Antonia finally said. "I think I'll give it to you. God knows when I'll ever be able to wear it." I knew better than to count on it. Everything she gave me, she ended up taking back some time later, saying that she never really had intended to give it to me. It was only on loan.

"Thank you, Antonia. I'll take good care of it," I replied, and I hoped that was true. I was very sloppy. I had spilled punch on a few of Carmella's dresses.

One of the best things that came from all of those dance lessons and dances was that our generation of boys and girls danced together. It wasn't just the girls out there while the boys watched. The last school dance turned out to be the biggest and the best. I hardly sat out a dance. I waltzed with Teddy Roosevelt and Jimmy Loveless, my true friends. William Keene only wanted to dance fast dances with me. When I was slow-dancing with Waldo, who still couldn't get the hang of it, Graham Wilson cut in. "Remember our first dance?" he asked.

"Yes, Graham, I do," I answered, smiling. "It was a long time ago, wasn't it?"

"I'll miss dancing with you in high school. I know you're going to be too popular to dance with me," he said, holding me and looking into my eyes. Little did we know that nothing could have been further from the truth.

Spring got a slow start that year. The rains kept coming all through April and into May. I was pretty isolated. I had no close girlfriend in my class. Elizabeth and Juanita were closer than ever, and Sharon Laity was with them. Margaret, still overweight, kept to herself. The rest of the girls had their own little cliques—Betty Sue and Christine, Grace and Ada May. The only friend I had was Julia Marshall, with her bruised-up arms and legs. She didn't dance or sing. I walked the school yard alone. At home I walked the damp hillsides and lowlands of Strawberry Fields alone. I thought a lot about my future, how I wanted my life to be. I started to think maybe I had a choice in how I wanted to live. I already knew for sure what I didn't want. I knew I needed a good job, to do important work, and to earn enough money to take care of myself. I dreamed of going to the big city. Chicago was the big city, but no one called it by name within a six-state radius. Ask anyone where they were going, and they'd say, "The city." Ask people where they were from, and "The big city" would be the answer. I would dine out in fine restaurants with friends and go to shows and dances. I wanted a nice apartment I could call my own, like the ones I saw on TV shows. I cut pictures of furniture out of the Sears and Roebuck catalog and pasted them on paper, making a room out of them with things in colors and styles I liked.

Besides the material things I craved, I wanted to be important, respected, and honored by others. Love was out of the question. I was too ugly to love. Love got you pregnant; it made you fat, old-looking, and tired.

Excitement surged through me that last week of school. We were given papers to take home and fill out for high school classes. When I looked at my forms, I was disappointed; my choices were so limited. If you weren't smart, there was no help or hope for you. The classes you were given were the most basic. I think the term they used was "remedial." They were classes for the slow kids.

Marco helped me. I had biology for dumb kids, general math, home economics, English for dumb kids, band (I wanted to be a majorette like Antonia), and gym. All freshmen were required to have a study hall. Antonia gave me her old baton, and I practiced with her at home when she had lessons. I was looking forward to band. "Well, you're not smart enough to take anything else," Marco said when I complained about the choices. "Next year you better take secretarial courses. I think you could learn to type and take shorthand. You must know the alphabet by now, so you could do filing." I didn't think a secretary was what I wanted to be for the rest of my life. I reluctantly agreed to Marco's plan. My future depended on high school. My escape from Strawberry Fields was resting on my ability to get a good job and make my own life work out for me. I hoped a miracle would happen, so I would be able to learn things and get better grades. I liked babysitting and caring for children. I was good with them when they were sick. I gave them their medicine and nursed them back to health on those rare occasions when they caught a cold or when they sustained an injury. I was always sent for to stay with them. But I was told that I was too dumb to be a nurse. It seemed I would grow up to be a receptionist or a secretary, not someone important in the world.

❧8❧

Lucy

I'M REMEMBERING LUCY TODAY. It's coming back to me, and it causes heaviness in my chest. I want to remember it right—how our lives were, how we came together, how we were back then. Old women need to go back to the beginning, those many years ago. Lucy deserves remembering. It's easy to recall her when the sunlight is bright. I can almost see her in my mind, dancing in the sun. She was always so full of life. Nothing ever got her down. Fun-loving, laughing Lucy, the life of the party. She was my oldest friend and the light of my life.

This is the way it began many years ago. I need to go all the way back. I must have been three, almost four at the time. My brothers and sisters were in school. I was worried that my mother would try to give me away again, so I was watching her closely as she worked. I was in the downstairs kitchen as she cleared the breakfast things from the table. "You no eat your food again this morning. I don't know what I can do to get you to eat. I think maybe you should go outside in the sunshine. Perhaps it will give you an appetite," she said. I saw an old Coca-Cola bottle under the sink as she reached down there to get some cleaning supplies.

"I'll take my milk in that bottle. I'm sure it will taste better in there," I said. Mama took the bottle, washed it thoroughly with hot soapy water, and rinsed it. She poured milk and fastened a piece of cloth over the opening.

"This is so it does not come out too fast," Mama said. "Now you go out and play." I took the basement stairs outside and sat on the cement ledge. It was a quiet morning. The chickens clucked softly in the yard as they pecked the ground. The rooster crowed very early that morning. I watched the sun dry the morning dew from the grass as I drank milk from the Coke bottle. My favorite doll was in my lap. Her name was Sandy. She was wrapped in a piece of old blanket; her cloth body was naked. I had no clothes for her.

I could hear the rumble of trucks on the big highway. If I stood up, I could see them too. There wasn't much between the highway, which was about two miles away, and Strawberry Fields Farm. I was lonely sitting out there. I couldn't go back inside and disobey Mama, for fear she would call someone to take me away. I watched the road for cars. It was something I would do all my life. There were none. I liked the sound of a passing auto, as it started out very quiet and got louder as it drew near, then grew quiet again once it passed our driveway and sped away. Time seemed eternal to me, so I'm not sure how long I maintained my vigil.

There was a ball of white light coming down the road that ran past our farm. I stood up again to get a better look. I knew better than to chase after it. I'd chased many things like it that turned out to be uncatchable or nonexistent. I used to try to catch shafts of sunlight through the trees in the woods next to our backyard. When I got up to them, they just disappeared, and I would be standing in light. On hot summer days I followed the blacktop, trying to reach pools of water that seemed so close. I longed to stick my hot feet into those black pools, but I never reached them. They would leave the earth in wavy, hot streams as I approached.

I watched the white ball of light move and stop, then move and stop again. When it came to the top of our driveway, I walked to the end of the driveway, just so I wouldn't lose sight of that ball. I wasn't going to chase such illusive things, although I was very curious. The ball was moving steadily my way. As it approached the bridge over the creek that ran through Strawberry Fields, it took the shape of a doll. I looked down to see my doll, still lifeless in my arms. The doll on the bridge was singing. My doll didn't sing, and it didn't move. I knew dolls couldn't walk. After peering over the edge into the water, the doll continued to move my way. Holding Sandy tightly in my arms, I watched as the doll, who was not a doll at all, came up the hill to face me. "Hello, I'm Lucy. What's your name?" the doll said boldly.

Staring straight into her eyes, I couldn't move or speak. It was the first time I had seen anyone smaller than I was. Like me, she wasn't pretty. Her brown eyes were deep-set. I could tell she had brown hair under the white bonnet. Her nose was rather large, and she had a bright, winning, friendly smile. I reached out and touched her to make sure she was real. She was wearing a white smocked dress and little white shoes. "Can't you talk yet?" she asked.

"Yes," I said, nodding my head. "I can talk."

"Is that your doll? Can I see it?" she asked, reaching for it. I gave it willingly. What was a silly doll, compared with a real child I could talk to and have for a playmate? She started to dance around with my doll in her arms. I began to dance too. I was so happy to have a real friend. We ran into the yard, dancing on grass in the sunlight. We went in circles, singing "Ring Around the Rosie" until we were dizzy and fell to the ground.

"What did you say your name was?" she asked.

"It's Evalina," I answered shyly as I sat next to her.

"Evalina?" she asked. I nodded. She started to dance again, singing, "Oh, Evalina, my sweet Evalina, my love for you will never, never die." She knew the song for which I was named! I didn't think anyone knew it but my family. We danced around some more. It was the happiest day of my life. I had a friend. She was smaller than me and not a member of my family. Most of all, she was funny! She liked me, and we weren't pretty children.

"Come," I said. "I want to show you to Mama." She hesitated

for a moment. I took her hand and urged her forward. She started to laugh and came willingly. We walked down the steps to the basement, where Mama was running a load of clothes in the wringer washing machine. "Mama, Mama, look!" I called. "I found a little girl outside. She is going to be my little girl. You will, won't you, Lucy?"

Mama came from behind the washer with a puzzled look. "Lucy, your mama, does she know you are here?" I was disappointed when Mama seemed to know Lucy. I thought I alone had discovered her. It hadn't dawned on me she might have a family and a mama too.

"Oh, of course she does," Lucy replied. I would learn very soon that Lucy could lie and tell the truth at the same time, making you believe every word.

"But how did you get here?" asked Mama.

"I walked," Lucy said very calmly.

"And your mama, she let you do this?" inquired Mama.

"Oh, yes, she lets me walk everywhere," Lucy answered. I could see that Mama still didn't believe Lucy. "Evaline, do you have any more toys we could play with?"

"Come with me." I took her hand. We walked up the inside steps to an empty room where Antonia and I played. There was nothing much in it. I had my other doll, Judy, and an old, slightly broken tin dollhouse, rusted on one side. There were a few little books and a couple of puzzles with some of the pieces missing. Lucy didn't seem to mind, and we played happily. I could hear Mama talking on the telephone in the downstairs kitchen. I stood up sometime later when I heard voices downstairs, but Lucy just continued to play as if she heard no one. "Someone's downstairs with Mama," I said. "Let's go see who it is."

"I'd rather stay here and play," Lucy replied. We played a little longer. We stopped when we heard footsteps on the stairs.

A woman burst through the door, calling, "Lucy, Lucy, why do you do these things and frighten Mommy so?"

"Oh, calm down, Gladys. I just wanted to come here and play with her." I was stunned to hear her call her mother "Gladys."

"I had no idea where you went. I was scared out of my mind! Come, Lucy, we're going home," Gladys said. I couldn't believe my eyes when Lucy threw herself on the floor and started to kick and scream at the top of her lungs. Gladys stood there, bewildered. I was scared for Lucy. I thought Gladys might try to give her away! I wondered why it didn't occur to her. Lucy had no such fear. Mama was standing in the door watching, saying nothing. I desperately wished she could see that I would never do this.

Gladys bent down and tried to pick Lucy up, but she rolled away, grabbing my doll Sandy. Holding her tightly and kicking her feet, she yelled, "No! No, I won't go home with you!"

"Will you come with Mommy if Evalina lets you take one of her dolls home?" Gladys asked. "We really have to go. I need to wake Daddy and get him off to work."

"You can get Howie off to work by yourself," she retorted. Again I was shocked to hear her call her own father by his first name. I knew what would happen to me if I called my pa Nino. Gladys gave a sigh of complete exasperation.

"Oh, Mrs. Rosario, sometimes I just don't know what to make of this child," Gladys said.

"Come, we have cup of coffee, and the children have milk, then maybe she go with you," Mama said.

"Good idea!" Lucy exclaimed. She walked out the door and went down the stairs. We all sat at the downstairs kitchen table, talking. Lucy clung to my doll. I was surprised to learn that she was more than a year younger than I was. She seemed much older and certainly braver. She was smarter too. I could never do the things she did or say the things she said. She was still screaming and crying as she clung to my doll when they left for home. I watched as they walked down the driveway and onto the road. I could still hear Lucy, even when I could no longer see them.

Lucy returned to Strawberry Fields the next day, and the day after that, without her mother's knowledge or permission. I was out of toys to give her, so she would return home with Gladys. She didn't return any of the toys. I didn't care. I would have given her the world. She made me feel alive and brought such happiness to an otherwise dull place.

The following week Mama took time to walk me over to Lucy's house. She stayed to talk with Gladys. I felt shy and a little out of place. I wondered if Mama planned to leave me there. I sat very quietly in a chair next to my mother while I watched Lucy tear around the house, making a mess everywhere. She ate her chocolate cookies as she went from room to room, smearing fingerprints all over the walls. She sang out in a loud voice, "What do you do with a drunken sailor? What do you do with a drunken sailor early in the morning?"

Mama and Gladys were deep in conversation. I sat listening to them discuss household chores—cooking, cleaning, and child-rearing. The house grew quiet. Mama and Gladys realized it at the same time. "I wonder where Lucy has gone," Gladys said. "Oh, Lucy, where are you?"

"I'm in the living room," she called out.

"What are you doing, and why aren't you in here playing with Evalina?" Gladys asked.

"Because I'm in here lighting a match. Oh, ouch! Damn it! That hurts!" Lucy yelled from the next room.

Gladys dropped the spoon she was holding and ran into the next room, just in time to see Lucy start a small fire on the coffee table next to the couch. "Oh my God in heaven!" she yelled, stomping out the small fire with her foot.

It didn't seem to make any difference to Lucy how many times she got a spanking; she still did all kinds of dangerous things. Some were funny and turned out well; others didn't have a good outcome. It never fazed her to have her mouth washed out with soap; she swore like a truck driver at a traffic stop. I think she might have ingested more soap than was good for any human.

A little more than a year later, Gladys had another baby boy she called Rocky. Lucy didn't like him. She tried to give him to me. I was visiting her house with Mama when she came into the living room, carrying Rocky by his head. "Here, you can have him. He cries too much." Gladys screamed and lunged for the baby. No amount of punishment seemed to deter Lucy from her bad behavior.

Her older brother, Lorenzo, was just like her. They looked alike and acted the same. He was five years older. He was in Antonia's class because he was held back a grade. Over the next few years, he and Antonia would engage in lots of harebrained scams that never seemed to land them in hot water as they did Lucy.

Mr. and Mrs. Cavetti were first-generation kids from parents like mine who came to America for a better life for their families. They were good, honest, hardworking people. Mr. Cavetti, Howie, worked at the Ford Motor Plant. Like my pa, he did shift work. Things in the car business were booming then, as they were in the steel mills. There was lots of overtime. While this was good for the pocketbook, it was hard on women like Gladys and Mama, who tried their best to keep their children in line.

Unlike Mama, who was shy and didn't like to mingle with the women of Sherman Acres, Gladys loved the social gatherings that took place in the neighborhood. She went to all of them. Wearing her best dress, she tried to fit in with big landowners' wives. They met at each other's homes for what they called "club."

When it was Gladys's turn to have club, she would run around for days, cleaning everything in her tiny house, including Lucy and her two brothers. Of course club time was the day and the very hour that Lucy decided to make mud pies in the field behind their house. She took, without asking, Gladys's best plates for her mud pies. Gladys was so busy greeting her guests and being a good hostess that she didn't notice the plates were missing from the beautiful table. The club meeting got under way when the ladies were seated. Lucy came tearing in the door, dripping with mud, holding Gladys's best plates with her beautiful mud pies on them. She offered each lady a pie and dripped mud into their laps. "Oh, Lucy, what have you done?" yelled Gladys as the ladies jumped up from their chairs, cleaning the mud from one another.

"Let's face it, Gladys. Your cooking isn't that good, and my pies are lovely," Lucy said. Indeed they were, because she had picked Gladys's prized pink roses and placed them in the middle of each pie. The club meeting came to an abrupt end. Gladys cried and cleaned the mess. Her tears didn't discourage Lucy.

Lorenzo was never outdone by his little sister when it came to embarrassing Gladys in front of her club ladies. One day he was playing with Antonia over in the creek. Tommy and Tadd from next door came over. It was great fun to float down the creek on a raft. Marco had taught them to make rafts. Boards were hammered together on a frame. An old inner tube was inflated and pushed up under it. The tubeless tire was still a thing of the future. These rafts were a great invention and could hold four or five small children. We were all small back then. (It is amazing to see old home movies. People are much bigger in today's world.) We played out there until supper. Lorenzo was no exception. He was having a lot of fun that day. He knew he probably should go to the bathroom, but what the heck, he didn't want to leave his friends. A sudden urge to go overtook him, and he messed all over himself—pants, socks, shoes, and even his shirt. "Oh no, what am I going to do?" cried Lorenzo. "I can't go home like this!" Tommy and Tadd voted him off the raft, or rather, they just threw him off; he smelled so bad.

Antonia was quite the inventor. She could come up with a plan to solve any problem. "I've got an idea, Lorenzo. You wait here. I'll be right back," Antonia said. He smelled so bad that Lucy and I went up the hill to play under the big oak tree in the front yard. Antonia emerged on the opposite hill, carrying a large brown paper grocery bag and a small shovel called a spade. Lucy and I watched from our hill as the drama unfolded.

Tommy and Tadd took the raft way down the creek, out of sight. It was just Antonia and Lorenzo there on the hill. "Go behind that tree, and take all of your clothes off," she commanded. When Lorenzo came out from behind the tree, he was completely naked and holding his soiled things in front of his private area. Antonia took a towel from the bag and gave it to him. "Go behind the tree, and drop those clothes. Dry yourself with the towel." He did as she said. Then he stood by, anxiously waiting for instructions.

Taking up the spade just like Pa would have, she began to dig a hole. After about fifteen minutes, Antonia inspected the hole with her feet by stepping into it. Her knees could barely be seen. Satisfied, she climbed out. "Now bring those clothes over here, and drop them into the hole. Go back behind the tree, and put this bag on," she ordered him. When he came out, Lucy and I fell to the ground, laughing. Antonia had cut holes in the bag for his legs, and he was now wearing it like a pair of underpants. She motioned for him to drop the towel, clothes, and shoes into the hole. She covered it with dirt.

"Come on, Lucy. Let's go home," Lorenzo said. Lucy was never one to be supportive of her brother when potential trouble lurked.

"I think I'll stay just a little longer," Lucy replied.

"Suit yourself," Lorenzo said, and he started walking up the long driveway.

"Let's wait until he's on the road, then we'll follow him home. I can't wait to see what will happen to him. If we wait, it will look as if we knew nothing about this, and we'll avoid any problems of our own with Gladys," Lucy said. I went along with her plan. When he got to the top of the hill and started down Sherman Acres Road, Lucy and I went to the field next to the front yard. We walked along the tree line, close to the woods, so Lorenzo wouldn't see us. Taking this route, we were hidden, and we watched. He entered the Cavetti's front yard. I knew instantly that it must be Gladys's club day. Cars were gathered in the driveway. Lorenzo held his paper bag around his waist and walked across the front yard and into the back, so he could enter through the kitchen door. He must have thought the ladies would be sitting in the living room. Still maneuvering ourselves along the tree line, we crossed the road, entered the backyard, and took our positions at the back door to watch.

A loud scream came from Gladys as Lorenzo entered the tiny kitchen, wearing nothing but the bag. All the ladies were sitting there, having lemonade and cake. We watched from behind the door as they jumped up and poured onto the lawn. "Lorenzo, what in the world do you think you are doing? And what is that awful smell?" Gladys yelled. "Get in the bathroom, and clean yourself this minute." Lucy lay on the ground, rolling in laughter as the ladies, unable to stand the odor, got into their cars and sped away.

"Good-bye, ladies," Lucy called out in between laughs. "Thank you for coming. Come again."

The following year, the Stayton's dug a pond in the middle of their woods. The beautiful forest was directly across the big field from Strawberry Fields Farm. It was across Sherman Acres Road, right in front of the Cavetti's little five-acre place. We were excited to see it! Antonia, Lorenzo, Lucy, and I were going together. A dirt road made by heavy equipment about a quarter mile from the Cavetti's had been used to remove the earth for the pond. Instead of taking the road, we decided to make a path through the woods from the road right in front of their house. The woods were beautiful and held many sights and sounds. There were giant oak and silver maple trees, along with many beautiful flowers of all kinds and colors. Birds sang in the trees all summer, creating a paradise in the middle of nowhere.

It took us the better part of the afternoon to make that path through the trees. Small forest creatures watched, keeping their distance. It was very hard work, but when we arrived at the little pond, it was so still and quiet, like blue glass instead of water. A tiny aluminum boat was tied to the little pier. We all felt it, that feeling of a magical place. Standing at the very end of the pier, it felt like we were floating on the water. We had to be very careful not to fall into the water.

Lucy and I sat on the pier, holding hands and dangling our feet in the water. Lorenzo was fascinated with the little boat. He wanted to take it out onto the blue-glass waters. "I'm getting in it," Lorenzo said bravely. I didn't think it was a good idea.

"Go ahead, Lorenzo, knock yourself out," Lucy replied.

Antonia stood by silently as Lorenzo untied the boat from the little pier. It only had one paddle. I knew he would not be able to steer the boat with only one oar. It began to drift on the water. He tried to paddle, but the boat kept going around in circles. Around and around it went, farther and farther from the pier. "Antonia! Help me!" he called. His voice echoed through the forest. "What should I do? I can't get the boat to go back to the pier." The boat had drifted more than halfway across the little pond. It seemed to be headed for the banks on the other side. Antonia started walking around to that side. It was such a small body of water that it didn't take her long.

"Hold out the oar. I'll get it and pull you to shore," she said. But the oar proved to be too short for her to reach. Antonia walked into the woods.

Lorenzo began to cry loudly as he drifted along. "Help me! Help me!" he cried louder and louder. After what seemed like a long time, Antonia emerged from the woods dragging a long, dead branch behind her. It was about twelve feet long, but it wasn't heavy. She held it out over the water.

"Grab it, Lorenzo. Pull yourself and the boat close to the shore," Antonia ordered. "You can jump out and help me pull it up onto the bank." Her plan worked. Lorenzo was rescued.

With the exception of this little mishap, we loved the Stayton pond. We went there often, no matter what the weather was like. We swam as soon as the temperature was warm enough, with and without swimwear. Our school picnics were held there. In winter we skated on it. I should say all the other kids skated on it. I watched; I couldn't stand up on skates. My ankles were too weak. I would sit by the big bonfire at the edge of the pond. It was warm and lovely on a clear night under the stars.

After that, things began to change. Lorenzo became more responsible and less daring. He worked harder at school, getting better grades. He and Antonia started to drift apart, playing together less. She seemed to play less with everyone.

A few weeks after the boat incident, I wanted to know how Lorenzo was faring. I walked alone to the Cavetti's in midafternoon. I hadn't gone far when the Creeper came along in his car. I wasn't to the point where I could duck into the field. I was reluctant to go into the woods, for fear he would leave his car and follow me. I walked faster. "Where are you going, little girl?" he said, slowing the black car to a crawl. "I can take you, if you just get in here with me. I promise." I broke into a run and didn't stop until I got to Lucy's.

She was standing in the screen door, looking out, as I approached, panting furiously. "What's wrong? Why so out of breath?" she asked. It was a few minutes before I answered.

"The Creeper was after me again," I finally said.

"Are you talking about the Fur King Pervert? He can't hurt you. He's just an asshole, that's all," she replied. I wasn't afraid of him when I was with Lucy. She called him all kinds of names. He didn't seem so sinister when she was around. His eyes softened, and he smiled and laughed when he saw her. I didn't know what the names meant. I was too afraid to say them out loud. Lucy used these and worse whenever she wanted. The Creeper didn't follow her or look at her the way he looked at me.

"Can you come out and play?" I asked.

"No, Gladys's underpants are twisted again today. She has me locked in here, like I couldn't climb on a chair and unfasten the stupid thing," Lucy replied.

"Why? What did you do now?" I inquired. It must have been something really good.

"The baby woke me, crying last night. When he didn't stop and Gladys didn't see to him, I got up and yelled at her," Lucy said.

"For this, she won't let you out of the house?" I asked.

"Well, what I said was, 'Gladys, get your lazy ass out of bed! The baby is crying!' Howie took his pillow, put it over his face, and roared like a lion with laughter. After Gladys got Rocky back to sleep, I was asleep myself. She came over to my bed and beat my ass with a paddle. She was yelling so loud, she woke the baby and Howie again. This time he didn't use his pillow. He just laughed and laughed. She's not talking to him. The good thing is there won't be any of the *bump,*

bump noise, bed creaking, and that 'Oh, Howie, oh' going on at night for a while. She's real pissed at him," Lucy said. I wanted to laugh, but I didn't want to make her mad at me.

"Where's your mama now?" I asked.

"She's in the shanty, doing laundry or something," Lucy replied. The shanty was a small white building in the Cavettis' backyard that had a basement where Gladys did the wash every Monday, just like Mama. The little house had all kinds of things stored in it, because the main house was so small. It only had two bedrooms, a living room, and a kitchen. Lucy shared a room with her two brothers. When Mariano was born, they built an addition.

"Lucy! Lucy, where are you?" I heard Gladys call. Lucy ignored her. I would have given the world to hear Mama call my name.

"Lucy!" Gladys called even louder.

"Keep your pants on, Gladys. I'm in the living room," Lucy answered. "You'd better go. I'll see you tomorrow. I plan to make her so miserable, she'll turn me out in the morning." It was true. Lucy got out the next day.

Over the years Lucy pursued fun things to irritate her parents and amuse others. At some point she learned to call them Mother and Daddy. We were inseparable during those years. No matter how many wild things she thought up, I was right there with her. I was her sidekick. I was always Ethel to her Lucy. Lucy was my Lucy.

Those unwritten rules still existed, so I couldn't play with her during school. After school and all summer, we raised a lot of hell. I couldn't have played with her at school, even if there hadn't been rules. Lucy was so popular; kids swarmed around her. She was one of those rare people to whom the rules didn't apply. She had friends in every grade in school, from first grade up through high school.

In rural Henderson County, there was no such thing as organized baseball. I'm sure it existed then, but we didn't have it. Baseball was our favorite thing to play every summer. After dinner, we met at the Sherman Acres School playground and turned it into a baseball diamond. This was before Waldo's brother tore it down. No adults supervised. We made our own rules. We chose teams and played the game with undying dedication. Antonia was always captain of one team and Lorenzo the other. I was small and not a good player. Lucy passed me up in size and skill. Lorenzo always chose her for his team. All of the boys wanted to be on the team with Lorenzo. Rosemary and Antonia used me as a bargaining chip. "I'll let you have all the boys if you take Evalina and give me Tommy," Antonia would say. It worked. Lorenzo fell for it every time. Antonia and Rosemary were very good players, along with the Loveless girls. They beat Lorenzo's team with only one boy, Tommy. He would do anything for Antonia. If disputes and fights occurred, they were negotiated between the teams. Everything was settled among us kids. Sometimes those games lasted all summer. It was great fun and a learning experience that proved helpful in adulthood.

I did my best to keep Lucy out of serious trouble. With her, it was never-ending, on and off the playground, in and out of school. We were all jammed in tightly on the bus, due to overcrowding. The county government knew that more kids came to rural areas every day, but it refused to get more buses. The motor gave a loud groan as it worked hard to pull the bus up that steep grade through Sherman Acres. Mr. Charles Bails was the driver. He had a serious look on his face as he steered steadily and carefully. We were all smashed up against one another. As the bus bumped and jerked, we got quiet. Then Lucy cried out, "Swing it into second, Charlie!" Everyone laughed, including Mr. Bails. She might have been a lot of things, but one thing was for certain: she was generous. Lucy always shared her beautiful blue bike. She taught me how to ride. We covered many miles of country roads.

There was a road that ran to the west and then bent to the south in the back of our farm. We used it to get to the back five acres of our property. There were a few small farms along the road, but it had no name. If you walked to the bend in that road and turned north, you would be in front of Faith Jones's and Crazy Elizabeth's places. The Browns' and the Gorman's little farms were on it. The summer before my freshman year in high school, the Gorman's sold their place after their only daughter died of leukemia. From the cement porch off the upstairs kitchen, I watched as new neighbors moved in. It was a man and his wife and their son. They had a beautiful palomino horse they didn't ride.

When Bobby Blaze began to fade from my fantasies, I noticed the Larsons' son, Eric. "A Summer Place" was playing on the radio as I watched Eric Larson pull out of his driveway in a silver-gray Cadillac car. The car was a beauty, and so was Eric. He was six feet, four inches tall, with reddish-brown hair and light brown eyes. His face was always red, like he had been out in the sun too long. I walked up Sherman Acres Road for a better look. When he rounded the corner, he waved. I waved back as he sped away. Who was this mystery man? He looked too old to be in high school, yet he lived with his parents. I wondered how I could meet this guy, who didn't look at me like most men did. I watched their home but saw only Eric and his father come and go at regular intervals. There were no guests or family gatherings.

"Lucy, meet me halfway on the road. I got something to tell you," I said on the phone one evening. We had an eight-party line. It wasn't safe to say anything. Any one of eight families could be listening in, or even all of them. We always met halfway between her place and mine. We would call out and talk to each other until we were out of sight of one another.

"So what's going on?" she asked when we met fifteen minutes later.

"Let's just walk awhile, okay?" I asked.

"Okay; what are we looking for?" she asked a little while later.

"Keep walking, you'll see," I replied. The Creeper came by. He didn't stop or slow down. He just smiled and waved.

"See, I told you he's harmless," she said. I gave her a look that said I knew better. The silver Cadillac turned onto Sherman Acres Road.

"Here he comes, Lucy!" I said. "Get ready! Smile and wave with me." As the Caddy got closer, we waved and gave our best smiles.

"Wow! Who was that?" Lucy asked. "He sure is a looker, all right."

"He's my new neighbor. They live in the old Gorman house. He has to be at least eighteen. He's not in school," I said proudly, watching the car until it was out of sight.

"So he's your new heartthrob, is he?" Lucy asked.

"Well, he's sure nice to look at. Trying to get to see him or talk to him will give us something to do. It will create a little adventure to look forward to all summer," I said.

So began the pursuit of Eric Larson, our elusive dream guy. For years he never stopped to talk to us. He only waved. Lucy and I spent many hours walking the road to get a glimpse of the man in the fancy Cadillac car. More than six years would pass before I came face to face with the handsome, mysterious man.

It happened when I was in nursing school. I saw him in a diner on the big highway one evening when I was with friends. I introduced myself. I even told him I had been chasing him for years. I hoped we could finally get to know each other. He was sweet and charming, even very amused by my story. He said he felt flattered that my friend and I had noticed him.

We started to date, but from the beginning, something wasn't right. He was a lovely person, always a perfect gentleman. He was a good boyfriend. I was still pretty naive and too afraid to go any further than a few kisses. Eric was so different, never trying that stuff, nor was he interested. We laughed and talked, but there was always a sense of distance between us. We went out to a show and dinner. We were sitting in yet another beautiful Cadillac when he began to say strange things. "You're so wonderful, so full of life and fun. I wish I could be the kind of man you deserve," he said. I looked into his eyes and felt confused.

"What do you mean, Eric?" I said. "I think you're a great guy. I've been in love with your looks since I was fifteen years old."

"Yes, dear, I understand, but what you don't understand is I have a problem. I don't know how to explain it to you. I would never hurt you for the world," he said, with real tears in his beautiful brown eyes. "I've been home all day, hiding out in the barn and drinking. I drink a lot, but I can handle it. I've been doing it most of my life. You know I work for my dad at his construction company. I didn't go in today. I love it when it rains. I can stay home and hide from the rest of the world." I understood pretty clearly then why he always had that red face.

"Oh, come on, Eric. A handsome guy like you can't have any problems. Why, you have it all—you have looks, you're a nice person, and you have a nice car. You're sweet, charming, and a real gentleman too. You could have any girl in the world you want," I said playfully, with a smile. I really enjoyed our relationship, because I never had to fight him off or explain to him that I didn't believe in sex before marriage. The looks he gave me were never the ones of a hungry man looking to be satisfied. The way he held me in his arms was beautiful, gentle, never inappropriate.

"I know all that, but that's the problem. I'm afraid I don't want any of them," he said, with tears now streaming down his face. "This will be our last date, sweetheart. Please don't hate me." Reality began to sink into my dense brain as I started to comprehend what he was telling me. I took him into my arms and held him while he silently cried. I was almost a graduate nurse by then. I knew about these things. I had to let those childhood fantasies go, move on with my life, and let Eric move on with his.

"I'll always be your friend, Eric," I said as I got out of the car.

"I know you will, and I'll always love you for it," he said. He was gone from my life forever. It was rumored all around New Moon Lake and Henderson that Eric was always looking for men. He disappeared from Henderson County altogether.

When I told Lucy the story of Eric many years later, she had a hard time believing it. She was married with a child then. We were both a little sad for him. We hoped he found some peace and happiness somewhere.

It didn't occur to me that there would be a time in my life when Lucy was no longer in it. We had been friends since I could remember. I was closer to her than to my own sisters. I didn't know that time has a way of changing everything and everyone. Spaces can grow between people, ones that can never be crossed. We lose the ones we love most when we take them for granted.

Dream girl

❧9❧

The End of Dreams for the Dream Girl

SUMMER AFTER EIGHTH GRADE, I felt as if I was on my way to becoming a grown woman. My scrapbooks of pictures of how my own place would look were growing. I walked around the back roads of Sherman Acres, still plotting my escape from this lonely place on the map.

Out of the blue, Crazy Elizabeth and Juanita started calling me. They were planning a bridal shower for Juanita's older sister, who had dropped out of high school to marry her longtime old-man boyfriend. Juanita asked me to help with the shower. The eighth-grade girls met at her house to make decorations and help plan the shower. Juanita was moving with her family to some high-class neighborhood southwest of the big city. They sold their home and little restaurant on the big highway.

Soon after they moved, I finally understood why they wanted to be friends. They wanted Juanita to stay with me. Elizabeth and her family lived in a virtual shack that wasn't fit for humans. Later that summer Juanita came to stay with me for a week. We visited Elizabeth every day. We went by Juanita's old house to visit the new owners. I was going to babysit their two little boys. I learned that Juanita had a mad crush on the brother of the man who had purchased their old place. He was very good-looking. Her mother wanted her to date such men. Juanita was scared of them—not scared like I was, but terrified. We were only fourteen, almost fifteen. I couldn't see why her mother pushed her so hard to date. At her sister's wedding, we were dancing and having fun when her sister came up and said, "Okay, Juanita, you have to dance with men now."

When I started to babysit for the new owners, the husband and his handsome brother pursued me constantly. They would try to trap me somewhere in the house, kiss me, and try touching me where I knew I shouldn't be touched. I became quite skilled at avoiding them, but it was getting to be just too much. I stopped babysitting.

Juanita's mental health became a big problem after she entered high school. She spent long months in mental hospitals until her death many years later. I never knew the true extent of her mental problems, but I knew they were serious and involved many delusions. She saw and talked to people that weren't real.

That summer before my freshman year, the country was abuzz with the fact that President Eisenhower's second term was about to end. Everyone was sure Nixon would be the next president. He ran the country during most of Eisenhower's last term. Then everyone started talking about a young man named John Kennedy. He was a senator from Boston, Massachusetts. He talked with a strange accent. Everyone in the family was for Kennedy. Enzo especially liked him. When Kennedy came to North End to give a speech, Enzo had to work that day, so he sent Nina to meet him. Later we talked about the time Nina got to shake hands with the great US president. I liked Mr. Kennedy too. I watched the whole Democratic Convention on TV. I didn't say much about him to my friends; they came from very Republican families. Henderson County was a great Republican stronghold and had been since the time of President Lincoln. Most farm folk's views were very conservative.

My freshman year in high school was another jolt of reality. I hadn't known there were so many kids in high school. Our class was the biggest in the history of the hundred-year-old school. There were one hundred and forty-eight kids in the freshman class. I was left alone in grammar school; high school was different. I was taunted daily by all the boys. I was so different from other girls and very conspicuous.

Being a majorette put me right out in front of the marching band at every parade and football game. I didn't realize what type of attention I would attract when dressed in that costume. It was the same style Antonia had worn. Then we were given new ones, more provocative and figure-flattering. I started to walk hunched over to hide my big breasts. It was the worst thing I could have done. Mr. Music, the band instructor, yelled at me in front of everyone. "Come on, you little hussy, everyone knows you got them big tits. Stick them out there!" He poked me in the back with his middle finger. I was humiliated! I just wanted to run away and hide. Teachers were always right. I felt dirty.

Taunting from the boys only grew worse every day. They would wait for me by their lockers and watch as I came down the hall. They would reach out, trying to touch my large breasts, saying things like, "Hey, do you put out like your sister?" They called out names like "Bedroom Babe" and "Sexpot." I didn't know what to do or say, so I said nothing. If I thought I could go to a teacher and complain, I soon learned that I had no ally in any of them. The male teachers joined in the fun. They seemed to enjoy it. The female teachers just looked on in disgust, treating me as if I were at fault. I walked with my head down, holding my books in front of me. When that didn't stop them, I started to go to class later to avoid them. Being late for class wasn't an option. Three times late, and a note went home to your parents.

A girl named Linda insisted she was going to be my best friend.

When we hung out together, she made fun of me too. I stopped being friends with her, and she had a senior girl threaten me. But I didn't back down. It was lonely.

After a few months, I became friends with an unusual girl named Lila Peace. She came from North End, where she attended the same Baptist church as Bobby Ray and his sister Janet. Bobby was in love with Lila. She was so beautiful, with blonde hair and pretty blue eyes. She was tall and wore lots of makeup, although she didn't need it. She was very sweet, without a mean bone in her whole body. She had a powerful imagination and could be someone different every day. For days she might be a Russian princess and speak with a heavy accent. She might be Queen Elizabeth and talk with an English accent. She was wonderful and fascinating. She would call me on the phone after school and continue the entertainment. She told wonderful stories about the places she had been and the people she met there. Lila Peace didn't stay at Henderson High. I think it was too boring for her. Her parents were missionaries with the church, and she had lived all over the world. She returned to a North End school.

My grades were not good, even in classes for slow kids. Some kids in high school were on the multiyear plan. They were still trying to pass courses required for graduation. A lot of the boys had jobs in the afternoon. Most worked in the steel mills of North End or at the Ford Motor Plant in South Heights.

One day in Mrs. Barrington's class, she asked, "Who in this class can tell me what success is and how it is determined?" I boldly raised my hand. After waiting to see if other students might have an answer, she finally called on me. "Yes, Evaleene, I guess you can answer," she said reluctantly.

"I think success is happiness. It doesn't matter if you're rich or poor. It only matters if you are happy. That's success," I said.

"Well, who else knows what success is?" she continued. In the back of the room, Sam Weeds Jr. raised his hand. He was a tall, lanky blond kid who drove a Thunderbird to school.

"Success is being a rich and powerful lawyer and doing whatever you want," he said. No surprise, coming from him. His father, Sam Senior, was the most successful lawyer in Henderson County. He handled mostly divorce cases. It was said throughout the area that Lincoln might have freed the slaves, but Sam Weeds freed the housewives for a king's ransom. When I grew older, I realized that he freed them into a life of poverty and dependence that caused them to run right into another bad marriage, or several, in order to feed their children.

After we heard from one of Dr. Hemming's boys, who said that being a doctor was the secret to success, a few of the girls said that success was either marrying well or becoming a movie star. Mrs. Barrington begrudgingly conceded that I had given the best answer. It didn't persuade her to give me a better grade. I still got only a C.

That fall John F. Kennedy was elected president of the United States. Everyone in my family had voted for him, with the exception of Carmella, who didn't care. Antonia wasn't old enough to vote; nor was I. There was something so strange about the fact that Antonia was married and had a child, but she wasn't allowed to vote. I kept turning this over in my head. It seemed to me that life in this great country was not always fair to females. We were taught that all men were created equal. I began to think that part of it might have been left out: the part that included women and people of color. Every time I heard that line, in my head I would add, *Some men are more equal than others. Freedom and justice only apply to men.*

I was still singing my country music that first year, but it wasn't with Grace Cain and her brother. Grace fell for a boy in our class, and they were going steady. In a going-steady relationship back then, the boy called all the shots. Eddie White refused to let Grace do any singing or go out anywhere with her girlfriends. He flirted on the streets of downtown Henderson with all of the wild girls.

I asked Richard Lively if he would play guitar for me, and he agreed to do it. We were seeing a lot of each other. He really wanted a girlfriend, but not one that was Catholic. I introduced him to Ada May Louis. They quickly became a steady couple.

Sammy and Marco were still keeping a tight rein on me. I was only allowed to go to special events. One of these was the winter formal dance. A boy in my class named Kenny asked me to go. I dreamed about it for weeks before it happened. I was so excited. Antonia borrowed a strapless formal dress of mint-green tiered ruffles for me to wear. It was tea-length, and it fit me well. As I left the house that night, I looked the picture of teenage innocence with my long, wavy golden-brown hair and a little baby-pink lipstick on my full lips.

Since Kenny didn't drive, we doubled with another couple. I was glad to discover that Kenny was shy. I didn't have to fight him off. We danced a few dances and had some punch and cookies. The drive home was a slow one through all of the back roads, with a stop here and there. The couple in the front seat quickly disappeared from our view. I really didn't want to see what they were doing. Kenny and I kissed a few times. It wasn't awful, but I was glad when it was over. I was home by the appointed time of ten o'clock.

After that I dated a boy named Billy, whose father was a teacher at Henderson High. All he wanted to do was kiss. It was the kind of kissing I hated. Boys like him stuck their tongue halfway down your throat. I got that feeling of being overpowered by them. I didn't mind kissing, really; I just hated that kind. I became very good at avoiding it and getting away from boys who wanted more than kisses. I knew every back road and dirt path in all of New Moon, Sherman Acres, and Henderson. When I said no and a boy tried to overpower me, I just let myself out and walked home. All that practice I got avoiding old men came in handy in high school.

In April of my freshman year, I was struggling to the end. I was doing my homework when Carmella called Mama. I listened to what they were saying. "She have a the chicken pox when she was a baby. Yes, I am sure," Mama said. When Mama hung up, she said, "Carmella, she coming for you so you can watch the little Katie. She has a the chicken pox. You had them, so you won't get them again." Carmella never could handle a sick kid. It cramped her style. She never liked staying home.

About three weeks later I started feeling sick and very tired. It was an effort to get out of bed and get to school. I just couldn't wait to get back home and go to sleep. I was sleeping a lot, which was very unusual for me. When I woke one morning, my skin felt itchy and hot. I was never hot. When I scratched at my skin, I felt rough bumps. I looked in the mirror and discovered I was covered everywhere in chicken pox. Never in my life had I been so feverish , and those blisters were everywhere. They were even in my nose and throat and other places I don't care to mention. I was out of school for a week.

Babysitting at Carmella's was getting to be quite an experience. Norman had lots of men friends around. He and his brother were running a gas station and auto repair place on the big highway. They were still working at the steel mill as well. I began to notice that those guys were really hanging around to be with Carmella. She was still so beautiful and flirtatious. One young man in particular seemed to have more than just a friendly interest in her. Just before Carmella gave birth to another little girl, named Liza, that young man was killed in a car accident. I thought Carmella took it awfully hard. I think she went a little crazy. She had been sure that her baby would be a boy, and she planned to name him after that young man. She had a hard time with the fact that Liza was a girl. When she came home from the hospital, she could hardly look at the infant. I carried Liza home in my arms.

Liza was a pretty baby with curly light-brown hair and big blue eyes. She didn't cry much. Carmella just couldn't cope, so I took care of her. That summer I took her to stay with me in my little room at Strawberry Fields Farm. I bathed her and dressed her in pretty dresses. I fed her formula from baby bottles. I took her for long walks in the buggy. I never let her cry. I never let her out of my sight for more than a few minutes, and only when Mama held her. I made a cradle out of an empty dresser drawer and a firm pillow. It worked great, and the baby slept all night, but I didn't. I was so afraid that I wouldn't hear her cry or that something might happen to her. I stayed awake the whole time she was with me.

Exhausted from no sleep one hot July night, I crawled into bed and went right to sleep. I was sure I heard the baby crying out in the middle of the night. I turned on the light in my room. The drawer had been replaced inside the dresser. I became frantic and started to pull out all of the drawers. When I couldn't find Liza, I started yelling, "Mama! Mama, the baby is gone! Help! Help me, the baby's gone!" Mama came running into my room.

"What is it? Why are you yelling like that?" Mama asked, very alarmed.

"I can't find the baby, Mama. She's gone. She was in the drawer, and now she's gone!" I began to cry and paced around the small room frantically. I was so upset that I started gasping for air, feeling as if I would pass out any minute.

"Look, there is no baby here," Mama said calmly. "We take her back to Carmella last night. Do you not remember this?" It all started to come back. I felt so foolish. The dream had been so real that it scared me. I couldn't get back to sleep.

I was still drinking a ton of coffee to calm my nerves. Those young guys kept hanging around Carmella's place. They started coming there when I was babysitting. "Carmella isn't here, and Norman is at the station," I said to a young man named Gene Berry one evening when I opened the door. He was a big man of about twenty years of age, with light brown hair and green eyes.

"I know," he said as he stepped into the tiny kitchen. "I came to see you. I'll help you put the kids to bed." I was tired, and I wasn't feeling well. I had taken Sammy's sunlamp and given myself a pretty bad sunburn. It rained all week, and I didn't want my tan to fade. I let Gene help me, and in less than an hour, both girls were asleep.

"That sunburn is bad," he said. "You'd better let me put something on it. I'll go up to the drugstore and get some stuff." When he returned, he put some cream all over my back, arms, and legs, which made me feel better.

"Thank you, Gene. That feels so much better," I said. Ordinarily I hated being touched by anyone, especially older men. I had surprised myself by letting him get that close. A sunburn, I had heard, could make you go crazy.

"I'll stay with you until your sister gets back, and then I'll take you home, if it's okay with you," he said.

"That's fine, Gene," I replied. When Carmella returned home at about eleven o'clock, she didn't seem surprised to see him. He drove me home and stayed to talk to Sammy. I went in to bed.

A few days later, Gene called and asked me to go on a date. I told him I wasn't allowed to date anyone yet. "Well, I talked with Sammy a few nights ago, and he said it would be all right, as long as we doubled with Carmella and Norman and got you home early," he said. Dating Gene was pretty nice. We went to the movies and to the beach in North End. I let him kiss me, but I pulled away and started to run when he tried to go a little further. Once, I bolted from the car and refused to get back in.

One evening we were sitting outside on the front porch, and Gene began to tell me something that made my blood run cold. "You know why I'm dating you? Well, I guess you don't. You're pretty naive." He continued without waiting for me to answer, "The truth is, your sisters wanted me to try and get you pregnant, but I can't do it. You're not willing like they thought you would be, and I'm no rapist." I was so shocked and hurt that I couldn't talk to my sisters. I never told anyone. The way Carmella and Antonia treated me, I was sure it was true. Gene had no reason to lie to me. He was fairly honest. Back then, men who got girls pregnant were never held responsible.

"Well, since that is never going to happen, Gene, I see no point in our dating," I said. He was disappointed in my response, but I didn't want to see him again. He wasn't the man of my dreams or even close. My dreams were still of a confident, successful, grown-up me.

I realized that my sisters probably meant me no harm. I think they wanted me to be more like them. But I wasn't like Carmella or Antonia. I didn't want a husband and children. I wanted freedom and the ability to make my own decisions, find my own way in the world. They thought I had a better life than they'd had when they were living at home, and perhaps still. It might have been true that I had a little more than they had when they were my age. Most girls in my class had much more than I did.

Antonia was expecting another baby that summer. She looked awful. She hadn't lost the weight from having Dean, and she gained more. She seemed never to want to fix herself up. I saved some of my strawberry money and bought her a maternity outfit. She seemed grateful, and yet she sort of expected it. Her attitude seemed to convey the message, *I have nothing, and you have everything, so you should share.*

My second year in high school was just as painful as the first. The boys continued their daily torment. Mr. Music, the band director, continued to say horrible things to me about the way I looked. One evening after a band concert and a performance by the majorette corps, I heard him telling another student's father something very inappropriate for a teacher to say. It was about my sister and me. I told him I no longer wanted to be in the band and majorette corps. I told him he had no right to talk about my sister and me that way. "You're supposed to be a teacher and set an example for the kids, not act like one," I said and walked away. The next day I went to the office to ask for a withdrawal from the band. I discovered that Mr. Music had already removed me. I was given another study hall.

I felt so bad about myself. I stopped talking to my friends. Crazy

Elizabeth and I were hanging out together. She was the only one who seemed unbothered by all the terrible things said about my sister and me. I went on trips to the big city with her and her mother. These would have been nice and even fun if we were allowed to get out of the car and explore a little. Mrs. Miller was so fat and sick that she couldn't walk. We just looked at the buildings from the car. Later I was in so much pain that I could no longer go with them. I kept my head down and refused to look at anyone. My friendship with Elizabeth became very strained. I became lonely and depressed. My grades were worse than ever.

That fall, Antonia gave birth to another baby boy. She named him Warren Lee Kenneth after her husband, but she called him "the Captain." Many years later, while going through some old photos, I found a picture of that little newborn boy. On the back, in my sister's perfect handwriting, I read his birthdate and the words "My Captain, the love of my life."

The Captain was a beautiful baby. He weighed ten and a half pounds at birth and continued to grow every time you looked at him. He had a full head of copper-red hair and big black eyes like his mom's. He had a very deep voice, and it would send me into fits of laughter when he said, "Dada." I now had four little nephews and four little nieces who were the light of my depressed life. After they tried to get me pregnant, I didn't babysit much for either sister. They complained again that my life was too easy. No one seemed to realize how hard things were for me, how unhappy I was. I turned to more coffee to steady my nerves.

Since I didn't have friends anymore and I didn't go anywhere, I started to do other things with my time. I bought some light blue paint and painted my room. I had Mama help me make some new curtains and scarves for the tops of my two dressers. I started to design my own clothes, and with Mama's help, we made a few things I designed. I had all the ideas but no talent to make them a reality. I relied on Mama. One of my creations was an orange sleeveless blouse with a sash, which I wore into town with a pair of black shorts on the first warm day. I was in the dime store, on the top floor, looking for materials. When I descended the stairs, everyone on the lower level stopped and watched as I came down. Most were high school boys. I lowered my head, causing my hair to fall. I walked out without purchasing anything. A simple trip to the dime store was a painful experience. Why couldn't I be like everyone else and just go to town and shop without causing a scene everywhere I went?

I still had some strawberry money left, and those majorette boots sat idle. I wanted to learn how to ride a horse with a real saddle. On a Tuesday afternoon I set out on foot for the Leila farm, where there were lots of horses to ride. Harry Leila was a big, strapping man of six feet, seven inches. He wore cowboy boots, jeans, and Western shirts with a Texas ten-gallon hat all year round. He thought he was a real ladies' man. Harriett, his wife, was a tiny woman with short, curly brown hair and blue eyes. She dressed in old housedresses with anklet socks and brown orthopedic shoes. She might have been pretty if she tried; she didn't. The Leila daughters, Iris and Amanda, looked just like their father. They were big, muscular girls that looked more like big boys. The boys, Johnny and Danny, on the other hand, looked like their mother, with small frames and fine bones.

Iris was the better horsewoman, but she had no patience to teach me to ride with a saddle. Amanda took the job and gladly pocketed the two dollars I gave her. After a few weeks, I was good enough to go riding alone through the fields. It brought me great pleasure! Avoiding Mr. Leila was a challenge. Fortunately, Mrs. Leila was always watching. She managed to keep her husband away from me. It was a hard job, but that little woman could handle that giant.

Those bad cramps I had were getting worse. Mama was afraid I would miss school. Dr. Hemming prescribed some very strong pain pills. I had taken only one or two of them when I suffered a bad reaction. I was walking upstairs to English when everything started to go black, and I thought I was going to faint. Mr. Foster, the choir director, caught me before I hit the floor. My heart was racing, and I was having trouble breathing. A loud ringing pounded in both ears. Fortunately for me, he was one of the few nice teachers. He stayed with me, gave me water, and let me skip class.

"She is just doing all of this for attention," Dr. Hemming said to Mama when she told him what had happened. I somehow knew, even then, that it was probably an allergic reaction. I wondered how Dr. Hemming ever got a license to practice medicine. Since he was the only doctor in New Moon and my father liked him, he remained our family doctor.

He almost killed Pa that summer when he gave him a dose of medication for his allergy to ragweed. Pa came home from his office so short of breath that I thought he might die. I didn't have a driver's license yet, but I was ready to put him in the car and drive him to the hospital in North End. After Mama got him to drink a few glasses of water, his color changed from a ghastly purple back to pink. I wasn't a good city driver yet, and in rural Henderson County, there was no ambulance.

Sweet sixteen was supposed to be the best time of a young girl's life. I was miserable, and Mama began to take note, not of my sadness, but of the fact that I wasn't gaining any weight. She worried that I wasn't developing properly. It was so absurd, because I had those big breasts measuring 34C. My waist was only eighteen inches around, and my hips were twenty-eight inches. When I was dating Gene, he always marveled that his hands could meet and touch when he put them around my waist. It was a gesture I hated.

It was back to Dr. Hemming for me again. "Look, young lady, I don't have time for your nonsense," he said to me sternly. "This is pitiful. You only weigh eighty-two pounds! You will start eating and putting on some weight, or I will put you in the hospital, put a tube down your throat, and force-feed you. Do I make myself clear?" All I could do was nod my head.

"Feed her whatever you can get down her," he said to Mama. "Bring her back in a month. If she hasn't gained any weight, then in goes the tube. Do you understand me, Mrs. Rosario?"

"Yes, but of course, Dr. Hemming," Mama answered quietly.

The threat of the tube brought another bad dream. I saw myself lying in a hospital bed, with a green garden hose sticking out of my mouth, attached to a big bottle of brownish fluid.

When Mama and I returned to Dr. Hemming's office the following month, I weighed in at eighty-four pounds. He seemed pleased. "Well, two pounds in a month is good. I won't need to see you again for another year, unless you're sick," he said. Nothing could have made me happier except never seeing him again.

≥10≤

He Came on a Horse Named Midnight

I T WAS A LONG time coming, but the rain finally stopped about the third week in March that year. A warm wind began to blow, drying the fields and the farms of Sherman Acres. The gravel and dirt roads became passable once again. Spring always brought a sense of hope and renewal. This season, it seemed different to me somehow. I began to feel that something good was going to happen in my life, although I had no sign of it. It was just a feeling. Things just couldn't get worse for me, here at the end of my first two disastrous years in high school. I managed to pass. I was going to the next grade level. I gained two pounds. All of these things were signs of better days.

I was a little more help to Pa. I could lift a bushel of corn, a bale of hay, or whatever he needed me to lift over my head and dump into the wagon. I had always been good at driving the tractor; I was too small to do anything else. I had been driving it since I was eight. I had to step on the brake with both feet to stop it. It never occurred to me or anyone that this might be a dangerous thing. All of my siblings learned to drive this way, at even younger ages.

Disappointment still stung sharply in my chest when I realized I still had no plan or means of escaping from this place, which I prayed never to see again someday. These two humiliating, painful years in high school had my self-esteem at a very low ebb. I desperately wanted to change my life, but I didn't know how to do it.

As I came out of my self-absorbed musing, I looked over at Lucy walking down the road beside me. I was still her Ethel and she my Lucy. She was much larger than me, at least four inches taller, and she outweighed me by forty pounds. Everyone said she had a woman's body, good for making babies. It always made us giggle when we heard it. I giggled a little now, on this gray afternoon with a warm wind blowing.

"What's so funny, Boobaleene?" she asked, looking at me. That was her favorite name for me. She was the only one who could call me that without making me feel bad and cry.

"Nothing, Lucy, I'm just glad to be out here with you, walking like this again," I answered. "It's been a long time." We were planning to do a few of her most beloved things. I never knew how she did it, but she could talk me into those things. I guess because I needed her approval so badly, I would do almost anything she asked. The first thing I had to do was steal some of Sammy's cigarettes for her. It was fairly easy: Sammy was a chain-smoker and wouldn't miss them. Marco didn't smoke. He was still trying to get out of poverty, and he didn't want to spend money on something you just burned. Lucy loved to smoke. No one in her house had the habit.

The second thing was Lucy's most famous game, which we were about to play. To her, it was almost like we were carrying out a public service. She was prepared with the items she would need. She had white business-sized envelopes and a black Crayola in her jacket pocket, and in her hand without the cigarette she held a bunch of three-foot-long sticks that she had collected along the road for the project.

We walked down the gravel road that ran just north of the bend in Sherman Acres Road. There wasn't much down the two-and-a-half-mile stretch. On our right was the Robinson farm, where the old horse Captain Tony had finally been laid to rest a few years ago. To the left, a deep, dark forest stood thick and silent. We never entered those four square miles of woods from this direction; nor did anyone we knew. This mostly dirt path was a great place for lovers to park, creating the perfect place for our mission.

"Oh, God, Lucy, is this a rubber?" I asked, bending forward slightly and pointing to the object lying at the side of the road. It was a gross-looking thing and quite large, I thought.

"Good job, Boobaleene!" she exclaimed, and she went to work. Taking an envelope and the black Crayola from her pocket, she wrote in clear block letters the name of the guy she was sure had used this item and shoved the envelope over the end of one of the sticks, bringing it down halfway. She poked the end of the stick into the used condom, making her infamous "rubber tree." She planted it on the side of the road, rubber side up, for all to see. We found three more, and she repeated the process. Walking back, Lucy was proud of her work. She had the overwhelming desire to name this lonely, deserted path "Rubber Tree Road." We laughed, because it had no name. I don't think any of the men or boys who might have owned these items ever objected to her handiwork. Some might have come along and taken them down, but we never saw them do it.

Something in the woods caught my eye. "Lucy, will you look at that?" I said, rather puzzled. "It looks like someone has made a path through there." We both stopped and stared at it. We knew how to enter the woods from the other north-south road about two miles due east. It went past Waldo's farm and the old school, which was no longer there. We used to enter about a mile from where the school had been. We walked through thick vegetation until we came to an old abandoned cemetery. We liked to read the old gravestones. One said, "Here Lies Captain John Parker Now in Devil's Land." "Baby Louisa Our Angel Lived Only One Day," read another. The one I never could stop staring at said, "Hattie May, Good and Faithful Wife." Her date of birth was 1859, and the death date was 1874. She'd hardly had time to be much of anything.

In that part of the woods were the remnants of an old building that legend said had once been an asylum for the mentally ill. It was owned by a rich psychiatrist from the big city. He used to bring his patients there for rest and treatment. He died sometime in the early 1900s. No one had returned to the building since, except for us kids. On Halloween, some said, you could hear the cry of those troubled and crazed people, if it was a full moon night.

"You know," Lucy said, "it looks kind of creepy."

"I know, but I really want to have a look, don't you?" I asked.

"Yeah, okay," Lucy agreed. We began our expedition down the crude little path. It got much darker in there, due to the dense forest of giant oak and maple trees. We must have gone about half a mile when we saw a well-made log cabin. I hesitated, feeling that caution was needed, but Lucy ran right up onto its front deck and looked boldly in the window.

"No one's in there!" she called out, trying the door, which opened so easily that she almost fell in. "Hey, this place is cool. Evalina, get in here!" Timidly I went in, and I couldn't comprehend what I was seeing. The cabin had four windows and two doors: one in front, which we came through, and one in the back. There were four beds; two were side by side, and two were bunk beds. There was a table and four chairs, as well as a potbellied stove in one corner, with a chimney leading outside. Along the back wall was a row of overhead cabinets without doors. Brightly colored dishes lined the shelves. There was some packaged food. On the counter below was a sink with an old-fashioned hand pump and more cabinets below. Coats hung in one corner of the spacious room. I looked out the back door's window and saw a stone path leading to an outhouse. Clearly someone had thought of everything in order to survive here in the forest.

"Oh, Lucy, someone must live here! We can't be in here like this, in someone's house without permission," I protested.

"Well, they aren't here now, and we are, so it's ours at the moment," Lucy said with confidence. I felt uneasy. I was invading another's private space. Lucy seemed right at home. When she found cigarettes in the pocket of a man's coat that hung there, she lit one. She lay back on one of the two beds, which were next to each other.

"What if they come in and find us here?" I said, starting to shake a little.

"Would you relax already? I read about places like this in mystery magazines. I think it's a hideout for some gangsters from the big city. I bet they bring the bodies of their murder victims out here for burial," Lucy said, taking another drag from her ill-gotten cigarette. I was sitting at the table, but I jumped to my feet and started pacing back and forth.

"Come on, let's get out of here and walk along that path some more," I said, heading for the door. With Lucy right behind me, we took the little path once again. We had gone about the length of one and a half football fields when we came to a high dirt hill.

"Let's go up it and see what's there," Lucy suggested. I followed, against my better judgment. When we got to the top, we both looked down into a big black hole and began to scream, clinging to each other for balance to keep from falling into the abyss. We quickly descended the mound of dirt and took the path back to the road.

Somehow the little place got into our blood, and we couldn't stop going there every chance we got. For Lucy, I think it must have been the free and plentiful cigarettes. It was like a glimpse of some kind of freedom for me. "It's gangsters, I tell you, that own this place. I can just feel it when we're here." Lucy said this every time we went into the cabin. It was never locked, and no one was ever there.

"Don't you think gangsters would want to lock their door?" I asked. She only gave me a dirty look and continued to smoke. We enjoyed the use of that cabin, free of its rightful owners, for a little over two months. It was like our little oasis in the woods, our secret place, our freedom from our everyday lives.

It was a warm day that first Sunday in June when we finally got a chance to get together and go to our little cabin in the woods again. It had been two whole weeks since we last visited. The planting season and a busy end of the school year had kept us away. We thought of the cabin as our own, because we had encountered no owner.

It was one o'clock in the afternoon. Church and the big noontime Sunday meal were over. The phone rang only once, to indicate it was for someone at Strawberry Fields. If it rang twice, then it was for the Cavetti's, three times was for our next-door neighbors, and so on, adding a ring for each of the places on our eight-party phone line. I lifted the phone and heard Lucy say, "Meet me on the hill." We always met at the top of the hill on the road between our two farms. I had two cigarettes tucked in the pocket of my clean white sleeveless blouse. I was wearing a pair of Marco's old jeans that I had cut off to just above the knee. His old clothes came in handy for me. He had grown since returning from the army.

Marco left Strawberry Fields right after the noon meal. Sammy, who was working the night shift, was asleep up in his bed. Pa and Mama were in the field down the hill behind our house. I was able to slip away undetected. No one would look for me until supper.

Leaving my hair hanging down, I walked quickly to the hill in time to see Lucy approaching it from her place. "We will walk with vigor," Lucy called out to me in her best President Kennedy accent, holding up an index finger. She had been saying this since we watched him on TV giving a speech about how Americans needed to increase their exercise by walking vigorously. We both loved President Kennedy and the way he talked.

Putting my hands on my skinny little thighs, I leaned forward, making my breasts pop out as I quivered my lips and sang, "Happy birthday, Mr. President. Happy birthday to you." Lucy laughed hysterically. It was my best Marilyn yet. Doing these voices made the mile-and-a-half walk go faster.

We were still laughing and talking when we entered the woods by the path from the gravel road. We were having fun chattering to each other. I stopped cold when I saw a man smiling at me, about one hundred yards away. Lucy saw him too. "Oh, God, let's run!" she said in an urgent whisper.

"We can't, Lucy. He's seen us already, and he is coming our way," I answered. As I gazed at the man, my fear seemed to diminish. A man with a smile like that surely wouldn't hurt us. He was slender and kind of wiry. He had dark hair under a white Stetson hat, and above that bright smile was a mustache. He wore tight-fitting jeans and a white shirt with the sleeves rolled up to his elbows. In his cowboy boots, he appeared to be around six feet tall. He sported dark, tanned skin.

"Hello," he called out as he approached us. "Welcome to the Tewlain woods. I'm Charles Tewlain." He held out his hand, and I took it. He had a nice, firm shake and a warm hand.

"It's nice to meet you, sir," I said quietly, and he held my gaze. I liked his friendly brown eyes.

"Oh, you don't have to call me sir. Charles will do," he said, still holding my hand.

Lucy extended her hand to him, and she gave him her most dazzling smile with her new capped teeth that Howie had worked overtime to purchase. "I'm glad to meet you, Charlie," she said, vigorously shaking his hand.

"Well, the pleasure is all mine," he said, giving a little laugh. "Come on and let me show you the house we are building." He led us down the path past the cabin, toward that high hill of dirt that we hadn't been back to since that first day.

"Gangsters, huh?" I said under my breath. Lucy punched my arm hard and mouthed the words *Shut up.*

"It is a little way in here, if that's okay," said Mr. Tewlain, looking back at us.

"Oh, it's just fine," we both said at the same time, picking up our pace. When we had gone the length of one and a half football fields, we saw it. The high hill of dirt had been replaced by a golden stone building with beautiful, high-arched windows, upstairs and down. It was magnificent! I realized we were standing on a hill overlooking a driveway. The steady downward slope ended at a corral with a large barn. We followed him around the big house in complete amazement. It wasn't like any other house in Sherman Acres or in Henderson County.

When we came around the back of the building, Mr. Tewlain pointed to a gazebo about two hundred yards away in the woods. "I built that for my wife so she could have someplace to paint. She is quite the artist. I had a real hard time cutting down any of these trees. I agonized over every one of them. I have made use of all of the wood they produced," Mr. Tewlain said. The gazebo was a peaceful, enchanted-looking place. I noticed all of the flower beds around it and the house. He saw me looking at them. "Do you like the gardens? My wife likes to garden. It's another one of her pleasures."

"They're really beautiful," I replied. We didn't know anyone in Henderson County who painted or gardened. Mama and Gladys and other women in the area had flower beds, but they didn't spend a lot of time in them like it brought them any pleasure. The women of Sherman Acres planted them just to make their places look a little nicer. Most of our flower bushes came up by themselves every spring, and Mama would hastily put some seeds in the beds, and they did their own thing all summer long. All other gardening was done to get food to eat or to sell for extra money. We sold our crops to heat the house in winter. It took a lot of coal to keep the house at Strawberry Fields warm.

Mr. Tewlain told us he had several businesses in the big city and they had done well. He'd always wanted a place in the country, and when he found the woods, he bought it for his family. He chatted on in the friendliest way as we walked down the hill toward the corral. He took a pack of cigarettes from his shirt pocket and lit one. The hunger in Lucy's eyes was unmistakable. "Would you like one?" he offered.

"Thanks, Charlie," Lucy replied, taking one from the pack he extended to her. It wasn't a crime back then to give a minor a cigarette, like it is today. It was way before cigarettes were considered hazardous to your health. Lucy talked to him and even flirted as we looked out into the meadow. I noticed that he treated her as if she were an adult, but he treated me as if I were a small child.

Sitting on the deck in front of the cabin when we returned were two women, or that's what I thought at first glance. When we got closer, I saw a woman and a young girl of about fifteen. "This is my wife, June, and my daughter, Mary Jean," Charles said proudly as we came up onto the small deck. After our polite greetings, I stole a look at Lucy to see if she had noticed anything about the two. I knew right away that she had noticed that Mrs. Tewlain was the opposite of her husband. She had snow-white hair and very pink skin. Her eyes were a deep blue, and she was very plump. Mary Jean resembled her mother, with the exception of her light-brown curly hair, her brown eyes, and her dark eyebrows, which were like her father's. They were both very nice, but they were quiet and reserved, not at all like Charles.

"This little one is so cute, isn't she, Mother?" Mr. Tewlain asked his wife, and he picked me up and held me as if I were a toddler. Lucy gave a muffled giggle behind us.

"Uh, sorry, Mr. Tewlain, but I'm almost seventeen years old. I'm practically a grown woman," I replied softly.

"You are? Oh, I'm sorry! You're so tiny, I thought you were younger," he exclaimed as he carefully set me back down on my feet.

"Lucy is over a year younger than I am," I said rather defensively, looking her way. She had a pleased look on her face.

When the cabin door opened and a boy of about fourteen came out, we all turned to look in his direction. At first glance he looked to be an ordinary boy of his age. He was two or three inches taller than I was. He looked to be a younger version of his father, but for two things. His eyes were his mother's deep blue, but softer, and he had her baby-pink skin. He was wearing tight-fitting jeans and a pair of black cowboy boots that could have been described as elegant. They were trimmed at the toe and heel with the finest Spanish silver, and so was the buckle of his black leather belt. He wore a bright white T-shirt tucked into his jeans and a big black Stetson hat that covered his dark, wavy hair.

Those blue eyes never left me as he shook hands with Lucy and said hello. When we were introduced, he took my hand and leaned in toward me. As I turned my head slightly, he placed a soft kiss just below the corner of my mouth. I wasn't sure where that kiss would have landed had I not turned my head so slightly. I was surprised but not offended by it. It was such an unusual thing for a boy his age to do. Most would have acted silly or barely spoken, but not Jimmy Tewlain. More chairs were brought out. We all sat around, talking and getting to know one another. He was as friendly as his father. He had lovely manners and spoke well. He sat next to his father, who sat next to Lucy and me. Mrs. Tewlain and Mary Jean were across from us. They said little, while Jimmy and his dad talked about life in the great woods.

Suddenly Mr. Tewlain began to laugh, and he pulled Jimmy into his lap and kissed him on the cheek, saying, "Why, you little rascal! That girl is so pretty, you can't take your eyes off of her!" Jimmy laughed too as his pink face deepened in color, and he kissed his father back while Lucy and I took in an astonished breath at the same time.

These people were clearly like no others we had ever encountered in our entire lives. Folks in Henderson County didn't act like this with their kids. Parents were mainly authority figures that gave orders and made sure you had food and clothes. I, for one, had never even seen my parents exchange any type of open affection with each other or with any of us. I had never seen them in anything other than their clothes. As far as I knew, they didn't sleep in anything else. When I got up in the morning, they were already up and at the table or out tending the animals and gardens. Physical affection was something that was just not done in my house or in the home of anyone I knew. The only kind of affection I knew was the kind those old men that came around our house kept trying to give me—the kind I hated and resisted. I have to admit, most physical attention made me uncomfortable.

The time passed quickly. Mr. Tewlain and Jimmy served us cold lemonade and cookies. I noticed that they waited on Mrs. Tewlain and Mary Jean as if they were the queen of England and her daughter. It struck me as both unusual and endearing at the same time.

When it was time to go, Jimmy and Mary Jean walked with us to the bend in Sherman Acres Road. "We hope to see you again soon," Jimmy said, still looking at me. "We're out here permanently now. We will be attending school here and everything."

"A bunch of us kids get together almost every night. We raise a little hell and have fun," Lucy said. "We will come and get you, so you can hang with us."

"That sounds like fun," Mary Jean said. "We would love to come along."

"I'll see you tomorrow, Eve," Jimmy said, taking my hand and looking into my eyes. I noticed his beautiful, very straight, white teeth as he smiled at me. He called me Eve. No one called me that, but when he said it, I thought it sounded like music in the wind that had begun to blow. I watched as he and Mary Jean started walking back toward the woods.

"Okay, so what did you think?" Lucy said when they were far away. "I think they're kind of queer."

"No, they aren't, Lucy," I said. "People act like that on TV all the time. You watch it, and you've seen them."

"I guess so, but I have never seen a father and son kiss like that before," Lucy replied. "As a matter of fact, I've never seen a father kiss his son."

"I think it's kind of endearing, and besides, he's just a boy," I said.

"Did you get a load of Mrs. Tewlain? My God, she looks more like Charlie's mother than his wife," Lucy said.

"Charlie?" I asked, giving her a sarcastic look. "I saw you flirting with him. God, Lucy, have you no shame?"

"No, I don't, when it comes to a handsome man like him," she said.

It was almost time for the evening meal when I left Lucy at the top of the hill. The evening passed slowly as I did the dishes and had another few cups of Mama's strong coffee. I lay in my bed, listening to the radio as a soft rain began to fall. I loved this kind of rain, because I would sleep well. There would be no visit from the man with the cigarette, and I wouldn't be running from the Creeper all night in my dreams. The rain kept them away. How or why rain kept those dreams at bay, I never knew.

The sun was already high when I woke the next morning with a start. I realized Mama was standing there, talking to me. "The sun has dried the fields enough, and we must pick now before it gets too hot and the heat destroys the strawberries. Get up and come to the field as soon as you can," she said, and then she was gone. I looked at my radio and saw it was seven-thirty. I had slept a full night, something I hadn't done in a very long time. I got out of bed. I slept in my panties and bra. I didn't want those big breasts to start sagging and hang down to my waist. I found a pair of dirty cutoff jeans on the floor and an old, ripped white blouse with stains on it. I didn't bother to wash my face or comb my hair. A quick cup of coffee and a biscotti and a brush of the teeth, and I was out the door and in the field. It was down the long driveway toward Sherman Acres Road. I didn't bother with shoes, because of the mud. I didn't wear them much in the summer anyway. My hygiene was lax during strawberry-picking time.

The mud oozed between my toes as I silently picked my way through a row of strawberries. The day was warm and promised to get warmer. It was early in the season. Mama hadn't hired any summer pickers yet. They were just local kids looking for an extra dollar or two. I was their only picker that first day. Almost two hours passed. I wasn't counting how many containers I picked. I didn't have any plans yet for the money I would make. I was pondering this when I heard the crunch of gravel in the driveway.

I looked up to see Jimmy coming down the hill on a bike that I was sure no other kid in Henderson County owned. It was gleaming with chrome and blue fenders, with saddlebags on the back. "Eve, hello," he called, and it sounded like music in the wind. Parking the bike at the side of the road, he walked directly over to Pa, extended his hand, and introduced himself to both my parents. "I came to help and then maybe get a chance to visit with Eve."

Pa immediately began to give him instructions on how to pick strawberries. I wondered briefly if Jimmy could understand anything Pa was saying in his broken English. My parents' gardens were the talk of Sherman Acres, because they were so perfect every year. It didn't matter what kind of fruit or vegetables were planted; they were in neat, very straight rows that contained no weeds. My parents used bolts of string wound around short poles to ensure that every row was straight. Weeding of the gardens was done daily throughout spring and summer. "You pick here in this row with Evalina," Pa said, bringing him over to the other side of my row.

"You really don't have to do this, Jimmy," I said. "I'm afraid you will get dirty."

"I want to help you," he said with a bright smile that showed his straight, very white teeth. "When we're done, maybe you can show me around. I hope it will be just the two of us. Besides, a little dirt won't hurt me."

"Okay, Jimmy, that sounds fine," I said, standing to face him. I was looking into those beautiful soft-blue eyes, and I was getting a little lost in them. He reached into his back pocket and took out a clean white handkerchief. He gently wiped a smudge of mud from the side of my face. It was the most tender and loving gesture anyone had ever bestowed upon me in my life. For a moment I couldn't move.

"Gosh, Eve, you're beautiful," he said softly. I became aware of how I must have looked. I was standing there, with mud clinging to my feet and lower legs, in those dirty cutoff jeans and an old, ripped, stained blouse, with my hair hanging down wildly past my waist. I must have looked like one of those wild minks our neighbor raised for fur coats for some company in New York.

"Thanks," I said, dropping to my knees. I was worried about Jimmy getting burned in the sun. He wasn't wearing his Stetson. I was afraid he would ruin those elegant black cowboy boots. I was amazed when Jimmy's skin never changed from baby pink. Mine turned a tawny brown every summer. Dirt never seemed to get on him much, either. I was a muddy mess. I attracted dirt.

Pa called out in Italian, asking how many containers we had filled. I stood and held up ten fingers, then opened and closed my hands four times to indicate that I had filled forty quart containers. When I turned to look at Jimmy, I noticed that he had picked as many as I had! I repeated the motion to let Pa know. He made a sign back, indicating that we were finished. "Come on, Jimmy, we will go up to the pump house and wash the mud off," I said. "My father will take the berries to market. Mama will put them in the cold storage." As I washed the mud off my feet, legs, and hands, I noticed Jimmy had only a little red staining on his fingers, and a quick wipe of his boots in the grass brought them back to their original luster. I was still a mess.

My pa was by the barn, trying to hook up the cultivator to the big Ford tractor. Jimmy was watching him. "I think I'll go and help your dad," he said. I slipped into the house, took a shower, and washed my hair. I put on clean cutoffs and a clean white blouse. I tied up my hair in a ponytail, using one of the special ties Mama had made for my hair. My hair was so thick—two and a half inches around when it was up. Mama sewed elastic into good-quality ribbon so I could wear my hair in that popular style.

I got out the heavy canvas bag Mama used for mushroom picking. I made two cheese sandwiches and filled two mason jars with ice water. I took a bag of fresh, clean strawberries from the refrigerator. I put everything into the bag and went out to find Jimmy.

In the back field down the hill from the barn, I saw Jimmy driving the Ford, making straight cultivated rows. Pa was sitting under a tree on the hill, drinking water from a jar, watching him. He seemed pleased as he signaled Jimmy to stop. I was amazed that Jimmy had done a good job. Pa thought the same, and he tried to give him money. "I don't need any money," Jimmy said, smiling proudly.

"I was just having fun." I thought all boys his age loved money, and so did Pa. He shook his head and put the money back into his pocket.

We walked to the driveway, where Jimmy's bike waited. He looked into my eyes. Not saying a word, he untied my hair from the ribbon, letting it fall to my waist, smoothing it like a fine golden-brown blanket. He carefully wound the ribbon around four fingers of his other hand and tucked it into his pocket.

He mounted the bike and turned to me. "Eve, sit right up here on the handlebars," he said.

"I can't do that. I'll hurt you," I protested.

"Of course you can," he said, laughing. "I ride like this with Mary Jean." I climbed up on the fender and sat on the handlebars. I pulled my hair over my shoulder to keep it out of the way. "Please, Eve, leave it. I love your hair. I want to feel it on my face as we ride. It's so beautiful, and it smells so good." It smelled of the cheap dime-store shampoo that Pa had brought home, but Jimmy came close and took a deep breath. "Hang on tight—this bike goes very fast." I didn't know a bike could go that fast. We must have been traveling about thirty miles per hour. Jimmy laughed as my hair blew all over him. We headed south on Sherman Acres Road, toward the Stayton woods and the pond in that magic forest. We stopped by the path through the woods and went into the thick forest. Lucy's house was right across the road. I hoped she wouldn't feel left out if she saw us. We parked the bike. Jimmy took my bag and one of those saddlebags from his back fender. He took my hand as we walked. The woods began to work its magic. Birds were singing, and the trees seemed to whisper a welcome to us. Jimmy started naming every bird we heard. He knew the scientific name for very plant and flower we passed. He could imitate almost every song the birds sang.

The blue, glassy water captivated us when we emerged from the woods. We walked onto the little pier. That feeling of floating on the water began to sweep over us. Jimmy put his arms around my waist to steady both of us. I noticed that he held me as if I were a fine china doll that might break. We were lost to the feeling of drifting. "This place is unbelievable, Eve. I could stay here forever, couldn't you?" Jimmy said, still holding me. We floated in a kind of dream.

"It's one of my favorite places. It sounds like the trees are speaking some secret language," I replied after a while.

"Your feelings for the woods are so like my own, Eve," Jimmy said, turning me around to face him. "I'm so glad. I could stay here all day." I found myself getting lost again in those blue eyes.

We sat on the pier and had our lunch. We placed our leftover bread at the end of the pier and settled ourselves in the grass to watch as the birds came to the pier and ate. There were lots of different birds. "Okay," I said, "I'll go to the end of the pier and point to one of the birds singing in the trees. You can sit here and tell me what kind of bird is singing." Jimmy got every one of them right. I was standing on the pier, pointing, while he watched me with admiring eyes. He took a small Brownie camera from his saddlebag and snapped a picture of me, a picture I wouldn't see for more than a year.

"The sun has moved into the western sky, Eve. I guess we had better start back," Jimmy said, taking my hand. We walked back through the forest to where we'd left the bike. When we arrived at the top of the drive, Jimmy looked into my eyes. "I had a wonderful time today, Eve. Thank you for spending the day with me." He leaned forward and kissed me softly, just below the corner of my mouth. "I think you're the most beautiful girl I have ever seen. I can't stop looking at you. Promise me you will never let anyone hurt you, Eve." I didn't know what to say, because no one had ever talked to me like that in my whole life. Jimmy might have been just a boy, but he was wise beyond his years.

"I'm sure that Lucy has called the others. We'll come and get you and Mary Jean in Teddy Roosevelt's red pickup truck," I said.

"Okay, Eve, I'll see you then," he said and kissed me again with those soft, sweet, pink lips. I knew he smoked. I saw cigarettes in his pocket, but he hadn't smoked around me all day, and he didn't smell like smoke. He smelled like the wind, sun, and soap. His breath was sweet, like that of an infant.

I went straight to my room. I looked in the mirror. I was trying to see what Jimmy saw when he looked at me. I was hoping, perhaps by magic, that I had changed into the beautiful girl he saw. Staring back at me was the same old homely face—two soft brown eyes, one smaller than the other, my father's Roman nose, and a set of full, pink lips. I still had a round face with a short little chin. Nothing had changed. I was still ugly. My long, cotton-soft brown hair was wild from the bike ride. "Don't take what that boy says too seriously," I told myself in the mirror. "After all, he's just a boy, and you're still ugly."

At sunset I walked past my parents' bedroom. Mama was sitting in front of the window, reading a magazine. "I'm going up on the road to meet Lucy and some of the other kids," I said, not stopping to hear her reply. I saw the red truck making its way toward me. It came to a complete stop, and I hopped into the bed. Inside the cab Teddy was at the wheel, and Jimmy Loveless was riding shotgun. We went on to Lucy's. Heading north, we picked up Big Mike Zabowski at the bend in the road. He had a thing for Lucy, but she ignored him. We went down the gravel road to get Jimmy and Mary Jean. They were waiting for us by the path. It was twilight when we got Scotty Brooks from his little house on the big highway.

Everyone was laughing and talking at the same time. We were going across the state line to get some old wino to buy a six-pack of beer for us for the price of a bottle of cheap Mogen David wine. We shared the beer between seven of us. We never worried about the police. There were so few in these parts. Most of them had done the same things when they were kids and would turn a blind eye to us, unless we showed signs of getting out of hand.

Driving down back roads, we would kill the lights and come up quietly behind parkers. Jimmy Loveless and one or two other boys would get out, sneak up to the car, and start rocking it. Then they would run like hell back to the truck, and we would take off in a cloud of dust. I can't recall why we thought this was so much fun. I guess we thought we were preventing some girl from getting pregnant. There were many shotgun weddings and premature births in Henderson County. Many children had "Broken Rubber" for a middle name.

When we parked the truck on a dark dirt path in the woods to hang out and finish the beer, Teddy Roosevelt fell instantly and madly in love with Mary Jean Tewlain. He was so smitten with her that he began to act totally crazy. It might have been the first time a boy had paid her attention, because Mary Jean seemed to fall for him. They looked like such an unlikely pair. Teddy hadn't grown much. With his raspy voice from too many choking episodes, his intense blue eyes, and his dishwater-blond crew cut, he looked to be a boy of twelve. He was about to turn seventeen. Not only was Mary Jean taller, but she also outweighed scrawny little Teddy.

The beer was passed around. Lucy drank about three cans. Jimmy and I split one. I was no beer drinker. Big Mike drank one can. Jimmy Loveless had brought his own supply. He and Lucy had the rest. Teddy never drank when he was driving. Scotty was no drinker either. When we got back into the truck, Mary Jean was in front with Teddy. Jimmy Loveless got in the bed of the truck. He was a daredevil, taking any risk for fun and entertainment. Everyone was smoking but Jimmy, Mary Jean, and me.

I don't know what possessed Jimmy Loveless, but he removed the gas cap and dropped a lit cigarette down the tank. A large flame shot out and caught his shirt. He jumped from the truck bed and rolled in the grass at the side of the road, trying to smother the flames. Jimmy Tewlain jumped after him while the truck was still going about ten miles per hour. I screamed for Teddy to stop. In one magnificent move, Jimmy Tewlain took off his own shirt and extinguished the rest of the flames. Jimmy Loveless was not seriously burned, but Jimmy Tewlain lay there in the grass, moaning, with his smoldering shirt in his hand. Lucy jumped down and ran to Jimmy's side. "Jimmy, you okay?" she asked, giggling a little. "I saw you hang your man parts on the side of the truck." Then she burst out laughing. Jimmy laughed too. The more she laughed, the more he laughed. "You laugh just like a girl!" Lucy cried.

"I know!" said Jimmy between bursts of laughter. Neither could get off the ground. When he finally regained his composure, I heard him say, "I didn't have much to begin with, and now I probably have less." He rolled in laughter again while Lucy lay there beside him, unable to control herself.

Jimmy Loveless never tried that trick again. We spent many nights playing in the woods. We were just farm kids making our own entertainment, as others had before us. No one ever got hurt; it was a miracle.

After that first night, Mary Jean and Teddy were together constantly. His love for her drove him to act silly and immature. He had a hard time letting her out of his sight. Although she was a very sensible girl, I was sure that Mary Jean loved him too. When he got too crazy, she would threaten to stop seeing him. He would offer an apology, and they would be together again. I think he was jealous and worried that he was not good enough for her. He was unable to express his feelings for her in a mature way.

Two days later Jimmy appeared at Strawberry Fields on that expensive bike. He helped pick berries, and he followed me everywhere. He wanted to help out wherever he could. I liked having him around. The time passed quickly, and the chores were less difficult. My parents and brothers didn't seem to mind him.

Early that afternoon, with canvas bag and supplies in hand, we headed for the Stayton woods and the little pond. We laughed and talked about nature. Jimmy was full of information about the woods, the sky, the sun, the moon, and the stars. He sat in the grass and watched me as I used the little pier for a stage, imitating famous people. He laughed and clapped his hands, cheering, "Bravo! Bravo!"

"Jimmy, I want to show you my tree," I said, taking his hand. "It's only a little way from this path." We walked silently. I stopped at an enormous oak that soared about one hundred and fifty feet into the air. It had a large trunk and great branches that were easy to climb. Antonia and I had climbed this tree together many times when we were younger. "Here it is, Jimmy. How do you like it?"

"Oh, Eve, it's beautiful. Let's go up." He went up first. I followed. Way up high there were two large branches that bowed out like arms. Sitting there on the one just below them, you could see everything. To the west was the glassy blue water of the Stayton pond. If you looked to the north, you could see the big open field and Strawberry Fields Farm. Looking south and east, you saw majestic forest. Sitting there was like being in Mother Nature's arms.

Jimmy walked between the arms and sat down. When he opened his arms to me, I went to him and sat down between his legs, with my back to him. He held me as if I were a delicate flower that might wither and die. He spoke softly. "It's amazing up here. It's like being in the arms of God. Oh, listen, Eve—the leaves are talking."

Leaning back into his loving arms, I replied, "You have such a way with words, Jimmy. I think you should be a poet." I was becoming comfortable with his affection. I relaxed into his arms as we sat listening to the forest sing. Being touched by him wasn't alarming.

A beautiful, large hawk came to rest at the end of the big branch. He had lovely brown, silver, gray, and white feathers. His beak was a sharp hook, his eyes shades of golden yellow that made him look regal. His wingspan was more than four feet. We watched him in enchanted silence. He didn't seem to mind that we were so close. He looked out and down to the ground, very still, almost like a statue of himself. Suddenly in one majestic swoop, he quickly descended to the ground and came back up again with a baby rabbit clutched in his large clawed feet. "Jimmy, oh no!" I cried out and tried to go after the eagle as he sped away over our heads.

Jimmy tightened his arms around my waist. "It's okay, Eve. Please stay here and let me hold you. It's okay, really it is. It's just nature and how things work here. I'm sorry you had to see it. Please don't be upset. I would have stopped him if I had known what he was looking at down there. He is a bird of prey, and that's just his way of survival," he said, gently rocking me in his arms. "It's okay."

We stayed in the large oak tree, holding each other, for some time. "I hope the mother comes back for the other babies," I said softly as we started down. "Let's not go too close to the nest. If she smells humans, she may not return, and the babies will starve."

When we got to the ground, Jimmy took me into his arms and turned my face to his. "It's what I love about you, Eve," he said. "You understand everything." He kissed me softly, sweetly, and tenderly. They were the kisses of a boy. When he said good-bye to me, he said it again: "Please promise me you won't let anyone hurt you, Eve."

"Okay, Jimmy," I replied. I didn't know why he said it or what he meant. He said it every time we parted.

Jimmy and I saw each other almost every day. At night we met up with the other small-farm kids and hung out. Although he laughed and joked, drank beer, and smoked, it seemed like he only did it to fit in. He was always at my side. I began to wonder if the other kids had noticed. I worried that they might tease him. He would drop his arm around my shoulders or waist in ways that looked natural. He seemed able to handle any situation, whether it was Teddy acting up or Jimmy Loveless doing something stupid. He put everything into perspective and made us better people. Maybe we wanted to be better because of him.

It was Mama who noticed. "The little boy, he is here all the time. I see if you take two step, then he take three right behind you," Mama said. "You better watch him so he no gets hurt." Little did she realize that it was Jimmy who was watching out for me!

I began to love all of the attention and affection he gave me. I relaxed in his arms. I even enjoyed those little kisses. I felt safe. I'd never liked being touched, but with Jimmy it was different. I started to think of him as my younger sibling. I loved that he looked up to me and admired me. No one had ever admired me. I loved hearing him say, "You're beautiful, Eve." Lucy only needed me for cigarettes and aid in carrying out her master plans for practical jokes. She didn't admire me or even treat me as if I really mattered in her life. I mattered to Jimmy.

His attention led me to start taking stock of myself. I started to be more meticulous with grooming and clothes. I took daily showers and washed my hair. My pa asked me one day if I was drinking the shampoo. "I have to buy you one every payday now!" he shouted. It was always Breck or Prell. In those days a bottle of shampoo was only about eight or ten ounces. There were no jumbo-sized bottles. It wasn't the custom to wash hair very day.

"I know, Pa, but my hair is getting dirty more with being outside so much," I replied. He only shook his head and walked away.

It was a Wednesday in late July. I was in the summer kitchen. I looked up at the clock on the buffet. It was twenty minutes after eleven. I tossed a summer salad of lettuce, tomatoes, and cucumbers. I sliced up a loaf of Mama's homemade bread and some salami and cheese. I took a chocolate cake from the oven and set it out to cool. I looked at the clock again. I was very anxious. Marco came thundering down the inside steps.

"What's on the agenda, ugly?" he said. "Ooooh, chocolate cake! Be sure you put a big piece in my lunch bucket." I ignored him and kept working. "Hey, moron, did you hear me?"

"Yes, Marco, I heard you," I replied, feeling my self-esteem sinking to a new low.

"Yeah, well, chop-chop, I got to go to work," he said and left. I frosted the cake, watching the clock. The summer pickers and my parents would be coming in for the noon meal. *Where is Jimmy?* I wondered. I hadn't seen him since Sunday! It wasn't like him to stay away for more than a day. I was worried and feeling very bad about myself again, like I had before we met. I needed him, his beautiful words and positive smile, like an alcoholic needed a drink or like a drug addict his drugs. I thrived on his attention. I made two pitchers of orange Kool-Aid, my pa's favorite. At noon everyone filed into the kitchen and ate quickly in silence. Since Mama paid them by how much they picked and not by the hour, they were hurrying to get back to work before it was too hot.

I sat listening as they left by the basement stairs and their voices faded into the distance. The clock said twelve twenty-five. Marco came tearing through, grabbed his lunch bucket, and headed for his car. The house fell quiet. I could hear Sammy snoring in his room. If I was going to make a move, it would have to be now. I cleared away the lunch things and went to the backyard. On the clothesline hung a pair of red shorts (another cast-off from Carmella), a white blouse, and my white Keds. The popular shoes were my favorite pair ever, and Mama worked hard on them to keep them white. I took everything and headed for the shower, where I washed my hair again. I dressed quickly and took a new red hair tie Mama had just made for me. I put my hair in a ponytail. I didn't want to do it, but it was so hot. If I got to see Jimmy, he would take it from my hair and put it in his pocket. I wouldn't see it again. I wasn't sure what he did with them, but I never got them back. I didn't know what to tell Mama when she asked me what had happened to them.

I left by the basement stairs. The sun was already very hot. The heat never bothered me much. Today I was glad of that as I started down the long driveway and headed north on Sherman Acres Road. No one saw me slip away. I prayed the Creeper wasn't out, since I had to walk past his house to get to the Tewlain woods. The hot tar was bubbling, and it made snapping sounds under my feet as I walked. The road defeated my mama's efforts to keep my Keds white.

I made it to the path in record time. As I entered the woods, the temperature dropped; it felt ten degrees cooler. I shivered a little, feeling hot at the same time. The cabin was a lonely sentry guarding the forest. No one lived in it now. The quiet woods brought calm to me as I made my way toward the golden stone house on the hill. When the house came into view, I saw Jimmy standing in the doorway, looking as I had never seen him look before. He opened the door as I came to the top step. "Jimmy, you look wonderful," I said. I was curious as to why he was dressed up. He was wearing a white shirt, a light blue necktie that made his blue eyes even brighter, black dress pants, and black wing tip dress shoes.

"Come in, Eve, quickly, out of the heat," he said, taking me into his arms and giving me a hug that was firm and not typical of him. Then he looked into my eyes, reached for the red ribbon, and loosened it. My hair fell around my shoulders and down my back. Again he wrapped the ribbon around four of his fingers and placed it in his pocket, strands of tangled hair and all. Seeing the puzzled look on my face, he said, "I put them under my pillow at night, so I can smell your hair. It's like having you with me." He took my hand and led me to the kitchen. "Let me get you some ice water. You feel warm."

I watched him as he got ice from the freezer and poured cold water over it into a tall glass. When he turned, I saw tears rolling down his face. I quickly set down the glass and took him into my arms. "Jimmy, what is it? What's wrong?" He laid his head on my shoulder and sobbed quietly.

"Oh, Eve, I'm just worried about my dad," he said. He pulled out a kitchen chair and sat down, bringing me to him and making me sit in his lap. "He works so hard for all of us. I'm scared something will happen to him. I'm dressed up because I'm going into the city to help him again today. Sorry I haven't been by to see you. He will be sending a car for me soon."

"It's okay, Jimmy. It's okay," I said, wiping the tears from his face with my hands. I hated to see him in pain. "I missed you, and I was worried."

"I'm sorry, Eve. I should have called you," he said. "Let's go sit out on the veranda and wait for Winston. Here, take your water. You need it." Jimmy never could stay indoors very long.

"Why didn't you call me, Jimmy? You know I would be glad to go with you and help," I insisted. "You're always helping me at Strawberry Fields."

"Oh, no, Eve, I would never want you to go to that big, dirty city. It's a terrible place! I couldn't think of you being there. When people live too close together, they sometimes forget how to treat each other and appreciate one another. You belong here in the woods.

That place is made of concrete, artificial lights, lots of cars, and car exhaust. Why, you can't even see the sky for all the buildings. There are no trees or greenery. Promise me you will never go there, Eve. I can't bear to think of you there." Before I could answer him, he kissed me and made me sit in the covered swing with him.

"Jimmy, it isn't fair that I can't help you. You're always doing things for me," I said.

"Yes, it is, Eve. I'll be a man soon, and I'll be taking over my father's businesses. I won't run them as he does. He's too nice to the workers. When they screw up, he gives them another chance, because he can't bear to put anyone out of work. I'll run things quite differently. I'll hold people accountable for their actions. I know how to hire good people. I have no problem letting those go that don't work out," he said. "You stay here, Eve, in the woods where you belong. It hurts me to think of you in that big city."

Just then we heard a car coming down the long drive. It wasn't just a car. It was a big, long limousine. A black man in a uniform got out and opened the back door as we came down the steps. "You ready to go, Mr. Jimmy?" the man said.

"Yes, thank you, Winston," he said, and he climbed into the back. He put the windows down immediately. They were tinted so dark that I couldn't see inside. "Eve, I'll be back tonight. I'll see you then. I have something to show you. Please wait at home for me, won't you?" he said, with such a serious look in his eyes.

"Of course I will, Jimmy." I put my hand through the window and placed it on his shoulder.

"Good. I'm glad," he replied. "Until tonight, then." I stepped back, and the car left in a cloud of dust. I started back through the forest. Jimmy hated the city, and I could think of no greater place. I loved concrete, lights, and the smell of car exhaust. I longed to see and hear all that went on in those places where Jimmy went. Mr. Tewlain owned nightclubs, restaurants, and theaters. I felt bad that I couldn't help Jimmy, after all he had done for me. He made me feel better about myself. Now I couldn't tell him how I longed to escape Strawberry Fields Farm forever, how I wanted to experience big-city life. I felt bad even thinking about it. I pushed it from my mind and walked on home. No Creeper today. I said a little prayer of thanks.

After the evening meal, I did the dishes. I took down Mama's canvas bag and began to fill it with things we might need tonight. I poured some coffee grounds into a paper bag, and I took a small pot from the downstairs kitchen. It wasn't the one Mama used; she wouldn't miss it. I cut two large pieces of chocolate cake and wrapped them in waxed paper. I put ice water in several mason jars and placed them in the refrigerator.

Marco was still at work. I went into his room, found that box of his old clothes, and pulled out a red and white checkered flannel shirt. I changed into a pair of cutoffs and my white blouse. I had no hair ties, so I had to leave my hair down. I tied the flannel shirt around my waist.

The sun was a red ball in the western sky. I sat on the front porch off the upstairs kitchen and waited for Jimmy. I worried about him. He was usually so in control, and seeing him cry today had made me very uneasy. I didn't like that I couldn't tell him my plans and desires. I couldn't tell him that I dreamed of a place where I felt wanted, accepted, and important. I was none of these things in Henderson County.

I wondered what Lucy might be thinking. She called after dinner to ask what I was doing. "I'm staying in and waiting for Jimmy to come over," I told her.

"Oh." There was a long silence. "All right, then," she replied and hung up. We hadn't hung out together much all summer. I was always with Jimmy. I assumed she was in town with friends.

The sun was almost gone when I heard hoof beats in the distance. Someone on a big black horse came into our driveway. When he came up the hill, I could see that it was Jimmy, on the biggest horse I had ever seen. I jumped off the porch and started toward him. Mama and Pa came from the back field, with hoes slung over their shoulders.

Jimmy dismounted. "Eve, this is Midnight! How do you like him?" he asked.

"Oh, Jimmy, he's amazing," I said. We went closer to admire Midnight.

"Look, he can do lots of things. He's really smart, and he knows what I'm saying," Jimmy said excitedly. "Midnight, give me a kiss." The horse nipped at Jimmy's face, and he laughed. "Now give Eve a kiss." Midnight nipped at my face. "Midnight, shake hands with Mr. Rosario." My pa, who'd been quite the horseman in his day, put out his hand, and the horse put a big right hoof in it.

"Okay, now count to ten, Midnight," Jimmy commanded, and the horse struck his right hoof on the ground ten times. "Take a bow, Midnight, take a bow." The horse went down on one knee and bent his head as we applauded. Pa asked many questions about the horse in his broken English, which I hoped Jimmy could understand. I went to get the canvas bag. When I got back, Pa asked me in Italian where we were going and when we would be back. He also cautioned me to be careful around such a large, powerful animal. I answered him in English.

"It always amazes me when you do that," Jimmy said, shaking his head. He wasn't the only one who said this. Almost everyone who came to Strawberry Fields mentioned it. My parents always spoke to me in Italian, and I answered in English. It was Enzo's rule. When he started school, he'd found that he spoke little English, and he was embarrassed. He vowed that none of us would go through the humiliating experience of not knowing the language.

Jimmy swung himself into the saddle. He extended his left arm to me and said, "Eve, take hold of my arm with both hands, and hold on tight." I did as he asked, and in one swift movement, he lifted me into the air. I swung my right leg over the horse and found myself seated in the saddle, right in front of Jimmy. We fit together perfectly in that saddle. My parents stepped back as Jimmy gave the horse a gentle nudge. Midnight took off across our front yard in a steady gallop. Then he jumped the fence between our front yard and the field with ease. He broke into a fast run, and we crossed the field to the Stayton woods. We took the road to the main entrance.

Venus was in the western sky when we arrived to set up camp by the pond. We built a fire and made coffee. Jimmy unsaddled Midnight, and we used the saddle and blanket to rest our heads. Midnight grazed contently as Jimmy talked about the sky and the stars; the horse seemed to know his role. We drank strong coffee and ate the cake. Jimmy wasn't a coffee drinker, but I made him into one. When the air cooled, he untied the flannel shirt from my waist and helped me put it on. We settled on the blanket, up against the saddle, in each other's arms, as the small fire blazed. "Let's look for shooting stars, Eve. Make a wish on it when you see one," Jimmy said. "Just keep looking. It takes a while, but you'll see one."

"Yes, there it is!" I exclaimed as I saw one, and quickly I made my wish.

"I saw one too, Eve," Jimmy said, turning to me. "Do you want to know what I wished?"

"No, Jimmy, please don't tell me, because then it won't come true," I pleaded, but he went on.

"I wished that you will always stay here in the woods with me, Eve, forever. I love you," he said, kissing me gently in that favorite spot just below the corner of my mouth.

"Oh, Jimmy, I love you too," I replied, surprising myself, because I'd never uttered those words to anyone! No one spoke them in my house. "You're just like the little brother I always wanted."

"Eve," Jimmy said softly, turning my face to his. "I know I'm just a boy, but I'll be a man soon. I will be taking over for my father. My dad is wealthy, and I'm sure I can become even more successful. Please understand I want to marry you someday. I know I can be the man you need, if you just wait for me. That's what I wish for, Eve, with my whole heart."

I was flattered, if a bit shaken. "Jimmy, you'll be starting high school. You'll meet lots of girls you might like to date. You'll forget about me. I'll be old by then," I said, believing every word.

"That isn't true, Eve. You're the only girl for me. I knew it the first time I set eyes on you. Look up into the sky—you see the moon and stars? I'd pull them right down and give them to you if you wanted them. I'd give you anything you wanted. I'm sure I can give you everything and make you happy. Just stay here with me, Eve. Please say you will stay. Please just stay," he said. He was so serious that I almost believed him. The lure and the pull of the big city was forever on my mind. It kept me from giving him any kind of answer. I was sure that Jimmy cared for me, but it wasn't enough to make me abandon my dreams. I stayed in his loving arms, giving no more thought to the future. He whispered all of these loving words to me under the stars of the heavens. It was wonderful, and magic was in the air.

We didn't realize we had fallen asleep in each other's arms until Midnight nudged Jimmy awake, just before dawn. Jimmy woke me gently, saying, "Eve, it is time to go. I'm sorry we both fell asleep. I hope your folks aren't worried." We killed the last of the burning embers, and Jimmy saddled Midnight. Guided by the morning star, the swift hoofs of Midnight took us back to the top of the drive at Strawberry Fields Farm. The soft gaze of Jimmy's blue eyes fell upon my face as I turned to him to say good-bye.

"Thanks for the magic. I love you now. I will always love you." he said softly.

I stood there without moving while he thundered away on Midnight; I felt like Miss Kitty watching Matt Dillon ride away. The doors to our house were never locked. I slipped inside and into my room as a new day was dawning. I fell fast asleep without another thought. I didn't think about how I felt about Jimmy. I only thought about how he cared for me, how he loved me, and how good it felt. When we were together, for me it was about the present, never the past or the future.

The following evening, Jimmy and Mary Jean came to Strawberry Fields on horseback. Jimmy sat high and proud on the giant black stallion. Mary Jean rode a painted mare named Paddy Cake. I couldn't get over the fact that the horses were so much like their owners. Midnight was high-spirited, lively, and always ready to run. Paddy Cake was gentle, quiet, and loving. We went with the other kids to the Leila farm. Mr. Leila had acquired quite a few horses. We saddled up and rode the meadows and camped out until late into the night.

Teddy Roosevelt had his nose out of joint. He didn't like to ride. He was so small that I think horses kind of scared him. Mary Jean was as good at handling a horse as her brother. When we were on these outings, Teddy was sort of left out. If he didn't find a horse that he was comfortable riding, then he followed us in his truck, if the terrain wasn't too rough.

Even though she was good with horses, Jimmy looked after Mary Jean as if she were the younger sibling. He cleaned her horse's stall, saddled Paddy Cake, and groomed her. "Why do you take care of Mary Jean's horse all the time, Jimmy?" I asked.

"Well, I don't mind. And besides, you know how special Mary Jean is. She's like my mom—intelligent and thoughtful." It was the first time I had ever heard a boy say things like that about his mother or his sister. Back then, the term "special" meant you were unique and unusual. The Tewlains were indeed unique and unusual.

I had been invited to have supper with Jimmy and his family one evening in late summer. The beautiful house was completed. As we sat at the dining room table, Mr. Tewlain said to Jimmy and Mary Jean, "I have a surprise for you two."

"What is it, Dad?" Jimmy asked as he served his mother and Mary Jean. Both looked questioningly at their father.

"Well, now that the house is completed, Aunt Bone will come here to live," Charles replied. Mary Jean and Jimmy giggled as they exchanged knowing looks and moaned a little.

"Aunt Bone? Oh, I can't wait," Mary Jean said rather sarcastically, rolling her eyes.

"Now, you two, it's not that bad," Charles said.

"I didn't know you had an aunt. What did you say her name was?" I asked.

"Well, you see, Eve, she isn't exactly our relative," Mr. Tewlain said. "She lives in our apartment building in the big city. I found her wandering around one day. She seemed lost, so I brought her back to her apartment. When it happened a few more times, I tried to find her family and discovered she didn't have anyone. I went to the police. I even hired a private detective. I found out her name, Genevieve Striker, but when you ask her, she will only say her name is Aunt Bone. The thing is, she really thinks she's my aunt, so we just went along with it. When she began to get lost every day, I put her stuff in storage and moved her in with us. Jimmy was good enough to give up his room. He slept on a roll-away bed in the dining room. That's why Jimmy has the biggest room in this house," he said, looking proudly at Jimmy.

"Oh, come on, Dad, it was no big thing," Jimmy said, looking a little embarrassed.

I thought it so typical of Mr. Tewlain for him to take in a complete stranger. One night as he returned from the city very late, he found a woman walking along the side of the road. She didn't wave at him or act as if she needed help, but what made Charles slam on the brakes was that she had no clothing on. "Pardon me, ma'am, but can I help you or give you a lift somewhere?" he'd asked, trying not to stare at her well-shaped, naked body.

"Well, sure, great, thank you," she said, getting in the Range Rover. She sat there high, straight, and proud, not the least bit embarrassed, and she asked Charles if he had a cigarette.

After taking a long drag from her smoke, she just looked out the window. Charles finally came to his senses and took his jacket off and offered it to her. "I'm sure you must be a little cold," he said. After some hesitation, she slipped it on. "Mind telling me where you're from? What you're doing out here in the middle of nowhere? If you don't mind my asking, what has happened to your clothes?"

"Oh, I don't mind at all," she replied. "I came out here with a gentleman, and when we were finished, I asked him for the money, and he tossed me out of his car without my clothes. I'm from the city, actually."

Charles fed the lady and called the authorities, who came and took her back to the city. Charles Tewlain would find many strangers wandering in his north woods with tales to tell. He did his best to help them. Mrs. Tewlain seemed to take his passion for lost and needy people in stride.

I returned to the Tewlain woods a few days later. I was in the kitchen with Jimmy when an old woman came into the room. Her thin, frizzy white hair was flying in every direction. Her glasses were on crooked. She was wearing a white cotton nightgown. One foot had a slipper; the other was bare. I stood there staring at her, and she said, "The admiral's cat is in my house, and he won't leave. Why does it keep snowing? I can't get it to stop." I watched intently as Jimmy walked up to her calmly and gently straightened her glasses and smoothed down her hair. He took a plate from the cupboard and a small glass, which he filled with milk. He added a few cookies to the plate. Holding both in one hand, he walked back to the old woman.

"May I walk with you, Aunt Bone?" he asked, offering her his arm. She wrapped both of her arms around it.

"My good boy," she said, stroking his arm. He gave her a kiss on the cheek, and then he walked her from the room, with me following close behind. We walked slowly past Mary Jean's room, which totally reflected her personality: white carpeting, pale pink walls, white furniture, and a white canopy bed. A white rocking chair stood by the large bay window of the small room. There were dolls and stuffed animals in the window, and pink throw pillows were everywhere.

Aunt Bone's room had no cat in it, and it looked just like a room that would belong to someone named Aunt Bone. It was identical in size and shape to Mary Jean's. It had white carpeting and a single twin bed with a white bedspread covered with wine-colored roses. A rocker with a soft, wine-colored cover sat next to the big bay window, along with a small white table. Jimmy set the milk and cookies on the table. He found her other slipper and put it on for her. A white robe was hanging on the closet door; he helped her into it and fastened it around her waist. He took a hand mirror from her dresser and held it up to her face. "Look, Aunt Bone, the queen has come to visit." The old woman looked into the mirror and began to giggle. She brought her fingers to her lips as she stared at her own image.

"Yes, the queen. How do you do?" she said, and they both laughed. He took the mirror and made its reflection dance in the sunlight.

"Sunlight, Aunt Bone—beautiful, glorious sun," Jimmy said, drawing the old woman's attention to the window. He rose from the bay window seat filled with pink, white, and wine-colored pillows. "You enjoy your cookies and milk with the queen now, and I will see you later." He handed her the glass, and she drank milk and ate the cookies with a look of utter contentment.

Jimmy took my hand and guided me from the room. "How did you know what to do for her, Jimmy?" I asked. "How did you know what she wanted?"

"I didn't, Eve," he answered. "I just try different things until I hit upon the right thing. Aunt Bone is harmless. My dad taught me. I just watched and learned to handle her—it frees Mom up." It was another lesson in life I'd learned from this extraordinary young man.

Word had gotten around New Moon and Henderson about the rich folks who lived in the north woods. People started to drive into the Tewlain woods. Every mother in the county wanted her daughter to marry or date Jimmy Tewlain, even if he was only fourteen years old. He seemed to be able to handle the girls and their mothers. He could talk to anyone. He always made them feel important.

Susie Anderson came speeding up the Tewlain driveway late that afternoon as we were about to go riding. She was twenty years old, for God's sake, and wanted a date with Jimmy! She was driving her father's red Thunderbird convertible. "Hi, Jimmy!" she called out, completely ignoring me. "I came to take you out to the movies and dinner. My daddy's given me the car for the whole evening, so we can stay out as long as you want." She was making goo-goo eyes at him, and I wanted to lean over and throw up in the driveway. Every mother wanted Jimmy for a son-in-law, no matter if her daughter was ten or twenty-five.

Jimmy walked to the car and leaned over, resting his arms on the door. "Wow, what a snazzy car! I bet you can cover some road in this!"

"Well, I'll let you drive, Jimmy, if you come with me," she cooed.

"Why, thank you so much, Susie, for the lovely invitation. I would love to go with you, but I have to stay here in the woods and watch the place. I look after Aunt Bone when Mom is out. But you go along, now, and have enough fun for the both of us," Jimmy said as he stepped back. She waved, and the car roared down the drive in a cloud of fine dust.

It wasn't just Jimmy who received this kind of attention; Mary Jean had many suitors. Every mother's son, whether age nine or ninety, came to the door, wanting a date. Waldo's mother led the pack. She wanted Waldo to marry Mary Jean. She even went as far as to send Mary Jean flowers from Waldo; they arrived at the Tewlain woods just before Waldo did. Since Mary Jean was very much in love with Teddy, she turned him down. His mother was heartbroken, but Waldo took the rejection pretty well. "But her family's rich," Waldo's mother said, "and this is the type of girl my Waldo needs to marry." She had no problem telling this to all of her neighbors and friends.

Not only did mothers and daughters admire Jimmy, boys and men came to the woods to ask his advice about many things. "Jimmy, what do you think of this girl? Should I ask her out?" "Jimmy, what do you think of my car? Should I put straight pipes on it?" "Jimmy, what do you think of my motorcycle? Should I give it some more chrome?" Jimmy didn't even drive a car or a motorcycle. He listened and seemed to know just what to say to everyone. He didn't date; he was just fourteen, always with me or his sister and family. He did his best for everyone and never made them feel any question was off limits.

Some other things seemed to set him apart from other men and boys. He wasn't interested in the things most boys lived to possess. Jimmy Tewlain was not wild for cars or motorbikes. He didn't talk sports. He never mentioned guns and hunting, the favorite pastimes of all males in Henderson County. Instead he spoke of God's great universe. He spoke of how he loved the earth, the wind, the sun, the sky, and his beautiful stallion.

On the rare occasions when I saw him smoke a cigarette, he would pick it up after putting it out. He place it in an empty pack he carried, never leaving them on the ground. He had such respect for the earth.

"Jimmy, what's your favorite song?" I asked one day as we sat on a rock by the creek that ran through the Tewlain woods. Midnight stood by, grazing in the grass on the small bluff. Jimmy was sitting behind me with his arms around my waist, holding me in that special way. Music was another thing I needed like a drug. I listened to it night and day on my radio in my room or in the kitchen.

"Oh, Eve," Jimmy whispered softly. "Just listen to the wind in the trees. It's the best music you will ever hear. It's the only music I need. It's what I love the most living here." In my short life I'd never heard anything so beautifully put that wasn't written in a book.

June Tewlain was sought after by the women of Henderson County. Gladys Cavetti wanted her to come to club. She went a few times, but it became apparent that she had little in common with social-climbing women. June gardened and painted. She read books and meditated. Social status was the farthest thing from her mind. She was as Jimmy had described her: quiet, thoughtful, and very special. Material things and ladies' gatherings were not high on her list. She just didn't need them. The woods, her family, and her devoted husband were all she ever needed.

Lucy had been dating Johnny Cummings, the son of a wealthy Henderson business owner. Johnny was a popular boy in my class. He was a big drinker. They were having some kind of trouble I didn't know about, as she never confided in me like she did her town friends. I tried hanging out with her a little more, but I found that I preferred Jimmy's company.

Early one evening Father Strickland, the priest from Christ the King Church, telephoned. "Good evening, Evalina. How are you, my dear?" he asked.

"I'm fine, Father. Thank you for asking. What can I do for you?" I asked.

"Well, I'm going over some church records, and I find you haven't made your sacrament of confirmation. May I ask why?" he inquired.

"No reason. I guess it just slipped by me. I go to public school, so I must have missed it," I said.

"Classes will begin at the rectory for you and a few others who have missed getting the sacrament. Please pick a sponsor and come to the rectory every Monday night for the next four weeks, and then you'll make your confirmation at the cathedral in Freedom Falls on the following Sunday."

"Okay, Father, I'm looking forward to it," I replied.

"That's my girl," he said and hung up. I called Lucy right away to ask her if she would do it. She accepted with great enthusiasm. It gave us a project we could do together for the next few weeks.

That Sunday in August we went to the cathedral for the High Mass with our group, and afterward we went out to eat at a diner on the big highway. I enjoyed it very much. When we got home that afternoon, Lucy took off her shoes and hat and threw them on the floor, declaring, "I've had enough church to last me a lifetime. Come on, Boobaleene, let's go raise some hell."

We changed into cutoff jeans and plaid blouses. We got a ride into town with Lucy's brother Lorenzo, who was going on a date. He was about to graduate from a prestigious university with an engineering degree. He was the favorite in her household. Lorenzo's girl, Lois, was a big landowner's daughter. They were planning a large, lavish wedding.

I didn't care much for Lucy's town friends. I wanted to please her, because she had gone through the religious stuff with me and taken her responsibilities seriously. I went along with her to met Alice and Babe. We walked around Henderson. They walked right between couples on purpose, not saying excuse me. They made mean remarks and comments about people. We went up to the high school and watched the new cheerleading squad practicing in the gym. Alice took a basketball onto the gym floor and started shooting baskets, daring any of them to stop her. "Lucy, it isn't right," I said. "Please make her stop."

"I can't stop her. Besides, she is only having a little fun with them," she replied. It was painful to watch. I walked to the upper gym doors and waited for them. When the cheerleaders ignored Alice, she decided it was time to go.

It was getting cool and dark. I wondered how we were getting back home. A bunch of those jock-type boys who made fun of me came along in a Cadillac convertible. "Come on, girls, let's go joyriding," one of them called out as the car came to a rolling stop. The girls got in, so I followed. Alice and Babe sat in the backseat. Lucy and I sat on the back of the seat, behind them. With the top down like that, it was a great place to ride. The car took off fast, and I almost fell off. I held on for dear life. When we got out of town, the driver hit the gas, and we were flying at about ninety miles an hour down a deserted country road. The girls were laughing and screaming. I was terrified. They had beer in the car and passed it around. I refused it. Lucy and the other girls drank it down quickly. I was hoping they would stop, at one stop sign at least, so I could jump out and walk home. My legs and arms were shaking uncontrollably when the car came to a stop at the top of the drive to Strawberry Fields.

I jumped out quickly. "Thanks for the ride!" The car sped away before I finished saying the words. Still trembling, I entered the downstairs kitchen. Mama was sitting at the table, drinking a cup of coffee.

"Whata happened to you?" she asked.

"Some of Lucy's friends gave me a ride home. They were driving so fast, it frightened me," I replied.

"Sit, and have strong coffee for the nerves. I get you two aspirin," Mama said.

Later I went to bed. Listening to my radio, I fell asleep, but I could still feel myself flying in that car. When I woke in the morning, my legs and arms felt tired.

The late summer air was crisp, and it smelled like fall when I stepped outdoors to go find Jimmy. I needed that feeling I had when I was with him, the feeling of having my feet solidly on the ground. When I arrived at his house, Jimmy came out to greet me. He seemed so pleased. "I'll saddle Midnight, and we will go for a nice run. Please stay here, Eve, while I saddle him. He gets too excited when he sees you, and it is difficult to get him to take the bit." It was true: Midnight loved it when Jimmy and I were both riding him together. The two of us were probably like a full-sized person. It gave him a sense of purpose to gallop like the wind. I sat on the fence of the corral to wait.

Just then a truck pulled up, and Mr. Tewlain came out of the house. I saw Old Man Swenson get out of the truck and shake hands with Charles. Charles was always being hounded by the locals for advice, and some actually asked for loans. They came walking my way. Swenson was talking to Charles like he was trying to sell him something. Swenson was a big man of about six feet and six inches. He wore bib overalls, work boots, and a big, floppy farmer's hat. "I don't know, Mr. Swenson," Mr. Tewlain was saying. "I'm not much of a farmer, and investing in farming can be a risky business."

Swenson looked over at me sitting on the fence. "I see you got one of them Eye-talian monkeys hanging around your place." I got down from the fence as Charles Tewlain came up to me.

"This is Eve, Mr. Swenson," Charles said. He put his arm around my neck and pulled me toward him. "This is Jimmy's girl." He kissed the top of my head as I stood with my arms hanging limply at my sides. I rested my head against his chest. I could feel my self-esteem draining from me. I must have really looked like a monkey. Charles had called me Jimmy's girl! He never seemed to remember that I was almost four years older than Jimmy. I was practically a grown woman.

"Looks like an Eye-talian monkey to me," Swenson said again, and he spat on the ground at my feet. Charles didn't reply. He stroked my hair with one hand and held me around the neck with the other. Just then Jimmy came thundering up to the fence on Midnight, who was indeed very excited. The horse reared up on his hind legs and gave me a loud greeting. "The horse is too wild, Charles," Swenson declared. "The boy will get hurt if you are not careful."

"He's just excited to see Eve, that's all," Charles replied. "Besides, Jimmy can handle him. He's a fine horseman." The horse pounded the ground under his hooves and pranced about. "Jimmy!" Mr. Tewlain called out as Midnight reared back once again. "You want this girl?"

"I sure do, Dad," Jimmy replied, and Charles lifted me into the air. Jimmy took me around the waist. I threw my right leg over the horse, and we were seated together, fitting like a glove. Jimmy gave Midnight a little nudge in the groin, and he reared up on his hind legs once again. He turned and leaped forward in one magnificent motion to fly across the meadow.

"That horse is too loco!" I heard Swenson call out again as the wind and sun filled my face and hair. We flew away, like children in a fairy tale, to the land of Nevermore.

When school started, I didn't feel the usual dread. I was worried more about Mary Jean and Jimmy and how they would fit in at Henderson High, where kids could be cruel to anyone who was a little different. When they boarded the bus that first day, they looked just like everyone else. Gone were those elegant cowboy boots, the tight-fitting jeans and T-shirt. Jimmy wore a brown, long-sleeved, button-down shirt; brown dress pants; and brown suede tie shoes. Belts and jeans were not allowed.

Gone were Mary Jean's dowdy, baggy clothes. She wore a pleated plaid skirt, a brown sweater, white Keds, and bobby socks. They sat together on the bus ride that first day and every day. When we arrived at school, they got off together, and I heard them wish each other well. "Have a good day," I said. "I'll meet you right here after school." They agreed.

The Tewlain family didn't seem to need anything but each other and their beautiful place in the woods. They had everything and needed none of it. They never went to football games or dances. They didn't stay in town and hang out like the rest of us. Everything they desired was at home in the woods.

I, on the other hand, needed everything. I needed clothes and shoes. I needed music and dancing. I needed to sing and be loved. I needed friends and the approval of others. I needed these things so badly that I was sure others could read the sad longing inside me, as if it were a story written on my sleeve. I stood up straight and walked past those boys who called me unkind names; I couldn't hear them. I put Jimmy's voice into my head, all those wonderful things he told me: *I love you, Eve. You're beautiful, Eve. Don't let anyone hurt you, Eve. Listen to the wind, Eve. It's the best music you will ever hear.* When report cards came out, I was proud of my two Bs and five Cs, even if no one at home noticed them.

I joined the choir and sat next to Janet Ray. She invited me to her house to sing with her and Bobby. I loved the Rays. Mrs. Ray and I talked as if we were old friends. I think she was lonely and needed the company. Mr. Ray, like my pa and brothers, worked two jobs to pay bills and keep the family fed. Janet and Bobby had an older brother who was severely mentally retarded and a younger brother in grade school. Lonnie James, the older brother, got very excited when he saw me. He would grab my arms and hold on tight, making loud noises. He couldn't speak; it was his only means of expressing himself. Mrs. Ray was afraid he might hurt me or scare me, but I assured her that he wouldn't. I liked Lonnie; he was harmless.

Janet Ray and I sang harmony as Bobby played the guitar. We blended together nicely, and we had a lot of fun. The Rays had migrated from the South. They knew all those wonderful old mountain tunes that brought such comfort and joy. Sometimes Mrs. Ray would join us in an old gospel song.

I got to see Jimmy on weekends. I didn't care who knew how close we were. We sat together on hayrides and at camp outings in the woods. We kissed when we parted, no matter who might be watching. He repeated his wonderful words: "Don't let anyone hurt you, Eve." I still didn't know what that meant. It comforted me and eased the pain of living in a house with two brothers who constantly berated me. When those boys at school made fun of me and called me names, I knew I was no Bedroom Babe or Sexpot.

Jimmy hated school. He did his homework on the bus. I guess he hated it because he was so smart and knew so many things. It must have been boring for him. "I'm just staying in school because my mother wants to see me graduate," he would say. "I already know what I'm going to do with my life. I'll manage my father's businesses and stay in the Tewlain woods until I die. Mary Jean will go to college and marry well—that's her destiny."

Winter came on with a vengeance; snow fell, making deep piles everywhere. I hated snow, but Lucy loved it. She begged me to go ice skating with her. I couldn't ice skate. When I went to the pond with her and her town friends, I was left out. The things they talked about shocked me. Most of those girls were already having sex. They didn't care much if I heard what they were saying. I was invisible to them. On a Friday night in early December, we all gathered at the Stayton pond. A large bonfire was set ablaze to keep us warm. The temperature fell to nineteen degrees. I just couldn't stand up on ice skates. Big Mike drove his car right into the meadow next to the pond and left it running, with the windows rolled down and the radio blasting. I chose to sit by the fire and sing with the radio while everyone skated.

"Oh, no, you won't just sit here," Big Mike said. He lifted me up onto his shoulders and skated around with me. It was fun, but after a while he tired and dropped me on the opposite side of the pond. "Now skate back on your own." I stayed there, because I couldn't do it.

Jimmy came and picked me up off the ground. "Jimmy, you'll hurt yourself carrying me," I protested.

"No, I won't," he said. "You're light as a feather. I love having you in my arms. Let's go sit by the fire and watch the stars. They're so bright; we're bound to see some really great things." The sky looked like twilight. He wrapped us both in a blanket, and we sat watching the stars and watching the others skate. Paul and Paula came on the radio, singing their signature song. "Now, there's a song I like," Jimmy said, burying his face in my neck. I laughed and kissed his cold lips gently. No one noticed. We held each other, enjoying the cold winter night in the magic woods. I was feeling like a princess in a fairy tale, with a prince at my side. Jimmy could feel it too. We didn't need words. It was all there in the night air.

≈11≈

1963: The Year That Everything Changed

AFTER CHRISTMAS, SAMMY TOOK me to the RCA store in Freedom Falls and bought us a record player and some records. I was excited, even though he said it was for the whole house. I knew Mama wouldn't care for it, and neither would Pa. Marco was too cheap to buy records and too busy working to listen to them. Sammy only let me get a few forty-five records that he approved. The rest were LPs (short for long-playing records) that he wanted. He picked mostly Johnny Cash and other country artists.

The record player sat in the upstairs kitchen, on the counter next to the windows. My typewriter sat on its little table in a corner of the kitchen. I had taken Marco's advice and enrolled in secretarial courses. At the end of my second year in high school, Pa and Marco thought my poor typing skills would improve if I had a typewriter at home. We had traveled about twenty-three miles down the big highway to a large secondhand store. I picked out a nice modern one that was easy to operate, similar to those we had at school, but Marco picked the one that he and Pa finally bought for me. It was an old clunker from about 1939. "If you can type on this," reasoned

Marco, "then you'll be able to type on anything." While the type-writer was a great asset to me, it only made me a mediocre typist, but it was a step up from being a poor one. I did some of my homework on it. My grades didn't improve, but I maintained them. I struggled hard to be average. With the record player, I could spend hours in the kitchen with my books. I didn't mind homework anymore. I even enjoyed some of it.

I came home from school one day in late February to find Carmella and Antonia in the downstairs kitchen with Mama. They didn't have the children with them, as I had hoped when I saw the car parked on the hill. "Get out of here, we're talking!" Carmella demanded when I entered the basement. I went upstairs to my room, where I could hear everything from the heat vent. "She is spoiled rotten, I tell you, Mama. You'd better stop buying her all of those luxury items, or she'll turn out bad," Carmella said.

"She already has a bad reputation at school because of the way she looks," Antonia added. "All the boys think she's easy."

I almost wanted to laugh. I knew the boys thought I was easy because of the way Antonia had gotten pregnant in high school. It wasn't anything I was doing. *Hey, do you put out like your sister?* Boys thought I would be like her. I don't think she was an easy girl. She had made bad choices. I was mindful and didn't want to make the same mistakes.

Mama said nothing; she only listened. She knew how hard I worked just to be an average student. I wasn't allowed to date. I spent my free time with a boy of fourteen, Lucy, and Janet Ray, who were both much younger than I was. I didn't spend time in town. Boys made fun of me on the streets of Henderson, where they hung out.

"I'm not giving her any more clothes, either," Carmella said. "She hardly comes to babysit anymore."

"You better listen to what we say, Mama, and do something about her before it is too late," Antonia said.

I had listened to enough. I went into the kitchen, closed the door, and started homework. I put a stack of LPs on the turntable, drowning out the conversation below. They left from the basement stairs. I was a little mad. Antonia, of all people, had no business saying a thing about me. She didn't even make it through her second year of high school. I was half done with my junior year. I didn't even have a boyfriend.

Later Mama came upstairs. "Pa is home, and the meal is ready. You come eat something. You no worry. I save money. I buy clothes you need." She knew I had listened. It was the closest Mama ever came to standing up for me against my siblings. She knew I wasn't spoiled. Others had much more than I did.

The promise of spring was in the air that Tuesday evening in early March when Pa took me to Christ the King Church School for CYO class. CYO stood for Catholic Youth Organization. If you didn't attend the big Catholic high school in Bishop Sheen or St. Bonaventure, you got religion class once a week. CYO was fun. Most kids treated me well, even the big landowner kids. I liked Mrs. Kelly, our teacher. She taught us about religion and how to be a good Catholic. Her son, Freddie, sat next to me. That evening, she kept me after class. "Evaleene," she said, "Freddie has something to ask you." She gave Freddie a knowing look and said, "I'll just wait right outside for you, dear."

Freddie was a typical farm boy, a big landowner's kid. He was shy and had a hard time keeping the manure off his big boots. He was a nice enough boy, a tall, lanky kid with a blond crew cut; black, horn-rimmed glasses; a big buck-toothed smile; and smooth, clear, baby skin with a few freckles across his small nose. When his mother left, he took my hand and said, "Evaleene, I would be honored if you would go with me to my prom on May seventh. We could start dating a little, so we get to know each other?" Freddie went to high school in West End, fifteen miles from New Moon and the church.

I was so surprised that I found it hard to answer. I hadn't even known he liked me or thought anything about me. "I would love to go with you, Freddie," I finally said.

His face was beet red. He breathed a big sigh of relief, with a large, toothy smile. "Oh, great, that's just great. How 'bout we go out this Saturday night? I can't stay out late because of church and the farm. We belong to the Grand Oaks Center. I could take you swimming if you like."

"That would be fine, Freddie. Just call me with the time." I thought quickly about the hot-pink one-piece bathing suit I had purchased last summer. I only wore it to sunbathe. I didn't want to ruin it in pond water. The Grand Oaks Center was down the hill behind Carmella's house. It was a beautiful place. When I was a girl, it had been the barn of a large farm. I couldn't wait to go swim in that beautiful indoor pool. Carmella went there because the man that owned it was Norman's father's boss. He also owned their rented house.

"I will; I promise," he said as his mother came back into the room with a questioning look.

"Evaleene, your father is out front," she said.

"Thanks, Mrs. Kelly," I replied. "Bye, Freddie. I'll see you on Saturday," I said, smiling.

Both Marco and Sammy had attended their high school proms. They agreed to let me attend prom with Freddie. They eased the no-dating rule when Mrs. Kelly called to say that Freddie would be picking me up at four in the afternoon and that I would be home well before eight that evening. That was Freddie's bedtime. A farmer's day started at four in the morning, every morning, rain or shine.

Freddie came to pick me up in his Studebaker. There was no need to worry about hanky-panky with Freddie. Mrs. Kelly had everything timed, down to the exact minute. Freddie picked me up at four. We arrived at the Center at half past. We changed into our suits and swam from five until six. We changed back into clothes and left. Freddie always took the long way back to Strawberry Fields Farm so we could kiss. He seemed to be happy with a few little kisses. He was shy and not one of those grabby boys who rammed their tongue halfway down your throat. We dated every Saturday night, right up until the prom. Sometimes we met on Sunday and went to church functions. When we did this, one of his younger siblings came with us. Mrs. Kelly and Mama seemed to have that "safety in numbers" idea in common.

"Don't go getting a big head now that you're dating and going to prom," said Lucy when I asked if she would do my hair for the occasion. Lucy was grounded for the rest of her life, according to Gladys. She and some of her wild town friends had painted lots of graffiti on the outside brick walls of the high school. They bragged about it at school. One by one, they were hauled in for questioning and told that if they didn't confess, they would all be expelled from school permanently. They all confessed, including Lucy.

"I'd pay you a hundred bucks to do it again!" Marco said, laughing loudly. He hated Henderson High. I was shocked, because if I had been in on it, he would have killed me. Lucy was sad and depressed because she couldn't stay in town after school. She was still allowed to come to my house.

Spring came early. We spent a lot of time riding the fields of the Leila farm on horseback with Iris and Amanda and camping out. Both girls were crazy for Jimmy. I was still the only girl he wanted. He knew I was dating, but we never talked about it. When we were together, we still had no future and no past. We only had the present and each other. "I love the smell of the campfire and shampoo in your hair, Eve," Jimmy said. I thought we would grow apart over time, but we were even closer.

One Saturday morning in early April, Pa took Mama and me into North End to go shopping for my prom dress. Mama had worked her magic to get money. She demanded five dollars a payday from Marco, Sammy, and Pa until she had enough. We went to only one dress shop. I tried on only one dress—the moment I spotted it, I knew it was mine. "I hope we have one small enough to fit you and also accommodate those large breasts. They're too big for a girl your size," the clerk said. I felt embarrassed. She went over to the misses' department instead of the junior girls' and brought back the same dress in a size two. Everyone in that store stopped to stare at me in the triple mirror.

I had a hard time believing what I saw. Was it actually me in that dress? I saw a young woman with long dark hair and dark eyes, wearing a beautiful ball gown of baby-blue ruffled tiers. It was strapless and very elegant, with a hoop skirt. It swept the floor as I whirled around. I heard another girl say, "I want that dress too!" When the store clerk mumbled something I couldn't hear, the girl said, "I'm not going to the same prom!"

The dress cost Mama twenty-five dollars. It was the most expensive dress I'd ever owned. Most of my dresses, if purchased at a store, only cost a few dollars.

Lucy was stunned when she saw me in the dress. She hardly said anything. She had a natural ability for doing hair, and she planned to go to beauty school. She was good at doing makeup too, but since I didn't wear much of it, I just applied some pearly pink lipstick.

Freddie said little when he came for me. He brought me a wrist corsage of white roses that I knew his mother had purchased. We were going with another couple. I thought the other girl's dress was magnificent. It was a sophisticated A-line style aqua dress with white lace trim and rhinestones on the top. "My dress pales compared to yours," she said.

The prom was held in the gym of West End High. It was decorated to look like a Japanese garden, with a bridge over a running stream and large, live goldfish. Thousands of beautiful flowers were everywhere. Freddie and I danced in utter enchantment. At eight, a dinner was served, so that kids wouldn't be traveling the streets. I turned to Freddie to start a conversation, but I found that he was fast asleep over his bowl of soup. I woke him gently, and he apologized. The life of a farm boy was early to bed, early to rise, and work, work, work. He'd spent all of his free time decorating the gym. He was very proud of the way it turned out.

We left right after dinner, because the boys wanted to go parking.

It was only nine-thirty, but Freddie had a curfew of eleven. When we got to a back road I knew well, I felt safe. I could find my way home. I didn't have to worry: Freddie was a good Catholic boy. All we did was kiss and hug. I accidentally glanced into the backseat and saw that the other girl had her dress off! The boy was on top of her. They never got up from the missionary position as Freddie put the Studebaker in drive. I arrived back home at exactly ten-thirty that night. I still have my prom dress!

My romance with Freddie continued throughout the summer. His birthday was in late June. His mother let him have a party in their barn, with music, a bonfire, and food. Of the attendees, I knew only the couple from prom and Freddie. He invited his whole class from high school. When the tables were set and the food was being served, he took my hand and led me into the barn and up into the loft. The late afternoon sun was streaming in the windows, and the wooden floor creaked under our feet. Somewhere a record played. Tab Hunter was singing, "They say for every boy and girl, there's just one love in the whole world...Young love, our love we share with deep emotion." Freddie took me into his arms, and we started to dance. He turned my face up to his. "I hope you don't mind, but I just wanted my birthday kiss," he said, and he kissed me slowly and sweetly. It was so romantic! I felt as if we were in one of those teen movies I loved to watch on TV. "I want to go steady with you, but my mom won't let me give you my class ring. You know you're my girl, don't you?"

"Sure I do, Freddie," I replied, knowing it really wasn't true, then or ever.

June brought the lavish wedding of Lorenzo and Lois. It was all anyone could talk about in the county. Lucy was the maid of honor, and Lois's married sister was the matron of honor. Lois's gown, purchased from a store in New York City, cost an unheard-of six hundred dollars. Lucy and the other bridesmaids were decked out in beautiful pink gowns of satin and lace. Lucy looked like a million bucks! I could tell she wasn't happy. Her big brother was getting all the attention at home. Gladys and Howie were so proud of their engineer son who was marrying well.

The wedding at Christ the King Church was well attended. All of the farmers and big landowners turned out for it. Six hundred people were in the main ballroom at Great Oaks Center. It had a massive, sweeping staircase and floor-to-ceiling windows overlooking the indoor "tropical paradise" pool. Unfortunately Lucy didn't make it through dinner. She drank more champagne than was good for any human. She didn't even know who I was in the receiving line. She couldn't stand up. When she vomited all over her beautiful dress, Howie gathered her into his arms and took her home.

Lois's parents built them a house on their ten-thousand-acre farm south of West End. The old saying that money can't buy happiness comes to mind. Although they were so in love, Lois and Lorenzo never got the chance to live happily ever after. During the wedding planning, Mrs. Hughes developed strange symptoms. Dr. Hemming told everyone that she was depressed over getting old and losing her baby daughter. I suspected that depression couldn't make you unable to hold things in your hands or make your legs stop functioning. While in New York buying the wedding dress, Marietta Hughes had seen a specialist who diagnosed her with multiple sclerosis. They said it was a slowly progressive disease, but seven months after the wedding, she was completely bedridden, unable to talk or feed herself. She didn't get a chance to hold any of Lois's babies. She died shortly after Lois's second, and Lois's father died seven months later.

When Lois was four months pregnant with baby number four, she and Lorenzo were the happiest and most in-love people I knew. Their romance and life was a fairy tale. Lorenzo could hardly wait to come home to his wonderful wife and family every night. While other men who worked in the big city hit the taverns and lounges, chasing other women, Lorenzo headed straight home to his personal blue heaven. The evening meal sat getting cold one night when the phone rang with the news. Lorenzo had been in a terrible accident less than three miles from home. Gladys and Howie were there with Lois at the hospital. They could hear Lorenzo crying out in pain behind the curtain in the emergency room. After an hour, all went silent.

The funeral was hard for me to take, but Lucy sat there calm and regal in a beautiful, full-length, camel-colored coat with a matching hat. We were in the middle of a nasty winter. The Mass at Christ the King was nothing short of majestic. The church was packed, and all the choirs were singing. In my mind I could see Lorenzo floating on the Stayton pond in that little boat, calling out to Antonia. I remembered him as witty, funny, and wonderfully full of life. Now he laughed and smiled no more; the golden boy was gone forever. He left a sad and stunned community behind, with a very quiet Howie and Gladys. Lois was left with four small children and a large farm to run. Gladys and Howie did their best to help her through the nightmare, as she fell into a severe depressive state.

A few years later, Lois married a big landowner's son who was eight years her junior. She was the type of woman that grew more beautiful with every pregnancy. Her new husband was immature and insecure. He was jealous of his wife and her money. He demanded a new home, and she gave it to him. She had two more children with him, but she couldn't keep him happy. They divorced.

One sunny June morning, I came down to have coffee in the downstairs kitchen. I found Mama at the table with one of my scrapbooks. She was turning the pages and studying them carefully. "Mama, what are you doing with that?" I asked with some annoyance.

"We going to fix up the house. I want to know what looks good. Maybe you come with me to the furniture store, and you help me to choose nice things," she said.

"All right, Mama, I can do that," I replied. I had no idea it would happen so fast. That evening after dinner, Enzo and Pa started ripping out a wall between Carmella's old bedroom and the downstairs kitchen, making a new doorway. It took them only one week to make it into a TV room. All of the furniture from the upstairs living room was moved to the TV room.

The next day we went to a Mohawk carpet factory in North End. I quietly nudged Mama and pointed to a beautiful, finely sculptured broadloom in a beige color. "Pa, I'm a think I like this one," Mama told him.

"It has no color at all," he said. "But if it is what you want, we will buy it." We had beautiful hardwood floors in our home back then, but we covered them up with carpet because it was considered a sign of poverty if you didn't have it.

The following week, after the carpet was installed in the upstairs living room and the dining room, we were back in North End, at a furniture store called Aristocrat's House of Fine Furnishings. The salesman kept showing Pa and Mama stupid-looking stuff that was quite expensive. I nudged Mama and pointed to a nylon-pile, three-piece sectional couch, in a beige that was a few shades darker than the carpet. It had fine wooden legs and matching throw pillows. "Please, mister, how much for this one?" Mama asked.

"Two hundred and fifty dollars," replied the salesman.

"I think it is very nice. What do you think, Pa?" she asked.

"Well, if you like it, we will get it," he replied. I could hardly contain myself. Not far from that couch was a mauve armchair in the same style and material. I poked Mama again and nodded toward it.

"Please, I want to know how much for this chair," she inquired.

"Ninety-eight dollars," the man said, turning up his nose, as if he smelled something really bad.

"I think I would like it too, Pa," Mama said. I moved quickly to the other side of the room, where I spotted a chaise longue that was almost white. It had a high tufted back and a round cushioned seat. It was the kind of furniture Jimmy's folks had in their house in the woods. It was like the stuff in those Hollywood movies. I had my hand resting on it when Mama came up to me. "Oh, this is quite nice. I would love to have it, Pa."

"How much?" he called out to the salesman, who came running over.

"It's one hundred and fifty dollars," he replied, and Pa nodded. "Now, how about some end tables and a coffee table, Mrs. Rosario? I have some mighty special ones right over here." I hated them immediately; they were cheap-looking but cost a bundle. I went over to a two-tiered dark wooden end table that had a little drawer in the upper tier. It was made of heavy wood, and it was less than a hundred dollars. The coffee table I wanted was of the same dark wood but round. I gave Mama the eye again.

"This set is of such fine wood, Pa, and reasonable price also," she said. I picked up a lamp with a gold base on it and a plain white shade. "I'll take the lamps too." I was pushing my luck, but I wanted one more thing. It was a new style of lamp called a pole lamp. It reached from ceiling to floor. It was twenty dollars. Because we bought so much and we were paying cash, the manager came out and gave Pa a big discount. We got all of that stuff for five hundred dollars. Pa counted out the cash.

A man came to the farm in a white station wagon with lots of samples of material. "What do you think?" Mama asked me. "We will get curtains made for the windows." Our living room had four sets of two windows: two sets in front, with the front door in between, and a set on each side wall. I flipped through the samples until I found the perfect material and pattern. It was a heavy drapery fabric of light beige, decorated with crab-apple tree branches with fine pink flowers and little green leaves. The fabric looked so alive that you could almost smell the flowers. When the man returned to hang them, he was impressed with his own work. The drapes had a wide valance at the top, and panels hung down to just below each window, given the room a very formal look. The dining room windows were on the other side of the stairs that led to the basement. Those draperies were longer, to meet the ledge of the carpeted stairs. When the furniture arrived, it looked as if we had hired an interior decorator.

"Well, I have to say your daughter has good taste. I never thought it would look this good, but it does. I could sure use someone like her," the drapery man told Mama. She was so proud of the room. Of course, we never used it. Only special company sat in there, but we showed it to visitors. I felt I could do this for a living, if I had half a chance. The drapery man said, "It's all wrong. The color scheme is all wrong, but it works so well. I don't know how, but I have to admit it does." He left, shaking his head and mumbling to himself.

By the second week in July, I realized I hadn't seen Antonia in a long time. She hadn't been out to see Mama, either. She wasn't at our Fourth of July hot dog lunch. It was the only time we ever ate that kind of food from a store. Enzo and Nina had brought all the kids. Carmella and Norman and their kids had come to celebrate.

"Mama, have you talked to Antonia lately?" I asked. I missed seeing the boys.

"I am sure she is busy. You give her a ring on the phone," Mama said. She left the downstairs kitchen and went up to her room to read.

I dialed Antonia's number, and the phone rang a long time before she finally picked it up. "Hello?" said a garbled-sounding voice on the other end.

"Antonia? Is that you?" I asked.

"Yeah, what do you want?" she asked. She sounded so strange. She sounded drunk!

"Are you okay?" I asked.

"Yeah! Just leave me alone," she replied and hung up. I called her back.

"Are you drunk?" I asked quickly when she answered.

"Yes! I'm drunk, and don't you tell anybody, you little twerp! Now leave me alone!" She hung up again. I called Carmella.

"What's going on with Antonia?" I asked. "She's drunk, for God's sake."

"Warren left her and the boys. She's all alone in the little rented house at Lake Calvin," she said. Rather calmly, I thought.

"Oh, no! That's just terrible!" I said. "She can't stay there by herself—she can't drive. How will she get around and feed the boys?"

"Beats me," Carmella said. "I told her she could come here for a few days, until she figures things out. But you know Antonia—she doesn't do anything. Everyone is supposed to do for her."

"Do Pa and Mama know anything about this?" I asked.

"No, they do not," she replied emphatically.

"Well, I'm going to talk to Pa. She can't stay there by herself. She and the boys will starve," I said.

"Good luck with that," Carmella said, laughing. "You know how the old man is." She hung up. The next night after dinner, I stayed in, waiting for Marco and Sammy to leave the house.

When he was settled in front of the TV, I went to him. "Pa, I need to talk to you," I said bravely.

"What you want? I watch my shows. Go to bed," he said.

"I need to talk to you about Antonia. I think she is in trouble," I said.

"You stay away from her! If she is in trouble, let her husband deal with her, not you!" he said.

"But Pa, he left her. She can't take care of herself or the children." Pa jumped out of his chair, swearing at the top of his lungs and pacing back and forth.

"She make her own bed, now you let her lay in it. You no interfere in her business. Let her figure it out on her own. You stay away from her, you hear me?" He yelled so loud that the windows of the house began to vibrate.

"But Pa, she isn't able to care for the children on her own. She can't drive, can't get to the store to buy food. She has no job," I said.

"This is not your problem, I tell you!" he thundered. "You stay out of it!"

"She and the children are your own flesh and blood, Pa. You can't turn your back on them and let them suffer like this." He jumped up again and switched off the TV, swearing and using words I could never repeat. Never in my entire life had I stood up to my father or talked to him this way. My heart was beating fast. I was afraid he would strike me, but I couldn't stop. "Think of the children, Pa. They don't deserve this," I said, talking in a calm and steady voice. I would give him back his own words, ones he'd said that night when he returned home from church: *You don't give away your own flesh and blood!* "Pa, what will people think?" I asked calmly. "They are your own flesh and blood. You can't turn your back on them and let them starve, or worse." My knees were shaking.

"Shut up! Shut up, I tell you!" he shouted. "Get out of here, and go to your room. I want to watch my TV!" He turned the set back on. I went up to my room, locked the door, turned on the radio, and lay down on my bed. The TV was playing loudly. Suddenly the house grew quiet. I heard Pa come upstairs and go into the bedroom with Mama. I could hear them talking in Italian. I don't know how long I lay there, but I must have fallen asleep. I woke with a start when Pa came banging on the door. "Come, we go get her. I wait for you in the car."

The babies were in bed. Antonia sat in the living room, looking dejected and alone. "Come on. You and the kids are coming home with me and Pa," I said.

"No, no, I can't do that. You can take me to Carmella's," she replied. I didn't want to argue. I went into the kitchen, and I found a bunch of paper grocery bags shoved between the stove and refrigerator. I went around the house, gathering up things they would need. I filled one bag with diapers and another with the boys' clothes. I went into Antonia's room. All of Warren's clothes were gone. Antonia had very little to wear. I took out underwear and socks, a few pairs of pants and blouses. I took some of the kids' toys.

I made several trips to the car, while Antonia smoked one cigarette after another. I carried the boys, one at a time, to the backseat.

"Okay, Antonia, get in the car," I said, standing in the doorway. She took her purse and a carton of cigarettes.

We took her to Carmella's that night, but Carmella called a few days later. "Come get her, or Norman and I will be in divorce court soon!" Carmella yelled into the phone. "She won't move! She won't do anything! She just sits smoking one cigarette after another. I got two kids of my own! I can't take care of hers too, and she won't do it."

"I'll see what I can do," I said, hanging up the phone. I went to my father, who was in front of his beloved TV, watching *Gunsmoke*, his favorite show. I stepped in and turned off the TV set, causing Pa to erupt into a volcano spewing words not fit for human ears.

"Pa, we have to go get Antonia from Carmella's. She can't stay there—the house is too small for seven people, four of them being children. Norman is upset with Carmella for letting her stay." My heart was beating loudly in my ears; my legs were shaking as I spoke fast and stood my ground.

"You see? You see now what you have done?" he yelled. "I told you, no interfere in your sister's business. Now you will pay—by God, you will pay! You go to your room, you take everything out. I don't care what you do with it. We will get your sister, and she will have your room!" The room was too small for us and the boys. I hadn't thought of where they would sleep. There were only four bedrooms in the house, now that the two in the basement had been turned into the TV room. Sammy and Marco would never share a room again. Sammy snored. They were grown men.

Mama took my things and put them in the bottom drawer of her dresser. My few clothes hung in her closet along with my prom dress. She said little regarding Antonia. She knew I was right. Pa said nothing when he helped me set up the crib in my room for the little Captain. Dean Martin would share the bed with his mother. The house at Strawberry Fields became a crowded place, with many mouths to feed.

Over the next few weeks, Antonia made no attempt to care for the boys. She sat all day, staring out the window and smoking, lighting one cigarette off the last. Mama and I took care of the babies, feeding and changing diapers. Little Cappy started to call me Mama. "I'm not your mama, Cappy," I said. But the little guy just looked at me, raised his chubby arms in the air, and said, "Mama!" He didn't understand.

Warren came to the farm one afternoon to see Antonia and the boys before Pa got home from work. He was crying, and he said he wanted to try to work things out. They got into his car and went to the rectory to see Father Norton. They were gone until after dark. Pa was waiting for them. He took his shotgun and went out on the porch. He pointed it right at Warren. He would not hear of reconciliation, and he ordered Warren off the property. Antonia sank to her knees on the gravel drive and cried. I ran to her, helping her to her feet as Warren sped away in a new car his folks had bought for him.

"You get in the house and take care of your own children like a grown woman!" Pa yelled.

Sam Weeds Sr. was a big, tall man with light hair and gray eyes. He wore a light tan suit all year round, with a matching Frank Sinatra fedora. He always had a cigar tucked into the side of his mouth. He was a hard man of few words. He worked his lawyer's magic, and Antonia and Warren were divorced in a matter of weeks. It cost the Kenneths a pretty penny. It cost Antonia nothing; she didn't have a dime.

There was a war brewing in a far-off land. It wasn't long before Uncle Sam came after Warren with a draft notice. My brothers thought it was the best thing that could happen to him. "It will help him grow up," they said. No one predicted the power of a mama like Warren's. She wrote a scathing letter to the secretary of the army. She attached a copy of a little-remembered bill called the Sole Surviving Son Act and a copy of her dead son's death certificate. She had given one son to the army, and she was not about to let them have her baby. Warren never knew the discipline of a military life. He continued to live as one of the bad boys of Henderson County.

Antonia seemed to blame our parents for all of the things wrong in her life. She'd acted of her own free will when she became pregnant and married Warren. Since she never discussed her feelings or her plans with anyone, we were never to know the real truth. She seemed to think that the world owed her a fair shake, but she never got it. You had to make your own fair shake in the world. Women received few of them, if any.

She received thirty dollars a week in child support. She spent it on cigarettes and candy, things the boys didn't need. Pa always got the mail, so one day instead of giving the weekly check to Antonia, he took it to the bank in town and opened up an account in her name. Back then, you could do things like that in a small town. "But I need that money to buy my cigarettes," she protested.

"You need to save, so you can take care of children, buy their clothes and food!" Pa yelled. Since she did nothing all day, Pa decided she should get a job. He took her to a truck stop on the big highway in West End, where he saw a sign saying WAITRESS WANTED. Since she didn't drive, we all took turns getting her there. I didn't see Jimmy anymore; I was so busy babysitting and transporting Antonia. I was tired from sleeping on the beautiful couch. That nylon pile hurt, no matter what kind of blanket or quilt I put over it.

After the divorce, Antonia started to date right away. I didn't think it was a good idea, but my parents favored it. Porky Potter was a nice guy in my class at school. Although he was Antonia's age, he was still trying to get a high school diploma. He loved the little boys. He got down on the floor and played with cars and trucks with them, like he was a kid.

What bothered me so much was this terrible mess that Antonia and Warren were creating, with the boys right in the middle. Warren was dating too. He came every Sunday with his girlfriend to get the boys. I was amazed that she looked just like Antonia. Antonia had Porky bring the boys out to his car. I really hated that kind of showdown every Sunday, with the boys flying back and forth like Ping-Pong balls.

Another one of Antonia's dates, Roger Manning, was the only one of Sammy's friends that I could tolerate. His younger brother,

Danny, was in my class. Roger was a well-mannered guy and a little older than Antonia. He really liked her, but she thought him boring. He wouldn't play the game of getting the boys from the car when Warren brought them home, and she dumped him cold.

When I could, I still slipped away to be with Jimmy in the woods. "Why do you hang around with that little boy?" Antonia asked. "You're a grown woman, for God's sake. Act like one, and date guys your own age. Where's your boyfriend Freddie been hiding, anyway?" Antonia liked Freddie. They both liked the Beach Boys. They liked listening to their records in the upstairs kitchen whenever Freddie came to call. I wondered if she was still hoping that I'd get pregnant. Seeing the mess she had made of her life, there was no chance that I would marry or have children.

"I date guys my own age when I'm allowed. Freddie is a farmer, a seven-day-a-week job," I replied.

At the beginning of August, we worked hard to get produce from the gardens to market. Now that there were more people to feed, we needed the extra money. On Friday morning I was going into town with Pa, to help him and to get my senior pictures taken. I was excited to be entering my last year of high school. I still had no escape plan. Being at home was really bad. Antonia fought with Marco, Sammy, Mama, and Pa. Because of the constant yelling, I was having trouble eating again. I had to start taking that green liquid medicine again.

The day before I went to town, Antonia came home from work and handed me a bag. "What's this?" I asked.

"It's for you to wear for your pictures." I pulled out a beautiful, baby-blue, long-sleeved angora sweater with a mock turtleneck. It was so soft!

"Thank you, Antonia! I love it," I exclaimed.

"I'll get up early and do your hair," she said. I hadn't thought about my hair or what I would wear. Lucy always did my hair for me, but I hadn't seen much of her lately. When I did see her, she seemed to be mad at me. The next morning, as I sat in the upstairs kitchen with wet hair and a towel around my shoulders, I was caught by surprise when Antonia whacked off a foot of my hair. She curled it, dried it, and then ratted it up in high-fashion Jackie Kennedy style. All the girls at school and every woman in the world wore it. It fell in waves and flipped up on the ends. She even put some makeup on me! The sweater had a little zipper in the back, so I could get it on over my head without messing up the new 'do. I put on a pair of tiny, very short, navy blue shorts and my white Keds without socks. A little necklace would have made the look more complete, but I had no jewelry.

Pa had the car all loaded with the produce for the store. I loved that car; it was black and white with big red fins on the back. It looked like a giant boat. The 1957 Dodge with push-button drive was the revolutionary car of its time and easy to drive. As Pa was listing all of the errands we had to do in town, Antonia came out of the house and said, "I need to go. There are quite a few things I need."

"But there's no room. The car is full," I protested. The backseat and floor held six bushels of tomatoes, potatoes, and melons. There were five more bushels in the trunk, and the last one was on the floor of the front seat. Pa handed me the list, the car keys, and some money.

"You two will go. I stay here with Mama and the boys," he said.

I had to get my pictures done first. I didn't think it would take very long. We were going in alphabetical order, and we each had half an hour. The man from the picture studio had his equipment set up backstage in the big gym. He just stood there, staring at me. He sat me down and posed me, taking an unusual amount of shots. Then he stopped, stared at me some more, and smoked a cigarette. He handed me something that looked like a white towel. "Go behind that screen, and put this on," he commanded. Once I got it on, I saw that it was a V-neck piece of material designed to look like the top of a low-cut dress. He stared long and hard when I emerged. I was getting very uncomfortable. He pulled the V-neck low on my shoulders and then posed me again, turning me this way and that, taking another bunch of snapshots. It took over an hour. The next person in line was getting anxious. "Well, I guess that's enough," he finally said. Antonia was pretty agitated.

"That asshole acts like he has never seen a woman before," she muttered as we left. I drove the car down Main Street. We went to the dime store for ribbon, elastic, and thread, so Mama could make my hair ties. Jimmy always took them, hair and all. He never returned them. Men began to pour out of the bank, the Rexall, and the coffee shop. They all stared in our direction. "Oh, for God's sake," Antonia mumbled. Quickly I got what I needed. The whole store was watching. I paid the dollar and twenty-five cents and headed back to the car.

I went to Ferguson's feed store next. When Lanny Ferguson saw me, he came up behind the counter and pushed his glasses higher up on his greasy, sweating face. He was the son of the owner, twenty-five years old and unmarried. He'd barely made it through high school. "Hi, Evaleene," he said softly, smiling with his big yellow teeth showing. "What can I do for you?"

"I'm here to place an order for my pa," I said.

"Will you be home on Tuesday when I deliver it, so I can see you?" he asked, practically swooning.

I thought I heard Antonia mumble something that sounded like "God, I can't take this." She left, calling out, "I have to shop. Pick me up at the Rexall." I watched her leave the store.

"I'm always at home, Lanny," I said, making myself a mental note to be gone when he arrived. I made the order and paid him seventeen dollars and fifty cents. I got back in the car and drove to Garden Food Market. I was feeling really bad. I hated the way those men all looked at me as if I weren't wearing any clothes. Every girl getting her picture taken was wearing almost the same thing. I couldn't understand what it was about me that caused so much staring.

I parked by the loading entrance, but no one was there. I went to the front of the store to find Mr. Bolton. Layton Cain came walking out as I was about to go in. He stopped dead in his tracks, and his hungry eyes looked at my thin, tanned legs; then they lingered on my chest and finally came to rest on my face. "Well, who have we here?" he said, removing every piece of my clothing with his beautiful dark-brown eyes. "Why, it's the youngest Rosario girl. My, my, but you have grown into quite the young lady now, haven't you?"

"Hi, Layton," I said, hanging my head. I knew my face was getting red.

"Yes! I believe I need to date you up now, Miss Evaleene," he said. He hadn't changed since his bad-boy days. He was divorced, and he had children that he didn't support. He had a less than honorable discharge from the army.

"I'm sorry, Layton, but I can't date, you know," I said, still looking down at my feet.

"Oh, that's right. I forgot about what happened to your sister. It's a shame about her, really. She used to be quite a looker too," he said. "Say, why don't you come by the house anymore and sing with Grace for your old buddy Layton? I'm sure she'd love to have you. It would be just like old times."

"Well, Grace is with Eddie now, and she doesn't have time. I'm kinda busy too, with my pa and the farm. As a matter of fact, I'm here now on a delivery, so I gotta go," I said. I couldn't believe I was talking so much.

"Well, you let me be the first in line when your brothers unlock that tower and let you out. You hear me, girl?"

"Good-bye, Layton," I called as I walked into the air-conditioned store. I was glad to get away from him, but my relief was short-lived. The hustle and bustle came to a stop as I entered. The cash registers stopped humming. I could feel my face getting very red again as bag boys stopped bagging and butchers stopped carving meat.

"Hi, honey!" my friend Patty's mother called from behind the bakery counter. Patty was a year older than me and lived just past the Leila farm on Sherman Acres Road. She'd gotten married last year, right after graduation. Mama and I attended the wedding and the reception. They had live music from a really good band. "You know that Patty's expecting any day now." Every bag boy and stock boy was staring.

"Tell Patty I'm happy for her. I'll visit her when the baby is born, Mrs. Hamilton," I said and kept walking to Mr. Bolton's office. I knocked on the open door. He rose from his desk. He was a large, heavy person. I could hear him breathing. He had the look of a man about to devour a feast. He actually started to drool, and he took a handkerchief from his pocket and wiped his mouth.

"Hi, Evaleene," he said, coming around the desk to shake hands. I stayed close to the door, so that anyone walking by could see us.

"I brought the produce, and I need some help unloading it," I said, stepping back through the doorway.

"We'll be right there. Are you parked in the back?" I nodded and went to the loading entrance, followed by every available stock boy. I knew exactly what they would have said, had Mr. Bolton not been present.

I went back into his office and collected ten dollars for each bushel of produce, a total of seventy dollars. Mr. Bolton put the money into my hand, and then he bent down and kissed my hand with his thick, wet lips. "It is always a pleasure to see you and do business with your father. Please tell him hello for me." I couldn't wait to get out of there and wipe my hand.

Back on Main Street, there was no parking in front of the Rexall. I had to park at the bank. Men came out of every building in the immediate area to stare. I found Antonia in the Rexall, smoking a cigarette and drinking a root beer float while reading a romance magazine. I didn't know why she still read them after all that had happened to her. There were a few old farmers sitting at the counter, having lunch, and they turned to look. "Can we get out of here now?" I asked.

She put out her cigarette. "Yeah, I'm coming." We drove back to Strawberry Fields in silence. I didn't bother to change my clothes after dropping her off; I started for the door. "You're babysitting for me tonight, so I can go out. You'd better be back here in time. It's the least you can do, after all the stuff I do for you and put up with from you," she said.

I was steaming! I did more for her than she ever did for me. I needed Jimmy! I needed his beautiful words and his reassurance that I was a normal person. I felt dirty, alone, and used.

Mrs. Tewlain answered the door when I rang. "Jimmy's up in his room, doing the books for his dad. Just go on up, Eve. He shouldn't be much longer." I went up slowly. I passed Aunt Bone's room and then Mary Jean's. The door of Mr. Tewlain's study was open, but no one was there. Jimmy's room was at the front of the house. It was the same size as the large recreation room just below it. It was so like Jimmy—big, bright, and alive. Two walls had floor-to-ceiling windows with only sheers; Jimmy always had to bring the outdoors inside. The curtains were open, letting sunlight spill on the floor. There was a large fireplace like the one downstairs. He had a king-size four-poster bed; Mr. Tewlain had made it. Under it was a large, braided woolen rug of dark forest green and wine red. The gleaming floor was oakwood. There was an attached bath and a large walk-in closet. Jimmy sat at his desk in the corner. He turned in his brown leather chair as I walked in. He didn't speak. He just stared.

"Jimmy, can I come in?" I asked. His lips parted, but he still didn't speak. "Jimmy? I hope I'm not bothering you."

"Oh, no, Eve. No, of course not," he said, getting up. I had to look up to see his face. When had he gotten so tall? I looked down and saw that he wasn't even wearing those boots that made him a few inches taller. When I looked up again, he wore a strange expression.

"Jimmy, you okay?" I asked. He just looked at me with those soft blue eyes.

"Sure, Eve, I'm just fine. It's just that you look so beautiful, you took my breath away." He ran his hands up and down the sleeves of my baby-blue sweater. "This is so soft." Then he noticed my hair. "You cut it! You're not going to cut it anymore, are you?"

"No, Jimmy, I won't. Antonia only did this for my senior pictures this morning," I said, smiling. Both of my hands rested on his chest. He leaned down and kissed me softly, but his face was rough. It caught me by surprise, and I backed away.

"I'm sorry, Eve, I didn't shave this morning. I've been busy with the books." He put a hand to his chin and rubbed it. Since when did Jimmy shave? "Gosh, I just can't stop looking at you. I don't know why, but you're different."

"Well, it's just this stupid makeup Antonia put all over me. I've been getting strange looks all day, like I just came from Mars or something. I had lots of errands in town today, and all these men kept coming out of everywhere, staring. Oh, Jimmy, I don't know why they have to look at me that way," I said, rattling off a mile a minute.

"Look, let me put these things away. I'll saddle up Midnight, and we will go for a run in the woods and talk, okay?" he asked.

I sat at his desk to wait. Under the glass was the picture he had taken of me on that first day we spent together in the woods. I was standing on the pier, looking up, pointing into the trees across the pond. My long hair was down past my waist. There was no hiding those big breasts in that pose. My face was turned toward him; I was smiling. I slipped it out from under the glass and turned it over. Written in Jimmy's neat, almost feminine hand were the words, "My Eve, my goddess in paradise." I felt as if I was invading his privacy. I quickly put the picture back.

We mounted Midnight together; it felt so good. We went flying across the meadow and took the trail into the Tewlain woods, where the creek ran cool and sang to us. I sat on the big rocks and took my Keds off. I dangled my tiny, child-sized feet in the water. Jimmy sat behind me. "Jimmy, I just hate Henderson. I can't wait to leave and never see it or those people again. You just wouldn't believe how they stared at me this morning. It was like I didn't have any clothes on. Every girl getting pictures was wearing the exact same thing. No one looked at any of them the way they looked at me." Jimmy stroked my hair and listened. "I can't wait to go live in the big city, where I can blend in and not be treated like an outsider. I'm sure they have people that look like me. I just want to live and have fun. I want to go to parties, the theater...taste new foods, and just live."

"Eve, I came from the big city, if you remember," Jimmy said gently. "I can tell you there's no one there like you. I think it might help if you looked at things differently."

"I don't know what you mean, Jimmy," I said.

"Well, those people in town may be somewhat unsophisticated and limited in their ability to express themselves. I think it's just their way of saying they like what they see," he said. I must have turned to him with a very astonished look. "Eve, I just don't think you realize how beautiful you are, how unique. I don't think you know what effect you have on others. You are a powerful woman. I just wish you could see yourself the way others see you." I looked into his eyes with disbelief. "Those people can't hurt you with their looks or their words. They can only hurt you if you let them. Don't you know that, Eve? It is what I've been telling you since the day we met. I saw what a gentle and sensitive person you are."

I pulled my feet out of the water, and I turned toward him.. I didn't know what to think. It sounded like he wasn't on my side anymore. It wasn't that Jimmy never kissed me on the lips; he had, many times. They were the soft, sweet, short kisses of a boy. I was surprised now when he took me in his arms and kissed me slowly, long and sensual. He kissed me more like a man. When we separated, I noticed his hands were shaking. "Jimmy, what is it? Don't you feel well?" I asked, very concerned.

"I'm fine, Eve. I'm just fine," he whispered. "I love you. Please don't leave the woods. I'll give you anything you want, Eve—anything, I promise. If those things you mention are what you want, and you think they will make you happy, then I'll get them for you. In three years I'll be running my father's businesses."

"I have to know if I can live on my own, Jimmy, even if I only try it for a little while," I said.

"Everything you need is right here, Eve. You just don't realize it," he said, looking into my eyes for a long time. "I think it's time to go." He took my feet and dried them on the leg of his jeans and put my Keds on for me, as if I were too young to know how to do it. "Just promise me you will think about everything I've said here today. That's all I ask."

"Okay, Jimmy." We kissed again in that strange way. I wasn't sure about it, and I didn't know what to think. He picked me up like a precious child and seated me gently in the saddle.

When we got to Strawberry Fields, it was almost time for the evening meal. "Thank you, Jimmy, for listening to me. Please don't ever change. I need you. I'm not sure I could get along without these talks—they make me feel better, for some reason," I said.

"Everything changes, Eve. That's the one thing you can count on. Everything will change, whether you want it to or not. Look in the mirror—you've changed already," he said, leaning down from the saddle. "Search your heart, Eve—all the answers are there. Everything you need to know is right in here," he said, resting his hand on his chest. He gave Midnight a nudge, and they were off like a thunderbolt.

I helped Mama with the meal. I bathed the babies. After reading them a few stories, they fell asleep. I lay down on the couch. I couldn't sleep. Jimmy's words were running though my head. I felt confused. Jimmy seemed to understand everything. Why didn't I know any of these things? I was older, but he was wiser. I wanted to believe him, but living here was very hard. I didn't have my own space anymore. I just got no rest on the couch. I heard Antonia come in at two-thirty in the morning. I could hear Sammy snoring.

Antonia seldom joined us for Sunday's noon meal. She went back to bed after Warren picked up the boys. "You will never guess who I ran into last night at Moon Over the Water Lounge," she said to me, after the food was passed around.

"I don't have the slightest idea, Antonia. I don't know anyone who goes there," I replied. Moon Over the Water Lounge was built right over a big pier out on New Moon Lake. You could dance under the stars, on the water. The place had big windows, and it felt like you were floating on the water as you danced. I had been there for country music shows and other family events, but you had to be twenty-one to go there when alcohol was served.

"Don't be stupid. You know lots of people who go there. Layton Cain and his band were playing there last night," she said.

"I don't go anywhere he goes," I said, getting a little irritated. Lack of sleep made me short with everyone.

"Huh, that's not what I heard," she said. I stared at her. "Well, anyway, Lyle North was there. I haven't seen him in a long time. We talked for quite a while. You know he has a thing for you, don't you?"

"No, Antonia, he does not have a thing for me. I've never even talked to him. I saw him a few times at the Cains' house when I used to sing with Grace." Lyle North was one of the bad boys of Henderson County. He wasn't really bad like the rest of them. He was rich. He drove a Corvette, like Harland Hicks. Lyle wasn't handsome. He had wavy brown hair and very intense blue eyes, but very bad skin. He came from a big landowner family, and he displayed a lot of self-confidence. Boys who claimed to have a thing for me only wanted one thing. I was sure that sex was the most disgusting thing in the whole world.

"Well, he talked about you nonstop, and he wants to date you." It wasn't a conversation I wanted to be having at the dinner table.

"Marco and Sammy won't allow it. Case closed," I said.

"Sammy was there, and he told Lyle it was okay," she replied. I looked at Marco.

"It's okay with me," Marco said. "At least the guy's got money, and I guess you could do a lot worse."

"So he's going to call you next week. Don't be stupid and turn him down," she said firmly. I didn't know why she was so insistent that I date Lyle. I remembered when she and Carmella had asked Gene Berry to get me pregnant. I never told anyone about it. I just had to be careful.

I didn't give her an answer, but when Lyle called, I was curious and a little flattered. I agreed to go out with him. A week before school started, I was dating him once or twice a week. He was a gentleman on those dates. He took me to nice places—good restaurants in North End and the movies in Freedom Falls. He loved kissing me, and he did it often and long. He seemed to take such pleasure in it. I hated it!

Mama thought my pictures turned out great. I was surprised when she bought all of them. I hated looking at my own pictures. It was hard for me to believe that it was me in those pictures. I never looked like that when I looked in the mirror. I was ugly.

Freddie had given me his eight-by-ten framed sepia senior picture. It sat on an end table in the living room, even though we were seeing less of each other. He was the only senior I knew who had a bedtime. He was going through some rebellion thing with his parents. Just before school started, there was a CYO dance for all of us seniors. It was the only time to do it; senior year was always so busy. I went with Freddie to the dance, but he acted like he didn't have a good time. His parents were the chaperones, and this upset him a lot.

After the dance, we went back to his house for homemade pizza. Pizza places were popping up everywhere in Henderson County. It was the new craze for teenagers and young adults. We sat at the kitchen table with his parents; his siblings were in bed. Mr. Kelly started to question me about my family. "How can your father afford to take care of all you guys, when all he has is that little place, and he doesn't speak English? I just don't understand how he gets along."

"My pa does quite well, Mr. Kelly. We do good with our produce every year, and he works in the steel mill. He has two full-time jobs," I answered proudly.

"Yeah, I think these foreigners are just taking over this country. They come here and start earning money hand over fist to send back to the old country. They don't contribute anything to our society," he said.

"Both of my parents happen to be American citizens, Mr. Kelly.

That was one of the first things they did when they came to America," I said, feeling a little defensive.

"Well, your old man is really getting up there in years, isn't he? How is he going to be able to send you to college?" he asked boldly.

"My father will be seventy when I graduate. Most say he doesn't look a day over fifty. His foreman at the mill says he works harder than most twenty-year-olds," I answered, a little irritated. "Besides, I'm going to work right after high school. I will go to college part-time to earn my degree." I had no idea where all that had come from. It just came spewing out of my mouth like hot ash from a wildfire.

Freddie jumped up and said, "Come on, I'll take you home." I could see he was upset. I didn't see much of Freddie Kelly after that date. He went into full rebellion against his parents. I heard he was dating fast girls. He went away to college after graduation and flunked out in a year. He opened his own car repair business. He married a girl who took everything when she divorced him. His mother died a few years after, from cancer.

We always started school after Labor Day, which was a big deal in Henderson, with a parade and all. I didn't go to it anymore. I wasn't marching with the band, and I thought the parade was rather barbaric. I got off the bus after that first full day of school. It was very warm and sunny. I found Antonia sitting at the top of the basement stairs, on the ledge. She was smoking, but she looked strange. "I have some bad news," she said as I approached. "Mr. and Mrs. Pullman were killed in an auto accident. They were headed downstate to visit relatives. There was no gate or stop sign at a railroad crossing on this back road they took. They didn't see or hear the train coming, and they were killed instantly."

I dropped my books and sat down next to her on the ledge. I felt dizzy, and my heart was racing. I started to cry. I loved the Pullmans. They had always been so good to me. As I sat there trying to make sense of it, Mrs. Pullman's words came rushing into my mind: *I think your sister is the best-looking one of all your siblings,* she always said to Enzo. *Please don't be so mean to her.*

Antonia grabbed my arm and shook me. "Get a hold of yourself, will you?" she cried. "You're going to Enzo's with Pa, to stay with Nina and the kids. Enzo has gone to help bring the bodies back."

The next few days were a nightmare. As Nina's family began to arrive for the wake and funeral, I was at Enzo's every day. I was expected to babysit all of the children; there were twenty-eight, ranging in age from fifteen years to a few months old. They were all screaming and crying at once, and the older boys were getting out of hand. My child-care technique of giving them everything they wanted to get them to behave and stop crying wasn't working. I didn't know what to do, so I called Antonia out at the farm. She had Sammy drive her to Enzo's. She took charge and started ordering the kids to settle down. They seemed to listen. She had a low voice and a gruff manner. I think it was the first time in her life she ever did anything for anyone that wouldn't benefit her somehow. I went to the kitchen and started cooking. I fried up four large chickens and made five pounds of mashed potatoes and gravy and a few pounds of green beans. They went through two whole loaves of store-bought bread. Most of the kids were asleep when the adults came back from the wake.

I didn't have much time to date Lyle while all of this was going on. He came the following Saturday night. He was kind and gentle. "Why didn't you call me?" he asked. "You know I would have come and helped you. That's what boyfriends are for." It was the first I knew he was my boyfriend.

Well, Lyle did come and support me when death came calling again the following week. It was the most devastating thing that occurred in Henderson County. There was a football game between long-time rivals Henderson High and Freedom Falls High. To this day, no one knows what happened on that deserted stretch of country road, but six teens were killed in a horrific accident. They were some of the best and brightest of Henderson County. They were all good kids and well-liked by the whole community. They were excellent students with great futures. There were two girls. One was a freshman that everyone loved, a pretty blonde who was a straight-A student. The other girl had graduated in the spring and was home from college, visiting, as was one of the boys in the accident. The other three boys were all shining stars of Henderson High. Tom Gray was a new senior in town—handsome, bright, and very nice. Gary Summers was a year younger than me, but he sat behind me in my Latin class. We used to pass notes back and forth that we wrote in Latin. It was great fun.

David Burns had been my classmate since the seventh grade, and he was Bobby Ray's best friend. David was a very gentle person who was sensitive and kind. He had a bad stutter, a problem for him all his life. He was a good student who took learning very seriously. He hated violence of any kind.

This terrible event shut down the whole school and town for more than a week, so that everyone could attend all the funerals. Lyle was a pillar of support and strength for me. He took time off work and came with me to every funeral and wake. He sat with me while I cried. He held my hand as I drank coffee, and he did his best to comfort me.

The funeral for David Burns was so large that it took all day. Everyone in the county turned out for it, because everyone loved the Burns family. Just like their son David, they were good, gentle, and kind. Mr. and Mrs. Burns and David's younger brother stood by his casket all day and offered comfort to all mourners who passed by it.

I was standing outside the church in the warm sunlight, waiting to go in. I was doing my best to hold myself together. Lyle stood by my side, as he had been doing all that week. When I saw Bobby Ray standing there on the sidewalk, with his hands in his pockets and tears running down his face, I stopped and stared. I couldn't move. When our eyes met, he came to me. We fell into each other's arms, crying and holding on to one another for dear life. Everyone turned to look at us, but it didn't matter. We held each other throughout the whole church service, and it was hard to let go. Until then I never had realized how close a relationship I had with Bobby Ray. I was at his house all the time, and he played guitar for me. We never spoke much when I visited, although he never said an unkind word to me. He was a particular boy. He liked his clothes neat and clean. He was good to his siblings, even if somewhat aloof at times.

After the devastating loss of so many people that I loved, I found it hard to concentrate and harder to sleep. Lyle did his best to help me through this very bad time in my life. He came to Strawberry Fields almost every day. He took me out for coffee; he knew I drank it to calm my nerves. During these outings he began to point out his wealth and dependability. He even went as far as to say that he would make a good husband. I had other things on my mind, and I wasn't paying close attention.

In late September, Lyle took me out for a fancy dinner to celebrate my coming birthday. He wanted it to be a special night for us—I had no idea how special until we were seated in that fancy restaurant in North End. Dinner was lovely. Over dessert and coffee, he began listing his attributes. He told me about the expensive house he was planning to build. He said, "I guess you know by now that I'm in love with you." He took a black velvet box out of his pocket and put it on the table. I was stunned. I didn't know what to say. He went on, "You'll be over eighteen in a few weeks. You can get married without your parents' permission."

"Lyle, I don't think I'm ready to get married. I'm still in high school, and I don't even know what I want to do with my life yet. All I've ever done is go to school, pick strawberries, and babysit. I haven't really lived. I don't know if I can take care of myself or be out on my own."

"Girls aren't supposed to worry about that stuff. That's what husbands do. Nice girls like you aren't going to work. They certainly don't live outside their father's house until they marry," he replied in earnest.

"Lyle, I don't know what is out there. I think I need to grow some before I make a commitment like marriage. Frankly, I don't know that marriage is what I want." The disappointment he felt was almost palpable. I felt bad, but I just couldn't lead him on. He was a nice guy and a good person. My future plans didn't include Lyle or any man. I wanted to be independent, a whole person on my own. We never dated again after that, but we remained good friends.

It was still warm on the first of October. There was a gorgeous harvest moon. We farm kids decided to have a hayride. For some of us, it would be the last one we would ever attend. It would be our last chance to live in innocence in the farmlands of our fathers, untouched by the cares of the rest of the world.

That evening after the meal, I took a shower and washed my hair. I combed it back, and it fell in waves down my back. It had already grown a few inches. I had no more of Mama's special ribbons for a ponytail. Jimmy had them. I put a headband around my head to hold the hair back from my face. I was wearing a new-style blouse that Antonia had bought for me. It was just like the one Ellie May Clampett wore on the TV show *The Beverly Hillbillies*. The red and white checked blouse had short sleeves, and it buttoned down the front. You could button it halfway, to just below the bustline, and then tie the ends in a knot. My midsection was exposed! My navel made a half moon on the horizon above the waist of my cutoff jeans. My white Keds with no socks completed the Ellie May look. I was so thin that you could count every rib. But those big breasts sat high on my chest.

We all met in the Stayton meadow that evening. I had no idea that the hayride would be so big. Word had spread, and everyone was ready to party. After so much death had devastated our lives over the last few weeks, we needed diversion. Everyone was there—big landowners' sons, sports jock types from town, and our small-farm crowd. The Leila girls, Bobby Ray, and Janet came. They never came to anything, only social events at their church. It felt like we were trying to hang on to something we were about to lose.

Mr. Tewlain dropped off Jimmy and Mary Jean. Teddy came with Jimmy Loveless in his truck; I thought it was rather unusual. Lucy and I walked there together. We were wearing almost the same outfit; two of the other girls wore it too. The boys still outnumbered the girls.

Two big landowners sent two large flatbed trucks with sides, filled with bales of hay. There was a pickup with food and a large barrel of ice water. A large pile of timber and brush stood in the middle of the meadow, ready for the bonfire once we got back. Several older boys, who were now in college, came to do the bonfire and to cook the hot dogs and marshmallows. They hid a few kegs of beer in the woods. Lucy and I climbed on the first truck. As Lucy talked to Jimmy, Mary Jean motioned me to where she and Teddy were sitting on a bale of hay. When I approached, Teddy got up and gave me his seat, saying, "Sit here. I'll be back." Mary Jean patted the place next to her.

"Come sit by me, Eve," she said. "I'd like to talk to you. I was wondering if you were fully aware of how my brother feels about you," she said.

"He loves me just like a big sister, and I love him too. He's the younger brother I always wanted, Mary Jean. I thank you for always sharing him with me and never complaining about all the time we spend together," I said, feeling so loved and proud of my relationship with both of them.

"Eve, you know my room is right across from my father's study," she said. "The door was open, and I overheard Jimmy telling Dad how much he loved you. He told him that he wants to marry you as soon as he turns eighteen, if you will have him. He was almost in tears when he asked Dad to support him in his decision."

I was shocked! I didn't know Jimmy had said anything to his dad or anyone. Until then, I thought it was only talk between us that meant nothing. I thought Jimmy would be dating other girls. I looked over at him now; he was surrounded by girls, all vying for his attention. But I saw his eyes on me. "What did your dad say to all of this, Mary Jean?" I asked.

"Just what I thought he would say," she replied. "He told Jimmy to be careful he didn't hurt himself with a girl like you, who was about to be a woman and probably had other plans for her life that might not include him." I could feel my face getting red and my heart beating fast. "Jimmy began to cry, and Dad held him, telling him he would support anything Jimmy wanted, but for him to be prepared if it didn't happen the way he wanted." She looked into my eyes and said, "I just wanted you to know, Eve."

I responded like a naive child. "You know I wouldn't hurt Jimmy for the world, but I just can't think about any of this right now, Mary Jean. I'm here to have some fun and live a little before I am a grown woman and have to lead a different life," I replied.

"Promise me you will give it some thought soon, Eve," she said quietly as Teddy reappeared.

Someone's car radio was blasting Little Eva's song "Locomotion." I looked up and saw Lucy keeping time to the music. "Hey, Lucy!" I called as I jumped up on the truck's railing. "Let's get this party started." She got up on the other side of the truck, and we did the Locomotion. The sun was setting in the western sky, hitting the gold highlights in my hair and making them glow. I swayed to the music as Little Eva sang, "You got to swing your hips now, baby, jump up, jump back. Well, I think you got the knack." I swung my hips and waved my arms in the air in time to the music. I was lost in it. My navel was now a full moon above the waist of my tight cutoff jeans. I was having fun. I didn't notice that everyone had stopped to watch us doing the popular dance. I was a good dancer, with perfect balance and limber moves, my skinny hips and big breasts swaying in time to the music.

The song ended. When I jumped off the truck, Russell Greer caught me in his arms, held me tightly, and kissed me, ramming his tongue halfway down my throat. He was bending me back and running his other hand up and down the skin of my exposed midsection. I was fighting, but I couldn't get him to release me. Then I heard Jimmy's voice, loud and firm. "Russ! Let her go!" Russell released me after what seemed an eternity. I quickly went to Jimmy's side, wiping my mouth with the back of my hand.

"Come on, Jimmy—she was asking for it, and you know it!" Russell said. Jimmy stood and faced Russell like a man. I noticed that Jimmy was a lot taller, but he didn't have the muscle mass that a football player like Russ carried.

"No, she wasn't, Russ," Jimmy answered him calmly. Then he did something he almost never did in front of me. He lit a cigarette. I noticed his hands shaking. With that cigarette between his lips, he came close to me. He looked into my eyes with those soft blue eyes of his, which looked even bluer because of his light blue shirt. He wore tight-fitting jeans, that Stetson, and his fancy boots and belt. He never took his eyes from mine. He reached under my big breasts, never touching them, and untied the Ellie May blouse and smoothed it down. He buttoned all the buttons correctly. "I'm afraid your skin will get scratched from the hay, Eve. Why don't you get a drink of water, then get on this truck? I'll be right there. Okay?"

"Okay, Jimmy," I answered.

As I moved away, I heard him say something that sounded like, "Okay, boys, the show's over. Let's move on." I looked back and saw him talking to Russell in typical Jimmy style. He couldn't have a dis-agreement with anyone without trying to right it. I saw them shake hands after a few minutes.

The sun was setting as I drank a cup of cold water. I saw Jimmy talking to Lucy, and it looked like they were arguing. Jimmy had both hand spread apart, holding them up. He was saying, "I got this, Lucy, I got it!" She said something I couldn't hear. He took her in his arms and gave her a hug. I was relieved! I couldn't bear it if my two best friends in the world didn't get along. I was happy to see that Jimmy would never let that happen.

The sun cast a red glow around him as he lit another cigarette. He was resting one foot upon a stump. He pushed back the Stetson, causing a lock of his dark, wavy hair to fall to his forehead. A sudden pain overtook me; I felt like I had been hit in the chest with a blunt object. As I looked at Jimmy, I realized that I was looking at a man! He wasn't the little boy I had known. Standing there with the sun setting behind him as he smoked, he looked like James Dean, James Garner, and the Marlboro man, all rolled into one. He was tall, handsome, and so beautiful that I almost cried. I didn't want this. I didn't want my little Jimmy to be a big, grown man. When had it happened? Where was I when he became a young man? I knew the answer deep down, but I couldn't let it into my conscious mind or risk saying it out loud. I had been standing too close, so close that I hadn't felt or heard the winds of change taking place. Now that the truth was before me, I couldn't bear to see it.

Quickly I disposed of my cup and almost ran to him. He put out the cigarette and got rid of it. I put my arms around his neck, and he lifted me to him. He took one giant step without effort, and we were on the truck. I was sitting in his lap. The stars were coming out, and Venus was in the western sky, shining brightly. Jimmy didn't let go of me. It was like it had always been with us. We had no past or future, only the present and the magic of night.

The campfire was blazing when we got back, and everyone was in high spirits. No one wanted to think about death or the end of our childhood. Janet Ray and I sang harmony on a few songs while Bobby Ray played guitar. "I want to drink my java from an old tin can and see the moon go sailing by. I want to hear the call of the whippoorwill, I want to hear the coyotes cry." It was an old favorite.

As the beer was passed around, some kids paired off into couples. I saw Lucy head for the woods with Johnny Cummings. I hoped it wouldn't end badly for her. Bobby Ray sang the most beautiful rendition of "Love Me Tender." I knew his mind was on Lila Peace.

Jimmy took my hand and led me to a blanket near the fire, under the moon and stars. He held me in his arms and said all those beautiful things again. "You're beautiful, Eve. I love you, Eve. Stay with me, Eve. I'll give you the moon and the stars, if you want them. Just stay here with me forever." I didn't want to think about what Mary Jean had told me. I didn't want to think about the future. I couldn't face Jimmy becoming a man. I wanted the little Jimmy I knew. I felt comfortable, safe, and loved. I was lost in the moment. I didn't want reality to touch us. Wrapped in his loving arms, I just let him rain down all his love.

All of those jock boys and big landowner boys kept coming to Jimmy. "Do you need any help there, boy?" "Can you handle all that by yourself?" I didn't know what they were talking about, or I chose to let it go over my head.

"Yes, I have it. I can handle everything just fine, guys, thank you." He kissed me in that strange way, like a man, but I wouldn't let my mind go there. I wanted that safe, loved feeling from him. It was one of the best nights of my life. It ended too soon. Headlights started to come down the dirt road to the meadow. The boys cleaned up everything and disposed of the beer. When I got in the Range Rover with Jimmy and Mary Jean, Mr. Tewlain said, "Jimmy, I'll drop you and Eve at her place. I'm going to take Mary Jean out for a Coke at the diner. You take as long as you want to say good night."

The grass in the front yard was dry and still warm. We sat under the moon and stars. I talked on about what a great night we'd had. I told Jimmy I was happy. "My birthday's in less than two weeks! I'm having a party to celebrate. You will come, won't you, Jimmy?" I asked. "It's going to be held in the new garage my pa and Enzo just finished. We're going to have music and decorations. Antonia will bake me her famous chocolate cake," I said. I didn't notice that Jimmy had grown very quiet.

We stood up as Mr. Tewlain pulled into the drive. "It's all up to you now, Eve," Jimmy said. I looked at him. "Your own happiness— it's all up to you." He kissed and hugged me, and then he turned to his dad, who was leaning against the Range Rover. Jimmy seemed to fall into his arms, as if in deep grief over a devastating loss. Mr. Tewlain hugged him close and kissed the top of his shoulder. Jimmy was taller than his dad.

"My Jimmy," he said softly. "My man-child, I love and admire the man you have become. It's fine, Jimmy. It's all just fine." Jimmy got into the car without another word. I was confused and about to speak, but Mr. Tewlain came forward. He took me into his arms; holding me tightly, he kissed the top of my head and said, "Eve, beautiful princess, I love you as if you were my own daughter. Go inside now, and sleep the deep sleep of one who is so loved." I didn't have the slightest notion what had transpired, and I didn't understand the meaning of what he'd said.

As I lay down on the couch, I didn't know what to think about Jimmy's silent and strange manner. I didn't want to think about the things Mary Jean had said. I couldn't bring myself to think of Jimmy as that grown man standing there in the setting sunlight. I did the only thing a selfish girl like me could do. Just like Scarlett O'Hara, I decided I would have to think about it tomorrow. I fell into a deeper sleep than I ever had before.

I didn't even know it was morning when I woke with a start—Pa was shaking me! "Get up now, or we will be late for church. I will wait for you in the car." It was ten minutes past nine. I couldn't remember a thing from that night of sleep. It was like waking from a coma.

I showered and dressed quickly. From Mama's closet I took a white shirt that had been Marco's when he was a boy. She'd sewed darts into it just below the bustline so it would fit me better. I rolled up the sleeves, turned up the collar, and left a few of the top buttons undone. I tucked the shirt's tail into my tight skirt. It was dark green and red plaid and had a white stripe with a yellow one running through it. Short skirts were in style; all the girls at school wore them. As we arrived at school, one of the teachers would stand at the door with a yardstick, measuring the length of every girl's skirt and making sure that it was no more than two inches above the knee. I found my garter belt and a pair of nylon stockings and put them on, along with my flat T-strap shoes that had a candy-apple-red patina. Jimmy had my red headband, so I put a bright yellow one in my hair and grabbed a rectangular piece of white lace for my head. Women were not allowed in church without their heads covered. I thought it was stupid, because men never had to cover theirs.

When I stepped from the car, I saw every man, even if he had a wife and a dozen kids, turn to stare. I wondered for the first time if my pa ever noticed the way men looked at me. If he did, he never said a thing. He greeted people as we walked into church. For some reason I wasn't bothered by those looks this morning. I sat in front with Pa, enjoying the homily by Father Strickland.

As I knelt at the communion railing, Father Strickland did something so different that it startled me. When I made my confirmation the year before, Father Strickland was there to deliver that little pat on the cheek after the bishop confirmed each of us. Instead of a little pat on the check, he had delivered a good pop that made me jump. Lucy and I had a hard time smothering our giggles. He thought it was cute and always did it after putting the communion wafer on my tongue. But that morning he took my chin into his left hand and turned my face up to his, looking deep into my eyes. Then he rubbed the side of my face with his hand before moving on to the next person. After Mass I found him at the back of the church. "What was that look all about, Father?" I asked.

"I was watching you during my homily, and you looked like a girl in love. I wanted to make sure you were still chaste." I frowned and looked at him, confused. "Don't worry. I see you are still the same. I'll continue to pray about it. Please see that you remain chaste until the proper time. Pray for guidance, my child." He moved on to greet more people. Father Strickland was always trying to guard every girl's virginity. He had to see daylight between any couple dancing a slow dance. If he couldn't, then he was right there, making sure the proper distance was kept. More than a few times, it crossed my mind that he never seemed to worry about the virginal status of boys.

Outside, I saw Lucy up ahead. I hurried to catch up with her. "Hi, Lucy. Great hayride last night, wasn't it?"

She looked me up and down. "Nice outfit, Boobaleene. You look just like a naughty Catholic schoolgirl," she replied.

"Oh, come on, Lucy, stop!" I said, trying to laugh it off.

"If I didn't know you so well, I would think this denseness of yours is an act. Don't you know you were almost gang-raped last night? What the hell is the matter with you, anyway? You looked like a fucking whore up there dancing last night. Whatever made you wear that outfit?" she railed.

"Lucy, you had on the same one, and so did two other girls," I pleaded.

"Yah, but none of us looked like you did in it, and we don't have your moves when we dance, either. God, what a prick teaser you are!" she said. I could feel my face getting red. "Poor Jimmy! Do you have any idea what you're doing to that guy? Everyone thinks you're doing him, and if I didn't know better, I would think that too. He must have to go home every night and beat off after being with you."

"Stop it, Lucy! Jimmy's just a boy, and it's not like that between us, and you know it," I replied, getting a little mad.

"He isn't a boy, for God's sake. Look at him—he's a man now. He is over six feet tall. He's almost sixteen years old. Wake up, will you? That guy's in love with you, and he wants to do you in the worst way," she snapped.

"That isn't true, Lucy. That's not how it is with me and Jimmy. Besides, I saw you go into the woods with Johnny Cummings last night. I thought it was over between you two. What the hell were you doing?" I demanded.

"It was just a little farewell moment. You know I'm with Big Randy now. Don't change the subject, you dimwit. Do something about Jimmy. I think it's time you love him or leave him. Let some other girls have a go at him. He won't even look at them as long as you're in the picture, and he thinks he has a chance with you," Lucy said angrily. "I got to go."

All through the big noon meal, I thought about what Lucy had said. I wanted to slip away, go to Jimmy, and talk to him. The table at the house at Strawberry Fields was filled to capacity. Enzo, Nina, and their four children were there; Carmella and Norman and the girls were all present. I loved playing with the children. After our spaghetti dinner, we played cops and robbers in the yard. I was still in my church clothes, and Enzo took moving pictures of us.

After everyone left, I went upstairs to do my homework. I would try getting away to the Tewlain woods before dark. Antonia came through the door with a tablet of paper and a pen. "We have to start planning the party. It's in less than two weeks. Now, tell me what you want at this shindig." I made myself a promise to talk to Jimmy at the party. I would try to get him alone somehow. I didn't know exactly what I wanted to say to him. It was hard for me to believe what Lucy and Mary Jean had said. I had to face the fact that he had grown over the last year and a half. I couldn't bring myself to give him up! I couldn't bear to think of our wonderful relationship changing. He talked to others about marrying me, but I was sure he would grow out of it.

Janie Lee, my good friend from town, was a sweet little blonde. She had been in love with Billy-John since seventh grade. They seemed to be able to break all the rules about who you could date. I was happy for them. They were meant to be together forever. She came to Strawberry Fields to help me get ready for the party. We had a great day together, laughing and talking like young women. I cried a few years ago when I received a letter from Janie recounting that wonderful day so many years ago. As we hung decorations from the rafters in the garage, she talked of her love for Billy-John. "I hope someday you'll meet someone you love as much as I love Billy. I hope you'll fall in love. Being in love with him is the best thing in the whole wide world," she said. I wondered how Janie knew she was really in love. We knew little of the world outside Henderson.

My town friends couldn't make the party, so it was only my small-farm friends. The party started out well, but there was a strangeness about the evening that even I couldn't deny. Mr. Tewlain dropped off Jimmy and Mary Jean. Teddy came in his red truck with Jimmy Loveless and Scotty Brooks. Big Mike drove his own car. The Leila girls and Lucy rounded out the group. When the Wilson boys and Ronny Raymond showed up, there were more boys than girls. We sang, danced, and played games, totally unaware that our lives would be altered forever after that night. We wanted time to stop and hurts to be extinguished; we were desperately attempting to fill the large void left by those we had lost. The deaths of our dear friends were never far from our thoughts.

Jimmy took me in his loving arms and kissed me. I laid my head on his chest. "Happy birthday, Eve," he said. "I love you." As Jimmy held me, I saw Lucy out of the corner of my eye. The look of utter scorn and anger on her face almost took my breath away. As I turned to go to her, she walked out of the garage and up to the porch. She sat there with Antonia and didn't return to the party, which took a strange turn.

After swinging from the rafters in the new garage and declaring that the place was mighty nice, Jimmy Loveless came up to me. "Happy birthday Evalina. I want you to be the first to know I'm leaving school and joining the army. I'm just a screwup. I don't have near enough credits to graduate. There is a war coming, you know. Maybe I can make something of myself there." He lowered his voice so no one could hear. "I'll miss you." I didn't know what to say. Before I could say anything, Teddy Roosevelt was at my side, pulling my hair.

"Hey, we have to talk. You're my oldest friend. I've known you longer than anyone in my life, other than my family. I can't do good in school. I'm going to join the army with Jimmy," he said, hanging his head and looking at the floor. "We've been together all these years. I guess no war can stop us now, can it?" I looked at him, shocked by what I was hearing.

Finally regaining my voice, I asked, "What about Mary Jean?"

"Didn't you know? She's breaking up with me. Says she wants to get serious about her life and start planning for the future. I guess that future doesn't include yours truly." He said it with such a hurt in his eyes that I could hardly look at him.

"I'm sure if you get a job and act a little more responsibly, she'll come around," I replied, trying hard to sound positive. Teddy had flunked out of school. He hung around the Tewlain woods and Mary Jean every day.

"No, she won't!" he said quickly and walked away. I thought I saw some tears in those intense blue eyes.

"I'm goin' too," Scotty Brooks said into my right ear. He still couldn't bring himself to talk above a whisper. I wondered how he would fare in the army, on a battlefield.

"Does your mama know?" I demanded. He only nodded his head and walked away. He went back to that group of boys talking and laughing together. He turned to look in my direction with pained light-brown eyes.

I felt a heavy arm upon my shoulder. I turned to see that it was Big Mike. "Oh, Big Mike," I said through tears. "Please don't tell me you're going to join the army too."

"No, baby, I'm not," he answered. "My time for that will come. I'll be drafted. I just wanted to say I won't be riding the bus with you next semester. I'm getting a job in North End, at the steel mill." He had a big arm around me, squeezing the life out of me. "I only need two more classes to graduate, so I'll be working afternoons."

Something changed that night as I stood there in the new garage, waving to my friends as they left, some of whom I would never lay eyes on again.

I never got the chance to talk to Jimmy the night of my party. I never knew just what I wanted to say to him anyway. Lucy wouldn't talk to me after that night. She preferred to come to Strawberry Fields and hang out with Antonia when she knew I wasn't there. I didn't know what I had done to make her so angry.

Scotty Brooks didn't make it back from the war in one piece. He was sent home to his mama in a body bag, in so many pieces that she wasn't allowed to look at him. He wasn't her only child.

He was the youngest of ten and clearly her baby. She stood there at Brady's Funeral Home, holding onto his casket with the American flag draped over it. I recalled thinking that no mother should have such pain in her heart.

Jimmy Loveless made it through the war and came home, but he was never the same. I went out on a date with him shortly after he returned stateside. He drank too much and raved on about my being the only girl he'd ever loved. The only reason he'd made it through that stupid, useless war, he said, was so he could lay eyes on me again. "The real kicker is," he said, "you still don't give a damn about me. Now you're in love with some guy who doesn't love you back. What I've heard around town is, he never will. I think you're getting just what you deserve out of this life!" I was stunned by this revelation. I started to leave the party we were attending with old Henderson classmates.

"You don't have to go, Evaleene," one of our former classmates said. "It's just the alcohol talking. War does things to guys like Jimmy. He never had much in the first place, and what little he had, well... it got left in Vietnam." I walked home alone. I never saw him again. He died a few years later of causes unknown.

Teddy never went to the army. They wouldn't take him; I never knew why. He followed Mary Jean everywhere, making a complete fool of himself. He would creep around the Tewlain woods and flatten the tires on every vehicle driven by any man that Mary Jean dated. Mr. Tewlain forbade him to return, filing papers with the state trooper's office to keep him away. The reason he died was unclear. He wasn't yet thirty years old.

The unseasonably warm weather continued during the month of November that fateful year. I stayed in town after school that second Friday night. I wanted to attend the football game and the dance. It would be my last. I went to Enzo's and had supper with the little ones. I changed into my red box-pleated skirt and my white blouse that was really Marco's old First Communion shirt. I wasn't getting castoffs from Carmella or store-bought ones from Antonia. I added my black high school sweater with the big white *H* trimmed in red on the pocket. I wore bobby socks and Keds. I headed back to school for the game around six that evening.

I met Janie Lee and Billy-John. Sarah was there with her little brother Larry, who was a freshman. He was very shy. Our families went way back. My mama and Sarah's mother were good friends. Sarah's mother grew up on a big farm behind ours. She married young. Sarah was the third youngest out of nine children. She took care of her younger brother and sister as if they were her own. The three of them shared a room, which she had divided so that each of them had a private space. When I smiled at him and said hello, Larry laid his head on Sarah's shoulder; he averted his eyes when he greeted me, even though he was a foot taller than Sarah. I wondered how they would get along without her when she married Nathan Miller. They were going steady. He would be coming for her after the dance.

I scanned the crowd and spotted Foxy Benton, and I waved. He saw me and smiled, making his way through the flood of people. Foxy was an interesting guy. While we weren't particularly close, he had been my dancing partner since freshman year. He had spotted me on the dance floor at one of Henderson High's many dances. He came to me and said, "I've been watching you. You're the perfect dance partner for me." We met at dances, where we were show-stoppers on the floor.

I didn't know his real name, or why he was called Foxy, until after his death. It never occurred to me that the boys never teased him about me or said those awful things to him about me. Everyone seemed to accept the fact that we were just dance partners. He was the only boy in a family with nine sisters. His twin and I were in majorettes together, but I didn't even know they were twins. I wasn't particularly close to her, either. "So here you are!" he said as he came forward and smiled. "We match. I'm so glad. I talked to your mom on the phone. She told me what you would be wearing." Foxy always talked to Mama on the phone. He always seemed to call when I wasn't at home.

He got home from school much earlier than I did, because they lived in town. I had that long bus ride. "Foxy, he calls you," Mama would say. "He want to know what you wear to dance tonight. I tell him it would be the lavender dress. He says he will wear gray suit with a tie same color as dress." So we always looked like we belonged together. He was a handsome guy who looked just like his twin sister, except for their eyes. Lillie's were light brown, and Foxy's eyes were green. Those conversations with Mama should have been a real clue into the mysterious life of Foxy Benton, but not for me. I was so naive.

When I was working as a nurse many years later on the south side of the big city, Foxy was managing the Woolworth's. We hugged and promised to get together. We lived so close to one another, but it never happened. I cried when I learned he'd taken his own life because living was just too painful for him. If I had known, I would have loved and supported him. He was many things, but most of all he was a decent person who always treated me well.

"Hey, I got to talk to some people over here, but I'll see you at the dance. Okay?" he said.

"All right, Foxy," I said. After our team won the game, my friends and I walked together to the gym. Foxy met up with us, and our little circle of friends was complete. When the music started, Foxy and I hit the dance floor, doing one fast dance after another. We covered that floor in our stocking feet. It was the best dancing we had ever done together.

When the DJ announced a slow dance, Foxy knew just what to do: he put me in the center of our little group so that jock boys couldn't get near me. He knew I hated dancing with them. It was a contest with them to see which one could get to me first, grab me, and push my chest up against his, doing a clumsy two-step while trying to cop a good feel of my large breasts. Foxy stood firmly behind me as our little group laughed and talked on one side of the dance floor.

In 1962, Andy Williams recorded and released the classic "Moon River." It was still a big hit in Henderson County. When the music started, I felt a hand on my shoulder from behind, where I thought Foxy was standing. I heard a low voice that I almost didn't recognize say, "Eve, may I have this dance?" I knew it was Jimmy, for no one but the Tewlains ever called me Eve. I was surprised to see him. I knew he wasn't a dancer. Jimmy and Mary Jean never went to dances or football games; their family and their home in the woods seemed to be enough for them. I turned to see Foxy standing there next to him, wearing a questioning look.

"It's okay, Foxy." I turned to Jimmy and smiled. He escorted me onto the dance floor, never saying a word. He held me like a real man. He looked down into my eyes with his soft blue ones, and our eyes locked. I had to look up at him; he was so tall and so beautiful. We started to dance the most elegant waltz of my entire life. Jimmy led, whirling me around the dance floor like a professional dancer. We didn't realize that everyone had stopped dancing as Andy Williams sang, "Moon River, wider than a mile, I'm crossing you in style someday. We're after the same rainbow's end waiting round the bend, my huckleberry friend, Moon River and me." I loved being in his arms. I didn't want the song to end. Like all good things, it ended too soon.

We still couldn't take our eyes off each other! He held me there in his arms. "Jimmy," I said softly, "I didn't know you could dance."

After what seemed like more than a few moments, he replied, "Arthur Murray. My mother insisted I take lessons with Mary Jean. Thank you, Eve. Good-bye," he whispered, letting me go. I watch him put on his elegant black cowboy boots. He was wearing a red corduroy shirt with the sleeves rolled up to his elbows. It was tucked into tight-fitting jeans with that black leather belt and Spanish silver buckle. When had he become such a perfect man? I didn't know. Something between us changed that night, forever. I could feel it somewhere deep in my heart. I watched him leave the gym, a thumb tucked in each front pocket, taking two stairs at a time and then disappearing through the doors.

Foxy was next to me, watching him too. "He's that rich kid who lives in the woods, isn't he?" he asked. I nodded, still looking at Jimmy. "So what was that all about?"

"I don't know," I said slowly. "I just don't know."

Death called again, like a total eclipse of the sun that would not pass. It was busy that November. The school took advantage of those of us who were too old to be in school. They used us as free labor. We senior girls in Miss Wilhelm's secretarial classes did all of the typing of tests and other documents for teachers and staff. We worked in the office, answering the phone and taking attendance. We posted grades for underclassmen. Everything that couldn't be done on a Smith-Corona was done by hand.

Miss Wilhelm was a strange bird indeed. She had thick black hair that she always wore piled high on her head. She came to school wearing three dresses at a time and twenty or so bracelets dangling on each arm. She was a tall, striking woman. She loved all the men who came to repair and maintain the office equipment in her department. She also loved Mr. James, who ran the art department just down the hall. She would shed a dress whenever she knew that one of those men was about to enter her classroom. She was loud and eccentric. She took to spitting out the window whenever the impulse struck her, whether the window was open or closed! Many were the days I sat watching a big hocker slide slowly down a sun-filled window. Miss Wilhelm would try to wipe it off, leaving an ugly smear. "All right now, girls, let's get squared around here," she would boom in her loud voice, preparing to dictate a letter that we were to take down in shorthand. She had many pens and pencils stuck into that big pile of black hair, but she was constantly looking for a writing utensil. The one thing we all knew about Miss Wilhelm was that she loved each and every one of us girls, so much that she would lay down her life for us. That's what she did every day. Teaching us was her entire life. She lived in one rented room in a house on Main Street. Until she died at the age of ninety-five, she never missed a day of school.

Girls in 1963 were not career-minded. We were never encouraged to be anything but good wives and mothers. Many girls were married and pregnant before getting a high school diploma. Some never got the document. Whenever a girl became engaged or tied the knot with her beau, Miss Wilhelm was excited for her. She was always encouraging. It was very unlike what you would expect from a woman who was such a career girl herself. "Let me see your ring, dear. Oh, my, it is lovely. Who is the lucky man?" she would ask. "Why, I've seen him around town. He is handsome." The few of us who planned to work after graduation were her pride and joy. Before we left school and her class, she would invite us up to her one room for tea. She seated herself at the table in front of her very own Smith-Corona. She would have us dictate facts about ourselves as she wrote beautiful letters of recommendation. Résumés weren't done. You got a job based on your letter—or letters, if you were lucky enough to get more than one teacher to write one. The letter and your diploma went with you on a job interview.

She was in rare form that November afternoon in 1963. She was loudly dictating a letter that we took down in shorthand. Every now and then, she would lean over the desk and bat her long eyelashes at the repair man servicing a machine. He blushed and laughed. We all giggled a little as we waited for her to begin again.

As she was about to continue, an announcement came over the loudspeaker. It went into every classroom, hallway, and bathroom, the gym, and even onto the football field. It was a male voice saying, "Stand down, everyone. Please stand down. Cease and desist all activity. Principal Stanly will come to your classroom to deliver an important message." I wondered if Lucy and her wild friends had done something else to the school. Everyone sat quietly waiting, even Miss Wilhelm, who couldn't stand to be quiet or stop teaching for a minute. She would be teaching as you walked into her classroom, and she wouldn't stop. When it was time to go, you just had to walk out as she raved on. She loved what she did. When she was lost in the moment, she just kept on going.

Mr. Stanly was wearing a charcoal-gray suit and a black tie that day. He was a tall, dark, stately man, well-liked by teachers, students, and parents. He entered the classroom and stood regally before us. "Ladies," he began. "I regret to inform you that our president, John F. Kennedy, has died. He was shot through the head with an assassin's bullet this afternoon in Dallas, Texas." The room went quiet, except for the humming of our Smith-Coronas. He took a handkerchief from his pocket and dabbed at his eyes. "The buses have been called. School will be dismissed. You may sit quietly until then." He left the room, but no one moved or made a sound. We were all in shock, including Miss Wilhelm, who was fazed by nothing. She looked stunned. Silent tears fell from almost everyone's eyes. The dead silence continued as we boarded buses for home.

I ran as fast as I could to the basement stairs and into the TV room. It was crowded! Everyone was glued to the set, where we stayed for the next five days. It was only the second time I ever saw Enzo cry. Even my pa, who always had something to say, was morbidly quiet. The horror continued to unfold before our eyes when they apprehended Lee Harvey Oswald. Then he was murdered by Jack Ruby. The mystery of that awful time lives on for all who are old enough to remember. People asked one another, "Where were you when you heard the news that President Kennedy was assassinated?" I don't think there is a person alive today who cannot tell you just where they were, what they were doing, and how the news affected them. It changed our lives forever.

I felt a profound sense of loss. I couldn't move. It felt as if the whole country was suffering a kind of paralysis. My world was spinning out of control. Too many of my friends and loved ones had died. Too many were off to face an enemy we didn't know. It all seemed unreal, except for the real fear of what the future might bring. Our little community was steeped in that fear. Christmas came and went without meaning for me. Lucy came to get Antonia to go ice skating with her.

"You coming?" she said, entering the TV room where I sat in front of the set with the boys.

"I think I'll just stay here," I replied, looking straight at the set. The Captain was lying in my lap, sound asleep. I stroked his red hair. Lucy turned and left. My president was gone! It felt as if hope had gone with him. I felt empty and so alone.

⇒12⇐

Letting Go of Jimmy

LETTING GO OF JIMMY didn't happen at any conscious level. It just happened. I need to stop here and explain what happened to our relationship. I'm going to fast-forward and tell you about it.

I never saw much of him after that night on the dance floor at Henderson High. I wasn't sure why. But in truth, I thought little about him. I was too wrapped up in myself. I know that I'm jumping ahead. I need to remember how I let him go.

The following fall, I hadn't seen him in almost a year when I was invited to a house party that he and Mary Jean were giving. He was a junior, and Mary Jean and Lucy were seniors. I don't recall why they were having the party. It wasn't something they did often. Lucy had made up her mind that she was never talking to me again. She claimed that I talked to her first that night. I didn't know why she was mad at me. Who talked first just seemed so unimportant.

Jimmy looked happy as he walked around, greeting everyone. He circled the room filled with pretty, flirtatious young ladies. Mr. Tewlain was showing me around, explaining about some new artwork he had acquired. I enjoyed his wonderful, lively conversation. He always treated me as if I was an important guest in their home.

As the party died down, I sat in a low chair next to the fireplace.

Jimmy made his way to me and sat on the floor by my chair. He rested his beautiful head of dark wavy hair in my lap. I stroked it lightly. My hair hung long, almost to the floor. Jimmy took a strand and brushed it over his face again and again. He used to do it when we were in the woods together. It was a sweet little-boy thing that was so like Jimmy. Then Lucy appeared, staring at me with that angry look. "I'm going now," she said firmly.

"Wait here for me, Eve. I want to take you home," Jimmy said as he rose and walked Lucy out. When everyone was gone, he took me into his arms. We were locked in the present in our special way. I babbled on, and Jimmy listened. The clock sounded midnight. "How about a ride home on the fastest horse in all of Henderson County?"

"I'd love it, Jimmy," I replied. As we walked with our arms around each other, the moon was bright, and the air was crisp and clear.

"Let's have a quick run to the woods and sit by the stream. I can't let you go yet," Jimmy said. Midnight had us there in a flash. We sat on the rocks by the creek, under the bright moon and stars. "Did you see it, Eve? Did you make a wish on that shooting star?"

"Yes, Jimmy." Then we held each other for what seemed too short a time.

"Come on, I'll take you home," he said.

I was in nursing school in the big city when next I saw Jimmy. I had troubles of my own by then. I was looking for old friends, someone to talk to, as I walked toward the diner on the big highway. I felt confused and alone. He just happened to be walking out. "Jimmy!" I fell into his arms. He bent down and kissed me. I knew immediately that something was terribly wrong. Jimmy didn't drink, but he was clearly drunk.

"I'm just a little drunk, Eve, that's all," he said, slurring his words. I took his keys. "Come on, I'm driving you home!" We got into the shiny, black, custom-made Jaguar convertible that Charles had given him as a graduation gift that spring.

"I don't want to go home, Eve. No one there likes me anymore. I can't blame them. Let's go somewhere and park, like when we were kids." He laid his head on my shoulder. I drove to a back road near the Tewlain woods with the top down. It was a beautiful summer night.

"Tell me what's happened to you, Jimmy. You're not yourself," I said.

"Oh, Eve, nothing is good for me anymore. I lost Midnight last fall, did you know?" he asked.

"Oh, no, Jimmy! What happened?" I asked, as the tears came. He took a deep breath, and slowly he began to tell me.

"No one was home that evening when I got back from the city, where I had been helping Dad. Mary Jean was away at college, and Mom had taken Aunt Bone into the city for a few days so she could see the doctor. It was getting dark. I felt so alone. I wanted to see Midnight. I walked down to the corral, but he didn't come when I whistled for him. I jumped the fence. I started to call him. It was so quiet. In the farthest corner of the corral, I saw something black. I knew what it was, and I started running, shouting his name, but he didn't move, Eve. He didn't move." Jimmy was crying now too, as we held each other. "When I got to him, I dropped to my knees beside him, but he was already gone. He was cold and stiff. I couldn't close his eyes. I didn't call the vet. I didn't want to know what had taken his life. It didn't matter. He was gone forever. I cried and yelled out, but nothing was going to bring him back. I ran to the barn for a shovel. I started to dig a hole to bury him. The ground was soft, so I kept digging and digging. It started to rain softly at first, then it got harder. When the hole was wide enough and deep enough, I used all my strength to get him in it. I propped my feet against the fence and pushed. I covered him with the dirt. I couldn't stop crying, and I couldn't leave him, either. I lay down on top of that mound of dirt, and I couldn't stop crying, Eve, just like now. My dad found me the next evening when he returned.

"'He's dead, Dad. He's dead. Midnight is dead. I buried him here, but I can't leave him,' I said to him. I felt hot and dizzy. I didn't know how long I was there before he found me. He carried me all by himself to the Range Rover and took me to the hospital. I spent a few days there with a lung infection.

"I can't do anything right anymore, Eve, because nothing seems right," he said, looking at me with those big blue eyes.

I didn't know what to say; no man had ever loved a horse more. I dried his tears, and he dried mine. "Jimmy," I said slowly, "one of the best things about you is your relationship with your dad. Go home, Jimmy. Tell him how much you love and need him, just like you did when you were a boy. Start to rebuild that wonderful relationship again. Heal yourself, Jimmy. I know you can do it." We parted that night with a promise to keep in touch, but it was not to be. I moved to the big city permanently and started living a different kind of life. Jimmy became the model son taking over his father's businesses. He married Guinevere when they were just nineteen years old.

Years later, when Charles Tewlain was found dead in his Range Rover, I couldn't go to Jimmy and comfort him. I was a broken woman. I was no good to anyone, including myself. I loved Mr. Tewlain. He had treated me as his own child. I just couldn't go. I was steeped in self-pity and shame.

The police investigation determined that it was a heart attack and not foul play that took Charles. He hadn't returned home for a few days. He often stayed in the city, looking after business. One of his long-time employees found him in the Range Rover, in a city parking lot near one of his nightclubs. His body was cold; he had been there for some time.

Life had become so unbearable for me. I couldn't even return to Strawberry Fields to visit Pa and Mama. Finally on a cold January day, some months after Mr. Tewlain's death, I put my baby and four-year-old into the car. The wind was blowing, and a light snow was falling, as I made that drive from the big city. The snow made swirling circles on the pavement in front of me. I wiped tears from my eyes. I cried all the time now—silent tears, so I wouldn't frighten the children.

My parents were glad to see us, but it stressed them out to see me this way. I was nervous. I couldn't even sit in a chair. I paced back and forth across the kitchen floor. Mama held the baby, and Sarah-Jane sat there drinking hot cocoa. "You know," said Mama, "Lucy is staying by the home of Gladys and Howie while they are away on a vacation. She is there with her little boy and her young brother. I think you should go visit. It would be good for you to spend some time with your old friend."

I couldn't bear the thought of any of my old friends seeing what had become of me. But Lucy had always been my ground wire. I would have to face people sooner or later. There was no hope of putting my marriage back together. "Okay, Mama, I'll go."

Lucy and I were happy to see each other! We hugged, screamed, and danced around the room. We visited while our children played on the floor. When Lucy's younger brother, Mariano, came home from school, he said, "I like little kids. You two go in the kitchen and have a good visit over a cup of coffee. I'll stay in here." He was very good with children.

Sitting in the kitchen brought good memories. Lucy pulled out old yearbooks. It started to be quite fun remembering old friends. But the reunion between us deteriorated when I picked up a yearbook belonging to Lucy's brother Rocky. Jimmy Tewlain had been a senior that year. I didn't realize it until I came to the senior pictures. *The Sound of Music* had been made into a movie, and the section was called "These Are a Few of My Favorite Things." Seniors listed their favorites next to their photos. Some were very funny and clever. Jimmy's read, "These Are a Few of My Favorite Things, by James Charles Tewlain Jr. Number one (and only) riding my horse, Midnight, in the Tewlain woods by the stream under the stars, holding Eve. These are a few of my favorite things." I started to shake all over. "What is it?" asked Lucy. "What's wrong with you?" I couldn't answer her.

She took the book from me, and she knew. "Those tears are no good now. I told you years ago. I warned you. It's too late. He's married to Guinevere. He's happy. Stop it!" she demanded. "Just stop!"

I couldn't stop. I couldn't speak. I was crying for myself. I was so alone and broken. Then Lucy did to me what she had done years ago when I was dating my now estranged husband. When he humiliated me and treated me badly, I would cry to her. Once it was so bad that I couldn't stop. I couldn't eat or sleep. I couldn't even swallow water. Now Lucy was at a loss as to what to do, so she did the same thing she used to do. She pulled me into Gladys and Howie's bedroom, farthest from the living room where the children were playing. She shoved me down on the bed and pushed my head, face down, into the pillow. Lucy always had been bigger and stronger than I was. "Now you scream, damn it, until you get it all out. Nothing will change things now. I warned you. Everyone knew that guy was in love with you— except you. No, don't get up, and don't stop until it's all out. It's your own damn fault you married a man who didn't love you. You stay in this room until you get a hold of yourself. Then go home and take care of those babies. Forget Jimmy." She started to leave the room. I tried to get up. She pushed me back down. "I'll lock you in here if I have to! I've done it before!" I cried with my face in that pillow for an hour before I could pull myself together. Lucy was right. I needed to face reality and get on with my life. But I didn't know how. I was crying for myself, for my girls growing up without a father. I was crying for my husband, who was never coming back to me. I couldn't run to Jimmy.

Jimmy never said or did anything to hurt me. But the last time I saw him brought only pain and heartache. It was a gray October Sunday. The leaves fell early that year. I was a registered nurse working in a major big-city emergency room. I was working nights and back in school full-time. Driven by blind ambition to give my children the life I'd never had, I was burning the candle at more ends than the candle could provide. "You're floating too many balls in the air!" my friends said. I hardly went to Strawberry Fields. My parents were upset about the life I was living. They were getting on in years, and they worried about what would become of me.

I turned down Sherman Acres Road, but when I came to the bend, an impulse took me in the other direction. I went down what was once the gravel road, now nicely paved. I was overcome with longing to see Jimmy. I hoped he still lived in the woods where he'd said he would be until he died. "This isn't the way to Grandma's!" my nine-year-old snapped. From the day she was born, she was too smart for her own good.

"I know," I replied. "We'll get there. I want you to meet an old friend of mine." I drove slowly as I passed the path that led into the woods. I went to the end of the road, turned right, and drove about a half mile. On my right were the black wrought-iron gates, each with a circle containing a gold letter *T*. I turned in, and the gates opened. I drove to the golden stone house in the woods.

"Who lives here, Mommy?" my five-year-old asked.

"A friend I used to know," I replied. I parked, and we got out. I had a child clinging to me on each side.

"This place looks kind of scary," the girls said almost at the same time.

Jimmy came down the steps. I froze there; I stared at him. He hadn't changed a bit. He was still beautiful, with dark wavy hair, baby-pink skin, and a thin, wiry body clad in tight-fitting jeans and a white T-shirt. He came closer, and I saw those soft blue eyes. "May I help you?" he asked. Before I could answer, our eyes met. "Eve?"

"Hi, Jimmy," I said as he took my hand. "These are my daughters. We're on our way to the farm. I thought I would say hello."

"Jimmy, who is it?" The voice came from behind him. A beautiful, tall, slim blonde came from the house. I noticed that she was about two inches taller than he was. Jimmy didn't answer. She came close and stood next to him. "Oh! You must be Eve! Why, I'd know you anywhere. Jimmy talks of you often. Please, you must come inside, have tea, and talk to me. I want to hear more about the things you and Jimmy did here as kids."

I looked into her marvelous green eyes. I saw the beautiful soul of a calm, giving, and loving woman who would be with Jimmy forever. "Eve, this is my wife, Guinevere," Jimmy finally said.

I swallowed hard and whispered, "Hello, it's nice to meet you." A cold wind blew and made me shiver.

"Oh, please come inside. I'll make us some tea," Guinevere replied.

We followed them into the house. Guinevere disappeared into the kitchen. Jimmy, the girls, and I stayed in the living room. He seemed nervous as he sat in a chair, staring at me with a look of pain in his eyes. I, self-centered and vain, saw only disappointment in that beautiful face. His dream girl had gone. In her place was a woman fast approaching middle age who had gained forty pounds and had a woman's body. She was a mother, a young teenage dream no longer.

His pained look was more than I could bear. I thought I might start crying. What was I seeing? Was it pain? Disappointment that I was no longer young and beautiful? I didn't know. I had to leave and never return. "Jimmy, I really can't stay. I have to get to the farm. Please apologize to Guinevere for me." I grabbed the girls' hands and headed for the door.

"Okay, Eve, but come back, we'll talk. Please." He followed me to the door, still wearing that same look of pain. I left the Tewlain woods, never to return, and I pushed Jimmy from my mind for years.

≫13≪

Today I Met the Boy I'm Going to Marry

A SEEMINGLY BENIGN AND simple decision can change your life in ways you never expected. The types of decisions I'm referring to aren't ones that you know will change things, like graduation, a marriage, or some other milestone; instead they are ones that will keep things the same. I returned to school in cold January 1964. The world had been in a centrifuge and been dumped out as something unrecognizable. I was too old to stay in school, but had no plan for my escape. I had more than enough credits to graduate. I didn't need to remain until May. I took seven classes every semester. I did all that free office work. January was no time to look for work; it just wasn't done. The situation with Antonia at home was growing more unbearable. I didn't want to be home with her and the fighting that went on. It would mean taking care of the babies full-time. It seemed logical to stay in school. I met with the guidance counselor, who provided little guidance and no counseling. I told him I wanted to stay in school and take college prep courses. He was more than happy to sign me up, as long as I got out of his office fast, so he could drink stuff from his thermos that didn't look or smell like coffee.

I was relieved that I wouldn't be at home with Antonia. She had stopped talking to me. She only yelled, falsely accusing me of doing bizarre things. She took a white sweater that she claimed I had ruined and stuck it up on the wall of our old bedroom with a bunch of hatpins. Every time I walked by, she yelled out, "See what you did? See what you did?" No one in the family seemed alarmed by her strange behavior; I alone thought it abnormal. They thought I was jealous, and I might have been years ago, but I envied nothing about her now.

Getting into town would have been a problem if I hadn't decided to stay in school. The bus provided transportation and escape. My pa believed that cars were for work, not pleasure. I could still be in the all-schools show taking place in the middle of March. If I got a good review in the local paper, I could perform at the county fair. Life seemed okay without Jimmy and Lucy. It felt like moving on, even if I wasn't really going anywhere.

Janie Lee and Billy-John went to the justice of the peace in town and got married. They lived in a three-room apartment in Billy's parents' house. They were in love and excited about the baby that was on its way. I missed Janie Lee in classes with Miss Wilhelm. We'd always sat together with Sarah. She had helped me when I was struggling. I didn't know who would help me after her midterm graduation. To my surprise, I didn't need help. We were doing legal secretary work the whole semester. I liked it and found it easy. Sarah was only in one class with me. She had a different lunch period. I didn't see much of her, as she always went right home after school with her little brother. She lived on a farm outside of town, in the opposite direction from Strawberry Fields. I started to hang out with girls from Lake Calvin. Two of them lived right next door to each other. Barbara lived on the other side of the lake, in a new house in an up-and-coming neighborhood. They stayed at school and worked during lunch, or we talked. They weren't popular girls who walked downtown.

Tryouts were scheduled for the first week in February. I called

Bobby Ray to ask if he would play for Janet and me. "I'm sorry, Evaleene. I thought you knew I took a job at the steel mill. I'm only in school a half day. I need the money. I'm planning to buy a new car, a Wildcat. Garrison Michael is going to play for Janet, so maybe you could ask him to play for you too."

"Oh, well. I'm happy for you, Bobby." I thought he needed money to convince Lila Peace to marry him. "I don't know Garrison Michael. I can't ask him. I'll call my old friend Richard Lively and see if he can do it, or I could ask Layton Cain. But I'd hate to owe him a favor, if you know what I mean."

"Say, I've got a surprise for you," he said, changing the subject. "Did you know Johnny Cash is going to be at the Civic Center in North End at the end of the month? I can't wait to go and see him."

"He is? I'd love to see him." I loved Johnny Cash. He was the king back then, especially in Henderson County.

"Well, I'm taking you. Lila's away that week, at some mission for the church. I'd love it if you would go with Janet, Mom, and me. Dad and my little brother are going to stay home with Lonnie James," he said.

"Oh, Bobby, I can't wait. I won't sleep a wink now until I see him." Bobby laughed. It was good to hear him laugh again; ever since the death of his best friend, he didn't laugh much.

After I hung up, I called Richard, who answered on the third ring. "Hi, Richard. It's Evalina."

"Hey, friend, how are you? It's been too long since we've seen you here at Lively Manor. To what do I owe the pleasure of this call?" he said. He was always full of fun things to say.

"Well, I was hoping I could get you to play guitar for the all-schools show. It's in March," I replied.

"Oh, I'm so sorry. I'll be working evenings the whole month. The foreman's getting a surgery done. I'll take his place. It is a lot of extra money, you know," he said, sounding a little disappointed.

"That's okay, Richard. I understand; really I do," I replied. "I was sorry to hear about your breakup with Ada May. I thought you two would be getting married." I knew the stories that flew around school. Ada May's mom had made them break up.

"Well, it is for the best, I think. I'm with another girl now, and it seems to be going well. We'll probably get married," he said.

"I'm glad, Richard. Keep in touch, okay?" I asked.

"Sure I will," he replied, but it never happened. I lost another good friend.

I took a deep breath and called Layton Cain. "Oh, baby, I'd love to do it, but I'm working two jobs. I got hauled into jail, and I got to pay that child support. My ex old lady, she got herself a good lawyer this time," he said. We both knew her attorney was Sam Weeds. I was happy for her. Layton needed to support those children.

"It's okay, Layton. Janet Ray has some guy I never heard of playing for her. She thinks he'll play for me too. His name is Garrison Michael," I said.

"Oh, sure, I know that guy. He's real good. I think you'll like him," he said. Why did everyone seem to know him but me?

I called Janet Ray. She said to come to tryouts, and she would introduce me to Garrison. "I know he'll do it. He's real nice, and he loves to perform. He has his own band, you know," she said. I didn't know, but she insisted it was okay. Tryouts were held in the gym at Henderson High. Some acts performed on the stage and some on the gym floor. We were gathered in front of the bleachers. Janet and I talked about the songs we would sing. I picked a Patsy Cline song.

Janet was an excellent singer. She could sing anything, and everyone loved it. She was very beautiful. She had a steady boyfriend who I thought was quite jealous of her abilities and popularity. But she was so in love with him, and she did her best to keep him happy. He didn't want her to perform, because it was time away from him. The year before, Janet had the lead in *Oklahoma*. It was one of the best school productions. Everyone talked about it for weeks, saying it was the best play in Henderson High history.

I saw a man standing about halfway up the bleacher stairs. He was staring at me. "Janet, who is that man standing there?" I asked.

"Oh, that's Garrison," she said, smiling and waving. I couldn't bring myself to stop staring. I guess he couldn't stop either. I wouldn't have called him handsome; I think "striking" is a more appropriate description. He was very tall, well over six feet, with a slender build. His black hair was in a crew cut. He had very dark skin. His dark brown eyes were large and sparkling behind a pair of black horn-rimmed glasses. He had well-chiseled facial features, with a slim nose and high cheekbones. He was wearing black dress pants, black patent leather shoes, a white shirt, a black tie, and a red cardigan sweater. He had on a black trench coat like all the male teachers wore; it was open. He descended the stairs very gracefully for a large man. He stood very close to me but said nothing. He was so close that I could feel his breath. Just then we were told to take a seat and listen to information about tryouts and the show. We sat in the first row of seats. Garrison was next to me, but he still didn't speak. I couldn't take my eyes off of him. I looked down at his feet and thought that no one I knew had such large feet. His hands were incredibly large, with long, slender fingers and well-kept nails. He didn't look like a schoolboy. He had a five-o'clock shadow, so I assumed he was much older. When I was finally able to turn my attention to the director, every time I stole a glance at Garrison, he was looking at me. He was sitting so close that it was giving me a strange feeling I had never felt before. It was almost like riding on the Tilt-a-Whirl at the county fair. I was getting dizzy, as if I were standing on the pier at the Stayton pond, floating on the water. When I noticed him looking at me, I expected him to drop his eyes or look away, but he didn't. He just kept a steady gaze.

When Janet introduced us, he still said nothing. He only gave a slight nod. "I hope it's okay that you will be playing for Janet and me," I said. Again he nodded without speaking. He was the first of our group to perform. I was surprised when he began to play the guitar, the drums and a cymbal with his feet, and a harmonica attached to a steel frame hanging from his neck. When he sang, I knew his voice! I remembered the great band that Mama and I had liked at Patsy Hamilton's wedding last summer. Garrison had been singing and playing the drums that night. I hadn't seen him sitting behind the band. Mama and I had left after only twenty minutes.

Janet performed next, and she was splendid. When it was my turn, Garrison started to play my Patsy Cline song in the right key. I sang a pretty good rendition of it. We came together to perform so naturally, as if we'd been doing it for years. I didn't know how he knew what key I needed. He hadn't said a word. I did all the talking. Little did I know that it would always be that way.

We had practice every Tuesday night. The following week went the same as the first. We arrived at school and waited for the doors to open, Garrison kept his eyes on me while smoking a cigarette, only nodding a greeting. Every week was the same.

The night of the Johnny Cash show, I got in the back of Bobby Ray's car with Janet. Mrs. Ray was in front. The drive was forty minutes, so we had time to talk. "Janet, don't you think Garrison Michael is different? I mean, he doesn't talk or anything. He looks so much older. Is he really a student at Henderson?" I asked, trying to sound casual. But in reality, I could think of nothing but Garrison.

"Well, he's in one of my classes," she replied.

"Really? I've never seen him before," I said. Mrs. Ray changed the subject and started to talk about Johnny Cash. We were very excited to see him in person. The Civic Center was a mass of humanity. There were many people, packed in very tightly. Bobby Ray and I held on to each other so we wouldn't get trampled or lost. Janet and Mrs. Ray held on too. Johnny's performance was outstanding. After the show he shook hands with everyone, talking to all who wanted to meet him. It was one of the greatest moments in my life to meet and exchange a few words with this extraordinary man in black. He was gracious and humble. It was hard to believe I was meeting the real Johnny Cash.

As the first night's performance of the all-schools show approached, I didn't want it to end. I was afraid I wouldn't see Garrison again. I hadn't seen him at school before the show. I was obsessed with him. I thought about him all the time. When we were in the same room, I couldn't stop looking at him, and he didn't stop looking at me. I wished he would talk to me. The night of dress rehearsal, I saw an attractive woman standing at the top of the bleacher stairs. She was holding Garrison's beautiful twelve-string guitar. He was on the gym floor, fixing his drums and connecting the amplifier. I saw an opportunity to talk to him. "Garrison, I see a woman standing up there, holding your guitar. Has she come to hear you perform?" I said.

He looked at her with a sweet smile. "That's Mazy. I just found out she's my sister." It was the most he had ever spoken. Before I could ask more, he was up the steps, retrieving the twelve-string. I thought it strange that he'd said he'd just learned that she was his sister. I had brothers and a sister much older than I was, but I knew them.

Both nights of the show went well. Garrison stood very close to me but said nothing. The reviews in the school paper and the local paper were wonderful for Janet and me. Garrison was described as a man of many talents in music and showmanship. It was the first and only time I was mentioned in the school newspaper—that was usually reserved for the popular kids of Henderson High.

I felt a big letdown on Monday. There would be no more rehearsals, no more shows, and no more Garrison Michael. I knew so little about him. I liked his looks and quiet manner. I liked the way he moved and the way he looked at me. I missed the way he smelled when standing so close. He smelled like a man: Old Spice and Marlboro cigarettes. His unforgettable voice entered my dreams! During lunch hour, I was making my way down the hall in a sea of people when I saw him. He was hard to miss. He towered over everyone, and he dressed so differently. I assumed he was one of those guys in his twenties trying to get a diploma. Suddenly it was as though I was seeing Garrison two or three times a day! He would say hello and nod to me. I hadn't seen him at school before. It didn't dawn on me that it might have been deliberate on his part. Reading between the lines wasn't something I had mastered. The following week I found him standing outside of Miss Wilhelm's department, waiting for me. "I was wondering if you would like to walk uptown for lunch," he asked. I was so stunned that I almost didn't answer.

"Uptown? Sure, okay," I finally said. He held my hand as we walked but didn't speak. We went to the local coffee shop. I ordered coffee and an egg salad sandwich. Garrison had the same. We didn't eat much. He sat across from me, watched me, and slowly smoked a cigarette. After I commented on the success of the show and the warm spring weather, we fell into a comfortable silence. Garrison said nothing, only nodding a few times and continuing his intense observation. "Garrison, I just have to ask why you look at me. What are you looking at? What do you see?" I was not offended by his gaze, only curious as to why he spent so much time just looking.

He took a long drag from the cigarette and spoke softly. "No reason. I'm just looking." He continued to smoke and watch me.

"Should I go powder my nose or comb my hair?" I asked, trying to get more words out of him. He didn't reply but only shook his head, never releasing me from his steady gaze. We went downtown almost every day. Sometimes we held hands, or he tucked me under one of his long arms, and my feet would barely touch the ground as we walked. It was cute, it was fun, and some days it was even funny! On the following Friday he asked if I would go with him and hear his band on Saturday night. I said yes without consulting my brothers. I was over eighteen. I could make my own decisions.

Garrison had his own car, a little Nash Rambler in red and black. He was dressed in a red sport coat and black dress pants with red patent leather shoes. He changed into the shoes after we arrived at a roller-skating rink about forty miles south of Henderson. "On, damn shoes!" he exclaimed. They were clearly too small! He wore size fourteen shoes.

"You sound like Macbeth," I said, laughing. We were reading it in my senior literature class, and it was my favorite Shakespeare play.

"I like *Macbeth* too," he replied with a slow, sweet smile.

"Can I ask you something?" I'd finally found the nerve. He was getting his equipment out of the trunk. He stopped and looked at me. "You have a job. You play in a band and have your own car. Why are you still in school?"

Barely speaking above a whisper in that low, beautifully toned voice, he replied, "Because I just turned sixteen." He turned away. I didn't know what to say. He was almost three years my junior. I was afraid to tell him. Besides, I was crazy for him. I didn't want to stop seeing him. I loved those walks into town, tucked under his arm. I loved the way he just sat across from me and watched me without speaking.

The skaters removed their skates and danced to rock and roll music. Garrison sang almost every song. He did a drum solo that was out of this world. He had the whole place jumping and screaming for more. Clayton Summers and John Fort were the other two boys in the band. Clayton, I learned, was the same age as Garrison. They had been classmates at school the previous year, before Garrison and his family moved to Henderson. John Fort was his cousin. He was twenty years old and married to one of Foxy Benton's older sisters. John's sister was also in the band. She was a heavy girl with crooked teeth, brown fuzzy hair, big thick legs, and large swollen feet. She had no rhythm when she played the tambourine. Her brother patiently showed her the beat to every song. As slow and imperceptive as I was, I could see right away that there was something between her and Garrison. I could tell she wasn't happy that I was there with him. I sat on a chair tucked behind the band. I didn't dance, because Garrison gave a mean look to any male that tried to come near me. The band played from ten until one in the morning. Then they all stopped for breakfast at a truck stop. It was fun listening to Clayton and John talk about music and where they would play next. Garrison said little, barely speaking above a whisper. The girl, Donna, stared at me. She didn't eat a thing or talk much.

That night I knew I only wanted to be with Garrison. He walked me to the door, took me in his arms, and kissed me in a way I had never been kissed before. It was a strange, wonderful sensation that I had never experienced. I felt as if I were walking on air! For days after, when I thought about that kiss, I got that feeling all over again. What was happening to me?

The next morning Sammy and Marco were angry because I had stayed out until three o'clock in the morning. "I'm over eighteen! I will be graduating from high school, getting a job, and leaving home soon. Leave me alone! I can take care of myself and make my own decisions!" I exclaimed. To my surprise, they said nothing more. I had never spoken that way before. It felt good!

I didn't see much of Garrison at school. Since I no longer spent time with Lucy, I started to see more of Big Margaret, who lived a few farms from Lucy. I had been in school with her since first grade. When her father died, I went to the wake and funeral to show my support. We became better friends. It was just Margaret and her mother at home. Margaret did all the shopping and driving everywhere.

Soon Holy Week came. I never liked Holy Week; it always made me feel depressed that we had done such bad things to God's Son. My depression always showed on my face. Last year it prompted Gladys to declare that something needed to be done about it. She made me sit in the kitchen with her and Lucy while we had cake and coffee. I didn't have that overwhelming feeling of depression this year, but I wasn't looking forward to being home for four days with Antonia. The boys were going with the other grandparents for the weekend.

On Good Friday, Margaret called to ask if I wanted to go with her to St. John the Baptist Church in Henderson for Stations of the Cross. I was feeling lonely. I wouldn't see Garrison for four whole days. He hadn't asked me out or called, so I decided to go with her. We were kneeling in prayer when I saw a tall man in a black trench coat with a short, heavy old woman. They went to the front of the church and sat down. I knew that tall frame and graceful walk. It was Garrison Michael, who was always in my thoughts. I remembered that kiss and that strange feeling! So he was a Catholic too! I was glad, since church and my religion were so important to me. He turned in my direction, and our eyes met. I smiled, and he nodded and turned away. I thought the next three days would pass like an eternity until I could see him again.

On Easter Sunday a blanket of new-fallen snow appeared, ten inches deep. Pa made Antonia go to church with us; even Mama came along. When we came out, Antonia was gone. We saw her walking toward Carmella's house. She was easy to spot, because she was wearing a coat just like mine. It was black and white in the pattern of a Holstein cow. I had bought it when Pa took me to a discount store. Before they came along, everyone shopped at J. C. Penney, Montgomery Ward, or Sears. Places like the Boston Store were not for people of our income level. Antonia made Pa take her there for the same coat. She never liked it when I had something she didn't have first.

Spring returned on Tuesday; the snow melted. It was April, and it dawned on me that I hadn't been asked to prom. I usually got several invitations from some big landowner's kid. The last few weeks I had spent my lunch hours with Garrison. I guess everyone thought we were going steady. He hadn't asked me to the prom! I heard a rumor that his band was playing for the Freedom Falls High prom. Donna Fort was a senior there. He had known her a lot longer. But knowing that he was probably taking her to prom left me feeling a little cheated.

A week before the prom, I discovered that the girls at our lunch table didn't have dates. Laura and Linda, who lived next door to each other, said at the same time, "We should have a party that night for all the girls who aren't going!" Everyone agreed it was a great idea. Linda's and Laura's houses were open. They lived right on Lake Calvin, with piers and boats. There were about twenty-five girls at the party; I came with Big Margaret. At Linda's we shot pool on a regulation table. Linda was an expert player and taught us how. We danced to rock music, laughed, and joked about those who were at the prom. We talked about who might wind up pregnant. Then we moved to Laura's, where her parents prepared a lovely meal. It was a great evening of fun and friendship.

Laura had invited one of her friends from a high school in North End who didn't have a prom date. She and Margaret formed an instant friendship. They were accepted into the nursing program at St. Mary's Hospital in that city. They would be moving into the nurses' residence at the end of summer. I wished I was going with them. My teachers and my counselor at school had told me that I just wasn't smart enough to be a nurse. I wanted to try it, so I could make my pa proud. He was happy that I was going to graduate high school!

After prom, Garrison began to seek me out. We resumed our walks downtown. He took me with him when he played Saturday nights. His sister Mazy took us to the big city to see a play. It was my dream to see a play at a real theater in the city. Mazy and his other sister, Ann, took us to see *Barefoot in the Park*, starring Myrna Loy and Richard Benjamin. I loved it! I enjoyed being out with them. I found it easy to talk to Mazy; Ann was less friendly. I noticed that Garrison was restless during dinner, but I thought nothing of it. I was having the time of my life. It was straight out of one of my best daydreams. I was walking on air when Garrison took me home and we kissed. I felt as if my life was finally getting started. I didn't want the roller-coaster ride with him to end.

Graduation day came so quickly! It was senior ditch day, and then we got out a week before everyone else. I came home from school to find Antonia sitting in the upstairs kitchen with her tablet of paper. She smiled at me. "So what do you want for your graduation open house?" she asked.

"I didn't know I was having an open house," I replied. Typical—Antonia hadn't spoken a civil word to me in months, and now she was planning my party.

"Well, let's plan this thing. You only graduate from high school once," she said, and we went to work on the details. "This is Pa's idea. He wants you to have the party." The next two weeks went by in an enchanted blur. Many kids came out to the farm to say good-bye and wish me well. I hadn't known that they cared one way or another about me. Some really nice guys in my class wanted to marry me! It hurt to turn them down. It was the first I had known that any of them knew I was alive. I went out with one I liked, but I knew my heart wasn't in it. My heart was with Garrison Michael.

Strawberry Fields Farm was busy the night of the open house. It took place on Friday after graduation. Roger Manning and his brother Danny came. I think Roger still wanted to date Antonia. They were such gentlemen. I was flattered. Many of my other classmates came in and out the whole evening. Big Margaret and I laughed and talked together about our plans. I felt bad that we hadn't been closer. I felt a little disappointed that Lucy, Jimmy, and Mary Jean weren't present. Garrison Michael called to say that his band was playing out of town and he would see me the following Saturday.

Only wealthy people gave gifts for things like graduations and birthdays. I was delighted to receive nice things and twenty-five dollars in cash. Even my pa bought a gift. It was a gift almost every senior girl got: a beautiful Lane Cedar chest called a "hope chest." Every girl had to have one. It was some kind of rite of passage into adulthood. You were to fill it with things for the home, like linens and towels, china dishes and silverware. Marriage still was not on the horizon for me, but I was thrilled that Pa wanted me to have such a nice gift. I don't know how much hope that chest ever held for me, but it was and still is a beautiful piece of furniture.

Garrison came to the farm a week later with a gift. He was dressed in a suit and tie. He had to play that night and wanted me along. I was impressed with the gift he gave me, even though I thought his mother or one of his sisters picked it out. It was a necklace and matching bracelet. I loved it. Mama had struggled to buy me a class ring—the only piece of jewelry I had owned until then! I was a little put out later when I saw that Donna Fort was wearing a very similar set. Garrison seemed especially proud to have me with him. I was wearing a baby-pink, tight-fitting, sleeveless dress and the white necklace and bracelet he had given me. I wore white high-heeled shoes, which made me a little taller: the top of my head came to Garrison's shoulder. He kept his arm around my waist when we went outside during the band's breaks. I put my arm around him. It felt like we were a real couple. It was the first time I had a chance to really talk to Clayton and John. It was kind of fun that they were interested in knowing me. "So why don't you do a few songs with us?" John asked. "I think it would add some variety and a little class to the band."

Before I could answer, Garrison answered for me. "No," he said firmly. I was astonished. I turned to look at him. "Only one of us will perform," he said. "It will be me."

I didn't know what to think, so I didn't respond. John seemed to feel the tension, and he changed the subject. My singing, with the band or anywhere, was never discussed again. By now I knew that Garrison was the youngest of twelve children He sang with his sister Nancy who was a few years older than he, but he never asked me to join them. I just assumed he didn't like my voice. My singing ended when I started dating him.

Over the next few weeks, it became apparent why Antonia was being nice to me. She wanted the two of us to join a local young adult club called Rural Youth of Henderson County. I really didn't want to, but she insisted. She didn't drive, so I would take us to group activities. Once we started attending, I could see other reasons why she needed me. I attracted lots of attention from the males in the group. Some of it came to her without offending the other female members. Club meetings were every week, along with dances, baseball games, and volleyball games. Antonia was a good baseball player. I was a good dancer. I knew the latest dances that she had missed when she married Warren, who was no dancer. It saddened her to realize that she had missed so many teenage things. She was very interested in an older man in the club. Redmond was probably at least thirty. The club members ranged in age from eighteen to forty. It wasn't long before she started to date him. I couldn't see what she saw in him. He drank too much and was kind of crude and loud.

Many nice young men belonged to the club. Some wanted to date me. It was nothing serious. I was having fun. Most were older children of big landowners who hadn't found anyone to marry in high school. Adulthood in rural America left little time for courting a mate. It was still called courting. Harold Anderson wasn't tall, but he was muscular from farm work. He had blond hair and blue eyes. He was shy and very quiet. At a gathering in the basement of Prince of Peace Church, many were playing a game called Truth or Dare. Someone gave Harold, whom everyone called Mickey, a dare. I was paying little attention. Mickey took me in his strong arms and planted a big kiss across my lips. I didn't know what to say. But everyone cheered, and all the guys shook his hand. I guess it was something he had wanted to do since Antonia and I joined the club.

I had a date almost every night that summer. Life was moving fast. I always tried to hold out for a call from Garrison. I hoped we would be dating each other exclusively. Although we dated a lot, I knew he was seeing other girls. It seemed like he was courting me all summer. We went to movies in North End and to nice restaurants. I went with him almost everywhere the band played. I was invited to their home for dinner. Garrison was the youngest. I found it fascinating that only recently had he learned the names of all his siblings and their spouses. Only a few were unmarried. He had nephews and nieces older than he was, with children. I was amazed to learn that Mazy was the eldest girl. She looked so young. She was divorced, with three little children. They lived with Garrison, his parents, and his other sister, Ann.

Although he said little, I loved my dates with Garrison. I did most of the talking, but he seemed pleased and content. He gazed at me with love and admiration, which led me to believe that I was special to him. He was fascinated by my long hair and my small frame. He would run his long fingers through my hair. He could hold me in the air with one hand. When he encircled my waist with his hands, his fingers touched. I didn't find it offensive.

Garrison had a job as assistant to the foreman on the Highlander farm. It was a commercially owned grain producer. It had two large houses, and there was an apartment above one of its many large barns. The foreman let Garrison stay there when he was drinking. The boys in the band all drank. The foreman was married and had six children. I think they covered for each other when they were hung over and couldn't work. Garrison took me to see the place. The houses and apartment were lavishly furnished. The job and playing in the band made it seem as if Garrison were rich. His parents were schoolteachers who had retired recently. They raised their ten surviving children on that income.

Garrison gave me many gifts over the next six months. It was turning into a courtship that every girl envied. The gifts weren't just anything; they were nice, well thought-out things, mostly articles of clothing. One evening when he came to pick me up, he draped a lovely, soft white sweater across my shoulders and said, "You're always cold. I thought you might need this." The cardigan was beautiful. He bought me many things; he bought me an orchid sweater with a matching straight skirt that fit as if it had been made for me! There was a soft, fuzzy goldenrod sweater with matching stirrup pants, so popular at the time. Antonia gave me a blouse with blue, red, and goldenrod flowers on a white background. The whole ensemble was stunning and fit perfectly.

"How do you know what to buy for me?" I asked. "Does someone help you choose these things? They all fit so well, as if made just for me!"

"Nope. No help. I pick them myself," he answered slowly, shaking his head. He never told me that I looked good. He never said I was beautiful. He only looked at me with that steady gaze of perfect contentment, like a farmer admiring a lush field of grain or a colorful sunset.

On a hot July night, we were sitting in Garrison's car. The sky was clear, with many stars in the heavens. We shared many long, powerful kisses that made my body tremble all over. It felt like being on a ride at the fair. My breath caught in my throat as his breath got heavier. Then, holding me tight, he whispered in my ear, "I love you, and I want you so much." I pulled back and looked deep into those large, dark eyes that seemed to swallow me up.

"I don't know what to say, Garrison. I think we may be too young."

He opened the car door, got out, picked me up, and said, "I'm not." He walked to the front door, set me on my feet, and walked away. I wasn't sure what had just happened, but something had changed. Every date ended the same way. Garrison's kisses made me feel things in parts of my body I didn't know existed. He would tell me that he loved me and wanted me. Slowly I realized that what I might be feeling was sheer sexual desire, the first such experience of my life. I had such mixed emotions about it. I didn't want to lose Garrison. I didn't want him to stop loving me. By August I was desperately in love. I never wanted him to stop telling me he loved me. I never wanted to let him go. I wanted Garrison to be mine! I quit going to the Rural Youth Group; Antonia had landed her man. I wanted to stop dating other guys. I looked at the calendar and noted that I had been dating Garrison nonstop for the last three months.

Everyone I knew smoked. No one thought it was bad. Garrison smoked a lot. I thought smoking would make me feel grown up. I lit one of Antonia's cigarettes and walked around with it in between my fingers. It made me look sophisticated and worldly. Antonia watched as I put it out in the ashtray. "If you're going to burn up all my smokes, you need to know how to inhale."

"Okay, show me," I replied.

"Look, this is what you do. Just watch me." She took a long drag. "Okay, you try it," she said, handing me the cigarette. I repeated just what she had shown me, and immediately I became very weak, dizzy, and nauseated. I had to go lie down. I felt sick all that day and night. Why would anyone want to smoke? I vowed never to do it again. It was the strangest thing I had ever experienced. I felt almost sorry for people who did it. It looked worldly on TV. But I knew I would always look like a girl just off the farm.

I was lost in my own thoughts when Marco came flying into the upstairs kitchen and found me listening to music. "Evie!" he called. I jumped, not knowing what I had done. He had a steady girl. Last spring Carmella made me go with her to the little truck stop on the highway where she worked, so we could check her out. She wasn't very pretty, but I could see Marco with her. She was serious and down to earth.

"What is it, Marco? What have I done now?" I asked, a little on edge.

"Nothing, stupid. I just need to talk to you," he replied, rather irritated.

"Please don't call me that anymore. I think we're adults now. We can talk without name-calling," I said. I marveled: that grown-up statement had come from me.

"Okay, well, here's the scoop." He straddled a kitchen chair and folded his arms over the back. "I'm going to marry my girlfriend next month, and you will be standing up in the wedding. Here is twenty bucks. Go buy yourself a dress," he said. I was stunned!

"What kind of dress, Marco? Can I talk to Bell and find out what she wants me to wear?" I asked.

"Yah, sure, call her if you want. Her number is 2768," he said, rushing from the room.

That night I was at Enzo's with the children. I wanted to call Garrison and ask him to come over. I hadn't seen him in a few days, and I missed him. The house was quiet with the children asleep. His sister Ann answered. I knew by now that she didn't care for me. "Garrison's in bed, asleep. He suffers from migraines. Mazy gave him some medication that will make him sleep. I'll tell him you called." Then she hung up.

I dialed Bell's number. There were no prefixes or area codes; four numbers were all you needed to dial to call a person. In the early

1960s the world wasn't obsessed with the telephone. It was only used for important information. "Bell, hi! It's Evalina—you know, Marco's sister. Thank you for asking me to be in your wedding. I'm happy to do it. But tell me, what are the dresses going to be like? I understand your cousin will be standing up also," I said.

"Yeah," she said. Bell was a woman of few words.

"Well, don't you want us to have dresses that match? Maybe we can all go shopping together?" I said, trying again to get a sense of what she wanted. "It might be fun to have a girls' afternoon outing."

"It doesn't matter. My cousin's a guy. He won't look good in a dress. Buy whatever the hell you want," she said, and she hung up the phone.

For the last month I had worked as a waitress with Antonia at the diner on the highway. I had some money. I probably could have worn my graduation dress. It was lovely, if a little too plain for a wedding. It was baby-blue taffeta with white eyelet lace over it. It had a square neckline, low in the back, and was fastened with four big blue taffeta buttons. The skirt was an A-line style. I needed to buy something more appropriate for the occasion. Pa drove us into North End, where I found a beautiful light pink dress in taffeta with a full short skirt and a white chiffon overskirt. The top was fitted pink taffeta with a low scoop neck and no sleeves. It was quite grown-up-looking. Since it was a little too long, Mama cut a piece of taffeta from the bottom and made a headpiece that looked like a queen's crown. She added a piece of pink nylon netting, and it was perfect.

I was spending a lot of time with Marco. I went to church with him and helped him make arrangements for the wedding. I don't think he had been to church in years. My guess was that confirmation was the last time. He didn't like dropping money into the collection box or listening to a sermon. He would rather be out flying his plane, which he had built all by himself. I wondered how Bell could stand him, since he was so cheap. I was sure he still had his First Communion money. The priest gave him hell for not attending church regularly. He wasn't pleased that Marco was marrying a non-Catholic.

There would be no High Mass, only wedding vows exchanged on that appointed September day. The wedding was finally all set.

I only worked at the diner for a few hours in the afternoon. I slept in most mornings on the couch in the living room, dreaming of Garrison Michael. I woke with a start when Pa came upstairs, yelling for me. "You no sleep a like a this all day and go out and stay out all night with all kinds of man. It is time for you to get a job and work to support yourself. You dress up now. I take you for a job." I had tried to get a job; all summer I went out looking. I tried for secretarial positions, but I was just too slow at typing, and I was a poor speller. There were no machines that spelled the words for you. Every job went to someone more qualified than I was.

"Where are we going, Pa?" I asked when I got into the car.

"Where you think? I take you for job," he said. I knew the building when we pulled up. It used to be a chicken coop. When Carmella first married Norman, they moved into that little apartment on this old farm. It was still owned by Mr. Hess. The coop was now a nursing home for the elderly and infirm who were unable to care for themselves.

We went inside. I was given an application to complete. My pa sat in a chair across from me with his hat in his hands. I sat at a wooden table. I set down the pen and took a deep breath. The door to the small office opened, and an elderly woman in a starched white nurse's uniform and cap entered. She looked very dignified. Behind her was an elderly gentleman with snow-white hair. He was plump and rather quiet, letting his wife do all the talking. She held my high school diploma and my letter from Miss Wilhelm. "So you're Evalina. How do you do? I'm Mrs. Liva B. Dunn, RN, owner of this establishment," she said. She turned to the man. "This is my husband, Mr. Dunn." He nodded. "Well, stand up, girl, so I can have a good look at you." She walked around me with her hands behind her back, eyeing me as if she were buying livestock. "Kind of puny, aren't you, now?" My heart sank. I knew how badly Pa wanted me to get a job. "But!" she exclaimed loudly, making me jump. "You have this, and this is golden." She was waving my diploma in the air. "I will hire you right now, if you want a job as an aide. I have no opening for a secretary or a receptionist."

"But I have no training as an aide, Mrs. Dunn. I'm afraid I won't be much help."

"Nonsense!" she shouted. "I'll train you myself. I can make a good aide out of you, and I believe I can make a good nurse out of you too. You'll start in the morning."

"But Mrs. Dunn, I'm afraid I can't do that," I said. "I'm standing up in my brother's wedding this weekend, and I'll need to be there for the whole thing." Behind me Pa took a big, deep breath, almost a gasp.

"It's okay," she said. "Supporting your brother is important, so you can start after the Labor Day holiday. Besides, you will have to do some shopping for a uniform, orthopedic shoes, and a good foundation garment that I expect you to wear every day to support your back. It is a necessary and vital piece of clothing in our business. The classroom is upstairs. Here's your key, the list of things you need, and the addresses where you can purchase them. I'll see you bright and early on Tuesday morning at seven." She left the little room, with her elderly husband following. At the door, she stopped. "I can only pay you a dollar per hour, and you will work a forty-hour week on a rotating schedule." She lingered a moment, waiting for me or my pa to protest, then left.

Pa gave a long sigh of relief. "Come, we go get Mama and go for the things." Ever since he'd retired on the last day of June, he had been driving me nuts, going here and there to shop or to visit his Italian friends. I wondered how he would pass the winter with no more work to be done in the gardens. The last of the livestock and chickens had been slaughtered. He wasn't planning to buy more.

Rehearsal for the wedding was Friday night. It was short and sweet. I liked Bell's cousin Raphe. He was a small, nice-looking man with a sunburnt face and bright blue eyes. His hair was copper red and wavy. He greeted me warmly. When it was over, Father Strickland kept Marco and me. We weren't going out for dinner; Marco was too cheap. "Since there will be no Mass for your wedding, Marco, I expect you to make a good confession right now. You will come to early Mass in the morning and receive the Body of Christ." He turned to me. "Evie, you will also make a confession and attend the Mass with your brother."

Marco's face was red with rage. It was too late for him to back out. The wedding would be called off if he tried to leave without doing exactly as Father Strickland asked. "All right, Father, I'll make sure we're here," I said. He went into the confessional. Marco entered first and was in there a fairly long time.

"I'll wait for you in the car," he said as I passed by him on my way into the confessional. We weren't doing face-to-face confessions yet. I wanted to sit with Father Strickland and talk about everything that was bothering me. He was a good priest, and he cared about us kids. He spent time with us at dances and other events.

After the usual "Bless me, Father, for I have sinned," I started to tell Father Strickland about my troubled feelings and how my body was responding to a young man that I was dating, whether I wanted it to or not. When I was finished, I braced myself for a dose of guilt and shame. I was expecting a long lecture on purity, chastity, and their importance. But that wasn't what I received.

"This may be the one, my child," he said. "This may be the man you love and marry. Pray, my daughter. Pray to God for guidance and strength. Keep yourself pure and clean until the day he makes you his wife. Go now, and sin no more." In the quiet church, I prayed harder than ever. I hadn't thought of Garrison as being the man I would marry. After Father Strickland said it, a light seemed to go on inside of my head. Maybe I was ready for marriage. Garrison told me on every date that he loved me and wanted me for his own. I would ponder all these things in my heart for months. I prayed every night for an answer from God. I always felt His presence and knew He heard me when I prayed. He answered most of my requests over the years. The answers weren't always what I wanted, but they seemed to work in the end.

The wedding was at ten o'clock that bright Saturday morning. Everyone entered the church, forgetting the bride in her uncle's big Cadillac car. I was trying to get her out of the backseat when her uncle came to help. Bell had the biggest dress, but it was gorgeous. She looked lovely. The wedding only took about ten minutes. It was attended by a few friends and relatives from both families. We drove to Fienberg's Studio for pictures. Mrs. Fienberg was happy to be doing pictures for another Rosario wedding!

When we arrived at the farm, Mama was in the upstairs kitchen, running around, clucking like a chicken. "Come, you help me with the table," she said. She was trying to get the traditional wedding breakfast of fried chicken and spaghetti on the table.

"Where's Antonia?" I asked. "She should be helping you." Mama didn't answer; she just kept working. I tied an apron around my beautiful pink dress and got to work. When it was time to take our seats, I slipped off the apron and sat next to Raphe. Father Strickland took his place at the head of the table. Marco and Bell sat at the other end. After Father Strickland led us in prayer, Mama ran around the table, serving us.

That evening at the reception, I walked into the hall on Raphe's arm. He was so sweet, and he was a gentleman. He told me funny little stories throughout dinner. My new sister-in-law was very loud and drank her beer right from the bottle while yelling greetings to all her friends and family from across the room. I was very surprised, since Marco was so strict with me about behavior in public. "Watch what you say and how you act, so you don't bring shame upon the Rosario family," he always said. His choice of a bride puzzled me. After the meal was done and the cake was cut, the gifts were opened. No one opens gifts at a wedding today.

The first dance was just Marco and Bell, and then Raphe and I joined them. He was a good dancer and kept up his steady flow of fun and interesting conversation. Since I wasn't allowed to bring a date, because it would interfere with my duties as the maid of honor, I thought I would be spending a boring evening by myself after that dance. "Well, I guess that does it for the duties of best man and maid of honor," I told Raphe. "Thanks for serving with me. You made it really fun."

As I turned to go, he took my hand and said, "Where are you going?"

"Well, I thought you would want to go sit with your wife and children, maybe dance with her," I answered.

"But I'm with you tonight," he said. "How would you like a drink? Let me get you one. What would you like?"

"But your wife is there. What about your wife?" I asked.

"Come on, let's go to the bar. I'll order you a highball." I could still see her sitting in a corner, tending to her three babies; it made me uncomfortable. But after a few seven-sevens, I forgot all about her. I danced the night away with Raphe, forever the selfish, unthinking girl.

Marco went to live with Bell on New Moon Lake, in a house owned by her father . When he came by a week later to collect his things, I begged Mama to let me have his room. It was the best room in the house. I loved it. Before Marco returned from the army, it had been our guest room. It had two windows that faced the backyard. The late afternoon sun filled the room. It had a big walk-in closet and blond oak furniture. "Please, Mama, let me have Marco's room," I begged. "I haven't had my own room for over a year. I just don't get enough sleep on that couch. Please, I need my own space. How will I get enough sleep and hold down a job?" Antonia started to move her stuff in. She was mad when Mama told her I would get the room. It meant she would stay in my old ten-by-ten bedroom with the boys. She had assumed that they would stay in there and that she would have Marco's room off the kitchen, right by the front door. It would have been convenient for slipping Redmond in and out in the middle of the night. She was madly in love with him, but I couldn't see why. He was nothing but a drunk, as far as I could tell.

I guess I'm no judge of good marriages, because Marco and Bell had a great marriage and remained very close. I admired that lasting, loving relationship.

I didn't see the pictures from Marco and Bell's wedding until more than five years later. I had the formal-looking one, where we all looked like statues or a lineup in front of a firing squad. Now I stared in amazement. Was I really that stunning-looking woman? I excused myself, went into the bathroom, and looked in the mirror. The same ugly face stared back. We were at Marco and Bell's home. Everyone was watching home movies and slides. I got up several times to look in the bathroom mirror. The face in the mirror and the woman in those pictures didn't look the same. It made me feel afraid, but I didn't know why. I stopped looking at the little movie screen. I looked past it, hoping no one would notice.

Before the wedding, Pa had taken Mama and me to North End, to department stores that Mrs. Dunn had recommended for the things I needed for my new job as a nurse's aide. The uniform, a light-blue nylon shirtwaist dress, was too big. The store didn't have one small enough, but Mama thought she could cut it down and make it fit. They didn't have a corset small enough. I ended up getting a girdle that fit more like a pair of Bermuda shorts. It had stays on it to hold the white nylons I had to wear. Only one pair of orthopedic shoes came in my size.

Tuesday morning I unlocked the door to the classroom with my special key. I found Mrs. Dunn there already, with books opened and waiting. She taught me how to take temperature, pulse, and blood pressure, as well as how to measure a person's respiration. I learned to make a hospital bed, even if a person was in it. Then I learned about catheters and feeding tubes. I didn't know eight hours could go by so fast. I took to my lessons quickly and easily. I liked learning how the human body works.

Since we only had one car, Pa drove me to work. During that first week, I spent my whole day in the classroom with Liva B. She was in her glory with a student like me, who wanted to learn everything. I had never had a one-on-one teacher, let alone one who was so inter-ested in teaching me things. I don't know how Liva B. knew I would do so well under her tutelage. I still marvel at how she took a chance on me and made me into a useful person. For the first time in my life, I felt that I could really do something and do it well.

⋙14⋘

Seeing Christ in the Faces of Others

T HERE WAS NO HARDER work in life than farm work, I thought, until I started working on the floor at the nursing home. I was put in the men's ward to start, because they were pretty much independent. For the first few weeks, I took their vital signs and made beds. I served them breakfast and lunch, if they didn't eat in the dining room. I helped them into the tub for baths. I thought seeing a man naked would scare me to death. I thought washing their private parts would make me throw up or run from the place, screaming. To my amazement, I did it with ease. Some of these men were loud, rude, and very demanding. They were unpleasant, dirty people. They used some of the foulest language I ever heard. Until then, I thought Pa, Enzo, Sammy, and Marco held top honors for swearing. Even Sammy and Marco didn't use that kind of language. My pa's cursing I wasn't quite sure about, because he swore in Italian. The words translated to "dogs," "devils," and "the blood of a potato." Another favorite saying of my parents translated to "May you get diarrhea." I guess that in rural Italy, to bestow such a curse on someone was the worst thing you could wish on them.

After that first four weeks, I was given a cap to wear. I learned to wind my long hair on top of my head in a bun. The cap fit over it. I worked with a plump old lady called Radamore Bolder. "Now, don't you work too hard or too fast, honey. I don't want Liva B. knowing how good we got it in this ward. If she knew, she'd make us rotate to the other units, where the care is heavy." I was good at the job. I was efficient. I wanted Mrs. Dunn to be proud of me, so I worked my tail off. Radamore hated me and told the others that I was a no-good show-off trying to get points with the boss.

The women working there ranged in age from girls a few years younger than me to a few grannies like Radamore. None had a kind word for me. It hurt to be left out of their little circle. I was very sad, and it showed on my face. Liva B. and her husband might have been old, but they didn't miss a thing. "Okay, spill the beans now. Why the long face?" she asked.

"Well, none of the others who work here seem to like me. They don't talk to me," I complained.

"Stay away from all of them!" she yelled. "They're nothing but a bunch of hussies, and they won't amount to anything. You, on the other hand, have it all. You're smart and pretty, and you have a high school diploma. It's more than any of those low-down, dirty women will ever have in their whole lives. You listen to me. You'll have your lunch with me, Mr. Dunn, and my daughter-in-law, the supervisor."

I worked my way up to being in charge of the comprehensive care unit with the sickest patients. I became depressed and lonely. The patients never got well. They never went home, and some left in bags in the undertaker's station wagon. Working all those long hours, for many days in a row without a day off, was getting to me. I worked four Sundays before getting a Sunday off. I went to church at five forty-five in the morning. It was a low Mass ending at six-thirty. I had time to pray before walking to the home, a block or two away.

"Why the long face, my dear?" Father Strickland asked.

"Oh, it is just my job, Father. I mean, I like the work and every-thing, but sometimes those patients are just too hard to deal with," I complained. I was thinking of Mr. Spalding. The day before I had given him a bath, and the floor was wet. I accidentally fell into the tub with him. He started to yell, "Bladder spasm! Bladder spasm!" And he wouldn't stop until the RN that covered for meds gave him a shot to calm him down.

"Oh, my child, look at you!" Father exclaimed, taking my chin in his hand. "You are young and strong, so capable. God has granted you many gifts. You must see that these people have little and they need you. Please promise me you will look for Christ in each and every one of them, for He is there. Look into their faces, and see our Lord. Remember you are doing God's work."

"Yes, Father, I will," I said. I began to find it easier to help the people in my care. I realized my life was a whole lot better than theirs and that I should try to make the world a better place for them. They couldn't leave the home and go places. Few had family that came to see them. Every day for them was just like the one before. Time seemed to stop in that place.

I was more in love with Garrison Michael. I had stopped dating almost entirely, so I could be available when he called. Now that I was working and he was back at Henderson High, we had less time to see each other. I had my own room again, and I could dream of him as much as I wanted. I realized that if I hadn't made the decision to stay in school, our paths might never have crossed. My life might have been much different without him. Things changed drastically that year after high school. I didn't see my town friends anymore, or the girls from Lake Calvin. They were married, having babies, attending college, or working.

We got paid at the home once a month. I took my first check to the savings and loan in Henderson and opened an account with half the money. I went to the new discount store and spent the rest on clothes. The quality of the merchandise was good. Things were still made in America then. I bought things that would last and work with other pieces I already owned. I purchased a straight black skirt, winter white stirrup pants, several sets of underwear, and black nylon stockings, some with seams and some with patterns on them. I purchased a new, very grown-up full-length coat from the Boston Store.

My birthday was the following month. I wanted it to be a special night for Garrison and me. We were to go to my cousin Mike's restaurant for dinner. I was excited, because Garrison bought me so many lovely things, and I wondered what he would do for my birthday. I knew his parents and sister Ann only tolerated me. I got on well with Mazy because she was a nurse, and we talked a lot about our work. But Garrison's sister Nancy was a different story altogether. Although she was married, she seemed to prefer Garrison's company more than her husband's. He was just as taken with her. When they were together, their behavior bordered on rude and obnoxious. It was the only time I heard Garrison speak more than a few words. He spoke softly but laughed a lot more and seemed more relaxed around Nancy. He was nervous when I told him about my cousin's restaurant. He said he would go if Nancy and Hardin came along. I wasn't looking forward to spending my birthday with people who didn't like me. I was upset and getting a bad headache, but I agreed to the arrangement. Since starting work, my weight had dropped. I was back down to less than ninety pounds. I did hard manual labor but remained unable to eat causing me to suffer from these frequent headaches.

Nancy and Hardin waited in the car while Garrison came into the house. He presented me with a box wrapped in shiny pink paper and a pink bow. He was silent and jittery as I opened the gift. It was a lovely pink pullover sweater with a boat neck and long sleeves. A small box in the larger one contained the most beautiful necklace I had ever seen. Hanging on a long silver chain was a crystal in the shape of a large teardrop. It flashed all the colors of the rainbow when I lifted it out of the box. "Oh, Garrison, this is the most exquisite gift I have ever received in my whole life!" I exclaimed. "You really don't have to take me out to dinner if you don't want to. You've spent too much already."

"I want to take you to dinner. It's okay," he replied in his usual quiet way.

"Well, I kind of have a headache anyway," I said.

"I think it's because you haven't eaten and it is getting late. I'd love to see you in this sweater," he said.

"I'll go and change." I went into my room and put on the pink sweater with my tight black skirt, black nylon stockings, and black suede high-heeled pumps. The crystal necklace sparked against the pink sweater and made me look as if I were going to the Ritz.

Garrison was dressed in a black suit, white shirt, and black tie. Together I thought we looked very classy. Nancy grumbled from the backseat, "I don't see why she can't just have a birthday at home. Why do we have to go to some dive and spend money on food we probably can't eat, anyway?" My head really started to pound, and my stomach was very upset. I knew that my cousin's place was quite good. I was afraid they wouldn't like it and the whole evening would be as uncomfortable as it was at that moment. Garrison didn't respond to her whining, and neither did Hardin. My mood went from happy to black.

Things improved when we arrived at the restaurant. I asked for Cousin Mike. He came out immediately and greeted us warmly. He was quite the host, telling me I was more beautiful every day. He shook hands with Garrison and Hardin. He seated us in the VIP dining room and had his wife come out to say hello. She was a quiet woman but kind and loving. We had a male waiter who couldn't do enough for us. He served drinks and then took our orders, saying we were to have anything we desired; it was on the house—boss's orders. When dinner was served, Mike came out with his little concertina. He played and sang, to everyone's delight. Garrison really enjoyed the music, and he relaxed. My headache got better as I ate my shrimp dinner. Even Nancy and Hardin seemed to be enjoying themselves. "Well, I take back everything I said. I guess this is about the nicest place I've been in. Your cousin's a great guy," she said, slurring her words. Since the beer was free, she drank a lot of it. I really didn't care whether she liked the place. I wanted Garrison to have a good time. He had told me that he loved and wanted me. I just couldn't bring myself to tell him I was in love with him too. I hoped to do it on Christmas. I thought I would have the nerve by then to say those words. I was planning to invite him to midnight Mass.

I was glad that President Johnson was elected that November. I really didn't blame him for President Kennedy's death, like most people in Henderson County. I thought he was kind of crude, like most farmers, but he seemed to be doing a good job for the country. I especially liked his wife. She was smart and refined. When he seemed to get a little out of hand or obnoxious, she would just lean over, put her hand on his knee, and give him a look that said, *Lyndon, you need to tone it down.* He always took her nonverbal advice. I liked the way he respected her judgment. His daughters were smart and attractive. One of them had a strong desire to be a nurse. I was disappointed when her parents discouraged it because nursing was considered beneath someone of her position. It was troubling. I thought all men were created equal, but some were more equal than others. It reminded me of my low position in life. I worked hard, and I paid taxes, but I could see that I was still a second-class citizen. In the eyes of the community, I was just another daughter of an uneducated immigrant.

Garrison's parents, I could tell, thought he was dating far beneath his level. They felt my parents were basically uneducated. Before he retired, Mr. Michael had been the principal of a school. They were very quiet people who talked about the weather and crops. Sometimes they discussed books they read. I had to sit quietly during these discussions. They thought I didn't read or have knowledge of good literature. Mazy was the only one who didn't act as though English was my second language.

In my family, you always knew where you stood with everyone. There was no question how we felt about each other and the world around us. We disagreed on many things, but we all talked to one another. In Garrison's family, feelings and emotions were never discussed. No one spoke above a whisper. I was always the loudest one in the room. There were many other differences between our families.

Alcohol was served openly and often in our home. No one was ever denied a drink. Sammy was the only one who drank to any extent. But in Garrison's family, his brothers and at least three of his sisters had serious problems with alcohol, yet it was never allowed in the Michaels' home. Mr. Michael once said he'd never tasted a drop of liquor in his life. It didn't occur to me that these differences had any affect on our relationship.

Garrison called to invite me to dinner at their home on Christmas Eve. He said it would be a fancy dinner of steak. Christmas Eve was a day of abstinence from meat, and my mama kept the tradition of serving fish on the night of our Savior's birth. "I don't think I can be there, Garrison," I replied. "On Christmas Eve we're only allowed to eat fish. But you will come to midnight Mass with me, won't you? We can come back here after and exchange our gifts under the tree." Reluctantly he agreed.

After dinner I dressed carefully. I put the top of my hair up in curls. I had a new winter-white dress made of a soft, fuzzy material, with a high waist, a scoop neckline, and long sleeves that ended in ruffles at the wrists. I put on nylon stockings that sparkled as I walked in my black pumps.

Garrison arrived carrying a very large box wrapped in white and silver paper with a big red bow. We set the gifts under the tree and left for church. It was always crowded at Mass on Christmas Eve. Garrison kept looking at me. "Is something wrong?" I asked.

He only shook his head and said a quiet "Nope." That night, as the choir sang and church bells chimed, Garrison held my hand, gazing at me. I turned and looked deep into his eyes. The moment had come.

"I love you, Garrison," I said. I saw so much emotion in his face. At first there was surprise and then relief. He held my hand to his lips and kissed it.

"I love you so much, Evie," he said. I was floating on air the rest of the night.

We sat under the tree to open our gifts. I had agonized over my gift for Garrison. I finally decided on a white shirt and a beautiful mohair sweater in a deep tan color with a brown tie. I had kept going back to the Boston Store to return what I had bought and to choose something else, until my pa said it was the last trip he would make with me to exchange the purchases. "So, do you like it? Will you wear it?" I asked anxiously.

"Of course, I love it," he answered. He seemed very pleased. He wore the set often when we were together. When I opened the big box, it was a perfect gift! It was an electric blanket. They were fairly new on the market and very expensive. I just couldn't tell him enough how much I loved it. I was always cold, with extremities carved from ice. It was the most wonderful Christmas in all my memory.

Things weren't so good for Antonia. Redmond came to the farm drunk and without a gift. The boys were with Warren for Christmas. They spent every other Christmas with their father. I heard her crying to Mama the next morning. "I don't know why she gets everything. Did you see that big box Garrison gave her? Red said that because he got me this big engagement ring, he didn't have any more money. I've had this ring for a few months. It isn't a Christmas present."

"I don't know what to tell you, Antonia," Mama said. "You have chosen him. You must deal with him."

As the New Year approached, I realized that Garrison hadn't asked me out for New Year's Eve. The band was playing at the roller rink down in Denton. Perhaps he was spending the evening with Donna Fort. One of the older ladies at work asked me at the last minute if I would be her nephew's date for the evening. He was staying with his aunt for the holidays, and they were all going to a party. Since he was from New Orleans, they wanted him to meet people and have a good time. I accepted the invitation.

I dressed in one of my most beautiful dresses. It was my favorite. Mama had purchased the designer dress, made in New York City, from a neighbor. Mrs. Hand was a wonderfully gentle woman who lived in a newly built house near the Tewlain woods. Lots of city folk were buying land out in Sherman Acres. She had a mentally retarded son, and she ran an organization that raised money for the care of people like her boy. She had been in the clothing business and had connections to the fashion district in New York City. Clothing shops there donated dresses that couldn't be sold, because they had been used for window display, and Mrs. Hand sold them out of her home in her designer dress shop. She would let anyone try on dresses and purchase them at low cost. Most were very tiny. Farm girls couldn't fit into them. I had my pick of any one I wanted. I chose a champagne-gold satin brocade dress with a plunging V neckline and off-the-shoulder capped sleeves. It was tight-fitting on top, with a bow at the waist. The flare skirt came to just below the knee. It was extremely elegant with gold high heels.

My date thought I was a model or an actress from the big city. He was very nice, but I think he knew I wasn't having a good time. I was miserable without Garrison; I didn't understand why he dated other girls when we were so in love.

A few weeks later, he called again. At the end of the evening, when he drove me home, Garrison began kissing me. He told me how much he loved me and wanted me for his own. "I just don't understand, Garrison," I said. "If you love me, why do you date other girls? I love you so much, and it makes me feel bad."

"Well, it's time you show me you love me and go all the way with me," he said. "If you don't do it, then I'll just keep getting it from girls willing to give it."

"Garrison, I can't do that. I'm a Catholic, and so are you. I have to be married," I replied.

"Well, if that's your answer I won't stop seeing other girls. And as far as I'm concerned, you can see whomever you like. Good night," he said. I was sure that I wouldn't see him again.

Since I worked so much, my pa, who didn't seem to ever have enough to do, started cleaning my room. He washed my sheets, changed them twice a week, and hung up my clothes. He mopped the hardwood floor and shook out the lavender rug that lay beside the bed. He made the bed every morning. He made my breakfast before driving me to work. When I cashed my check, I would keep some money out and put it in my drawer for safekeeping. The rest he took to the bank.

It was against the rules to get personal calls at work unless it was an emergency. I was working a split shift when I received a call from Garrison. "I'm sorry to bother you at work, but I have to see you. I called your dad and told him I would pick you up from work today. Is it okay?" he asked.

"Sure, Garrison. But what's wrong?" I asked. "I haven't seen or heard from you in a while."

"I'll tell you tonight when I pick you up," he said and hung up. I really didn't want him to pick me up from work. I smelled like the home after working there all day, cleaning up human waste. When I got in the car, he seemed so glad to see me that I forgot he hadn't called in a long time. Garrison parked the car at the top of the drive at Strawberry Fields, took me into his arms, and kissed me tenderly, saying he missed me and couldn't live without me. I felt so happy and relieved. "I hope you can help me," he said. "I'm in a bit of a jam."

"What is it, Garrison? You know I love you and want you to be happy," I said eagerly. I was so glad to have him back.

"Well, I got caught speeding. I was driving drunk, and they took my license. I don't have the money to pay the ticket and get it back," he replied, hanging his head as he spoke. In those days, drunk driving wasn't a big deal, even when you were only sixteen, like Garrison.

"It's okay, Garrison. I have some money in my dresser drawer. I'll go get it. We can go to the justice of the peace, pay him, and get your license back," I said without a thought. It never occurred to me that he was just using me. "How much is it, anyway?" I didn't ask why he didn't have the money. He played in the band almost every weekend. Since his summer job at the Highlander farm was over, he worked at the dime store in town as a stock boy after school.

"It's the maximum one hundred dollars," he replied. That was almost a full month's salary for me. "I only need fifty. I got the rest."

"I'll go in and check my drawer. I'm sure I have it," I said. I went in through the upstairs door, went straight to my room, and pulled open the drawer, but there was no money in it. I was frantic. "Mama, my money's gone!" I shouted. "It's gone, and it was right here in my top drawer!"

"Quiet down. Pa took it to the bank for you this morning," she said, coming out of her room, where she had been reading a magazine. I began to cry loudly. "What a is wrong with you?"

"I need that money, and I need it now!" I continued to cry as my pa came into the room. "Why did you do it? Why? Why?" I yelled.

Instead of getting mad at me for yelling at him, poor Pa just looked very hurt. "I just thought I was helping you. Tomorrow is your day off, and the bank is open. I will take you to get the money." I felt really bad for yelling at my parents. I never did that sort of thing anymore. They were both a little surprised.

I washed and dried my face and went back out to Garrison. "I'm so sorry, Garrison. My father took the money to the bank. Maybe you could come tomorrow after school. I'm off, and I'll get the money and go with you to pay the justice."

"That would be great!" he replied. "I'll see you then. I got to go now." He drove off, leaving me standing there. I was happy that I would get to see him again the next day.

In a small town like Henderson, everyone knew everyone else's business. It wasn't long before word got out that I was seen going into the JP's office with Garrison. "What a sap you are!" Enzo yelled at me a week later. He told Pa and Mama what I had done. "I thought you were smarter than that, but I guess I was wrong."

"It is none of your business. Garrison's already paid the money back," I answered.

We had been dating again, but the way Garrison kept begging me for sex made me very uneasy. I wanted him as much as he wanted me, but my Catholic upbringing stopped me. Every time he brought it up, my mind flashed back to Antonia in the hospital with her body swollen beyond recognition, her face a moon with slits for eyes, and I shuddered. "Well, I think we should both date other people," he said.

Henderson had a new community center just outside of town. It had a big outdoor pool, a gym with a stage in it, and a kitchen. It was the perfect place to have any type of celebration. John Fort wanted the band to hold a dance there and sell tickets for a dollar. They planned to decorate it and advertise in order to become better known in the area. It cost one hundred dollars to rent the place. They spent another fifty on decorations and signs to advertise the dance. They paid an off-duty town cop to be present for the whole thing. I helped them decorate. We worked nonstop. At ten that night, we still had stuff to do. The chief of police came and made us leave. He went out to his car to wait. John Fort had a brilliant idea. He noted that the cop hadn't counted how many of us were there, so he hid under the stage. We got into our cars and started to drive away, and the cop locked the doors and left. We circled around town a few times until he went in the opposite direction. We returned and parked the cars in a field behind the place. John was there to let us in. We worked until one in the morning, getting everything ready. It was great fun. Best of all, we were never found out.

The next night I dressed carefully in a beautiful cream and powder-blue crepe dress with a full skirt and long sleeves. I had blue sling-back heels and a blue headband. Garrison said nothing about the way I looked. When I descended the steps from the upstairs porch, one of my heels came off. I was wearing nylon stockings, and I hopped on one foot so I wouldn't tear them. Garrison came to my rescue. He stooped down and reached for my foot, holding it in his hand. It fit perfectly. "You've got the smallest feet I've ever seen—like a little kid's," he said, slipping my shoe back on. He made me turn around for him a few times but said nothing. That admiring look was the only way I knew he liked the way I was dressed.

The boys in the band and the ones helping to run the event all stopped moving about and stared at me. I smiled at them and said hello. Breaking their silence, almost every one of them said something to me about the way I looked. It would take me another year and a half to learn my fatal mistake. Garrison didn't speak to me or look at me the rest of the night. Acknowledging compliments from other males was a capital offence to him. I grew tired of just sitting there. I danced with a few guys I knew from school. That was another large mistake. The dance was a big hit, but it rendered no profit or new business. At least two hundred kids and young adults came. The police started turning them away when the center reached its capacity. After expenses, there was nothing left. I didn't see Garrison again for a few weeks.

When he graduated in May, I bought Garrison a beautiful men's watch with a chain-link band. His other girlfriend gave him a cheap two-dollar Timex. When I gave him the expensive timepiece, he took hers off and wore the fancy one. I was hurt and upset.

Graduate nurse

⇒15⇐

The Graduate Nurse

MARCO AND BELL'S BABY was born in March. Mama said nothing about the fact that it had only been six months since the wedding. The baby cried a lot, which upset Bell. She didn't like it when Marco came to the farm to do things for Pa. He was still working hard to get out of poverty and didn't have much free time. Since I had been working, I saved most of my money to buy a car. Marco was going to help me choose one. The afternoon he came to take me to a large car dealership in North End, a light snow was falling. I saw the car of my dreams: a 1957 Chevy, black and white with turquoise on its back fins. What a snazzy car! Marco test-drove it. I thought it ran just fine, and I liked the price. It was four hundred and seventy-five dollars; I had the money to buy it. "Oh, Marco, I like it so much, and I have the money. Don't you think I should buy this one?" I asked.

"You don't need to buy the first car you see and spend all your money," he said. I was disappointed when we left without the cool '57 Chevy. Marco was so frugal. I was even more let down when he showed up at the farm a few weeks later with a car he said was mine, telling me I owed him three hundred dollars. The big, white, four-door 1959 Chevy Bel Air was a stick shift, which I wasn't used to driving anymore. "Be sure you practice in the driveway before you take her out on the road," Marco warned as he climbed into Bell's waiting car. With the baby screaming in the backseat, they drove off. Well, I had a car now, even if it wasn't the Chevy of my dreams. My pa continued to drive me to work.

On Easter Sunday, everyone gathered at the house at Strawberry Fields for the noon meal of ravioli. Mama always made them by hand. "Mama and me, we going to make a trip back to the old country to visit for one last time before we get too old," Pa said. I couldn't believe what I'd just heard. I wouldn't be going with them, although they made it clear that they wanted me along.

"Perhaps you will meet a handsome and rich man on the ship going over, or we could go to Rome. I have cousins there who work at Banca di Roma, and one works at the Vatican. I sure they would be glad to show you around and introduce you to some nice young men," Mama said, trying her best to talk me into taking the trip.

"Well, I can't leave my job," I said quietly. I could have left it in a heartbeat! It was Garrison I couldn't bear to leave behind for three or four months. I was afraid he would forget me. I was happy for my parents. Pa hadn't returned to his homeland since coming to America in 1929. Mama went back only one time when I was in fifth grade. I hoped I wouldn't have the depression and loneliness I had suffered then.

I remembered that terrible day in the winter of 1962 when my grandmother died. Mama cried for days, but she didn't return to Sicily for the funeral. Her brother had written her a letter to tell her of it, and the funeral was long over by the time she received it. He hadn't telephoned; I'm not sure he had a telephone. That day I had come home from school and gotten the mail. It was a fairly nice winter day, cold but sunny. I was planning to go for a long drive with Elizabeth and her mother.

"I'm sorry, Elizabeth, but I can't go out with you and your mom today," I said when I opened the door to her. Mama could be heard in the background, wailing mournfully. "I just found out my grandmother in Italy has died." My mama saw her mother only one time, in 1956. It was the only time she was able to visit her in her adult life.

As spring turned into summer, there was an problem so obvious that we couldn't miss it, not even me. Antonia was pregnant! It was obvious by the end of June, when Pa and Mama were about to embark on their journey. "I have things under control, Mama. I'll handle everything," Marco assured them. "You guys leave on the first of July, as planned." I did my best to ignore it. I didn't want any of my friends or Garrison to know. I was ashamed. I didn't want Garrison or other guys thinking I was easy.

Marco's plan to get out of poverty must have been working. He purchased his first house in Henderson. He turned it into a two-flat and rented out both units while continuing to live at his father-in-law's. He paid cash, and he did the renovations himself. The upper level of the house was for Antonia and Redmond once they married.

I was spending more time with the girls from Lake Calvin when I wasn't with Garrison—rather, I should say, when he was dating other girlfriends. I tried dating Laura's older brother, Raymond, but my heart belonged to Garrison.

After my parents left, I began to get sick. I had never been sick; I'd only had bad cramps and that thing with my esophagus. This was different, I couldn't breathe through my nose anymore, and my head felt stuffy. It was hard to concentrate on anything. A friend suggested that I see an ear, nose, and throat specialist. The doctor said I had two problems. I had a bad infection, which I must have picked up working in the nursing home. He said it was a bacterium common to those places. I took antibiotics for two months before it started to improve. Also I had lots of allergies. The doctor had a vaccine made so that I could give myself allergy shots. All of it was a lot of work and a lot of money. For the first time in my life, I began to sleep all the time. I felt so tired that I stopped being so upset over Garrison. I felt so bad all the time. After a date with Garrison I went in and went right to bed.

In mid-August I was exhausted. I came home from work and took a shower. I lay down on my bed and went right to sleep. I didn't hear it start to rain and thunder. Sammy was at work, and he usually went out afterward, or he did a double shift. He didn't get home until really late, if at all.

Sometime during the night I could hear someone calling my name. It sounded very far away. I was so tired that I didn't care to respond. The voice grew louder, and then I heard a loud booming that I couldn't ignore. I sat up in bed. It was very dark, as if I were in a black room—or maybe I had lost my eyesight! I shook my head and listened. I heard the voice calling me again. It was Garrison's voice. I tried to stand up. Why was it so dark? I managed to walk to my bedroom door and unlock it. I heard Garrison's desperate cry for me. The front door was open, but the heavy storm door with the screen was locked. I always locked the doors now that I was alone. "I'm coming, Garrison. What is it?" I called out.

"Open the door! Oh God, are you all right?" he yelled. I didn't know he could produce such a loud voice.

"I'm just fine," I said. "I was asleep. What on earth do you want? It's the middle of the night." He came inside and took me into his arms, lifting me to him as if I were a sleeping baby.

"I'm so glad you're safe," he said, holding me tight. "When the storm came and all the electricity went out, I tried to call you, but the phone was dead. I thought something must have happened to you." This was the longest sentence I had ever heard Garrison utter.

"Garrison, what you are talking about? It's the middle of the night. I was sound asleep. What storm?" I inquired, still a little foggy from sleep.

"A tornado passed through here. Well, actually it was several of them, and they left a path of destruction three miles wide and one hundred fifty-five miles long across this state and the next. Are you saying you didn't hear any of it?" he asked.

"You know that medication makes me so tired. All I want to do is sleep. Put me down so I can turn a light on," I said.

"Honey, there are no lights—no one has them. The storm has caused a major power outage for two states," he said. "I don't think you can stay here by yourself. You need to come home with me," he insisted. "We don't have power either, but at least you won't be alone."

"I'm not leaving Strawberry Fields, Garrison," I said. I looked down at my glow-in-the-dark nurse's watch. "It's after three, and the sun should be rising soon. You can stay with me until then, if you like. I think I can find a candle in the kitchen drawer."

The sun came up to reveal massive devastation and destruction everywhere. President Johnson declared the area a national disaster zone and sent in the National Guard to help clean up. Except for some debris, downed tree branches, and the power being out, Strawberry Fields was virtually unharmed by the storm. It took the electric company five days to get the power back on in Sherman Acres. All the food in the freezer had to be thrown out. I had dinner a few times with Marco and Bell, and sometimes I went to Enzo's or to Carmella's. Mostly, I just didn't eat.

I returned to my new doctor and asked him what was in those pills that caused me to sleep like the dead. He felt it wasn't just the pills but also the infection causing such fatigue. He was amazed that the farm and I were left unharmed. He worked even harder to clear the infection. I felt depressed, and I just didn't seem to care about anything.

In September Antonia married Redmond at our church in New Moon Lake. It was all arranged by Marco and the pastor from Redmond's church. I didn't go to the wedding; I had to work. In truth, I didn't want to go. I went to the church and helped with the reception that evening. "Well, it's about time you showed up," Bell said as I went into the kitchen to help with the meal. I still felt unwell, and I really didn't care what she thought.

My one-year anniversary of working at the home passed with no raise or recognition. The previous spring, Liva B. had declared that she had taught me everything she knew. I had the infection, which was lurking throughout the home. I had slept through the biggest natural disaster ever to hit the Midwest. All of this, I was sure, meant that I should move on with my life.

I went to the university extension in North End and applied for their practical nursing program. All my teachers, and other adults in my life, had done a good job of convincing me that I could never be a real nurse. The only one who thought otherwise was Liva B. Most people thought she was just old and crazy. I cried hard a few weeks later when I received a rejection letter from the school, stating that I failed to meet the minimum test score for entrance.

A young woman named Pat worked part-time in the comprehensive unit, and sometimes we talked. She asked me why I was working there, when I could work at a hospital for more money and under better working conditions. She told me about the big hospital in West End. "You should go there for a job. My sister worked there and loved it."

It was on a large parcel of land set apart from the rest of the town. I met with the director of employment, and I was hired that day. I gave Liva B. a two-week notice. She said, "Well, you can come back whenever you want. You're young and need to try different things, but you really need to go to nursing school."

"Thank you, Mrs. Dunn, for all you have taught me." I left quietly. When my parents returned in November, I was glad. I didn't like coming home to an empty house. It was a busy month. My friend Sarah from high school married her longtime boyfriend. Janie Lee was standing up for her, and I took her to Mrs. Hand's for a dress.

Since Janie Lee was very tiny, it was easy to get a beautiful gown. She was the perfect matron of honor for Sarah. I was glad that Mama came with me. Garrison refused to go. "I don't go to weddings unless I'm playing the music. I'm not going to just sit around with you," he said. It was nice that Mama got to visit with Sarah's mother, renewing their long-standing friendship.

"I can't believe our babies are growing up so fast," she said to Mama after greeting her warmly. The small wedding gave me ideas for my own. I got another scrapbook and started to write things in it.

That November, Bobby Ray married Lila Peace. I went to the wedding alone. Garrison said he had to play and refused to go. Lila was a beautiful bride. I was so happy for them. I sat with Mrs. Ray and the rest of her family at the reception. "Evaleene," she said, "I'm so worried about those two. You know they haven't even been on speaking terms for the last two weeks. I don't know how this marriage will last." In my heart, I knew that Bobby Ray loved her so much that he would do anything to keep her forever.

Later, I lost contact with them and the whole Ray family. I saw Janet at the bank in New Moon when I went to make a car payment. I was a nurse and living in the city. She was pregnant with her second baby. Our only other contact, or near contact, was years later, after the breakup of my marriage. I was in Henderson during the fall festival when I heard Janet singing over the PA system. "That's Janet Bledsoe singing," Carmella said. "Weren't you good friends with her at one time? She used to be Janet Ray. She sure has a beautiful voice." I couldn't bring myself to go talk to her. She had been the one who introduced me to Garrison. That same day, I ran into Lyle North. He had married a girl in Lucy's class, and they had a little girl about the same age as my younger daughter. Lyle made a big deal over seeing my beautiful daughter and me. Mrs. North was not happy. I did my best to be polite and get away from them quickly.

That busy November month of weddings also brought a new baby for Antonia and Redmond—another boy. He was exceptionally beautiful! I thought they were so lucky to have three boys. Redmond continued to drink and grumble about all the mouths he had to feed. They never had money for rent or food. I wondered how long Marco the Thrifty would put up with the rent not being paid.

Lucy and I started to see each other again. She completed her course to become a beautician and worked at a shop in Henderson. She settled into her relationship with Big Randy. In late December I was going with Garrison to band practice at the Forts' in Freedom Falls. Lucy called, wanting to do something that night. "I thought maybe we could go raise some hell, like old times," she said.

"Well, Garrison has band practice tonight, and he asked me to go with him. Why don't you come with us? I always wanted you to hear his band," I replied.

"Randy has some big church thing tonight. I don't want to go with him and his parents. I guess I could come along. It might be fun," she said. I was glad, because I wanted her and Garrison to get along. So far I hadn't been successful in making that happen. I'd really made things tense last spring when I suggested that Garrison take Lucy to the prom. The rules had changed. If you weren't in high school, you couldn't attend the prom. Freshmen and sophomores weren't allow to go either. Garrison's other girlfriend was a freshman. At first Lucy considered it. I was never sure what really happened when he asked her, because she said no.

We picked Lucy up and headed for the Forts' home. Everything seemed to be going all right. I guess Lucy and I together could be a bit much. We talked and laughed loudly, doing a few of our imitations of famous people. After practice got under way, I didn't know if Garrison was nervous or just unused to having someone there he didn't know well. He completely ignored us! He became totally wrapped up in conversation and even flirted with Donna Fort. He went into her bedroom with her. We could hear them laughing and talking together. I was so embarrassed and humiliated. I felt just awful. The ride home was very uncomfortable.

I guess all of his bad treatment finally got the best of me. When he took me home, I hung my head and began to cry. I really didn't mean to; it made me feel even worse about myself. I started to go for the door, but he stopped me. His reaction to my tears was something I'd never expected. I really didn't understand it. I thought he would be mad and tell me to stop it, or maybe even apologize for being rude. Instead of being uncomfortable with my tears, Garrison was delighted with them. They fell from my eyes like water from the pump house. He was fascinated! The tears rolled down my face and landed in my lap and on my hands. With the wonder of a child seeing his first new toy on Christmas, he watched me cry. He touched my tears and tasted them. He ran his fingers through them gently as they covered my cheeks. The more he took pleasure in them, the more I cried. "Garrison, why do you hurt me so?" I asked. "I love you so much, and I try so hard to make you happy, make you love me back, but you just treat me so badly." He didn't answer me or apologize. He started kissing me all over, as if we hadn't seen each other in a long time.

After that night, however, Garrison didn't even try to treat me better; he only treated me worse. He left me at tables by myself. He would go to other tables, sit with other girls, and flirt with them. I cried more, and he seemed to enjoy it more each time I broke down. I decided to ignore his rudeness. I started to talk to other guys and even dance with them. He behaved even worse toward me. One night he left me at a dance and took another girl home. I had to get a ride from one of the other guys in the band. Every time one of these episodes occurred, I was sure our relationship was over. Then Garrison would beg me to come back. I never could resist him. There were times, I have to admit, that I was the one calling him and asking him to come back to me. Garrison was fascinated with my emotions. He had grown up in a home completely devoid of them. In his house no one laughed, cried, hated, or loved. Everyone spoke in the same quiet way. Feelings were considered the work of the devil.

My job at the big psychiatric hospital was good. I didn't have to work as hard. I had hoped to be on the medical surgical floor, but I was trained by the hospital and placed on the women's double-locked psych ward. Some of the patients were dangerous, and some had even committed murder. I wasn't afraid of them. I realized that the women had very sad lives. They were just lost and confused. They didn't seem to matter to anyone as people, only as wives and mothers. The institution viewed women that way, reflecting the world in the mid-1960s. A lot of the women shouldn't even have been locked up.

I liked my head nurse. She was very smart, and I learned a lot from her. When I asked her about the way these women were treated, I was stunned by her answer. "It is a man's world out there, missy— you better learn that. You need to learn how to navigate it, or you will have a miserable life ahead of you. Learn to manipulate a man, so you won't end up in a place like this, dearie." Why were women not as good as men? We were paid less, and our opinions on things didn't matter. I began to see that all men were not created equal, especially the female ones. There were few men in the psych hospital. There was only one small ward for them, which had twenty-five beds. There were over two hundred beds for the women. It was a Catholic institution. The first floor was for convalescence of sick priests and nuns. Most of the priests were alcoholics, young and able-bodied. The nuns were old women that could no longer take care of themselves; most of them were in their eighties and nineties.

There were licensed practical nurses there; an LPN wore a white uniform decorated with a pin with a lamp emblem, and a nurse's cap with a gray stripe. I asked one of them where she had gone to school. "The program's in the city. It's part of the public school system, and it's free if you live there. I'll give you the address. You can apply, but you might have to move there in order to get in." In early summer I took the train into the city all by myself to take the exam at one of the city colleges. I didn't sleep for four weeks until that letter finally came. It wasn't a rejection letter, exactly. It only asked that I come to the school and talk with Mrs. Bingham, the admissions coordinator for the practical nursing program. I was nervous. I didn't want to go alone. I cooked up a story in my head to tell Carmella. I called her to ask if she would accompany me to the big city.

"Hi, Carmella, I was wondering if you could go to the big city with me on the train next Thursday. I need to pick an insurance plan my job is offering. I have to go there and sign some papers. I missed the representative when he was at the hospital," I said.

"If I get Norman's mother to babysit, will you buy me lunch and pay for the tickets to ride the train? And can we ride in a cab too?" she asked.

"Sure I will. Dress up pretty, because there're all kinds of people down there. We need to try and blend in," I replied. Who was I kidding? We certainly didn't blend very well. We looked just like who we were: two country girls in the city for a day.

Mrs. Bingham was the kindest lady I had ever met. She was warm and friendly. "Come in, and please sit here," she said, and I took a seat across from her at a small table in her office. "I'm not allowed to show you your test scores, but I think I have your problem figured out. I don't think you read well, my dear," she said.

"I'm not sure I know what you mean," I replied.

"Well, you only completed half of the test. I think it's because you don't read well," she continued. "I have a plan for you that I think will work. I've signed you up for a reading course at one of the city colleges. Here's the address and time you are to be there. It's six weeks long, once a week, and it's free. I want you to return here and retake the exam. What are your thoughts, Miss Rosario? Are you willing to try it?"

"Yes, ma'am, I am. I want to be a nurse," I said.

"And you will be, my dear. You will be if you just work a little harder than anyone else." Mrs. Bingham showed me to the door. I left with the envelope she placed in my hand. Once a week I took the train into the city and attended my reading class from five until eight. I loved the train ride and the city. I felt so grown up. The class was fun. I actually started to like reading. I bought books I had always wanted to read. With the new method, it was so enjoyable to read a whole book that I did it almost every two weeks.

My troubles with Garrison continued, like the summer heat. Some of the girls from Lake Calvin admitted going out with him when I wasn't around. I was hurt; they were my only friends. I finally let them know my feelings. They didn't do it again.

The Michaels' home had been the rectory for the old Saint John the Baptist Church before the new one was built. It was a large, stately house with six bedrooms, a wraparound front porch, and a large backyard that faced the street behind it. There was a gravel drive wide enough to park several cars. Janie Lee and Billy-John moved to an apartment in a house directly across the street from that backyard. When I was there, I could see the house clearly. I discovered that it was the perfect place for Garrison to meet women for late-night, low-cost rendezvous.

Judy Sands was a friend of Garrison's sister Nancy. She was a wild woman with a reputation for sleeping around. She was twenty-four years old. I discovered her there with Garrison one night as I left Janie's apartment. I was very distressed. I tried confronting Garrison. "Well, as long as you aren't giving it to me, I'll get it where I can," he replied. I thought he had learned his lesson when last September he was caught having sex with Donna Fort up in his room. They took his car away for a week. Donna was no longer welcome at the Michael home, but I was sure that he was still seeing her for sex.

With nowhere else to turn, I went to the one person in the world that I thought I could rely on and trust. I went to Mama. I found her in her room, reading one of her many romance magazines. I sat down and poured my heart out to her about my troubles with Garrison. "I don't understand why he does these things. He knows I'm Catholic. I won't do it until I'm married. How can I keep him from going with other girls? I'm sure he cares for me as much as I care for him."

"Oh, the men. This is just how they are. They will have relations with all kinds of women, but they won't marry those kind. You just keep yourself pure for the one you marry. Men want to marry a woman who is untouched, not one that has been used," she told me. I couldn't imagine my pa being like that. I comforted myself with the fact that I was the marrying kind, as Mama suggested. I turned a blind eye to Garrison's behavior with other women. I had the sound advice of Mama and my priest. My friends told me the opposite. I decided that friends weren't the best people to give guidance. Lucy told me what a little fool I was, but I didn't believe her.

Lucy quietly married Big Randy at the Baptist church where his father was a minister. She was expecting a baby. For as wild as she had been, she settled into married life very quickly. I didn't see much of her after little Randy was born.

Life started changing fast for me when I returned to the big city and retook the exam for the practical nursing program. Mrs. Bingham was so pleased with my results. "I knew I was right, my dear. I just knew it!" she exclaimed. "Now, you have a lot of things to do before you join your class. You need a physical exam and a dental exam. You need vaccinations as well. Here is the address of the bookstore and the store where you will need to go for uniforms. Oh, I'm so excited for you, dear, and I'm so proud. You will make a great nurse! Don't you worry about the residency requirement. I had it waived, along with the out-of-city fees. You don't have to pay a thing. Just show up every day and do your very best!"

Changes came to Garrison's life. After graduation from high school at the tender age of seventeen, he enrolled in college that fall, but he didn't even make it through one semester before dropping out. He hated school. That winter he stayed at home with his mother, and they played cards. It never occurred to me to think it was strange behavior for a grown man. Finally John Fort got Garrison a job at the factory where he worked. I don't know what transpired between them, but the following summer, Garrison left the band. He joined with a couple of older men who played music at Moon Over the

Water Lounge in New Moon. The band played all kinds of music. It seemed to suit Garrison's talent. Since he looked so much older, no one questioned a teen playing in a bar and drinking. He had access to even more women. When I went with him, I sat in the background. He was surrounded by older women.

Garrison didn't want me dating anyone else, but he wanted to continue seeing girls for sex. I made up my mind to stop seeing him. It hurt me so badly that I started to have headaches again. I made another trip to the city for my books and my uniforms. I signed all of the final papers. I was all set to start the program the following month. Coming home on the train, I was feeling lonely, and my head was pounding. I went to a phone booth in the train station and called Garrison. I just had to see him one last time. I learned that he and his band were going on tour for six months. Their agent had booked them into clubs throughout the South and the Midwest. "Hi, Garrison. I was wondering if I could see you tonight. I know you're leaving to go on tour and all," I said softly into the phone.

"Where are you?" he asked.

"I'm in the train station at North End. I just got back from the city. Everything is set for me to start nursing school next month," I said. There was a long pause. "Look, Garrison, could you meet me at my cousin's restaurant for dinner? It's my treat. Since we're going our separate ways soon, I thought it might be nice to see each other one last time."

"I'll meet you there in about an hour," he said and hung up the phone. I felt really bad for asking him to see me. I just didn't know why I couldn't move on. But I felt really good too, at the same time. I didn't know how to get along without him. I wanted him even when he treated me badly.

My cousin was his wonderful, charming self. He gave me two aspirin for my headache and told me to order whatever I wanted, on the house. He brought Garrison to me when he arrived. We were seated in the dining area with the big water fountain. I sat there rubbing the side of my head. "The headache will go away soon. Cousin Mike just gave me some aspirins," I said.

Garrison sat close to me and took my hand. "I just think you need to eat," he said softly. My guilt over calling him started to fade with my headache. He had come when I called, so he wasn't ready to let me go yet either. We had a lovely dinner. He gazed at me and stroked my long hair. A few times, he said very quietly, "You know I love you, don't you?" I was lost in his spell. We left the restaurant and walked to a large park in the middle of North End. It was a beautiful, warm night for October. I was turning twenty-one soon. I had to start growing up.

"I just know going to nursing school is a good move for me. In a year, when I'm done, I'll be able to get a good job and my own place," I said, more to reassure myself. I wanted to show Garrison that I too could move on.

"Old Man Waters is giving us a going-away party at the lounge on Saturday night," he said. "He's going to serve food and everything. Why don't you come with me? I'm feeling good about this road thing. I have a feeling it's going to be our big break." We sat on a park bench, holding hands. Garrison was more excited than ever about his career.

I dressed carefully for the party. I wanted Garrison to be proud of me. I wanted him to remember me while he was away. Carmella had been to Mrs. Hand's basement shop and purchased a dress that she later gave to me, saying, "It's just too old-looking for me. I think it would be all right for you." I should have been insulted: she was thirty-five years old. She always bragged about looking younger, but she was fourteen years older than me. The dress was very unusual! I guess if a woman in New York City wore it, no one would take notice. In Henderson County it was very noticeable.

I put the top of my long hair in curls, sweeping it up on the left side and pinning it with two rhinestone combs shaped like stars. The rest of my hair curled down in big ringlets to my waist. I put on my garter belt with a pair of silk stockings that shimmered like silver. The dress was short, a good four inches above my knees, with a high waist. It was tight-fitting, with a scoop neck and capped sleeves that fell off the shoulders. It was made of a silver material that sparkled as I walked. The thing that made it so unusual was the black lace over-skirt attached to the dress from the high waist, slit open in the front. It was a little longer than the dress, giving it the look of a negligee rather than a dress. In the mid-1960s the only place you would have seen black lace other than a house of ill repute was on a widow's head at her husband's funeral. Black lace was only for widows and whores; it wasn't for a young woman from a small farm in Sherman Acres. I was taking a terrible chance as I slipped on my silver slingback high heels. Those high-waist dresses sure made my breasts look even larger. I applied a little eyeliner and some red lipstick. I put a little blush on my high cheekbones. My teardrop crystal glistened as it hung from the silver chain around my neck.

Garrison said nothing as he entered through the upstairs kitchen. He stared and then made a motion with his hand for me to turn around. I put my hand on one hip, pulling open the black lace, and I turned around slowly for him a few times. He kept staring at me. "Well, is it all right?" I asked. "Should I go and change?" He shook his head.

The place was already very crowded. There must have been about one hundred and fifty young people, more women than men. We walked around the lounge, greeting people. Garrison was holding my hand. I hoped he was proud of me. Since I was unsure, I walked behind him a step or two. The bar was loaded with men, since women were not permitted there without a male escort. Some of the men shook his hand and commented on his fine female friend. Someone asked, "How did you land her, Garrison?" "Some women look good in black lace," I heard another say.

He took me to a table by the stage and left me. He moved on to his adoring female fans, who were lining up to greet him. I was the perfect accessory for Garrison the rock star. At some level I became aware that we made a stunning pair. It was equally apparent that he hated the attention I received from other men. I don't think it was the attention he didn't like; rather it was the way I responded to it. If

I acted as if I hadn't noticed or heard the comments, he was fine. If I smiled and responded to any one of these admirers, I could expect to be humiliated and left sitting at a table alone. I sat on a high stool at that table, ordered a drink, and sipped it slowly. I sat straight, with my head held high, and crossed my shimmering legs as the black lace fell away, cascading down the side of the chair and exposing more leg than probably was appropriate.

"Whoever said black lace was just for widow ladies? My God, Evaleene, you sure can turn a man's head." Layton Cain came up behind me, taking in every inch of me. He was dressed in a black tux, like Garrison and the other musicians. I didn't know he would be performing.

"Hi, Layton," I said. Not wanting to encourage him, I gazed around the room.

"I swear you could make a grown man weep for mercy," he said as he ran his fingers up and down my silky leg, giving me a chill. I shivered. He threw back his head and laughed. "I bet you ain't as cold as you want us all to think, now, are you?" I gave him a mean stare. "Okay, I'm goin'," he said, putting both hands up. "The booze is free tonight, so I'm ready to enjoy it."

I sat alone for a while and then made a trip to the ladies' room, to kill some time and check myself in the mirror. When I came out, Foxy Benton was standing there in a stylish gray silk suit that flattered him. "Why the hell are you still with that guy? He treats you like shit, and everyone knows it. They laugh at you behind your back. What's wrong with you, anyway? Don't you know you're much better than that? Wake up, lovey. Smell the horseshit around here, and get out while you can," he urged. I knew he was right. I felt ashamed for the way I always let Garrison treat me. I just couldn't stop it. Being with him and having him treat me badly was better than being without him. It was what I told myself when he was ignoring me.

"I thought maybe you came to dance with me, Foxy, just like old times," I said, trying my best to be cool and to ignore the awful truth he'd spoken.

"I'm getting out of here. I can't stand to see you destroy yourself for the entertainment of others. Call me when you get some self-worth back. I really can't watch," he said angrily and walked away.

Garrison was standing among a group of young women, with his hands in his pockets. He was smiling and laughing as one of them put her arms around him. He looked so handsome in that tux. He was now a diehard Beatles fan, and he had grown his hair long, combing it in the style they had started. I walked back to my table by the stage and sat down again. All eyes were watching me cross that dance floor. I knew they were watching to see how this situation would play out. Determined not to embarrass myself, I perched on that high stool and held my head up, keeping my back straight. I really didn't care now how much leg was showing. Garrison wasn't paying any attention.

The band started playing. Layton Cain took the stage right in front of me. I could see he had way too much to drink. His eyes were glassy and bright. That beautiful voice of his filled the room as he looked directly into my eyes and sang to me one of the most beautiful love songs ever written. "You are my special angel sent from up above. The Lord smiled down on me and sent an angel to love." It was one of my favorite songs, and he knew it. I couldn't help smiling at him. I wasn't prepared for what happened next. I was getting caught up in Layton's shining dark eyes and hypnotizing voice when suddenly I was lifted off the high stool! Garrison was twirling me around on the dance floor. It was the first of only two times he ever danced with me, in all the years we were together; the second time was at our wedding. He was only a two-step guy, but he held me firmly with one arm around my waist, tucked under that black lace overskirt. I could feel everyone watching us, especially the many women who would have loved to have been in my shoes. It was a lovely romantic gesture. Garrison always said, "I play the music. I don't dance." It was a very special moment, if only done to get me away from Layton. I didn't want that moment to end.

"Oh, God, here she comes," Garrison muttered after the music stopped; he was still holding me. It was Melody Lotus. I loved her, but Garrison always said he hated her. She lived next door to him. She put her arms around us and picked us up off the floor, hugging us tightly and crying. She was as tall as Garrison, but she outweighed him by at least a hundred and fifty pounds.

"Oh, you two, please tell me that you will stay together always! You are the most beautiful pair in all Henderson County, and I love you both so much," she cried.

"I love you too, Melody," I said as I struggled to get out of her grasp. The poor thing just overreacted like this all the time. I empathized with her, because she was so cruelly treated by the good folk of Henderson County. She had been just as big in the fifth grade. Her parents took her out of school, because the teachers said that she couldn't learn anything. I knew it was because they couldn't teach her anything. She was by no means slow and uneducable. She was just different. The one thing she had that everyone loved and wanted from her was a voice that could fill a stadium without the aid of a microphone. Like Garrison, she had perfect pitch. The school board wouldn't let her go to school but wanted her to sit backstage and sing for every concert and school play while some skinny, popular girl took the stage, pretending the voice came from her. Melody did it because she wanted everyone's approval. She even laughed and joined in when kids made fun of her. It was heartbreaking for her parents and for those of us who loved her. She was the singer with Garrison's band and going on tour with them.

The last time I saw Melody Lotus, it was an emotional time. It was more than ten years after that going-away party. I was finally able to hold my head up in Henderson and New Moon. I came back to attend my high school class reunion. Someone talked me into going to Moon Over the Water Lounge for a drink. I was sure Garrison wouldn't be there. I was dressed to the nines in the latest style, in a purple dress with thin straps that required no bra. My hair was cut very short, and I wore a matching flower in it. Melody was onstage, singing. I sat at the bar with a few old classmates. I didn't think she would see me. I was so wrong. She picked me up in her huge arms and cried all over me. Big tears fell on my purple dress as she sobbed. "How could he let you go?" she demanded.

"Things happen. People change, Melody. They move on," I said, easing myself from her strong arms.

"Well, I don't," she said, loud enough for the whole place to hear. It was true that Melody never changed. If she loved you once, she loved you always.

When Garrison took me home that night, it wasn't the sweet sorrow of parting I had hoped for. He was angry with me. He still couldn't stop looking at me and playing with my long ringlets of hair. How could he love and hate me at the same time? When I tried to get him to talk to me about it, he held up a hand and said, "Have a nice life."

I took to the nursing program like a duck to water. I loved it! I was good at it, thanks to Liva B. I thanked God for Mrs. Bingham, who had believed I could do it. When the roll was called, I stood and answered to the name of Mary for the first time. It sounded so much better to me than Evaleene or Evelyn; I despised both. From then on, I was Mary the nurse.

I loved the big city. Ignoring my family's pleas and warnings of danger, I drove myself there every day. Before school started I practiced it by doing a dry run there and back several times. All the worry about the drive was brought on by the fatal car crash of the Creeper's wife. It frightened Mama and Carmella. "Well, we don't know how she will do, driving there every day for nursing school," Mama said to our next-door neighbor, who was the mother of the dead woman. I was glad the Creeper wasn't at the wake. The death of his wife didn't detour him from his creeping ways. In no time at all he remarried, to his first and true love, some said. She and her son moved into the house with him. It was as if nothing had changed for him. One wife was gone, and he replaced her with another in less than a year.

Jimmy Tewlain was right about a lot of things he said about life in the city. It was true that I didn't blend in and I didn't look like everyone else. I still attracted lots of attention from men, but I became better at handling it. I was so determined to do well in school and learn everything. I had no difficulty turning down dates and unwanted advances.

I was still going out to lounges and dances with my friends from Lake Calvin. We hung out at bars and waited for guys we knew to get off work and come in for a drink. There were signs that said, "Unescorted ladies are not permitted to sit at the bar." But my friends and I did it anyway, much to the dismay of bar owners. One of the places we especially liked was on New Moon Lake. It was rustic and charming, with a big fireplace. It also had a full-size pool table. Linda was an excellent player. She had the same regulation table at home. She and her dad played all the time. One evening we met up with a couple of guys we knew in high school. We asked if we could join them in a friendly game.

"So do you girls even know how to play?" Joel asked.

"Why don't you show us?" begged Linda, batting her long eye-lashes and flipping back her blonde hair. We watched as he demonstrated a simple shot. "You mean like this?" Linda picked up her pool cue and cleared every ball from the table. Then she took a cigar from her coat pocket and lit it, smoking it slowly as the bartender leaned across the bar, glaring at us.

Valentine's Day came, with no date and no one to send me candy or flowers. Garrison had been gone from my life since he left to go on the road. I tried hard to forget him. Sometimes in the middle of the night I woke to the ringing of the phone. Once I was able to get to it in time, and it was Garrison asking if I was all right. He didn't say much, but it was nice to know he thought of me.

"You need to go and look at the big box on your bed. I don't know who it is from," Mama said when I came home from school. I had no idea what she meant. When I saw the big white box with a red ribbon, I didn't know what to think. It contained two dozen long-stemmed red roses and a red envelope. Mama stood behind me as I opened it. The card had a long-stemmed red rose on the front. When I opened it, there were only four words written on it: "I love you, honest." It was signed by Garrison. I didn't know where he was or how to call him to thank him.

"Do you mind if I take them and try to preserve them?" Mama asked. She put them into a special wax she made, then hung them upside down on the clothesline in the basement. After a few weeks of drying, she put them into a vase. They stayed beautiful for many years. I kept that card for a long time. I read it when times were bad for Garrison and me.

Garrison didn't return to Henderson at the end of his tour. In late summer I heard he was drafted into the army. That crazy Asian war was raging. I was dating other guys again, but I just couldn't bring myself to accept any marriage proposals. Garrison's beautiful words haunted me. *I love you, honest.* What if he really meant them? After graduation I took a job at Liberty Hospital, which wasn't a hospital at all. It was like a giant nursing home. The pay was good. I lived in the nurses' residences for a year. Every man there, old or young, blind, crippled, or just plain crazy, knew my name.

Garrison spent his overseas tour of duty in Germany, far away from the battlefields of Vietnam. He was a cook, and when he wasn't working, he did what he pleased. I guessed the army had its way of knowing who was able to serve in battle and who would best serve his country by flipping pancakes. It only took one little letter from him to send me running to the airport when he returned. I had thought I was completely over him. In his letter it was clear that he was certain nothing had changed between us. While it was full of his love for me, it was also full of his confidence that I would enter into a sexual relationship with him. I was still living in the nurses' residences at Liberty. There was only one phone in the hallway. When it rang late one night, I knew it was Garrison. "My plane will land in the big city about two in the afternoon. Will you be able to pick me up and take me back to Henderson?" he asked.

"Of course I will, Garrison. I'm looking forward to it," I replied. He hadn't seen my new sports car. It was a blue GTO with a stylish rubber bumper on the front. My pa had helped me get it, which caused a lot of hard feelings in the family. He never helped the others buy a car. Fashion had taken a big turn. I couldn't be missed in a micro-mini dress in colors of orange and yellow and the same color blue as my car. The dress barely came to the middle of my thighs. I wore knee-high, high-heeled go-go boots with a bright yellow patina. My long hair fell in waves down to my waist. I had no doubt left when I spotted Garrison in the airport. His hair was cut short again. He looked so handsome in his uniform. I ran to him, calling his name. He lifted me to him, and we kissed a long time while others looked on.

The party at the Michaels' home was anything but celebratory. Nancy got pregnant while Hardin was in-country, fighting that awful war. I could tell he was having a hard time accepting the baby. Thirteen-month pregnancies were commonplace. Nancy was her usual obnoxious self, and she was drunk. She planted cold beer out in the bushes in the backyard. It wasn't long before Garrison was glassy-eyed too. Hardin said nothing as he sat rocking the baby. Nancy and Garrison still preferred each other's company to anyone else's. They ignored me.

I went out to the backyard to get some air, and Garrison followed. "Let's go to a motel for the night. I've got money," he said. I was still a virgin. I hoped he would ask me to marry him first, but that didn't happen.

"No, Garrison. You know I have to be married first," I said.

"Susie's here, and she don't care, Garrison. You go with her and have fun," Nancy said as she stumbled from the bushes, so drunk that she fell. "Let your little virgin hang on to it. She's getting so old, no one will want it soon." Susie appeared at the back gate. Garrison, also pretty loaded, started to walk toward her.

"Good-bye, Garrison," I called as I went around to the front of the house. I drove back to Liberty, crying. Things hadn't changed! The perfect accessory for Garrison the rock star and Garrison the soldier was also the perfect convenience. It was just a week later when he called to ask me to take him to the airport for a standby flight to Boston, where he would be stationed for the rest of his tour. Poor little fool that I was, I did it. Bad Garrison was still better than no Garrison.

Bride-to-be

≈16≋

Big-City Woman

DEPRESSION AND LONELINESS WERE overtaking my whole life as I struggled with the grueling work at Liberty Hospital. I discovered a new hospital, Our Lady of Light, that was a real hospital, and I planned to apply there for a position. Garrison started writing to me, and sometimes he called. His letters were full of his love for me and his need for sex. He even talked of us getting engaged when he came home for Christmas that year. His letters brought me no comfort. I knew he was still seeing other girls.

Jimmy Tewlain was right when he told me that I didn't realize the effect I had on other people. I went to the hospital called Our Lady of Light, dressed in the latest fashion. I wore a bright yellow minidress with a matching coat and black high-heeled shoes. My hair was down past my waist. It was a sunny day. I put on a pair of big sunglasses like Jackie Kennedy wore. People stared at me as I walked down the street toward the main entrance of the building. I still didn't understand their staring. I dressed like every other young woman. Women gave me dirty looks, and men were always trying to talk to me or grab me.

My intention was to put in an application, go shopping, and visit some of my friends back in Henderson. I hoped to spend a little time with Mama. She seemed to be very lonely ever since I had moved into the nurses' residence at Liberty. I had no idea the director of employment would be so impressed with me. She insisted that I meet with Sister William Catherine that day. "Sister, this is Mary Rosario. She is a licensed practical nurse. I think she would be a good fit for our new floor opening up next month," she told the tall, stately nun, who gave no reply, only looked me up and down very slowly.

I began to shake a little, and I felt my face getting red. "Do you actually possess a license to practice nursing, Ms. Rosario?" she finally asked.

"Oh, yes, ma'am, I do. I really do," I replied very nervously.

"Good. You come back tomorrow and bring it. Meet with me at three-thirty in the afternoon," she said and slowly left the room.

"I assume you have a suit of a darker...shall we say, more conservative color you could wear tomorrow?" the employment director said.

When I returned the next day in my dark green suit, with my hair up and my sensible heels to match, I was hired on the spot. Sister William Catherine was so gracious to me. She treated me like a friend and a respected colleague. I felt like a real nurse and a grown woman for the first time. I would be working two jobs until my contract at Liberty ended. "I want you here working full-time the minute your contract expires," Sister told me.

That December I started to go home to Strawberry Fields a lot. I wasn't feeling well. There had been a big flu epidemic going on since November. I didn't know if I had the flu or if I was just a bundle of nerves. I wanted Christmas to be a memorable one for Garrison and me, since I was expecting an engagement ring.

I had lots of ideas for decorating the house. I wasn't good at making things, but Nina and Antonia were experts. We made beautiful stars out of clear plastic medicine cups that we dipped in glitter glue and tied together with craft wire. Someone at Liberty came up with this idea. Everyone liked them. We were given a large supply of the little cups so we could make them.

"Antonia," I said, "I want to have all the names of our family on the tree as decorations. Can you help me? You have the best hand-writing. You will write them on heavy white construction paper. Nina and I will cut them out. Then we'll glitter-glue them in silver and hang them on the Christmas tree. We will start with Pa and Mama at the top. Enzo and Nina will come next, then their family, and so on, right down the whole tree. I think it's going to be beautiful." I had the ideas but not the skills to pull them off. I needed Nina and Antonia. They agreed to do it. They even thought it was fun. Their days were spent sitting around, smoking, and moaning about their miserable lives. I guess it gave them a purpose and something to take their minds off their problems. The tree, cut from our own farm, turned out even better than I had hoped. My nieces and nephews still talk about how beautiful Grandma and Grandpa's tree was with all our names on it. The names were placed on the tree every year. Antonia took pride in adding new ones as new babies were born to our extended family.

When Garrison came home, I met him at the airport and drove him to Henderson. We were in the coffee shop on Saturday morning. "I guess we'll go shopping for that ring you want," Garrison said.

"You don't have to buy it for me if you don't want to, Garrison," I replied, feeling very sick inside.

"It's Christmas, it's what you want. I intend to get it for you. We can go right to the jewelry store across the street," he said. I really didn't want to go there. It would be all over town in minutes if we purchased one or just went in to look.

It wasn't exactly the romantic proposal of my dreams. But I was blinded by my desire to move our relationship forward. "Okay, Garrison, we can go look at rings." The store seemed busy with all the fine folk of Henderson out shopping. When several of the locals heard Garrison ask Norman's uncle, who owned the store, to show him engagement rings, heads turned in our direction. Voices fell to quiet murmurs. Some of the rings had diamonds so small you could barely see them. When Uncle Lars brought out a set made of white gold, I knew it was made for me. They were beautiful corrugated bands. The engagement ring was a thinner band with a diamond in a setting like a flower on a stem. The wedding band was thick, with a circle of diamonds, and the engagement ring's flower-shaped diamond fit into it. It was unique. I think Garrison purchased them because they made me so happy. He told Uncle Lars that he would be back to get the engagement ring. He would make arrangements to pay for the wedding band on time. I was walking on air! I failed to see that Garrison was anything but happy.

We were supposed to go out that night, but Garrison stood me up. I didn't know what was wrong. I was scared something had happened. "I just can't go through with it," he said when he called the next day. "I'm sorry, I just don't want to be engaged," he said and hung up.

I was so distraught that I couldn't eat or drink anything without throwing up. I couldn't stop crying. I told no one what had transpired between us. Mama was worried that I had contracted the deadly flu that had been sweeping most of the Midwest. She called the doctor. Luck was on my side: it wasn't Dr. Hemming. I couldn't stand seeing him ever in my life, and certainly not in my present state. It was Dr. Lewis, a young, very good-looking man whom everyone loved, especially the woman he treated. Carmella lived right next door to him. She talked about him all the time.

"Would you like to tell me what's going on with you today? I don't think it's the flu, like your mother said when she called me, is it?" asked Dr. Lewis. I shook my head, and tears came pouring down my face. He took both of my hands in his and looked into my eyes. "Come on, now. Out with it."

"I was supposed to get engaged on Christmas Eve, and he called it off," I said softly, hanging my head.

"You mean that guy in the band I always see you with? What's his name, Garrison Michael?" he asked. I nodded slowly. "I don't know why a great-looking little nurse like you is so hung up on a guy like him. I used to hear all the doctors talking about you when you worked at the local hospital. You know, you could have had any one of them you wanted." I began to cry even harder. "Look, I got something that will fix you right up. You can't work like this. I know you don't want to spend Christmas crying, do you?" I shook my head. "These little yellow pills are the best on the market. Take one every four hours if you need to. I guarantee you won't feel a thing with them. I promise." He kissed me on the cheek, put the prescription in my hand, and left the room. It read, "Valium, 5 mg by mouth every four hours as needed #90."

By Christmas Eve I was numb and not crying anymore, but I couldn't say I felt happy. I couldn't say I felt anything. Garrison called to ask me to his home for dinner. "Why?" I asked. "Why would you want me there? It won't be any fun for either of us."

"Well, I haven't stopped loving you. I just don't want to be engaged, that's all," he replied. I swallowed another Valium and said yes. I put on the special dress I had bought for the evening. It was beautiful. The color was Garrison's favorite. The high-waisted dress was of a soft, creamy lavender crepe, and it had a belt made of silver and rhinestones. It was short, with a scoop neckline and long sleeves with wide tapered cuffs at the wrists.

When Mrs. Fienberg's son took my engagement picture, I was wearing the dress. He was so excited to be doing it instead of his mother. It was to be in the local paper, to announce our engagement. But after Christmas was over, I refused to let Antonia put it in the *Henderson Times*. I can't identify with that girl I was in 1968; it's another photo that scares me. The only one I can tolerate looking at is the one taken in my nurse's cap. I can identify with her. That's Mary the nurse. That is what everyone called me. I can't ever remember looking like the others. I only remember the ugly duckling I saw in the mirror in my room in the house at Strawberry Fields.

Christmas Eve passed in a blur. I was so doped up with Valium that I didn't even feel bad when Nancy berated me in front of the whole family for wearing such a fancy dress to dinner. "None of us are impressed with your wardrobe. I don't know why you bother," she said. I think she was mad because she had a new boyfriend, but he wasn't allowed at the Michaels' home. Hardin had quietly divorced her. She wasted no time hooking up with another alcoholic like herself. The baby's father was only a high school boy who wanted nothing to do with a baby. Nancy was twenty-five years old. I wasn't sure what she was doing with such a young guy, but I guessed it was for kicks. She and Garrison did a lot of things just for a laugh. A baby was no laughing matter.

"I happen to like my dresses, and that's why I wear them," I said firmly, surprising myself. She didn't reply. I think she was a little stunned because I had said something so terse. I was glad. I wondered if those Valium pills were always going to make me vocal. It could be a dangerous thing.

After dinner Garrison asked me to come upstairs with him. Reluctantly I went. I didn't like being up there. I knew he would try to get me into his bed; he had tried it before. We were sitting on the back porch, which had been converted into a TV room. A famous choir was on TV, singing beautiful Christmas carols. Garrison looked handsome in his army uniform as he sat next to me. He took my hand in his and said, "Merry Christmas, my darling." He placed a little black box into my hand. I knew it was my engagement ring.

"Garrison, you didn't have to do this. You said you didn't want to be engaged." I tried to hand it back to him.

"I love you, and I want you to have it." A few moments passed. "You don't look happy," he said, with a concerned look in his eyes.

"I'm so doped up on these pills my doctor gave me, I can't really feel anything. I'm sorry, Garrison. Thank you. I do love the ring very much. I love you more than I love anyone else, including myself," I replied, looking into his shining black eyes. I think those were the truest words I had ever spoken. That Valium made me a brave soul. It was a reality I had never admitted to myself, let alone anyone else.

"So when will be the wedding?" Mama asked when I showed her the ring the next day.

"I don't really know, Mama. We haven't talked about it yet," I replied. A worried look came into her green eyes as she sat at the kitchen table, peeling potatoes for the big noontime meal. I couldn't tell her that Garrison had refused to attend the meal. I made the excuse that he needed to be with his own family. He said we would see each other that evening. It never occurred to me to be concerned because my dearly intended didn't want to have even one holiday meal with his future in-laws. He never had felt comfortable with my family.

The next day I took Garrison to the airport for a stand-by flight back to Boston. He told me he didn't want to be engaged, and he said I could keep the ring. I watched him as he ran to catch his plane. I had tears in my eyes and a pain in my heart that no pill could have stopped.

Things at Liberty in January were worse than that horrible Christmas. My head nurse was mad at me for being off sick a whole week over Christmas. She didn't want to hear that it couldn't be helped. "And by the way, you look like hell, too," she added.

By the end of the day, the Valium was kicking in again. I stuck my head into her office. "My contract is up today," I said. It was Friday. I would be going to Our Lady of Light to work. Almost everyone there loved me. They didn't care that I was gone for a week. They would be glad to see me. I needed people who were happy to be with me.

"Wait, I'll have you sign another one," she said.

"Don't bother. I've packed all of my things, and I left the key in my room. I won't be back," I said.

"You can't just leave like that!" she yelled, getting her large body to its feet. Her blonde hair bounced under her nurse's cap as she came around the desk.

"Just watch me." I walked out. I hated it there, even though the money was good. It was a hard place to work. For someone like me, who always needed to give at least 110 percent in order to feel good about myself, I just couldn't cope with the way the patients were treated . . . or not treated. I needed to be needed and wanted, by people other than the patients.

I drove to Our Lady of Light Hospital in a blinding snowstorm. I went to Sister William Catherine's office. She was busy. When she saw me, she came right out. "What's wrong?" she asked with concern.

"Nothing's wrong, really," I said. "My contract was up at Liberty today, and well, here I am. I even pack all my stuff into my car." I knew that if I said too much, I would start crying.

"Good, I'm glad," she said, putting a hand on each of my shoulders and smiling at me. "Now, if you need a room for the night, I can arrange to give you an on-call doctor's sleeping room. The weather is bad. I don't think you'll make it to the farm tonight. I need you here tomorrow."

"Yes, Sister, I'll be here," I said. Not wanting to argue with her, I left. I didn't want to spend another night in a single room like the one I had spent the last year in at Liberty. I would go back to Strawberry Fields and commute until I could find the little apartment of my dreams. There was nothing to stop me now. There was no Garrison Michael and no engagement.

My parents were worried about my driving all that distance. They always tried to wait up for me. They made late meals. I really hated being a burden to them. I knew Mama still waited on Sammy, but I couldn't stand it. She and Pa were growing old. They should have been able to rest without worrying about grown children who should be caring for themselves. A few weeks later, some friends at the hospital told me about an apartment for rent on a street just down the hill. It was so close that I could walk to work. The landlady rented it to me right away, since I was a nurse.

I couldn't afford the rent and all the things an apartment needed. I asked my old friend Linda from Lake Calvin to move in with me. She was working for a bank in the big city and taking the train to work from North End. It was a long commute. There was a train station right behind my apartment building. I talked her into sharing that little three-room place. I was always so wrapped up in myself that I didn't notice Linda was miserable and probably having some problems of her own. We parted after a few months. It wasn't a big deal, since everything in the place was mine. But I still needed help with the rent.

It wasn't long before I found the perfect roommate, or so I thought. She was an aide in the ICU at Our Lady of Light. She was kind of shy and reserved. I was just the opposite by then. I could talk to anyone. I was even brave enough to ask guys for dates. It was a fun time in my life. It was a time when I thought I had it all. I had a great sports car and an apartment I had furnished to look like a big-city woman lived there. I had a great job where everyone loved me. They depended on me and respected me for my work. I worked very hard. I took every challenge that came my way. It felt so good to be needed and wanted.

My roommate Joyce and I had many parties at our little apartment. Everyone came, from doctors down to the kitchen staff. We were one big, happy family of coworkers. Joyce was a good cook. We invited our neighbors to our functions. They all came and loved it.

That river of men was still flowing right to my door. I had all the dates I wanted. I was having a lot of fun. Men no longer begged for sex or made inappropriate advances. When the occasional date would ask about sex, I would tell him I had never done it. Most were surprised, and all declined to be the first. So I dated and had fun going to all kinds of fancy nightclubs and restaurants. I was leading the life I had dreamed of on the farm. Now I had it, as long as I didn't think too much about where it would end.

The sexual revolution was in full swing. Sex was easy to get anywhere. All the girls were doing it, including Linda, who got pregnant. She married one of her coworker's younger brothers. Even conservative, retiring Joyce was having sex with every Tom, Dick, and Harry who came to the door. She liked telling everyone I was wild. "Well, it may be all right for you to wear those short dresses and flirt with men, but I just can't do it." She said those things in front of everyone, including me! I was shocked when I found out she was sleeping around. I was so dense when it came to this stuff. Joyce was also a closet alcoholic. She hid vodka bottles everywhere. When I found them, she lied and said she only did it that one weekend I went home and left her alone.

"Excuse me? I left you alone? What on earth are you talking about? I'm not your mother or your babysitter. I visit my parents every other weekend. They're good to me, and I like them." She didn't get on with either of her parents. Her father was a terrible man who drank daily and had tried more than once to rape her. Her older sister had been raped several times by him in his drunken state.

"Well, when I'm all alone, I don't know what to do with myself. I get so lonely. That's why I drink and have sex with so many men," she admitted.

"Does it make you feel better to constantly belittle me, as if I'm the one who has loose morals, when it's really you?" I asked. She started to cry and apologized to me for the way she had acted. I tried hard to understand her.

In order to protect myself, I set some rules. When I was there, she couldn't have men in the apartment for sex. Her parents weren't welcome. Her father was dangerous, and her mother whined and cried, calling at eight in the morning, and the phone was ringing when we arrived home at eleven. "Joyce, please ask your mother to stop calling here before nine in the morning," I asked.

Most of the young men that came to our door smoked marijuana. It was very popular among the young adult crowd that hung out in local bars and coffeehouses. We frequented them to listen to folk music, which was very big, thanks to Bob Dylan. I was in love with him and his music. If I had the opportunity to meet him, I would have wanted him for my own. He was so much like Garrison, and Garrison was so much like Bob.

When I was alone, I thought of Garrison and how I loved and missed him. The little yellow pills with the heart-shaped hole in the center were gone. I had thrown them away; I was no pill taker. The engagement ring sat in its box in my dresser drawer, in the bedroom I shared with Joyce. We had little twin beds and matching spreads. We had our own blankets and teddy bears denoting our separate spaces. My bed was along one wall and hers by the other. Each of us had a side of the closet. My side was stuffed full of beautiful suits and dresses, blouses and skirts. The floor was filled three feet high with shoeboxes. Joyce's side was half empty. She had a few pairs of shoes. Every drawer in my dresser was full, with sweaters, matching sets of undergarments, sets of pajamas, and nightgowns. I was still selfish, vain, and immature. I took my laundry home to Mama. She washed, starched, and ironed my white uniforms. I always looked the part of the well-put-together nurse. Mama liked all my fancy clothes. I guess I got my eye for them from her.

One of the first things I did when I moved into the little apartment was to call Garrison and give him my address and phone number. I was such a fool. He would call occasionally or maybe drop a line or two. There were long periods of time when I didn't hear from him. The silence prompted me to seek out Nancy in Henderson. She was actually nice to me. I guess I was a cheap babysitter. It was a small price to pay for the latest word on Garrison. Nancy was working at the dime store in town. She was living in a little apartment in the same building where Antonia had lived when she first married Warren. She was still with that boyfriend she had last Christmas who wasn't allowed at the Michaels' home. They got on well, having one drunken brawl after another when the baby was asleep. "You know, Garrison has been sleeping with all of my girlfriends since he was about thirteen years old. I'm four years older than he is. When I moved out on my own after graduation, he used to come stay with me in the apartment I rented with my friends. We had a lot of great, wild parties," she told me.

"Well, I still don't intend to do it until I marry," I replied.

"Suit yourself. But Garrison likes sex, and he'll have his way with any woman who wants him. I think you're wasting your time on him if you think he'll marry you. Sex is just like cigarettes to him. He has been smoking since he was five years old, and he can't give them up either," she admitted.

My pa was turning seventy-five years old. I wanted to do something very special for him. I thought a big party at Strawberry Fields would be just the thing. I went to the one person that I knew would like the idea: Enzo. I found him at old Mrs. Kincaid's farm, in the barn, tending one of his racehorses. "Well, if it isn't the big-city woman! What are you doing here?" he asked.

"I came to see you. Pa's turning seventy-five in July, and I want to do something special for him. I want a big party, like a picnic at the farm. What do you think? Will you help me?"

"You know, that's not a bad idea," he said. "I have some friends who do these big outdoor things. They make a firepit and roast a whole pig. What do you think?"

"It sounds perfect! You take care of the pig. I'll get everyone else on board to help me with the rest of the food and the liquor," I replied excitedly. Getting my other siblings to agree on anything, even the weather, was hard. They all liked the idea, but there were fights about who was doing more than someone else. Antonia and Carmella finally agreed to do the salads and baked beans. Nina took care of getting all the paper products. We all got together and made the decorations and worked on the guest list. Nina sent the invitations. I took care of the cake and the liquor. Marco and Sammy donated money.

As the smell of barbecued pork filled the air, Pa suspected nothing. I never knew what story Enzo gave him about why those men were out there all night with that big fire. Practically everyone who lived in Sherman Acres attended. All the folks from Italy that came over on the boat with Pa were there, as well as our whole family. In the family picture taken that day, we all look so young!

The people came and went all day and into the night. There must have been at least one hundred and fifty guests. Pa was very happy and surprised. Everyone ate, drank, laughed, and had a good time. Some of my old friends came: Big Mike, Lucy, and the Leila girls, as well as their father, who was still very full of himself. I was glad to see Lucy. We talked just like old times.

The relationship between Lucy and Big Mike was still strained. He was such a good friend to me that it made me feel bad. I remembered that Christmas Day the year I graduated from my nursing program, when I was driving home from Linda's house. A car had been following me. It was almost like mine. I rounded the bend on Sherman Acres Road, pulled off to the side, and stopped. The car following me did the same. When a big man got out, I knew right away that it was Big Mike. "Hey, I like your car!" he said. "I wanted one just like it, but I couldn't afford it. I guess nurses make a lot more money than factory workers. Slide over, and let me try it." He got in behind the wheel. We drove around the old neighborhood, laughing and talking. "Say, why don't you come home with me and see the family? We're just going to sit around, play games with Busha, and have a few drinks." I remembered that Christmas evening as one of the best times in Sherman Acres. Mike's grandmother, whom he called Busha, was so much fun. She told many jokes in her Polish accent, and we all laughed. That day and Pa's party were the last contact I had with Big Mike. He still lives in Henderson. It saddens me a great deal that we can't be friends now, when we need each other even more than when we were kids.

After Big Mike left the party, Lucy and I got a chance to talk. "Are you happy, Lucy?" I asked. "Being married, with a kid and all?"

She didn't answer right away, but then she said, "You know, Boobaleene, I just never think about what makes me happy anymore. I just live." I thought the answer was strange, but truly happy people don't spend a lot of time thinking about whether they're happy. Lucy had grown up and left me without an anchor.

A few guys Linda and I used to meet at bars in New Moon after work, friends of Sammy's, came to the party. They wanted to renew old friendships. Ben was very pleased to see that I hadn't married. "We would have made the perfect couple, and we still would, if you married me," he said. "I believe this with all my heart." Ben was a great guy, very handsome, with green eyes and light brown hair. He'd lived with his mother until her death in a farming accident. He was left with the entire estate. He would have been a great husband and provider for me, but I wasn't in love with him. Ben was so wonderful that I often wished I could be the perfect woman for him. I never could pretend to love someone. After that day at Strawberry Fields, more than ten years would pass before I reunited with Ben. I stopped by his farm one day on my way to visit Pa and Mama. It didn't go well. I had children then, and he wasn't interested in them or in me anymore. He never married and has since retired to a warmer climate with another man! I don't know how I missed that. We self-absorbed people only see what we want to see.

Another special event had me returning to Henderson again the very next month. It was for my five-year high school class reunion. I dressed in a silver micro mini in an A-line style with long, wide sleeves and a scoop neckline. I wore silver pantyhose that had just come on the market and matching silver heels. My hair was longer than the dress. "Where on earth did you get something like that?" Ada Mae asked. She was married to the older brother of one of our classmates.

"Why, it's the latest thing, don't you know?" I said proudly while she examined the material.

I danced all night and had fun with all my old friends from Lake Calvin. All the guys in my class that had tormented me were married. They were standing at the bar, watching me dance in that short dress. *Eat your heart out, all of you,* I thought to myself as I danced with one man after another. If they were making fun of me, then I didn't care anymore. I knew life beyond the boundaries of Henderson County; I didn't think they knew it. I thought I was the smart one after all. I was more blind and selfish than ever.

It was rumored around Henderson that Garrison Michael was coming back from the army. He had been discharged. I hadn't heard from him in a while. The last time was back in spring, when I found out he was in an army hospital in Boston due to a severe case of mononucleosis. He spent more than a month there. After he left, I had no way of reaching him. It seemed like I was a lot happier without him.

I was off that weekend in September. My roommate was spending time with her sister. I decided to slip into Henderson and see if I could run into Garrison. I told no one I was going. I didn't go to Strawberry Fields, either. When I left the apartment, I didn't lock the door. Neighborhoods in the big city's south side were very safe back then. Everyone knew each other and looked out for one another. I made a few casual inquires and found out nothing. I called the Michael home, but his mother said she didn't know his whereabouts. I knew she wasn't telling the truth, but I just thanked her and hung up. Nancy had moved from town. I didn't have her phone number.

After attending Mass at my old church, Christ the King, I started back to the city. Father Strickland had been transferred to another church. I was sad about not seeing him. But I saw him in the most unlikely place more than thirty years later! I was in the Army Nurse Corps, attending Mass with officers from my unit. We were at a facility in southern Texas, which is the army capital of the nation. I saw him at the altar, saying Mass. I was disappointed that he only vaguely remembered me from my younger days at CYO. I had changed greatly. He had been so many places since we last met, but he hadn't changed. I would have known him anywhere.

When I arrived back at my apartment, even before I walked through the door I knew something had changed. I had a strange feeling that my life was about to change again forever. It was a perfect, sunny, hot September day. The sky was a clear blue. I lingered in the courtyard for a little while. Sometimes when I did this, neighbors came out. We would sit and talk. The place seemed deserted that day. No one came, not even my little friend Julie, who lived in the apartment across the way with her husband and her small son. She was a teen bride because she had been pregnant. Hers was a troubled marriage. I played marriage counselor and referee many times for them.

I walked up to my bright blue door, and it was ajar. I pushed it open slowly. Garrison was lying on the couch, fast asleep. He was wearing a pair of bell-bottom jeans and a colorful shirt. He had no shoes, and his feet were very dirty. His hair was very long, and he wore some beads around his neck. A leather bracelet was on his wrist. His black horn-rimmed glasses had been replaced by a pair of gold wire ones. Dropping to my knees next to the couch, I stroked his hair and called his name. "Oh, Garrison, it's really you," I said softly, not wanting to wake him and wanting to at the same time.

"Maybe you were expecting someone else?" he said softly as he opened his big, dark eyes.

"How did you find me? How did you get here?" I asked in amazement.

"I have a car. I drove all night and half the day from Boston. I have your address and just stopped a few times for directions. I was too tired to drive anymore, so I just went to sleep," he said.

I felt so glad inside. "You go and call your mother. Go have a shower, and I'll make us some coffee," I said. Like me, Garrison loved coffee. I don't think he ever drank it until we met, but he quickly learned to enjoy it. He took his duffle bag and went into the bathroom.

I went into the small galley kitchen and started to prepare coffee. My hands were shaking, and it took me a long time to get calm enough to pick up the pot, fill it with water, and measure out the grounds. When I turned around, he was standing there in the doorway, just looking at me. I rubbed my shaking hands on my miniskirt. I took a few steps toward him. He picked me up into his arms and began to kiss me like he hadn't in years. They were hard, forceful kisses, filled with passion and want, making me respond to him. I felt things I never thought I could feel. Garrison's big hands were everywhere on me. I couldn't get him to release me until finally the smell of burning coffee filled the room. I tried to get loose from his grip. "The coffee—it's burning," I said.

"Just leave it!" he replied, kissing me again even harder. When I smelled smoke, I finally got free from him and turned off the flame under the pot. Garrison was right behind me, grabbing me again and touching me everywhere.

"Garrison, we have to stop," I said firmly. I was starting to get hold of myself again, remembering that this was the man who refused to marry me. I straightened myself and assessed the damage to the coffee pot. It was pretty charred. My shaking hands started to run some water into the sink. I added some soap to try to wash the pot.

"I'll do that," Garrison said, coming up behind me. I left the kitchen and went into my bedroom. I wanted to cry, but I didn't want to do it in front of him. I remembered how much he loved it when I broke down. I changed from my beautiful little navy-blue sailor minidress into shorts and a white tank top. It was hot in the apartment. I sat on my bed with my back against the wall, resting my head with my eyes closed. Why did I always let him get to me? I was still very much in love with him. I never had those desires with any other man in my life.

I could smell fresh coffee brewing when the bedroom door opened and Garrison walked in. He sat on the bed next to me. I moved away from him. The bed was very small, so there was nowhere to go. "Where's your ring?" he asked. I pointed to the top drawer of my dresser, where I kept my few pieces of jewelry. The room was so small that he just reached over and opened the drawer. He took out the little black box that held my dazzling engagement ring. He removed it from the box, took my hand, and placed the ring on my finger. I only looked at him quizzically. "I'm not ready to get married, but I love you and want you for my own. I don't want you to date other guys. I've been out of the army for more than a month, just knocking around Boston, trying to find myself. I don't know what I want from life or what I want to do. You always seem to know just what you want, and you go after it, and you get it. This apartment, it's real nice. And your job, you seem to like it so much."

Once again, it wasn't the proposal of my dreams. I was upset by what he'd said, even though I was glad that there was finally some dialogue between us, for the first time in all the years we had known each other. "I work hard for everything I have, Garrison. It didn't just fall into my lap, you know."

"I know, but does it make you happy? It seems to me you aren't really happy, are you?" he asked, looking into my eyes.

"I'd be a lot happier if I had you as my husband," I replied. Immediately a look of confusion and resistance appeared on his face. "Let's don't talk about it. Why don't we just be together and enjoy each other's company? You take your time sorting out what it is you want out of life. I'll wear the ring, and I won't date any other men." I didn't know the rule was only supposed to apply to me. I didn't realize he had no intention of being engaged to me. I was supposed to be engaged to him so I couldn't date anymore. Women desperately in love may agree to do desperate things. I was no different from any of those women. I just didn't want to admit it.

I was fairly happy with the arrangement while Garrison tried to get his life together. He took a factory job in North End. He was living at home with his parents and his sisters Ann, Mazy and Mazy's three children. Ann, I realized, was like a second mother to him. Garrison went back to playing music with a few of his old bandmates. He spent the night on my couch when he came to see me. "You don't know how hard it is for me to do this," he complained. But I did—it was just as hard on me! So we argued a lot, and I cried a lot.

I wanted that Christmas to be special and very memorable for us. I wanted us to have matching outfits. I found a pattern for them. It was a new trend then to dress alike. I wasn't an expert seamstress, but Joyce was practically a professional, and I talked her into making them. They were so cool! I still have the vest from mine. I have no idea what Garrison did with his. I think he might have pawned it. Joyce was a good egg about it. She worked on those things day and night for over a month. The vests were a shiny paisley material in multiple colors of brown. They were long, with gold chain-style buttons down the front. We had matching brown bell-bottom pants and white long-sleeved turtleneck shirts. The pictures of us are striking. We were part of the new generation with the "mod look."

We disagreed on everything, bickering over every little thing. Garrison said it was because we weren't having sex. I felt it was because we hadn't set a wedding date. I think it was both. It never occurred to me that Garrison only wanted sex from me. Marriage, a home, and children weren't in his future plans. He just said those things, hoping I would give in to his demands. Premarital sex, that's what it was called. Everyone was talking about it on the news, in magazines and books. Everyone had an opinion on whether it was right or wrong. Almost all people polled who were twenty-five and under saw nothing wrong with it. Almost everyone over that age thought it was wrong. I knew where I stood on the subject, even if I wasn't yet twenty-five.

In January, Garrison quit his factory job and went back to college full-time on the GI Bill. I was proud of him. He intended to major in music and chemistry. He had an IQ of one hundred and eighty-five! If he liked something, learning it came easy to him. Although he didn't read a note of music, he could play almost any instrument and any song he heard. He had an amazing ear for it.

Some of the things that made our relationship work were the things we had in common, like our love of music, nature, and antiques. Hiking in the woods was a favorite thing. We went downtown in the big city to hear the symphony play. Estate auctions were fun for us. We bought some nice things that we would put in our own home someday. We loved all the same movies. The ones we saw together still warm my heart. I can watch them over and over again. We loved *Funny Girl* and *Butch Cassidy and the Sundance Kid*. When I see them, I remember how happy they made us.

I pressed Garrison about a date for our wedding. "Why don't we get married in August?" I asked. "By then you'll know how school is going, and we can take our time planning the wedding." To my surprise he agreed. I was walking on air. But he only agreed because he thought it would make me give in to sex, and it didn't. I didn't want to be a statistic, pregnant before marriage. In February I took a second job doing home care for an elderly man in my neighborhood, for four hours in the morning. I saved all the extra money for the wedding. I had a scrapbook full of plans. I even knew what kind of dress I wanted.

I went to Strawberry Fields for Mama. She came to the big city so I could try on wedding gowns. It was only the second dress I put on. The first one was too big, and it cost more than I could afford. We ended up a local shop in South End. They had the very gown I had seen in a bride's magazine; Alfred Angelo was the designer. It was a lace gown, very full, with long wedding sleeves, a scalloped neckline, and a fitted bodice that came to a point just below my waist in front and back. It had tiered ruffles and a long train, and it was covered in crystals. It fit perfectly! "Huh!" said the store clerk as I came out in the dress. "That dress is only designed to go on a mannequin, but it fits you perfectly. It doesn't require any alterations." I bought a dress made for a store dummy!

Millinery shops do not exist anymore. You could find them all over the city; hats and other headgear were made to fit your every specification. In the window of the shop in South End was a crown made entirely of crystals. I bought it, along with special tulle, for twenty-five dollars. The ladies in the shop were excited to make my veil. I went to the stationery shop down the street and ordered invitations. It was a small, family-owned store. They did most of the work by hand in the store. Now we have computers that can make such things in an instant. Antonia wrote the invitations. She was good at it. She was living at Strawberry Fields again with Redmond and the four boys. Since Garrison didn't like making wedding plans, I was glad for her help. Lots of nurses at the hospital were busy planning their weddings. They all complained that their future husbands didn't want to help, so I wasn't upset that Garrison wouldn't discuss plans with me. "Just do it, and let me know where I'm to be and what I'm supposed to do," he said.

I wanted the reception to be at the country club in Freedom Falls where I had first heard Garrison's beautiful voice. Antonia did her best to get it for me, but we couldn't find anyone there. We went with the Knights of Columbus hall.

The bridesmaids were fitted for their dresses. They were being made by the most famous dressmaker in Henderson County. Eccentric Mrs. Kerry always took on more than she could handle. She had been known to sew a bride's hem as she walked down the aisle. She worked from her home until the day she died. Dresses and material were everywhere in her big, beautiful home. She sewed day and night. I designed the dress myself, but I lacked the talent to draw a picture of it. As I explained the dress to her, she drew the exact dress! It was an A-line shape with a high waist, a scoop neckline, and sheer, wide sleeves gathered in wide cuffs at the wrists. It was a typical design of the day, but with a twist: I wanted them in every color of the rainbow. I had six bridesmaids. Joyce was my maid of honor. Her dress in light blue had a train. She wanted blue because she had red hair. Carmella wore yellow, and my little neighbor Julie wore lavender. My niece Susie wore pink. Katie and Sally, who were almost the same age, walked together as junior bridesmaids. They wore peach and mint green.

I found flowers for their hair to match the dresses. I wanted them to carry umbrellas to match their dresses, but we couldn't find any. I came up with the idea to make them by purchasing child-sized ones, removing the plastic, and replacing it with tulle, ruffles, and flowers.

Joyce worked night after night, making the umbrellas to my specifications. She could have earned a living doing it. I asked her once why she didn't go into the business. "Then it wouldn't be enjoyable or relaxing. It would be a job," she answered. I didn't understand. I rarely did anything for fun or relaxation. I only knew work and more work. It was the way I was raised. I had been taught that making a living wage and caring for yourself and your family were the most important things in life. Everything else was secondary. The following year, all kinds of umbrellas appeared in bridal magazines and store windows. I was always just a little too ahead of the times.

I knew that Garrison still cheated. He admitted it, and he tried to call off the wedding. But then he came to the apartment late one night and said he was sorry. He still wanted to get married, if I would still have him. I thought of those wedding vows as magic that would make him stop cheating after we spoke them. As the wedding drew near, Garrison, who was always a man of few words, became a man of fewer words. He did as I asked and ordered his tux. I wanted the latest style, called the Edwardian tux; it matched perfectly with the bridesmaids' dresses and my own. I think Garrison had a good time going to the formalwear store with Norman and Buddy and Joel, who were standing up with him. They all had a good sense of humor, and they made it a fun outing.

Garrison and I went to order flowers and the cake. It was a rare day of fun for us. Things got a little tense at the florist's in Henderson. Mrs. Kyle exclaimed, "Well, isn't it wonderful! You're finally getting married! I bet your mama's proud! You'll still be able to have a baby or two at your age." Garrison turned white, so I had to say something.

"Why, yes, Mrs. Kyle, she is very proud! I'm only twenty-five, so I think I can still have babies if we decide to have them. I believe you and my mama were in your late thirties when you had your last babies," I said, smiling.

"Well, what would you like, dear, for the wedding flowers?" she asked. Her face turned a little green as she started to look through wedding books.

"Daisies," I replied. "I want plain white ones in a cascade-style bouquet. I want them in all colors of the rainbow for each bridesmaid." I loved them. They grew wild on the farm along with buttercups and purple snakegrass. I used to make beautiful bouquets of them.

"Daisies are so cheap, my dear. Are you sure you want them and not some nice white roses for you and these pastel ones for the girls?" she asked in her most polite voice.

"She wants the daisies!" Garrison, the man of few words, said it in a firm, sharp voice that made Mrs. Kyle and me straighten our backs. "They're her favorite." The order was written swiftly.

We went to a bakery in Freedom Falls. "I'd like one of those fountains in the cake that actually has water in it. Blue water," I said to the owner.

"Well, I know what you're talking about. I've seen them, but the problem is, I never made one myself," he replied.

"I'm sure you can figure it out, sir," I said as I handed him a bag with all of the figurines in it for the cake. "I want stairs going up to the fountain, and these little bridesmaids and groomsmen going up the stairs, and the bride and groom on top. I want all the flowers on the cake to be in these colors."

"All right, lady, I'll try my best," he replied, scratching his head. We shook hands and thanked him.

Garrison chuckled as we got back into the car. "I don't think that guy knows how to make that cake. I hope you aren't going to be disappointed," he said.

"Oh, I think he'll figure it out, since everyone I know who is getting married now is asking for the same one," I replied.

"Yah, well, you live in the big city, and this is Freedom Falls in Henderson County, remember," he said. "I just don't want you to expect too much, that's all."

Joyce and I went to the mall so I could get a wedding ring for Garrison. He said he didn't want one, but I wanted him to have one. I found a beautiful, wide white-gold band with a single diamond in it that had grooves around it like a starburst. It would complement my set perfectly.

Everything for the wedding was in place. I was happy. Every time Garrison and I were together, I chattered on and on about the wedding. He became more silent and remote. I refused to think about it or let it dampen my high spirits. When we went to see the priest for premarital counseling, I worried that Garrison wouldn't go through with it. He was so nervous, and he seemed angry about having to go. To my surprise Father Southerland, the new pastor at Christ the

King Church, was very nice. He seemed to like Garrison a lot. He spent a lot of time talking to him about the sacrament of marriage. We had sessions together and then separately. I wasn't supposed to be listening, but I could hear what he and Father were saying. They were joking around a lot, but then it came to that serious question, "Is anyone forcing you to marry?" I held my breath, but Garrison answered a firm no. When we left, I said that I thought our premarital interviews went well. To my amazement, Garrison agreed.

He seemed pleased when I showed him the wedding band. "Oh, no, Garrison," I said as he tried to hand it back. "Take it home, and put it with mine, so you can give them to your brother. He will give them to us during the ceremony."

"Okay," he said reluctantly. His sad look seeped right into my heart. I had a hard time blotting it from my mind.

≈17≈

Storm Clouds Gathering

THE SUN WASN'T SHINING the day of that fairy-tale wedding, or for many days after it. Instead, storm clouds gathered the night before. They were gathering in my life as well, but I refused to see them. Everything went well at the rehearsal and the rehearsal dinner. Father Southerland laughed and joked with everyone. We went to the Knights of Columbus hall and decorated it in all the colors of the rainbow. We were all in high spirits. Garrison seemed relaxed and happy when we said our good-byes.

Joyce and I were staying at Strawberry Fields. Julie and her husband, Tim, were at a motel in New Moon. I couldn't sleep, and Joyce couldn't either. I found her on the front porch off the upstairs kitchen, getting some fresh air. It was a hot night with no breeze, moon, or stars. I couldn't see Venus. "I think it is going to rain, Joyce," I said with disappointment I couldn't hide.

"I know," she said. "I can feel it too."

"As if the rain isn't bad enough, I started my period tonight," I said, feeling very let down.

"Well, Garrison will understand. I have a feeling he's the kind of guy that won't care," she replied, to my surprise. "Come on, now, let's get some sleep." We went back to bed, but I didn't sleep. When we got up, we couldn't eat Mama's large breakfast. Joyce and I drank our beloved coffee. She was a constant coffee drinker. The girls arrived at the house early so Julie could do everyone's hair.

I talked Mama out of having that traditional wedding meal she always served. I told her it just wasn't done anymore, and we were having an afternoon wedding anyway. We were ready when Mrs. Fienberg's son came to the farm to take pictures of us in Mama's beautiful living room. It still looked brand new. We all look so young and small in the pictures. The girls in their rainbow dresses, holding those umbrellas, with the matching flowers in their hair, looked like young Hollywood.

The storm clouds continued to gather as we left the car and walked to the front doors of Christ the King Church. Joyce was behind me, carrying my train. Pa and Mama were on either side. I suddenly felt calm and happy! This was my wedding day. I wanted to enjoy it. I no longer cared if it was perfect. I just wanted to marry the man that I loved with all my being, and to be forever known as Mrs. Garrison Michael! As Pa walked me down the aisle, I saw Garrison standing at the altar. I smiled brightly at him, and he smiled back, looking happier than he had in all the years we were together. When we approached the altar, Pa placed my hand in Garrison's. We turned to face Father Southerland. He leaned toward us and said to me, "That is the biggest dress I have ever seen in all the years I've been doing this." We both started to laugh!

We had the full traditional High Mass. Garrison's mother claimed until she died that she never heard Garrison say, "I do." For years I joked that I'd said it for him: "Oh, he does, he does." It was a funny story that all our friends loved to hear. "Ave Maria" filled the whole church, flowing down from the choir loft. Since Vatican II, the rules about what type of music you could have in church were relaxed. Besides that traditional song, the soloist sang "As Long As He Needs Me," from the popular movie version of *Romeo and Juliet*. The song would have profound meaning to me later.

A light rain was falling by the time we finished with the pictures.

I'm looking at the picture of Garrison and me sitting in the backseat of my pa's brand-new Chevy Impala. There are raindrops on the windows, but we look happy. "You won't believe the cake when you see it," I remember him saying.

"What are you talking about, Garrison?" I asked. We pulled out of the church parking lot. Garrison's brother was driving the decorated car. He and Joyce blasted the horn.

"Well, the guy from the bakery called me this morning at home. I still had the key to the hall. I had to go there and let him in. The cake is so big, we had to take it apart to get it through the door," he said. I looked shocked. "Don't worry, you're going to love it! I've never seen anything so beautiful. Well, maybe you in that dress." That may have been the only time Garrison ever said that to me. I was distracted by the news that there might be a problem with the cake.

It was six feet tall and had six layers. The baker told Garrison that he had to build a base for the fountain that could house the motor underneath, so it wouldn't be seen. "So don't cut the bottom layer," he said. "It's fake." I'm still amazed when I look at the pictures. That cake only cost one hundred dollars. Today such a masterpiece would be about ten thousand dollars.

Garrison and I greeted our guests together. All of our friends and our entire families were in attendance. Everyone laughed, talked, and had a good time. Dinner was family-style and very good. Antonia had chosen the caterer, and I had selected the menu. I actually ate! I was hungry for the first time. I realized I hadn't eaten in days.

Music filled the room when Garrison's band began to play. They did it as a wedding present. They'd hired a drummer so Garrison wouldn't have to play at his own wedding. We danced the first dance together. I didn't know it would be the last time we would dance. At the end of the evening, the band played "Let Me Call You Sweetheart." Our friends and families circled around us, singing. When the song ended, we left to begin our new life.

My parents and siblings did a lot of background work to create the wedding of my dreams. Antonia and Mama thought of everything.

After the dinner, Mama and some of the other ladies packed the leftover food, the gifts, and the box with all the envelopes. They took everything back to the farm. Redmond decorated my car and drove it to the reception. The exit picture of us leaving the reception tells a story in itself. Garrison is behind me, with his tie gone, wearing a big smile. I have my big dress hiked up. Smiling, I'm pulling him toward the door as our guests wave.

When we arrived at Strawberry Fields, the fairy-tale princess wedding continued in royal style. I entered the house through the upstairs kitchen with Garrison to find Sandy Smith waiting for me. "Your parents hired me to watch the farm. I'm to help you change out of your dress into your going-away clothes. I've stacked the gifts in your room, along with the cards box. After I help you change, you and Garrison can go through them. You two can count the money. I'll write the amount in each card so that you can send thank-you notes," she said.

Sandy was a sweet girl. She was in grade school when I was in high school. She lived with her family on that little stretch of road behind our farm. We used to ride the same school bus. "Thank you so much, Sandy, for doing this and giving up a Saturday night."

"Oh, it's nothing! You've always been my idol ever since I was a tiny girl. I was delighted when your sister called me. You're so beautiful in that dress," she replied, blinking back a few tears. I had to bite my lower lip so I wouldn't start crying.

Garrison made himself comfortable at the kitchen table. Sandy and I went into my room to see if we could figure out how to get me out of the big dress. It had over a hundred tiny, lace-covered buttons fastened by little loops down the back. Joyce had buttoned them with a crochet hooks.

"Just let it fall to the floor. I'll get it when we're done," Sandy said once all the buttons were undone. I carefully took my arms out of the long lace sleeves, and she slipped the new cream-colored short high-waist dress over my head. It had long, wide sleeves fastened at the wrist and a little green vest with cream-colored embroidery around the edges. It fastened under the bust with an embroidered button. I stepped from the gown and sat in front of the mirror. Sandy removed my crown of crystals. She brushed my hair and handed me a tube of lipstick. "It's all you need. You're so pretty without makeup."

I stepped into the kitchen, and Sandy followed, carrying the box. Garrison looked pleased but said nothing. We opened the envelopes and found that we had enough money to take a trip. While I put a few more things into my suitcase, Sandy took care of the princess's dress still lying on the floor in my room. She carried my suitcase to the car and would not hear of Garrison doing it. I saw him put a ten-dollar bill into her hand.

We planned to spend the night at a large hotel on the big highway. From there we would map out our trip to Denver. I was excited about seeing mountains. I thought the magic would continue when we got to the hotel. Happiness flowed through me like electricity when Garrison said, "I'd like a room for my wife and me." He signed us in as Mr. and Mrs. Garrison Michael.

My heart was pounding when I came out of the bathroom wearing a white Grecian-style negligee with nothing on under it but a tiny pair of briefs. I still had my period. Garrison stared. Then he got up and went into the bathroom. I got in bed and covered up. I was filled with fear and desire. This turned into incredible disappointment when he returned and said, "I think we should get some sleep. It's been a long day." He slipped into bed and took me into his arms. The fire ignited! I thought there was no turning back. The skimpy white briefs were torn off in seconds, but when Garrison tried to enter me, I had no idea anything could hurt so bad. I stifled a scream by putting my fist into my mouth. He immediately backed off and repeated his plea for sleep. The fairy tale I had been living all day came to an abrupt end. I don't think I slept much, but Garrison slept soundly. I had a lot to think about. Reality began to set in as I started to see my life ahead of me, how ill-equipped I was to handle it. All I knew of sex came from my anatomy and nursing books and from eavesdropping on conversations between Carmella and Antonia. I only knew the mechanics and nothing else. I would learn that Garrison only knew about sex with fast, experienced women.

There was blood everywhere the next morning. Garrison cleaned it up and me too. He did it swiftly and gently helped me into the shower. "I'm sorry, Garrison. I didn't know it was going to hurt," I said once we were in the car on our way to Colorado.

"It's okay. It will get better," he said softly. I wondered if it would. I sat silently recalling my trip to the doctor a few weeks ago. I had done my best to prepare myself for that internal exam, but it never happened. When Dr. Castro discovered I hadn't had sex yet, he'd refused to do the exam.

"Let your husband have you first, the lucky man! Then you come back here, and I examine you. I give you pills, yes?" he asked in his heavy Cuban accent. Birth-control pills were new on the market, and all the girls I knew who were getting married were taking them. Some started them months before their wedding.

"No, I'm Catholic, and I don't think I want them, but I'll take the spermicidal foam instead," I said. I had read about it in a bride's magazine. I thought it was the better choice for a Catholic girl. Reality was never my best subject. Birth control was still birth control, no matter what kind. It was against all teachings of the church.

"Suit yourself," he said, chuckling a little while writing the script. "You are very beautiful girl. I hope your husband know what a catch you are." Thinking about my conversation with Dr. Castro, I realized I hadn't used the spermicidal last night. But I had my period.

In Wyoming it didn't go any better than the night before. I found myself crying and apologizing to Garrison again. He was gentle and understanding for the next few nights, but each night was more painful than the last. The foam made me itch and burn. I was so uncomfortable. I was starting to have trouble walking.

"Garrison!" I called out as we were driving. "Look, I think I see mountains." It was one of the high points in our life together. We reached the Rockies and saw snowcaps. I have a picture of me pointing toward them with my hair blowing in the wind, and one with Garrison looking through binoculars.

By the fifth day of our adventure Garrison reached the limit of his patience with me. That night he pinned me to the bed and entered me with force. I screamed and cried for an hour. I couldn't walk well for an entire day. I couldn't imagine how our relationship was going to work. "I'm sorry I had to do that," he said, helping me into the shower again. "Maybe it will be better now." It wasn't.

Denver was beautiful for sightseeing. We went shopping and bought each other wedding presents. What I purchased for him slips my memory. We went into a downtown department store. He just walked up to a rack of clothes and pulled out a purple and gray pantsuit. "Are you entirely sure it's what you want to buy for me?" I asked. He nodded. "Shouldn't I try it on, and shouldn't we look around a little more?" He shook his head.

That evening I dressed in a short white minidress with tiered ruffles and orange polka-dots, a high waist, a low-cut V-neck, and long, puffy sleeves. Garrison loved it. We went to a popular night spot in the heart of the city. We saw Bob Dylan's band perform. They called themselves the Band. It was a wonderful evening.

The next day I put on the pantsuit. To my amazement, it was a perfect fit and quite flattering. I never would have chosen it. "I just don't know how you do it. You always seem to pick the right thing for me," I said as we went to visit with an army buddy of Garrison's. Gary lived in Denver with his mother. He tried getting his life together after returning from the war. He and Garrison had met in a ward at the army hospital in Boston. It didn't bother me that Garrison wanted to see Gary; it was his trip too. When it came to my husband, I was willing to paint everything a rosy color. The damage done to Gary was quite evident. He was a tall, thin man with long red hair and a red beard. His hand shook the whole time. He continuously wiped his watering eyes as he and Garrison smoked one cigarette after another. He was so thin. There was no help for soldiers with his kind of wounds. Men like him had to cope on their own. Most of them turned to drugs and other forms of destructive behavior to stop the horror playing over and over in their minds. He and Garrison wrote to each other often.

After a week and a half, Garrison thought we should start for home by a different route and visit other places. After a few days on the road, we were homeward bound. "I can't wait to get home," Garrison said. "I miss my family. Don't you miss yours too?" There should have been a big red flag flying, a loud drum beating. I chose to brush the rosy paint over it again, too afraid to ask myself what kind of man misses his family on his honeymoon.

Back in our own apartment, without Joyce, I hoped we would settle in and be the kind of husband and wife I saw on TV. Garrison grumbled; the apartment didn't feel like home to him. The place had flooded once, and it was a constant worry that it would happen again.

I woke early one Sunday morning. Garrison hadn't returned home from playing the night before. I wanted to make him a special breakfast when he arrived. Suddenly I became so dizzy and nauseated that I fell to my knees in the bathroom, vomiting violently into the commode. I was sweating profusely. I could hardly get up. I felt better after about an hour. I got dressed and went to the store. I don't know what made me look at the bulletin board, but there was an ad for a house for rent. It was just past the bridge and over the railroad tracks, a few blocks from the hospital. I memorized the address and phone number. "Garrison, I found an ad for a house for rent! Can we go look at it?" The old couple was retiring to a warmer climate. They agreed to rent it to us on the spot because I was a nurse and I worked at the hospital. It bothered Garrison that it was because of me that we got the place.

I immediately made another appointment to see Dr. Castro. The discomfort wasn't going away. I felt very tired, as if I had the flu. "I think I'm allergic to that foam, so maybe I should take that pill," I said to Dr. Castro, who sat patiently listening to me tell him about the pain, the rash, and the fact that I was tired and feeling sick.

"No, my dear, I can't give you the pill," he finally said.

"But of course you can. We talked about it on my last visit, and you suggested it," I replied.

"I can't give you, my beauty, because you are pregnant," he said calmly.

"What? I can't be!" I exclaimed, jumping to my feet.

"Why? Haven't you had penetrating sex yet?" asked Dr. Castro.

"Well, yes, but we used the foam," I replied, crying now. "How do you know I'm pregnant, when you haven't examined me?"

Dr. Castro jumped from his chair and grabbed me by my shoulders, shaking me. "Look!" he said softly but urgently. "You are not going to die. You are just going to have a baby. Go to the lab, if you want, and get a urine test. I can tell you it will be positive, and if you want me to examine you, I will." I went behind the screen and prepared for the internal exam. "I can't do it," he said after getting me in the stirrups. He removed his gloves. I took my feet down, and he helped me sit up. "Your hymen is still intact. Go home and enjoy your husband, now that you don't need pills or foam." Smiling, he bent down and kissed me on the cheek. "You don't know how I envy that man."

I was sitting at the kitchen table in our new little house, crying, when Garrison arrived home from band practice. I was shaking with fear. "Oh, Garrison, I'm so sorry. I'm pregnant," I said, putting my head in my hands, sobbing uncontrollably. I didn't like saying this to my husband of five weeks.

He started laughing and went down the hall to the bathroom. I followed him. He opened the medicine cabinet, took the spermicidal foam, and tossed it into the garbage. "We don't need this anymore, and now we can really have a honeymoon." He carried me to bed. My husband had a good time; I did not share in the fun. It was still so very painful. I was sick every morning and most of the day for the next seven months. I was miserable. My constant state of nausea and fatigue began to wear on him. I was working the day shift. I made it through my eight hours, but I could do nothing but go to bed the minute I got home. Garrison felt alone and deserted. He was such a kid, used to living in a large family where he was cared for and looked after.

Garrison took a job as a cook in a local restaurant. Three weeks later I came home from work to find him in bed, the lights off and the curtains drawn. He was having a severe migraine headache. He got them when he was under stress. He was very sick for two days. "Garrison, you don't have to work," I said. "I earn enough money. Just concentrate on your studies at school." It never occurred to me to ask him where his money went. The check from the government came every month he was in school. I started a savings account with it. I deposited my pay into our checking account. Garrison paid the bills. I just took a little money for gas and groceries.

I was very embarrassed to be pregnant so soon. I didn't want people thinking it had happened before the wedding. Most folks in the city didn't care. Back in Henderson and New Moon it was all they could talk about. The word spread quickly as I began to show. Another Rosario girl pregnant? Well, what else is new?

Being the naive child I was, I had failed to put Garrison on my insurance and change us to a family policy before I found out I was pregnant. Insurance companies didn't cover pregnancy for unmarried women. As far as they were concerned, I was unmarried. We had to pay the doctor and hospital out of pocket.

I returned to the doctor the following month, and this time I got Dr. Castro's partner, Dr. Madrid. He was such a lovely gentleman with beautiful manners. "Oh, Mrs. Michael, I see you often at the hospital. You are a beautiful woman, and look, you only gain a few pounds. How nice," he said in his lovely Spanish accent. I had totally psyched myself up for the exam. "My dear, I am afraid I do no exam today. You still have hymen intact. You go home to husband, and everything will be all right, that lucky man."

I cried the rest of the afternoon. Julie came by to see the new little home. "What's wrong with me, Julie? I'm married for more than two months, I'm pregnant, I'm sick all the time. I still have an intact hymen, and sex is so painful. I didn't know it was going to be like this," I cried.

"Well, I've seen things you can buy in a magazine. They're call vaginal dilators. Why don't you get them, see if it makes it better for you?" she asked.

"Julie," I said, staring at her, "have you really looked at Garrison? He wears a size fourteen shoe. I don't think I need them!"

Garrison quit his job as a cook. I became the main breadwinner. Even though I was always sick, I went to work. I worked harder than ever as a practical nurse at Our Lady of Light. Things were changing fast. I had to go with the flow if I was going to keep a roof over our heads. I worried about everything—bills, the baby, work, and motherhood. I worried about Garrison. How would I ever be the wife he so obviously needed?

We purchased an expensive crib and matching changing table from a salesman who came to our door. There was no such thing as the privacy act. Everyone knew your business. We didn't have computers or Internet. Instead, sales and marketing people hung around doctors' offices and pharmacies. For a few bucks they could learn all the names and addresses of those who needed their products. These point men hung around your neighborhood. We bought the crib because we were young and had no idea what a baby needed. We didn't know that the only thing infants need is two loving, stable parents. "Babies need so many things, Mama," I complained. "I hope I can earn enough to pay for it." Garrison didn't want me working overtime, but he wouldn't let me go to the clubs with him either.

"You no worry. I save money for baby things, and me and Pa, we take you to get," Mama said. I didn't go near Antonia and Carmella. They were delighted to hear of the coming birth. They were happy that I was like them: married, with child, and miserable.

I saw Dr. Castro one month and Dr. Madrid the next. I was in love with them. They were so different from one another. Every time I saw Dr. Madrid, he sang my praises, saying how beautiful I looked and how pleased he was that I hadn't gained weight. When I saw Dr. Castro he warned me to watch everything I ate. "You don't want to lose that lovely body of yours. Your husband won't be happy." I wasn't sure how he knew, but he was totally right.

After six months I could taste food. I began to like it. I was becoming a pretty good cook, thanks to my mother-in-law. She wasn't a good cook, but she gave me her Fanny Farmer cookbook. It was so comprehensive that you could be a complete idiot and learn to cook.

I checked myself in the mirror every day for signs that I was looking like Antonia when she was pregnant. I was never able to forget what pregnancy did to her body. I was unchanged, except for a little bulge just below my waist. Garrison said it looked like I had stood on a basketball court, looking up with my mouth open during a free throw, and accidentally swallowed the ball. By my ninth month I had gained twenty pounds. I put on my favorite bathing suit. The leopard-print bikini still fit. I was so obsessed with my figure and getting it back that six weeks after Sarah-Jane was born, I was back in that bikini! My breasts grew a cup size bigger. Garrison took my picture to show all his friends. It was the only one he carried in his wallet.

I didn't think the fact that people were counting the months on their fingers was bothering Garrison. It bothered me a lot. He was allowing me again to go to clubs he played. It was fun for him to see guys come up and ask me to dance. When I stood up and they saw the basketball in my abdomen, they would apologize and step away. On our nine-month anniversary, May 8, we were having dinner. "Happy nine-month anniversary, Garrison," I said. I had baked a little cake for the occasion.

"Have we been married for nine months?" he asked.

"Yes!" I replied.

He went to the phone and dialed a number. "Hello, Sharon," he said. "Guess what? I've been married to my wife for nine months, and she is still pregnant. Isn't that amazing! Now you can stop counting the months every time you see her!" He slammed down the phone. I was shocked. Garrison was never given to such outbursts. It never occurred to me that gossip would bother him.

My parents and I shopped for baby items at a big discount store. We still lacked many things. The next day, after work, I went to my head nurse's house for a wedding shower for my friend Janet. To my surprise, it was a shower for both of us. I was so grateful to my friends from Our Lady of Light. They truly were like family.

A week before the baby's birth, Garrison insisted that I go with him to New Moon, where the band played three nights a week. Carmella worked at that restaurant. She and Antonia came together. "Well, welcome to the real world. You look fat and pregnant," remarked Antonia. As young women walked by, Carmella pointed out the ones that she knew followed my husband around.

"See that one there?" she said. "I saw her sitting in his car last week. I'd go tell her to leave him alone, if I were you. Tell her you'll beat the hell out of her if she doesn't stay away from him." Carmella had always been the fighter.

"Carmella, I don't think I'm in a position to beat up anyone. I'm about to have a baby," I said calmly.

"Well, don't say I didn't warn you when he runs off with one of them," she replied.

At the end of May, the basketball bump moved even lower. It made me have to use the bathroom all the time. I didn't want anyone at work to know my time was near. I wanted to work until I delivered. I cleaned and painted our second bedroom at night, since I couldn't sleep. I was nervous, restless, and afraid. How would I handle motherhood and a full-time job, and keep Garrison happy? I wondered how other women did it, but I was too ashamed of my ignorance to ask. I feared I would be looked upon as insecure and immature. I was all those things that I tried to hide. As Garrison prepared to leave for the club, I told him, "I feel like I'm having contractions. I think I might have the baby tonight. Is it okay if I call you at the club to come home?"

"Well, okay, but try to hold out long as you can, so I can get paid for the whole night," he replied.

"I guess I'll call Julie and see if she wants to come over and keep me company. In case something happens, I won't be alone," I said, feeling like a burden on Garrison.

Julie came with soda pop and snacks. "You don't have to watch what you eat anymore. I think it will make the time pass faster if we dance, eat, and have ourselves a little party."

Garrison came home at two in the morning, very early for him. "You're still up. I thought you would be asleep. We're going to bed. You need rest," he said. I couldn't sleep. I felt a surge of high energy that wouldn't let me relax. The contractions started coming regularly. I was terrified. I wanted Garrison to sleep. He had final exams that morning. At seven I got up and took a shower. When you went in to have a baby, they did terrible things to you. They shaved all your pubic hair and give you enemas until the water returned clear. I did it all myself at home. The nurses in the delivery area were shocked. They couldn't imagine how a pregnant woman could accomplish these things alone. I was a dancer and very limber.

Garrison slept, while I labored with little or no progress. "It's going to be a while before she has this baby. If you have somewhere you need to be, you could go," the nurse told him.

"I'm going to take my last final exam. I'll be back," he said. I felt very alone. I knew the mechanics of childbirth. I had even delivered an infant in nursing school. I was aware of the things that could go wrong, and there was that picture of Antonia still in my head.

"Well, now we can get started," said an older nurse, adjusting the Pitocin drip to run faster. Just then Dr. Madrid came into the room.

"My darling, I hate to do it, but the baby is face up. I will attempt to turn the infant in utero, so don't be alarmed," he said. I had never experienced such pain in my life. I began to scream.

"Shut up!" yelled the nurse. "You'll scare all of the other mothers in labor." I apologized between screams. The baby didn't turn. The Pitocin made the contractions stronger. I lay there screaming and saying how sorry I was for doing it. Garrison came back, dressed in scrubs. He leaned over and kissed me.

"I got back here as fast as I could. My instructor gave me the test right away. I think she is just as excited about the baby as I am. I saw Dr. Madrid, and he told me to come with him and get dressed in this. He's letting me into the delivery room." Fathers were not allowed in the delivery room. The nurses were upset because Dr. Madrid let Garrison stay. They thought he would pass out or worse, but he handled it well.

"What time is it?" I asked.

"It's almost one in the afternoon," he replied.

I refused to be sedated. "Garrison, come," Dr. Madrid said. "We will get this baby out! Mrs. Michael, you will watch in the mirror up above you." I had never seen so much blood in a delivery. I was strapped down and couldn't move. Dr. Madrid took a large pair of special forceps and popped the baby's head out. Sarah-Jane was crying before the rest of her was out. She was face up, with the umbilical cord wrapped around her neck. In Dr. Madrid's skilled hands, my baby was just fine. I was drained but happy to have a girl! Garrison left shortly after the baby was taken from us. Dr. Madrid had a lot of repair work to do. The placenta didn't come and had to be removed surgically. I had many stitches. I was so ashamed and embarrassed that I screamed. I felt so inadequate. I was staying only one day, because we were paying out of pocket. Garrison didn't come for me until Saturday morning, and only after I called home about one hundred times. He had stayed out all night, and he refused to tell me where. It wasn't the first time, and it wouldn't be the last.

The baby cried all the time, and I cried with her. I couldn't sleep, for fear of something happening to her. Garrison did his best to help, but the responsibility fell on me. In six weeks I was going back to work the three-to-eleven shift. Garrison would watch the baby when he wasn't playing music. We also hired a neighbor from a few houses down. I was depressed, and I lost focus. I couldn't make a simple decision. I had always been the one in control. We needed a rocking chair, but I was so uncomfortable in every one I tried that I left the store without one. "I just can't find one, Garrison," I said when I arrived home after two hours. He left and came back an hour later, followed by a delivery man with a big overstuffed rocking chair. The baby cried for about six hours straight, every afternoon and night.

Garrison was at the end of his rope with me and the baby. He said it to his mother on the phone. His sister Mazy overheard. She told him what was wrong with me. She told him he shouldn't worry, it would pass. "I have just the book to help you," she said. Dr. Spock's book on baby and child care helped me to understand my baby and myself as a mother. After about six months, things were better with the baby but not with me and Garrison. I didn't enjoy sex, and he seemed to want it at the most inconvenient times. I struggled to please him, keep my job, and care for the baby.

Work seemed to be the only place I felt in control. I was still the main breadwinner. I did the cooking, the cleaning, and the laundry, with a wringer washer that required a lot of muscle. I shopped Monday mornings before Garrison and the baby woke. I was exhausted. It was hard to believe how quickly my life had changed. I went from being the big-city woman, dressed in the latest fashion, to a life consisting of work and more work. I saw little of my family. Garrison visited his family two or three times a week. He spent many hours away at school and band practice. Little changed for him. There was plenty of evidence that he was seeing other women: the smell of another's perfume and love marks on his neck. I reached my breaking point and confronted him. "I know you're cheating on me, Garrison. I'm not blind! Why don't you leave and go live with your girlfriend, or go back home to your family? That's where you spend most of your time anyway."

Garrison started yelling at me. "You never pay any attention to me! I might as well not be here! If you're not at work, you're cooking, cleaning, doing the laundry, or holding the baby. It's your fault I date other women!" I didn't know he could yell.

"I have to work to support us so you can go to school and get your degree. I'll quit once you're done. I'll be glad to stay home once you have a good job."

"I never intend to get a good job. I like school and studying. I don't ever intend to work at a boring nine-to-five job. Music is what I'll do for the rest of my life," he said. Until that argument, I didn't know what my husband wanted out of life. It may have been the first time he knew. I didn't know anything about the man I married. Suddenly I recalled a recurrent dream I had before our wedding. I was dressed in my beautiful gown, smiling, walking down the aisle to meet the man I would marry. When I reached him, he had no face. My subconscious mind had told me that I didn't know him.

"This isn't what I thought married life would be like, Garrison. I thought we wanted the same things—a nice home and three children. We would grow old together, watching them grow. I didn't know I would be married to a man who is never home," I replied.

I wasn't a big person. I couldn't easily forgive and forget. I couldn't see that these were only threats to a marriage. I didn't know how to make a relationship survive. I did laundry and cleaning. Garrison followed behind, watching me work. "I didn't have sex with her, if you want to know. I couldn't do it. All I could think about was you and Sarah-Jane and my responsibility," he said, hanging his head. I should have believed in him, trusted him, taken him in my arms and forgiven him. I should have said, "Let's start again, treat each other better, and work together." I couldn't do it.

"That was real big of you, Garrison," I replied. I couldn't bring myself to speak to him. Forgiveness was long in coming. It was too long for Garrison. I didn't speak to him for weeks, and it was months before I could allow him near me. Every time he left the house, I wondered where he went and with whom.

❧ 18 ❧

The Heart Won't Lie

I KNEW THERE WAS another woman in Garrison's life. After the birth of Sarah-Jane, I went on the pill in spite of my Catholic upbringing. I went to church carrying my baby. Garrison hadn't set foot in church since our wedding. "I don't believe in any of that stuff," he said. "I only went along with it for my folks and you, but I don't want to pretend it means anything." I was never more alone than I was when I was married to Garrison. We were leading separate lives. I visited my family at Strawberry Fields; he visited his in Henderson. We rarely went together. I refused to listen when my sisters told me about the other woman.

The sex act was still a problem. I heard about a new book entitled *Everything You Ever Wanted to Know About Sex (But Were Afraid to Ask)*. It was a well-written practical manual for people like me. I read it from cover to cover. Garrison read it too. Sex got better, but Garrison wasn't satisfied. He went from one extreme to the other. He would ignore me for long periods. Then there were times he wanted me at the most inopportune moments. If I was cooking dinner, watching it carefully, he would come into the kitchen and take me by force. If the baby was waking from her nap and crying, he would carry me off to bed. If I was the one who wanted sex, he would be totally unable to perform. He said it was my fault. If I refused him, he left home for hours or even days. Since our lovemaking was so sporadic, I had a hard time remembering to take the pill. It led to a miscarriage, which was sad and painful for me. I think Garrison was relieved.

I tried making life easier for us. "Garrison, I've been saving money, and we have enough to get an automatic washer. It would save so much time for us."

"Suit yourself. I don't think we need one. It's a waste of money. The wringer works just fine. Buy it if you want, but don't expect me to hook it up. I don't think it will work in here." I finally got him to go shopping for the Maytag, but he seemed indifferent, even resentful.

The post–World War II bungalow didn't have the modern hookup for a washer, but the men who delivered it said it was an easy fix. I went next door to see how my neighbors had installed theirs. "Garrison, I figured it out. Here are the things you'll need from the hardware store for the hookup. Mr. Jameson next door said he would help you, but I think it looks pretty easy." To my amazement, the washer did save a lot of time, but it wasn't time that my husband chose to spend with me. It seemed to free him up to stay away from home longer.

The Jameson's retired and sold their house to a young couple with a girl a little older than Sarah-Jane and a baby boy. We knew each other instantly. "Mary, you took care of me when I was in the hospital with a blood disorder, when I was pregnant with Molly!" Sandy exclaimed.

"I remember you. I'm glad you're well. It's great that we will be neighbors," I replied. I could spend time with her while our children played together. Sandy was a stay-at-home mom.

Since I worked afternoons and Sandy's husband worked days, she and Garrison spent a lot of time together with the children. She wasn't much of a housekeeper, neglecting it weeks at a time. Jerry complained. Garrison thought it was great. He got along very well with Sandy but not Jerry. She took Sarah-Jane over to play with her children. "They play so well together, it frees me to do a few things around the house so Jerry won't yell." Sandy and Jerry didn't get along, but there would be no talk of a divorce, because of the children. She told me they didn't sleep in the same room. "You're so lucky to be married to a guy who loves you." I was too ashamed of the way we were to tell her that things weren't as they appeared. I couldn't tell her I was miserable and unhappy. I couldn't tell her how alone I felt. I saw Jerry come home evenings, and he was there every weekend. I never heard him speak a mean word to Sandy, although she said they fought all the time.

After our second anniversary, Garrison dropped out of school and went on the road. The band had a new agent who got them jobs all over the Midwest. Mr. Hilbert promised them that touring would lead to a recording contract once they got to California. I was alone more than ever.

Around two o'clock one morning, I heard someone at the door. I sat up in bed. The door opened and closed softly. Footsteps fell on the hardwood floor in the hallway, coming closer. Sarah-Jane was asleep in her room. As the sound of the intruder grew closer, I thought of jumping up and running to her. The door to our room opened slowly. I reached for the lamp on the bedside table, and light flooded the room. I stared in horror as Garrison stared back at me. "Oh, my God in heaven, it's only you!" I finally said.

"Of course it's me. Who else would it be?" he asked. He had been on the road for more than three weeks. I thought he wouldn't be back for another week. He seldom let me know when he would return.

"Well, Sandy and I have had problems with a prowler. We got a good look at him one night when she decided to put the dog into the garage." Sandy's dog, a large greyhound, couldn't bark, but he scared the man away when he tried to enter. I caught sight of the man peeking into our bedroom window. The police never could catch him. He jumped the fence one night and ran away as they were in pursuit. The shocked look I gave him, combined with news of a prowler, prompted Garrison to love me as never before. He was very attentive to Sarah-Jane and me. But Monday morning he left again. I knew he wasn't alone on those trips.

In the early 1970s, I was into the feminist movement. I went to a few meetings, trying to learn about it. Women were treated as second-class citizens. I hoped it would change. If we were buying car insurance or a new washer, salesmen talked to Garrison, even though I was paying the bill. Big transactions were dealt with by men. Women weren't considered smart enough to make large purchases. You had to have a man. First it was your father, and then it was your husband. The meetings helped us understand the movement. They didn't advocate that every woman should get a job or work like a man. They were fighting for our right to choose to be a construction worker or the director of a large corporation. They wanted equal pay for equal work. Even in nursing, a man was paid much more for doing the exact same work. For thousands of years women have been oppressed and objectified. Freedom and equality for women is still just a concept.

By the following spring, I had saved enough for a down payment on a house. I longed for another child. I thought that if I had a boy, Garrison might stay home. I was screwy and unrealistic. It took a while to convince Garrison. We started to look in South Side. "I don't know why we have to live here. I want to be in Henderson," Garrison complained.

"Because I work here, Garrison. I'm supporting us. It's too far a drive. I won't be able to work overtime. We'll need the money when we own our own home. We won't have a sitter, and we have so many wonderful ones here," I explained.

"I could support us if you would let me," Garrison replied.

"But you never put any money in the checking account," I stated.

"You have the government check every month. Isn't that enough for you?" he answered, seething.

"It's for the down payment on the house and emergencies," I replied.

The search continued all spring. I wanted a two-story house with high ceilings, at least three bedrooms, and two baths. We needed a yard and a garage. Finding it on a limited budget was difficult. We secured a VA loan that required a smaller down payment.

When Garrison played locally, I didn't go with him. I hated it the last time I went. I saw a woman who followed him everywhere. She stood by our table and stared at me. He ignored her. The band knew her well. Those guys said unkind things about her. I thought it was because she was so unattractive and overbearing, hanging around them.

The band stopped touring and just played locally. They were more popular in the area, drawing large crowds. The small amount of money I took from his wallet Monday mornings for groceries was all I saw of the three hundred dollars he earned every week. I cooked a big meal before work. On my days off, I cooked an evening meal and set a beautiful table. I tried to have a conversation with my husband. He said little and ate less. I was sure that once we found the ideal house, things would be better.

It wasn't unusual when Garrison didn't return home after playing. I didn't question him when he came in at around noon that day. It was my day off, and I had other things on my mind. "Do you think Sandy would mind if you took Sarah-Jane next door so I could talk to you about something?" he asked.

"No, I don't think she'll mind," I replied. I thought he wanted to go over the information on the last few houses we saw. "I'll take her over and be right back." I went to Sandy. She was always cheerful and full of fun information.

When I returned through the back door, Garrison was standing in the kitchen, pouring coffee. "I fixed your coffee the way you like it," he said. Since having Sarah-Jane, I now liked my coffee with cream and sugar rather than black. My husband had never made me coffee before.

"Thanks, honey," I replied. Garrison leaned against the counter and stared at me. It was so quiet that you could have heard a cat walk across a gravestone.

"I can't live here anymore. I feel trapped. I don't have anything here I can call my own. I need to live by myself—find out what it is I want out of life," he said calmly in his quiet manner.

My heart started to pound in my chest. "I don't know what you mean, Garrison. You have me and Sarah-Jane. We have a home and two cars, and we love each other. What is it that you think you don't have?" I asked.

He sipped his coffee slowly. "No, you have all these things. You wanted all of this, you pay for it."

"Well, I could quit working, and you could take over," I replied.

"No, it won't work. I need to be alone, figure things out for myself. I rented a sleeping room in North End. I've already moved most of my clothes there," he said.

Shock and disbelief began to set in. I started to cry and tremble. "You can't do this, Garrison! We need you. I can't live without you, and neither can Sarah-Jane—she adores you."

"That's the problem. You can live without me. Everything here, you paid for it. You buy my clothes and food, and you pay my car payment. I have nothing to call my own," he said sadly.

It was true. I thought he wanted it that way. He had the best clothes my money could buy. I spent a lot of time shopping and paying for them. I didn't buy things for myself. My wardrobe consisted of jeans, uniforms, and a few good dresses. My things that went out of style went to charity. "Garrison, whatever it is you think you need, I'll get it. I don't understand what has changed. Is it another woman?"

"No, no, it's not!" He lied straight-faced, without blinking an eye.

"We're buying a house, Garrison. We're a family. I think we can work this out like two adults. Just tell me what I can do to make things better," I pleaded.

"I told you, it won't work. I need to be on my own," he said again. I cried and pleaded, telling him how much I loved and needed him.

"I don't think you really love me," he said, "and I know I don't love you. I don't think I ever did. I just wanted to have sex with you. Even before I met you, I heard about you. The guys at school always talked about you and that come-on look you always had in your eyes. When I saw it for myself, I knew I had to have you. When we dated, I was the envy of all those guys. I just couldn't leave you alone. When I realized you hadn't been with other men, I was obsessed. I would be your first and only! It was a powerful turn-on." It was more words than Garrison had said at one time in all the years I knew him.

"Well, I guess I don't need these anymore." I reached into the cabinet for my birth-control pills and threw them into the garbage. My self-esteem was gone. I would have done anything he wanted.

"I got to go now," he said softly, standing very close to me. "I'll call you when I get a phone. I'll come back every day when you leave for work and stay with Sarah-Jane. We can keep the same schedule. We can still get the house. I'll sign the papers with you." At that time a woman couldn't buy a home unless she was someone rich and famous. Banks didn't lend money to women. Most credit cards had to be in your husband's name.

He slowly took off his beautiful wedding ring and placed it on the table. "I need one of the cars and about three hundred dollars, if you have it," he said softly.

I still had my GTO, and it was paid off. "You can have the new car. You'll make the payments," I replied flatly. I got the payment booklet and three hundred dollars in cash. I set them on the table in front of him. He took them and walked away. I ran to the bedroom and threw open the closet, revealing emptiness that matched the hollow space in my heart. The pain in my stomach was so great that I went into the bathroom and threw up. It took a long while before I could regain control of myself and go next door for Sarah-Jane. "Garrison left, Sandy. I don't know what will become of me and Sarah-Jane." She called her mother to come sit with the kids. Then she took me home and sat with me while I cried.

"Look, I think he's just scared. He'll come around once you get the house. I know he will. You bring Sarah-Jane to me. I'll keep her and not charge you a thing." She was such a good friend and probably one of the best people I knew in my whole life. I can't remember a time when she let me down. For days I was in a state of shock. I was glad she was there for me.

I wasn't good for anything but nursing. I wasn't a good mother. I couldn't hold onto my husband. My experiences pointed to one fact: I was a survivor. I lived through those last few days of shock. I couldn't eat or sleep. I lost fifteen pounds. I went through the motions of daily life: working, cooking and cleaning, caring for my child. I cried each night.

"Get the house," Sandy said. "Everything else will work out." I started working every day, some days for sixteen hours. I turned off lights. I didn't need light; Garrison had to have them on. I had all the phones taken out except for one. The grocery bill was cut in half. I started selling things I didn't need, small wedding gifts and then some big ones. I sold our piano and stereo system; I didn't play piano, and I didn't have time to listen to music. The piano was a gift from Mazy. Garrison hated it because it couldn't be tuned to his sense of perfect pitch.

"Do whatever you feel you need to do. I'll help you if I can. You know I've been through plenty, and I understand," Mazy said when I finally called. I went to Henderson to visit her folks. They were very cold and offered no advice or support. "Well, you knew they wouldn't," said Mazy. "Garrison is their baby. The sun rises and sets on him."

I stayed away from Strawberry Fields. I didn't phone them. I wrote Mama a letter every two weeks, letting her know I was all right. I told her I was working to buy the house. I said nothing about my husband's desertion. She wrote me a few words in English, saying that getting my letters eased her mind. She began having heart problems. The thought of living without her frightened me. Although we weren't close, she tried to be there for me after Antonia left home.

At first Garrison kept his promise and came when he wasn't playing in a club. He took Sarah-Jane next door to Sandy. Then he took me to bed. We were having more sex than when we had lived together. He knew I wasn't on the pill. We did nothing to prevent a pregnancy. Sandy knew what was going on. "I only hope he comes to his senses," she would say. I was desperately hoping for a reunion. Love leads you to act in ways you never thought you could.

In mid-August I looked at a house in South Side, in a neighborhood where we hoped to live. It was the house of my dreams: an old, two-story, slate-shingle frame house with twelve-foot ceilings, four bedrooms upstairs, a living room, dining room, kitchen, and den downstairs, one bath, and a full unfinished basement. It had an enclosed back porch, and the backyard was fenced. There was a garage off the alley. I called Garrison. He loved it. I hoped there was a real chance he would come back. We made plans to buy the house on Sunny Side Avenue.

A week later I returned home early in the morning after a sixteen-hour shift. I barely made it into the drive. I had to open the car door quickly and throw up. I was dizzy and nauseated and sweating. I had to lie down. It was the third time I had experienced that feeling. I knew immediately that I was pregnant again. I didn't tell anyone. I gave little thought to my own health. As long as I had coffee, I required little food, but eating curbed the nausea. I gained weight! My breasts were larger and very sore. Those thing hadn't happened until very late in my first pregnancy and not at all in the second, when I had lost the baby. I was so uncomfortable that I went right into the shower each night and then put on a loose-fitting robe. I didn't work overtime when Garrison watched Sarah-Jane. I zipped the front of my robe and hurried to the kitchen to make Garrison some coffee and give him a slice of cake. He came up behind me, running his hands all over me. He caressed my large, firm breasts, and he ran his long fingers down my growing belly. He stopped abruptly and tore open my robe. "You're getting so fat! Don't you care about yourself?" I could feel my face getting red and my self-esteem drain away.

"Garrison, I'm pregnant." The robe slid off onto the floor, and he took me right there in the kitchen. The feeling passed for me; only sadness remained. Garrison didn't notice, enjoying every lust-filled moment. As the time for closing on the house drew near, he seemed happy about it and the new baby coming in March. The baby was really due in April. I didn't want anyone knowing I got pregnant after my husband left me. I clung to the hope that he would return.

Two weeks later, unable to hide my growing belly, I started to wear maternity clothes. I couldn't put off going to Strawberry Fields any longer. Enzo was standing by the garage when I got out of my car. Sarah-Jane darted for the house, her grandmother, and her uncle Sammy, whom she adored. Enzo stared at me. "What's wrong?" he finally said, coming toward me. The floodgates opened; I couldn't hold back the tears any longer. "He left you, didn't he? Well, didn't he?" Enzo yelled. He knew! I supposed everyone in Henderson and New Moon knew. He took my arm, and we walked to the upstairs kitchen. "Come on, let's sit and talk. Mama! Pa! Get in here—we need to talk." Sammy took Sarah-Jane out to play.

"I'm sorry I didn't tell you before. I thought it would pass and he would come back," I said slowly. My pa mumbled that he had never liked Garrison anyway. Mama looked at me with such sadness that it hurt.

"What will you do now?" she asked.

"She'll come home!" Enzo stormed. "I'll come with my truck and pack your shit, and you'll live here, where you belong."

"No, Enzo, I can't do that! South Side is my home and where I work. I'm planning to buy a house," I replied. I wasn't going to be another Antonia, running home to Mama and Pa every time something in my life went wrong.

"Don't be stupid. You know nothing about caring for a house, and you can't afford it on your own. I don't have time to maintain it for you," he said. He had a florist business, and he was supporting Antonia and her four children. They were living in one of his houses.

We all sat down to one of Mama's great meals. I was amazed that I could eat. "You should get rid of that while you can," Sammy said, pointing at my growing midsection. "It's legal now, you know."

"You're crazy, Sammy! I would never do that. I want another child, and anyway it's none of your business," I retorted.

"Yah, well, I can't babysit two kids," he replied. I ignored Sarah-Jane's questioning look. She didn't know about the baby yet. I thought it was too soon to tell her.

"No one is asking you to do that," I said.

"All right, shut up, both of you," Enzo chimed in. "Well, you do what you want, but you're going to need a lot of support we can't give you, being so far away." I wanted to go home right then. I was more determined than ever to make my plans work.

If I didn't feel bad enough already, I felt worse when Marco walked through the door. "What's going on?" he asked. I sat with my head down as Enzo and Sammy filled him in on the details of my broken life. "Oh, don't be stupid. You don't know how to buy a house or handle one if you had it. You'd lose your ass. Just rent an apartment by the hospital, so you'll be close to both home and work."

"What makes you think my children don't deserve to be raised in a home of their own, Marco? You're raising your kids in a home you own. Kids need roots—they need to be in a place they know is theirs," I protested. It was the first time I had put this idea into actual words. I would fight for what I thought was the right thing for my children. Those women's lib ideas were a major part of who I became.

I sold more things at a garage sale. I tossed out and burned even more. I destroyed all of Garrison's love letters to me. I shed more tears over that beautiful card that read, "I love you, honest." I tossed that old bouquet of red roses, faded to a nondescript color. There were boxes of things in the garage that had belonged to Garrison. I took the liberty of going through them. After reading all those letters and cards, I burnt them one by one. Some were from Garrison's old army buddy. Some were in my own hand; others were from women I didn't know and a few I knew. I'd had no idea they knew my husband romantically. Once the fire got larger and burned brighter, I began to feel better. I was burning a painful past that I refused to carry into my uncertain future.

On December 4, at the closing for the house, I was as big as a house. I was still telling everyone the baby was due in March. I felt like an unwed mother, something I had been careful to avoid. When I looked into the mirror, I saw Antonia as she was when she was pregnant with Dean Martin and his brothers. My face was swollen. My abdomen was large, and my arms and legs were pudgy. The hormones of pregnancy kept me cheerful. Happiness flowed through me as I held Garrison's hand. We left the big-city title and trust company with the keys to our new home. We did some window shopping. We laughed and talked like any other married couple. "I'll be by sometime tomorrow to help you move. I just don't know when yet," he said when he dropped me off at home. I was disappointed that he didn't stay.

Packing was another one of Sandy's talents. She did a lot of packing for me. She kept Sarah-Jane while the move took place. My nephew Buddy was coming to help me. I sat in the kitchen at dawn that morning, looking out the window, waiting for him and Sammy. I was excited to be moving, even as anxiety and uncertainty loomed. The hours passed slowly as I waited for Buddy. He had grown into such a fine young man. Sam Weeds had gotten Buddy a divorce from his first wife, and he had custody of his young daughter. He wasn't used to city driving, and he got lost several times getting to my little house in the city. Sammy arrived, but it was impossible for him to move furniture alone. When moving finally got under way, I lifted as many boxes as I could before going to work. That whole evening, I could think of nothing but the move. I could hardly wait for my shift to end.

When I arrived at the new house, I found Garrison there, with Sarah-Jane safely tucked in her little bed in her new room. I wandered from room to room, looking at how everything fit. Garrison carried a few boxes to the basement and put things away. "I guess I'll take a shower," I said. I was so swollen, and it felt good to get out of my work clothes. I slipped into a shift robe with a front zipper. My heart was singing as I brushed my long hair. We were in our very own home together. I thanked God and prayed everything would work out for my little family. In the living room, I saw Garrison sitting in the big rocking chair by the fireplace. He was reading a book and smoking a cigarette as the fire blazed. I went in and sat at his feet, resting my head in his lap. The wind blew outside our door, and a light snow began to fall. I sat there quietly watching him and listening to the sounds of our home. Anyone looking in would have seen the perfect family, living a normal life. He looked at me and smiled. I went into his arms. We made love on the living room floor, softly and tenderly, not like the Garrison I knew, who took me by force, leaving me bruised and bleeding. He was loving and gentle. I couldn't release him when it was over. He pulled away, gently replaced my robe, and led me to the divan. I sat down, thinking he would join me and talk about the future and our new home. Instead he walked into the foyer and put on his coat. He walked out the front door without so much as a good-bye. I pulled back the drapes in the large front window and watched the wind blowing the trees and the snow falling. My heart felt a profound loss. I was utterly alone in the world. I had thought he was coming home to stay, but I was alone.

Christmas was coming. I had to be happy and cheerful for Sarah-Jane, but everything inside felt broken. I wanted the one thing at Christmas that I knew always made me feel better. I thought it would drive out the loneliness. I bought the biggest tree I could find. I dragged it from the car onto the parkway in front of the house. I got the biggest knife from the kitchen. In the snow and cold, I tried my best to make the end of the tree small enough to fit into the stand. I was sweating and breathing heavily. I didn't look up when a police car came to the curb. I heard the car door open and close. "Should a woman in your condition be doing all that?" a voice behind me asked.

"I'm not sick, feeble, or dying. I'm only pregnant, so leave me alone," I said without looking up. He got back in the car and left. Good! Good riddance, I thought to myself. Cops! They think they know everything. My hands were freezing, so I went inside to warm up. I looked out the window at the nine-foot tree, thinking I might have overdone it. The cop came back with a large meat cleaver and began to whittle at the bottom of the tree. I ran outside.

"It was the only thing I could get my hands on in a hurry. I can't get into my garage—the door's frozen shut," he said without looking up at me. In a few short minutes he had the tree in its stand.

"I thank you very much, sir," I said, taking the tree by the stand and dragging it up the front steps into the house.

"Hold on! Hold on there, now. I'll help you," he said.

"I don't need any help," I replied. I closed the front door after the giant tree. I could see him from the window as I got the tree upright in front of it. The lights on the tree burned brightly, but they didn't lighten my heart. I had to work on Christmas Eve, so Garrison took Sarah-Jane to his parents in Henderson. She was in bed, asleep, when I got home.

Garrison was waiting at the door with his coat on. "I have to go."

"I'll see you at your folks' house tomorrow," I said.

"No, you won't. I'm not going there," he replied and quickly left.

Mazy was at work. I had a very quiet, uncomfortable meal with the Michael family. They said little, making no eye contact. They seemed annoyed as Sarah-Jane sang and danced around their living room. After a reasonable amount of time, I went to Strawberry Fields, where the whole clan was assembled. I couldn't sit there either, as Enzo pumped me for details on my situation. I could only answer, "I don't know, Enzo." I drove back to Sunny Side Avenue with a heavy heart. Other than that Christmas I had spent without Mama, the one before my second child was born was the loneliest of my life.

After the New Year, I filled my head with the fantasy of my husband's return. I worked hard preparing for the new baby and fixing up the house. I cleaned it and decorated it in the latest style. On the days Garrison watched Sarah-Jane, she was tucked in bed, asleep, when I got home. We continued our sexual relationship. He didn't seem to mind that I was so big and that we were limited to only a few positions. I couldn't bring myself to refuse him; he seemed to need me so much. I never could see that it was only sex he needed, not me.

On a cold night in February, the phone rang in the nurses' station at work. "It's for you, Mary," Colleen said. "It's your husband. He sounds upset." I took the phone.

"Garrison? What's wrong? Is Sarah-Jane all right?" I asked anxiously.

"She's fine, but I have to leave right now. You have to come home!" he demanded.

"Well, what is it? Are you sick?" I asked with deep concern. "I have two more hours to go on my shift."

"I don't care," he said and hung up.

"Just go, Mary. It will be all right. I'll tell Mrs. Peckenpack you had to go home." Colleen was such a big support for me during those awful years. She had her own troubles with an alcoholic husband at home and a wild teenage daughter.

Garrison was standing in the kitchen doorway, on the phone. He would press the receiver, dial a number, and then do it again. "What is it, Garrison? What's happened?" I asked gently.

"I can't watch the kid anymore. I won't be back here. Hire someone. I'll give you a little money if I can," he said.

"Please, Garrison, tell me what I've done to make you so angry." I took his arm and tried to get him to sit at the dining room table.

He jerked away and yelled, "You don't understand! I have an emergency. I have to go right now!" Shocked, hurt, and afraid, I began to feel my large abdomen contract into a hard mass. I sat down and took a deep breath as he left. I called Mazy to ask if she had any idea what was happening to Garrison or what his emergency might be. I like to think that she didn't know or didn't want to upset me. The news might have brought on labor. The Michaels knew. They claimed to know nothing.

Sandy encouraged me to go talk to the priest. She said it might help me, even if Garrison didn't want to go. I rejoined St. Jude Church across the street from the hospital. The priest was popular with everyone at work. He had performed almost every wedding ceremony for them. Father Fiery was a young guy who prided himself on being a modern priest. He had futuristic ideas and ideals. I sat on the couch in his office, big as the back end of a city bus, crying my eyes out, telling him my husband had left me with a toddler and with a baby on the way. "I think there may be another woman. I'm not sure. He's been acting strangely. I'm trying to keep a roof over our heads and take care of my child, and the new baby is due in a month. I don't know where to turn," I said through my many tears.

He leaned back in his big chair behind his big desk. He said the most bizarre things I ever heard a priest say. Gazing straight ahead at nothing in particular, he said, "Well, Mrs. Michael, I think you should just let him go. He may have found the love of his life and moved on. You should do the same." I wondered if the man had looked at me. I could barely walk, let alone move anywhere. "I, for one, can't wait to meet the woman of my dreams as soon as the pope decides we priests can marry. You know, my ideal woman would be blonde and ..." He continued talking, I sat there stunned, demoralized, and totally destroyed. It was as if he didn't see me. I left in a daze. I lay down on my bed and did my best to put the whole experience out of my head. I quit going to that church and attended St. Luke Church on the opposite end of town. I continued to cling to the fantasy that the baby would bring Garrison home.

Mazy was a great support to me. She called almost every day. We made plans for the delivery. She volunteered to be with me, so I wouldn't deliver alone. I would tell the staff that my husband was out of town and couldn't be there. Mazy had been through a painful divorce herself, and she encouraged me to seek legal advice. She went through bad times in the early sixties when a Catholic woman couldn't be divorced from her husband unless the Vatican thought she had a good enough reason and plenty of money. Douglas was divorced from Mazy, but she was only separated from him, so she could remain a practicing Catholic. "You need to protect your rights and assets," Mazy told me. "I know how much you love my little brother, but it has nothing to do with the financial aspect of things. Do this, please," she begged. "I lost everything when Douglas divorced me. I got the three children and our clothes. If my father hadn't taken us in, we would have been on the street. My husband has never paid a dime of child support. He never held a job." I knew she was right.

I sought legal counsel with a prominent attorney in South Side. I briefed him on the situation by phone. I told him we had purchased the house jointly. "A pregnant woman can't get a divorce in this state," the lawyer informed me when we met. "I had your husband here, and this is what I have done to protect your assets. He signed a quit claim deed to the house and signed off both of your accounts at the bank. Everything is only in your name. I'll get you the divorce as soon as the baby is born. I'll be the lawyer for both you and Mr. Michael. This will save a lot of money."

"But I don't want a divorce, sir. I want my husband back," I said through tears.

"I'm afraid that's not going to happen," he replied. "If it's any consolation to you, your husband sat here in my office and cried for his children. He isn't taking this any better."

"We still remain as a married couple, if you know what I mean," I answered.

"I know what you mean, and sex does not a marriage make, young lady. I'll get you fifty bucks a week for the kids, and he will get them every weekend. You're tough and hardworking, I know—I've heard all about you at the hospital. I'm on the board of directors. I feel that it's your husband who is getting a raw deal. I never saw a guy cry like that," he said. I knew from past experience that Garrison was a crier. He did it well and often, when he felt backed into a corner and he was losing a disagreement. It always gained him lots of empathy from authority figures like his parents, his sister Ann, and his sergeant in the army. With a copy of the quit claim deed and bank accounts in my name only, I left the lawyer's office in a daze. I had thought he was going to be my lawyer. What raw deal had Garrison received? I was paying the lawyer; why was he worried about Garrison?

I called Mazy back. "Well, don't you worry," she said. "You're having a baby. You need to keep your spirits high. Don't do anything—don't sign any more papers until you're ready." The wonderful hormones of pregnancy kicked in. I sailed through the next few weeks as these God-created things protected me and my baby. I didn't return to the lawyer.

I enrolled Sarah-Jane in a preschool program at the park two mornings a week. I felt terrible, because she was all I had. I talked to her like an adult. At the park I saw a woman who was expecting. Before I could talk to her, another young mother asked me to go to Walgreens for breakfast so we could talk while we waited for our little ones. She was friendly and bubbly, but I was sad without my girl. I watched the clock the whole time. She talked about how she was divorced, with two boys, and had just gotten on welfare. She had a new boyfriend whom she felt was Mr. Right. I couldn't bear to hear more. I didn't want my life to be like hers. I avoided her after that first day.

Out of the blue, Sarah-Jane told me she wanted to name the baby Cathy if it was a girl. I had already picked Jenna-Lisa, but I knew my subconscious mind was hoping for a boy, whom I would call Eric.

Garrison told me to name the child whatever I wanted. He begged me to stop asking him to choose a name. "Why do you want to call her that?" I asked my little girl.

"Jenny's mommy is calling her new baby that, if it's a girl," she said. When I picked up Sarah-Jane from the park the next day, I saw Margaret Ann walking along the sidewalk with Jenny.

"Excuse me, but would you like a ride?" I asked.

"Why, it's very kind of you," Margaret Ann said, and she and Jenny got into my car. "It looks like we're due about the same time."

"Well, I'm due any day now," I replied. She invited us in, and we visited with her for a while. They lived about four blocks away from us. After our first meeting, we were together almost every day. I confided in her a little. I told her that I hoped my husband would come to his senses and return. She was a good and kind person. I realized that she was just as lonely and abandoned as I was. Her husband drank when he wasn't at work. He wouldn't let her drive his car. We came to depend on each other. Although she believed in equal rights for women, she was very subservient to her husband. We talked about rights and politics.

On April 8 I began to lose my mucus plug; contractions were coming more frequently. I was scared and alone. I was under the care of a new doctor in Dr. Castro's growing practice. I didn't like her. She was impersonal and didn't care that I had gained so much weight. I went to her the next day before work and begged her to get the baby out of me. "Well, you're dilated two centimeters already. I stripped the membranes, so you should be ready to deliver in the next twenty-four hours." I complained that my last delivery had been very hard and long and the baby had been in the wrong position. "Oh, relax. I don't know why you're so worried. It's a small baby, smaller than your last. You just gained too much weight. I'll probably see you in the hospital tomorrow."

When I got to my floor, I called Mazy, letting her know I was in labor. She said she would pack a bag. Sarah-Jane was staying with good friends from the old neighborhood. I was working with a very young, squeamish nurse. I didn't know she heard me telling Mazy the time was near. I went down the hall to care for my patients. The evening supervisor followed me. "This hospital won't be responsible for anything that happens to you. You should go home. This is no place for you," she demanded.

"Yes, it is," I replied. "The delivery room is right down on the next floor. I worked right up until I delivered my last child." She stormed away.

Mazy slept soundly in the room I'd prepared for the live-in nanny I hadn't hired. I couldn't sleep. I tossed and turned, worried about everything and the mysterious absence of my husband. I had called him earlier to tell him I was in labor. He said, "I hope it goes okay. Call me when it is over." He hung up without another word.

Mazy was the best coach for any laboring mother. The labor was hard and long, and the baby was turned the wrong way. I wondered why doctors never trusted a patient to know her own body. Since my tongue had swollen after a shot of Demerol during my last labor, I couldn't take it. When things were rolling pretty well according to Mazy, the nurse gave me a shot of something else that made me feel like I was watching the whole thing from somewhere up on the ceiling. The labor stopped, but through my fog I asked them to catheterize me, as with my first delivery. It worked, and the labor proceeded.

A miracle happened, and the baby turned around after that catheter was placed. The nurses refused to let Mazy stay for the delivery, even though they knew she was a very experienced nurse. Although the delivery was difficult, it wasn't dangerous. A nice, healthy baby girl, weighing eight pounds and one ounce, came out crying at the top of her lungs. Then things got a little complicated. As Dr. Styles was trying to get the afterbirth to dislodge, a large mass of tissue came tumbling out. Upon closer examination, she declared that it was a six-pound undeveloped fetus. I hemorrhaged, lost consciousness, and had to be resuscitated with IV fluids, oxygen, and a medication to stop the bleeding. I accidentally touched one of the delivery room nurses. She flew into a tirade and strapped me down to the delivery table so tightly and brutally that my legs and arms had bruises. They were so swollen that I could barely walk or bend my arms. When I became conscious in the recovery area, I was allowed to see my new baby. She was perfect and so beautiful. She looked just like my pa, like a Rosario.

Garrison came the next day. I was very sick with an infection. I didn't look my best, as I had hoped. "She's really pretty. Congratulations," he said quietly, as if visiting a stranger.

"She's your baby too, Garrison," I replied.

"Yep, I know she's mine," he said with a faraway look in his eyes. He barely looked at me, mumbled an excuse, and left.

Five days later I was released. A neighbor took me home with Sarah-Jane and my new baby. I was all alone. Mama was too ill to help, and Sammy was mad because I had kept the baby. Antonia and Carmella were saying I'd gotten just what I deserved. My husband waited a whole week before he made his appearance. I looked into the mirror and was horrified. The circles under my eyes made me look as if I had black eyes. My hair was wild and unmanageable, and the rest of me resembled a large burlap sack of potatoes. Where was the dream girl, the graduate nurse, the bride-to-be? They were alive only in pictures.

Garrison promised to spend the whole day. I made plans for getting my life back. First, I needed a strict reduction diet, a haircut, and some new clothes. When I returned home from the beauty shop, he and Sarah-Jane were reading books. I entered the living room in a pair of new jeans and a shirt in the latest style, wearing makeup and a very short haircut. Garrison got up and walked around me, staring. He took a comb from his shirt pocket and ran it through my soft, short curls. "I think I'll go out in the yard and play," Sarah-Jane said. Many years later she recalled that day, telling me that she didn't know me. It took her a few days before she was sure I was still her mommy.

Over the next five weeks, I worked hard to get rid of the bag-of-potatoes look. It was only five weeks, not the six it should have been, when Garrison and I resumed our sexual relationship. He was careful to avoid penetrative sex. We engaged in all of the others, which he didn't consider sex. It was easier for him to leave me.

On a rainy late April evening, a truck pulled up to the curb in front of my house. Its lights were flashing. I saw the shadow of a man placing cones to block off the area behind it. When he walked under the streetlight, I knew it was Enzo. He unloaded equipment and brought it to the back porch. When I opened the door, he said, "I came to fix the back door. It can't stay like this with a newborn in the house."

Our babies were born the same day, April 10, but in different hospitals. Margaret Ann and I resumed our friendship. She encouraged me to get Jenna-Lisa baptized at St. Luke Church. I called the rectory and spoke to a nice lady who said she would make all the arrangements. She told me to come to the church that Sunday morning in the middle of May. She called my former church and got all my records sent over. With all my friends helping me, the party after was to be a great success. Garrison refused to come. My babysitter and her husband agreed to be godparents.

We gathered at the baptismal font Sunday morning: Mr. and Mrs. Polkas, Margaret Ann, my friend Laurie from work, Sarah-Jane, and me. I was against the traditional long, white baptismal gown. Jenna-Lisa was dressed in a pale yellow dress that accented her dark skin. When Sarah-Jane was baptized, I dressed her in a little pink ruffled dress. There were three other babies and their families as well. We were first at the baptismal fountain. The priest stared at me. "So why should I baptize this child? Do you belong to this church? And where is your husband?" he said very loudly.

I was stunned and angry. "Well, yes, I do belong to this church. I registered when the nuns came to my home just after the baby was born. I called to make arrangements for the baptism. Your secretary said she would take care of the paperwork. She said it was all set when I talked to her last week," I replied, feeling all my courage slipping away. I hung my head and added, "My husband and I are separated at present."

He harrumphed and said, "Well, let's get on with it." After all the bad advice I had received from priests over the years, and with this priest acting like he was doing me a favor, I began to wonder why I was still a Catholic.

The party was a complete success. Everyone came: Mama and Sammy, Marco and his family, Enzo's wife and children, Carmella and Antonia and their families, and my friends from the hospital. No one from my husband's family came. Mazy had to work. She was a single mother of three teenagers.

In late afternoon the house grew quiet. The baby slept in her bassinet, and Sarah-Jane napped on the divan. I rocked gently as the sun came through the windows and the trees swayed outside. A lovely pattern danced across the floor. I drifted off to sleep. I heard the front door open; it was Garrison. He carried me off to the den. We had sex for the next hour and a half, while the children slept in the living room.

Later, he helped clean the party things and stayed for dinner. We went through the things the baby had received for her big day. I thought of us as a normal, happy American family celebrating and living life. We bathed the children and put them to bed. After more sex, I fell asleep in the arms of the man I so desperately loved. Sometime during the night, he left me again.

I was walking on air the next day, feeling closer than ever to getting Garrison back. It was another bright, sunny day. When the children took their naps, I planned to sit at my desk in the dining room and pay bills. I was on maternity leave for another six weeks. I was hoping Garrison would come back and work, so I could stay home with the children. I started with the phone bill. It looked unusually high, so I went over each item. I noticed a few calls to a number similar to Garrison's. I called it, and he answered. "Garrison? You have two phone numbers?" I said, confused.

"Well, I can have two numbers if I want," he replied tersely and hung up. Reality slowly began to sink into my thick head. Before I had moved and after Garrison moved out, my phone rang often, with no one saying anything at the other end. I got a new number when I moved, but it continued. The babysitter told me that while I was at work, a woman had called, asking for Garrison. I questioned him, but he'd said that he had no idea who would call him. I recalled several times last fall when Garrison took Sarah-Jane to band practice. She returned home talking nonstop about someone named Carol who came to practice and played with her.

"Who is she?" I had asked.

"I don't know, Mommy," replied Sarah-Jane. "She's not pretty like you, but she is really nice." When I had questioned Garrison, he became defensive, saying she was just a waitress at the club. More reality set in as I began to think about the woman in the club that followed Garrison everywhere, the one Carmella said I should know. I suddenly recalled her. I ran upstairs to the master bedroom and found an old Henderson High yearbook. I looked though the freshman classes and found her. I dialed information and asked for her phone number, and it matched.

I called Mazy, waking her from a sound sleep. "I'm so sorry, honey, that you found out this way, but I guess it just couldn't go on without your discovering it. I learned about her that night in February when Garrison left your house in a hurry. I knew why, but I was afraid to tell you, thinking something might happen to you and the baby. Besides, it was his responsibility to tell you, not mine." She paused before saying, "The emergency he had was Carol finding out you were expecting another baby. She went all to pieces and called Garrison, telling him she was leaving him. Obviously it didn't take much for him to talk her out of it."

After hanging up with Mazy, I called Sandy. "Did you know about her?" I demanded.

"Oh, Mary, I'm so sorry. She came to the house next door when you were at work. I thought she was Garrison's sister. I only figured it out that night in February when he called here so upset. He wanted me to come and stay with Sarah-Jane, but it was late, and Jerry was bowling. Can you ever forgive me, Mary? I tried to get him to come back. I got a sitter, and I drove to Henderson and confronted them. I told them they were wrong and treating you unfairly." She sobbed. I felt bad for her. Her friendship had gone far beyond what I expected.

"It's not your fault, Sandy," I said. "What I don't understand is, if he is so in love with her, why does he still come to my bed? I'm sorry, but you know what goes on between us."

"I think he fancies himself in love with both of you. He would have kept up this charade forever if you hadn't figured it out," she replied. "I thought my husband was bad, honey. You got yourself one mixed-up man." I may have been a fool, but I was a survivor. I called the sitter, took a shower, and got dressed in my best clothes.

"Please, ma'am, I need my old job back," I said in between sobs as I sat in the office of the director of nursing at Our Lady of Light Hospital.

"Come, now, don't cry," she said, patting me on the back. "You know you'll always have a job. You can start tomorrow on the night shift, on your very own floor." I did what I had to do to survive. Work was the only answer.

When it came to my husband, I had no sense of pride. I did what every desperate and devastated woman in my position would do: I called the other woman. "How can you do this to my family?" I demanded. "What kind of person are you? You must know what goes on. We're still a married couple. We have sex, and then he leaves me and goes to you."

"I know how you tricked him into getting you pregnant to get him back, but it didn't work. He's with me now, Mrs. Michael. He doesn't love or want you. I know the things you say are all lies," she said. Carol would be with Garrison no matter what he did. She was willing to believe anything he told her. How I could trick my husband into sleeping with me was almost a joke. I wondered how he explained to her how I forced him into sex, when he was more than a foot taller and outweighed me by one hundred pounds.

The only time I didn't cry was at work, where people depended on me. It was beginning to affect Sarah-Jane, but I just couldn't stop. I made an appointment with a psychiatrist. His advice was sound, but I just wasn't ready to hear it. "You must stop crying, for the sake of the children and yourself. Don't call your husband anymore. Call me when you need to talk or when you feel you want to call him. The damage you're allowing him to do to you could result in bad consequences for you and the children. You need love and support. You need your friends, your family, and me. Listen to me, and let me help you. Don't run to one who has betrayed you. He will keep hurting you. He isn't considerate of your feelings or the children's. You need to regain some self-esteem. You only have control over your own actions. They are the ones that count. You must work on your own feelings and let him deal with his own mess," he told me. "You need to become a whole, functioning person again."

I didn't know how to be a whole, functioning person. This man's help came at a high price. Most insurance companies didn't cover the services of a psychiatrist. People who consulted them were considered unfit. It carried a stigma that could affect one's whole life, professional and private. I couldn't trust priests or lawyers, and I certainly couldn't trust my husband. I didn't know if psychiatrists were trustworthy. His help would put me at risk in ways I couldn't afford. I never went back.

Signs in my life showed me that the Father, the Son, and the Holy Ghost hadn't deserted me. Somewhere deep inside, those spirits were with me. Priests were only men, humans. They made mistakes and had weaknesses. With help from the Holy Father, I began to see that I was the one person who should never let me or my children down. I had to learn to depend on myself.

When Sarah-Jane was hit by a car while crossing the street, I considered it a miracle when she recovered without signs of permanent damage. I knew that the Father was with me, helping me. My baby showed signs of a weak immune system; after three months she was ill with one infection after another. She required the same monthly shots as Sarah-Jane. Through my grief and despair, someone was always there for me—the Spirit, friends, or my family. I seemed to be getting by with a little help from all of them.

I knew that cop was watching me. "Did you know you can't park in front of your house?" he said to me one fall day as I put the kids into my car. "See that sign there?"

"Look, buddy, this is my house. I'll park in front of it if I want. My baby's sick. I'm taking her to the doctor. I'm not parking in the garage—it's too hard to get the kids in and out. Write me a ticket if you want, but I don't have time for you and your nonsense," I replied.

"It's Tom. My name is Tom. I can give you a police escort to the hospital if you like," he said.

"No, Tom, I don't like. I'm taking the baby to the clinic," I retorted. This guy couldn't leave me alone! I knew he drove by my house several times a day when he was working.

The country was soon gripped in a recession affecting everyone, as gas prices skyrocketed to a dollar a gallon. There were long lines at the gas pumps and signs everywhere that said No Gas. The Watergate scandal had devastated the country the previous year. Jerry Ford replaced the disgraced President Nixon. I too was disgraced in 1974. I couldn't return to Henderson for my high school reunion. I was pregnant, with no husband and an uncertain future, as I watched Mr. Nixon on TV give the peace sign and board the plane back to California. Now joblessness rose to an all-time high. People stopped going to clubs. Garrison found himself out of a job. It had no effect on me or the children; he'd never supported us. I had all the overtime I could handle. Even in a bad recession, people got sick and needed care. I was never without work.

The only thing Garrison did for us was to come every other Friday to stay with the children while I went for my check, paid bills, and did banking and grocery shopping. I went to a local coffee shop for a little time to myself. Then I cooked dinner for my family and had sex with my husband. He stayed for the dinner and intimacy but didn't offer to buy even a gallon of milk. He said it was my fault that he didn't support the kids. "If you want money, all you have to do is let me take them to my house once in a while. We'll watch them there."

"It will only happen over my dead body, Garrison. I'll never let you take the babies to your whore's house. This is their home, and we're their parents. We're a family!" I said.

"Well, I don't want to be a family with you anymore. I'd like nothing better than to never have to see you," he said angrily—right after we had sex!

"Be careful what you wish for, Garrison. You just might get it," I retorted. I was sure he thought it an idle threat.

Ann came to his defense and wrote me. She had cared for Garrison since the day he was born. She was an old maid with a physical impairment and a nasty attitude toward life, me, and the children.

Evie,

You need to leave my brother alone and stop this terrible behavior of yours. I don't know how you could have allowed yourself to get pregnant and carry on with Garrison when you knew he had another in his life. You hurt him very badly. All you care about is those kids. You never loved my brother. You only used him to have kids and get yourself a house. By the way Sarah-Jane looks awful. She's getting fat! Stop feeding her so much. Grow up and leave Garrison alone!

Ann

I cried to Mazy. I felt so dirty, yet I was Garrison's wife. I had married him in the church, in front of God, friends, and our families. "You've no reason to be ashamed. Garrison is your husband, and you have every right to sleep with him," Mazy replied. "Carol should be ashamed, and Garrison too. I blame her more. If women like her would stop pursuing men like Garrison, more marriages in this country would be saved. Women like her, who hang around men like Garrison, good-looking and full of themselves, will continue to destroy families like yours. Look around you, Evie. You're not alone."

My life was like a TV soap opera or one of those cheap romance novels I hated. I didn't spend time dreaming of the house with the white picket fence, the kids, and the husband. But like all good American girls, it was what I ended up desperately wanting as it slipped away.

My tears began to dry after two and a half long years. I lost weight and looked like my old self. Men noticed me again, lots of them, on the street, in the stores, and in the park. They came to my door and asked for dates. Some wanted to help when I did yard work. Even old men who were barely able to walk came to my door. Most of them wanted a little more than friendship. Even so, I'm ashamed to admit that it took me five years and his divorcing me without my knowledge before I stopped sleeping with my husband. I learned from Marco that Garrison married Carol. He saw an ad in the *Henderson Times* that said, "Not responsible for debts contracted by Mary E. Rosario Michael as of this date." I blotted out the rest.

I had to compete in the real world to survive. I went back to school and earned a two-year registered nurse's degree at the community college. I was a big hit with all the young men on campus. I dated a few, managing to keep it platonic. It didn't seem to bother them that I was in my midthirties and almost old enough to be their mother.

❧19❧

Illness: The Great Equalizer

I FOCUSED ON THE children and my career. I had to work hard in order to keep the house and maintain it. I gave the children everything I thought they needed. A lady who lived across the street in the large apartment building became my babysitter. She had only an eighth-grade education. The girls loved her. Many nights I wondered who was watching whom.

Garrison thought I was responsible for him, no matter where he was living or with whom. "Honey, do you still have me on your insurance policy?" I had a family policy through my job. I didn't take him off it.

"Why do you ask?" I inquired.

"Well, I was skiing yesterday and injured my hip. I want to use the insurance card, see the doctor, and get an X-ray," he replied. I probably would have given in to him if I hadn't discovered that he took a life insurance policy I had for him. I stopped the payments, but I wasn't sure how long I had been paying another of his bills.

Garrison began to fade from our lives after he married Carol. Sarah-Jane cried and begged to see her father. In her child's mind, she thought I could make him visit her. "Honey, your father knows where you live, and he knows your phone number. If he wants to see you, he will." I regretted saying those words. She missed him on every holiday and special occasion in her life. No matter how special I tried to make them and other milestones, she longed for Garrison.

Just before I completed my registered nurse program, a girl I worked with introduced me to her sister's ex-boyfriend. "Maybe you can help him get over her," she said. "My sister dumped him, and he's taking it pretty hard. You seem to have recovered quite well from your breakup with Garrison." I was flattered that she thought I was over him. Stanley Zewicki was a handsome guy and the mayor of a small village. There was no romantic attraction for either of us. We decided that a friendship would last longer. It was one of the best decisions I made in my life, because we're still friends. I came up with a plan for him to get over his old girlfriend. I couldn't make it work for me, but it worked well for Stanley. Being a mayor of a small village wasn't a full-time job; Stanley worked full-time for my congressman, and he introduced me to him. I owe Stanley a great deal of credit. He got me involved in the community and in politics. I was invited to many social events with big politicians. I learned a lot about how government really works. I was invited to many cocktail parties, not because of my political prowess, but more for the way I filled out a cocktail dress. The first of these engagements was a large gathering for First Lady Rosalynn Carter. I bought a sleek white dress, form-fitting, with a V neckline and a large wine-colored sash at the waist. It cost one hundred and twenty-seven dollars—a large sum of money in a faltering economy. I looked like someone going to a fancy nightclub instead of a political function.

I felt like a visiting queen when the gentleman sitting next to me realized I was alone at the party. He was attentive to me and his wife, who was sitting on the other side of him. She was a gracious lady. I enjoyed a lively conversation with them as we had dinner and then waited in line to meet Mrs. Carter. Over the years I met many of our nation's great leaders. I really liked Jimmy and Rosalynn; they were so down-to-earth. They talked to you like a neighbor. I was devastated when he lost the election to Ronald Reagan the following year. We were blindsided by that vote. We never thought the country would elect an out-of-work actor to be president. It seemed to me that Mr. Reagan thought he was just playing another role in a movie.

I was standing next to former vice president Walter Mondale one evening in the early fall of 1984. While we waited for the photographer to reload his camera, I said, "Mr. Mondale, I will be taking two weeks of my vacation from the hospital to work on your campaign. I hope it's enough." He knew I was a nurse and a single mother.

He turned to me with real tears in his eyes. "Mary, you would do this for me? Use your precious time off to work for me for free?" In our picture, his eyes are shining from those tears. I was as overcome as he was. He had picked a female vice presidential running mate. That was all I needed to know about Mr. Mondale. He knew that women needed recognition.

For the next thirty-five years, the Carters never missed sending a Christmas card with a few kind words in it. I broke the relationship in 2008. I thought the Democrats treated Hillary Clinton unfairly, taking votes cast for her in the state of Michigan and giving them to Barack Obama. It was done because he wasn't on the ballot in that state. Harold Ickes Jr. was head of the party. He and I were the only ones having an episode of apoplexy over it! I wrote to President Carter and asked him why he didn't intervene in this unfair decision. I knew he was for Obama and didn't like the Clintons. Maybe he thought they had too much power in the party. He went to other countries to ensure that elections were fair; I needed to know why he didn't do the same for the United States. His answer was vague and short. The cards stopped coming.

When I completed the ADN program and became a registered nurse, I went to work in the emergency room. I loved emergency care. The fast pace and quick turnover of patients was very uplifting. The doctors loved me! The other nurses and my supervisor did not. I got lots of attention from all the men that came to the department. Doctors, policemen, firemen, and paramedics asked for me by name. They hugged and kissed me, no matter how I tried to avoid it.

One young South Side cop caught my eye. He was tall, with smoky blue eyes and rosy pink cheeks. He was quiet, unassuming, and twelve years younger than I was. His fellow police officers called him "the lawyer," because he was in law school. I flirted with him; he flirted back. Mr. Smoky Eyes in the blue uniform came to the emergency room often, making a point of talking to me. One weekend night in the middle of summer was especially busy. We had a rush of many ambulances from a large accident in which five people were mortally wounded. They were badly mutilated; blood was everywhere as we worked to save them. Brian was helping with the notification of family members and identifying bodies. It was a grueling twelve-hour shift. We were covered in blood when it was over. "I have to wash this blood off, but I don't think I can sleep. I'm doing another twelve-hour shift tonight. What about you?" he asked.

The children were visiting at Strawberry Fields. I planned to work all weekend. "I won't be able to go right to sleep either. Do you want to come over and talk? It might help us get ourselves back together for another shift."

"Sure, I'll be there as soon as I sign out and take my shower," he replied. I went home, showered, and dressed in a pair of short shorts and a tank top. I made a large pot of coffee. I heard a knock. I poured two mugs of the black gold and let in Brian. We sat at the dining room table in the early morning sunlight and tried to come to terms with the last twelve hours.

"Man, I don't know how you do it, working in that slaughterhouse every night," he said, looking into my eyes with his smoky blue ones. "I admire you. I love watching the way you move with such confidence. You always have a kind word for us cops." It had been many years since a man had told me he admired me for anything other than my body parts.

"It was a hard night, and I don't think I'll sleep much," I replied, hanging my head. "I don't know how well I handle anything. I really feel bad we couldn't do more. It makes you realize how little control you have over life." He leaned over and kissed me.

I knew what was coming. I don't know if it was sex I needed or the touch of another human being that understood me. After so much death, I needed another's touch, the feel of a man's skin on mine. I knew, at some unconscious level, that the hurt I was feeling was pain from all the hurts in my life. I realized that they never really go away. You just learn to live with them.

Brian carried me up to the master bedroom. Red satin sheets were on the bed that sat in the middle of the room, before two large windows facing the backyard. He removed the holster that held his Glock and gently placed it on the dresser. I shivered. I was still afraid of guns, especially big, dangerous ones like the Glock. Slowly and gently he undressed me, without taking his eyes off me. He dropped his jeans and the half-buttoned shirt onto the floor. He made love to me with the sun streaming in the windows. He was excited but shy and respectful. He didn't mind using a condom. He seemed surprised and amazed at the passion we aroused in each other. When we were both finally spent, emotionally and sexually, Brian said, "This has been the worst and best sixteen hours of my life. I don't think I'm likely to forget it." It was a sweet thing to say.

We saw each other quite often. I think we needed one another's support. I was going to school, and he was working on his law degree. I joined the Army Nurse Corps reserves in the early 1980s. He helped me become a marksman with the M16 rifle we officers were required to carry in times of war. I was one of the few women in my unit that could handle it. I hated it. Brian taught me, drilling me every time we were together, until I could manipulate that weapon like a pro. He was a quiet man. I enjoyed his company as we studied toward our separate goals. He had a girlfriend. She wanted to marry, but he said he wasn't ready. How I knew that story! I commented, "A young man like you should marry. I'm sure you'll want children, Brian. I know that isn't what our relationship is about. I won't be hurt or offended if you stop seeing me and marry her."

We never had sex after that first time. Brian sometimes talked about it. "I don't think I'll ever be able to forget that day. I've never had sex like that before or since," he would say.

"Well, there's more where that came from," I said. He was a shy guy. Maybe he just thought it wouldn't be like that again. Sometimes a memory can be more satisfying than reality. I could tell that he truly admired and was in awe of me. It was great for my self-esteem, which could still crumble at any given moment.

Late one night, a year later, I was home alone, working on my last classes before I graduated from the university with a degree in industrial environmental psychology. The girls were having a sleepover at a friend's house. There was a soft knock at the door; it was Brian. I hadn't seen him in some time. I was busy with school, the army, working two jobs, and my girls. My free time was limited.

"I saw your lights on. I thought I would stop and chat for a minute. Is it okay?" he asked.

"You know I'm always glad to see you, Brian," I said, letting him in.

"When you're away, I come and check on the place. It's a good idea that you let the police department know when you're out of town for army duties," he said.

"Thanks, Brian. I appreciate that very much," I replied. He sat at the dining room table, gazing at me without saying anything. "Can I get you some coffee or some other beverage?"

He shook his head and continued to stare. I was getting a little uncomfortable, so I tried some small talk. I closed my books and looked steadily into those captivating eyes.

"We had choir practice last night. I was there," he said finally. "Do you know what that is?" he asked.

Of course I knew. Everyone in town knew. Late on a designated night, the cops met at an undisclosed location to drink and talk about cop stuff and women. Most of them were womanizers and had several girlfriends, a wife, and a few ex-wives. They loved to compare notes and conquests. It was a guy thing.

"I know," I said flatly.

"You know me, and you know I never go to those things. But I was working with a partner last night, and he wanted to go sit in for a little while on our break," he said, staring some more. "Your name came up."

"I'm sure it did. Tell me, what was it the good cops of South Side had to say about me?" Whatever they had to say, it wasn't true. I knew none of them had anything to brag about. I was friends with many but had slept with only one. Tom, the older man, was good to me and the girls. He had even proposed once. He drank a lot. I couldn't see him as anything more than a friend. I was friends with Jason because of our kids. We met often after work for coffee and kid talk.

"When your name came up, every man was asked if he had been with you. They all said no. They all looked at me and asked if I had been in your bed," he said, and those rosy cheeks turned a bright red. "They all seemed to know you once had a thing for me." He hung his head.

"And what did you tell them, Brian?" I asked. "I'm sure you could have given them a good story."

He shook his head. "I couldn't do it. I knew then I was the only one who had, and I couldn't say it. I just couldn't brag. I'm not that kind." He paused. He knew it was true. Men like that never would have missed an opportunity to tell of a conquest. "I just have to know why. Why me, out of all those guys that would give anything they owned, even a vital organ, to have been in my shoes? Why on earth you did pick me?"

"Well." I took a deep breath. "I thought we picked each other. You're a good and honest person who wouldn't kiss and tell. The other reason is, I like you," I replied.

He married his girlfriend that year. I thought it was over with us until he began to call. He talked about that day we'd spent together. "Brian, you need to stop this!" I told him. "It isn't good for you or your marriage. It isn't good for me. What might you be doing when we're having these conversations?" (I was finally becoming a little worldly when it came to the ways of men.) "You keep asking me if I remember that day! Yes, I do, but please don't remind me anymore. You have moved on." He stopped calling for a while. Curiosity got the best of me one night after my shift. I don't know what made me drive by the house. I saw him through the window. The phone calls resumed.

Kyle Baines worked for Danny Wilmot's trucking company when I met him a few years after Garrison left. He was just nineteen and a mixed-up kid, but he thought I was the one for him. By the time he became a cop in town, he had been married and divorced several times. These facts didn't stop him from prowling around my house at all hours. Because of his track record with women, I kept him at a distance. I have to admit I was taken with him. He was handsome and sweet in a "bad boy" way. One night I kept seeing the same squad car go by and shine a light in the window. About eleven I opened the door. I noticed that the car was parked. It was Kyle. "Hi, beautiful," he said, and he leaned in through the open door and kissed me. He was cute and a lot of fun. I couldn't resist a kiss or two. He branded my neck, and I didn't know it until the next day.

I worked on the mayor's reelection campaign. He appointed me to the library board. I helped out with other community activities. I had a political meeting that morning. I was the only woman at those gatherings, and I worked at keeping an air of professionalism between those men and myself. No amount of makeup could hide the mark. It was noticed by all at the township office. They speculated for weeks about the man's identity. Kyle loved it! He was so proud. I made sure he never got that close again.

Transportation was big business. Danny Wilmot was very rich. He was my friend's boyfriend. When she dumped him, I decided he needed me as a friend more than she did. I knew he wanted more than a friend, but I wasn't interested. He was clingy and too needy. He was kind and generous, showering me with gifts. He was good to my girls, gentle and understanding with them. He displayed patience I sometimes lacked. He had a lot of friends who became my friends. He lived on the other side of town in an apartment complex with young couples. I came to know Gary and Belinda through Danny. I met Gary first. He needed extra space, so I rented him my garage. I didn't use it, and renting meant extra spending money. The children were standing by the back door in their pajamas, watching Gary out in the garage. I was trying to get them in bed so I could sleep a little. "Can't Gary come in and say good night to us, Mommy?" Sarah-Jane asked, standing there in her Dr. Dentons.

"I don't think so, honey. He's very busy," I replied.

"Can't you ask him, please?" she begged. I was so tired. I needed sleep. I went to the backyard and asked him to come inside and say good night to the girls.

"Well, I'm not much for kids. I don't know anything about them. I'm an orphan myself," he said.

I tried again. "I think it would make them feel safe if they knew you. It will only take a moment, and I would appreciate it so much."

"Okay, I'll come around to the front door and talk to them there," he said.

The children were sitting on the staircase leading up to the bedrooms when Gary entered the foyer. They started to have a easy conversation. Jenna-Lisa was only about a year old at the time, but she seemed to enjoy the encounter. Sarah-Jane had the vocabulary of an adult. She took charge of the conversation. Gary was very impressed. She talked him into reading them a story, and the time just seemed to fly. He had such an easy way with children; I was surprised that he thought he didn't know much about them.

A few months later, when Gary came to move his things out of my garage, Brenda came with him. I opened the front door to a smiling Brenda and a Gary who looked pleased but a little embarrassed. "I just had to come and thank you for getting me pregnant," Brenda said.

"I beg your pardon?" I said, feeling a little dismayed at this remark.

"Well, Gary didn't want children until he met your two. He's talked about them nonstop ever since. Now I'm pregnant, thanks to you and your two girls," she said, smiling. I still keep in touch with Gary and Brenda. We write to each other at least once a year. They are retired and live in another state. We exchange letters about our grandchildren.

It took me eleven years to earn two degrees from the university. I worked hard. I was on the dean's list. I earned a degree in industrial environmental psychology and a nurse practitioner degree. We students practiced on each other to learn to do physical exams. As my lab partner was doing my exam, our instructor came into our room to watch and grade her progress. "Oh, my goodness!" she exclaimed as Judy was examining my chest. "Did you know you have an inverted sternum?" I looked at her with fear in my eyes. "Well, don't worry. It's only a normal variation." I was concerned. When I got to the hospital that afternoon, I called down to the ER for Dr. BJ. He was my friend. I went to him when I had a medical question. He was smart, but I didn't think people appreciated him. "BJ, it's Mary. Can I come down and see you? My instructor at school says there is something wrong with my chest."

"Of course. It isn't busy yet," he replied. "I can see you in Room Two—it's empty." I went to Room Two, stripped down to my waist, and paced back and forth, looking in the mirror on the wall. I was nervous and worried. I always had known that my breasts stuck out too far. This must have been the reason for it all these years. I was more concerned when BJ knocked and entered the room, looking very shocked.

"Oh, God! So what do you think, BJ? Am I badly deformed or what?" I said anxiously.

With hands quivering, he walked over to the cabinet and took out a hospital gown. He draped it gently around my shoulders, with the opening in the front. Still shaking badly, he began to examine my chest. "Mary," he said gently, closing the gown around me, "I don't think there's anything to worry about. Your sternum is inverted, but it isn't one that needs surgery. It isn't interfering with your heart or lungs."

"Well, you really scared me with that look you gave me." I removed the gown, walking back and forth with my hands on my hips. "Are you sure I don't look deformed? That instructor sure seemed to think so."

"Mary, please put that gown back on, for God's sake! I may be a doctor, but I'm also a man, and you just about shocked the living hell out of me standing there like that. I know we're friends, but sometimes you just don't realize what you do to men. I don't mind caring for you, but my God, please be a little more discreet," he said, still trying to control the shaking.

"Oh, I'm sorry, BJ. I just wasn't thinking," I replied. "But you think I look all right? You know, I've never been sick much, and I'm getting older."

"You can get dressed before I have an embarrassing accident. You're fine. You don't look a day over twenty. Get the hell out of here!" he said, shaking his head and rolling his eyes as he left the room.

If it hadn't been for the support of my friends, I never would have been able to accomplish so many things. I worked two jobs. I went to school almost full-time. I was in the army reserve. I owe a lot to people like Mr. and Mrs. Polkas, who supported me. No one is completely alone in the world. We need other people to help us along the way. No one achieves goals on his or her own; everyone has help getting to the top. I was no exception. I stayed away from Strawberry Fields, and especially away from my sisters. They were convinced that

Pa and Mama were paying for my schooling. Our Lady of Light had a policy for full-time employees. You could get tuition paid entirely by the hospital. I took advantage of the program. I thought that when I finished, they would give me a promotion.

When I graduated with both degrees, Sarah-Jane graduated from high school. She left for college at the tender age of sixteen. That spring Carmella called me with bad news. She was always the bearer of it. If anything was wrong, she called. "You won't believe it! Henry Miller is dead! He was killed at work. He rigged his machine so it would go faster by taking the safety feature off. The part he was working on came off and went right into his neck, killing him instantly." Henry Miller was Antonia's third husband, a good husband and father figure to her teenage boys. I felt bad for my sister, although we weren't close. Such a tragedy shouldn't happen to anyone.

I attended Henry's service alone that day. No one spoke to me, only Enzo and Marco. I asked Marco why Mama and Pa wouldn't talk to me. "Antonia and Carmella told our parents you intended to put them in a nursing home and take their money."

"Marco, you know that isn't true. I make more money in a year than Pa ever made in any ten-year period in his whole life. I don't need his money," I said, trying to remain calm.

"I know. Our parents are old and will listen to anyone who visits them. You aren't there to defend yourself. Your sisters are able to fill their heads with lies," he replied. I felt I couldn't do anything to change the situation.

Another year went by before I heard from Carmella again. Her husband Norman was diagnosed with terminal cancer. He'd looked like a walking corpse at Henry's funeral.

I earned a good living, and I sent my girls to good schools. I had a bad time in public school, and I wanted better for them. Sarah-Jane started Catholic school, but she was so far advanced for her age that they didn't know what to do with her. They were far from kind or Christian to her or to me. I sought out a private school, a Montessori school. She did well, but it was very expensive. I didn't feel she was getting everything she needed. I heard about a school located on a farm about ten miles from South Side. I took Sarah-Jane for an interview. They grilled the child for over an hour while I sat watching in horror. The principal said, "We will take her into fourth grade. I feel it's best."

Since the school only went to the sixth grade, I had to find a new school again a couple years later. We tried the Catholic school in town, but it proved a disaster. I felt bad for Sarah-Jane; they were unkind to us. I moved her to a Christian school far from town. She did well and entered high school at thirteen and struggled to fit in. After two years she switched to an all-girls Catholic school in the big city, where she thrived and made many friends. Jenna-Lisa was able to stay at the Farm School through the eighth grade. She went to the same all-girls high school. Both girls did well, making me proud. My hard work was paying off.

I started my first job as a nurse practitioner the year Sarah-Jane went away to college. Life was looking up for the dream girl from the farm. I was a practicing nurse practitioner and a captain in the US Army Nurse Corps Reserves. I was a community leader. I worked for my congressman in my spare time. I kept my job at Our Lady of Light, because I felt I could return to regular nursing if needed. It was always in demand.

Scores of men hung around me—doctors, lawyers and cops. I took none of them seriously. I knew deep inside that I would always fall for the same man, that handsome, tall, dark, womanizing charmer. I liked being single and making my own decisions. I had to survive and raise my daughters. I was a real modern-day Scarlett. The year Garrison married Carol, I received five proposals of marriage. Danny Wilmot used to say it was because I had the body of a seventeen-year-old. I gave little thought to my health. I thought I would remain that homely little girl with the big breasts and small waist. Carmella, who was fourteen years older, still looked as if she were thirty. I still had trouble recognizing myself in pictures. I hated looking at photographs. I was afraid to admit that I couldn't recognize myself.

I ran six miles almost every day. Physical fitness was required for the army. I did all of this with ease until working in the big city became very stressful and demanding. The position I had in middle management was not ideal. Not only was I the nurse practitioner for the entire hospital and university, I was expected to hire and fire those who worked in my department.

An ad in the local nursing news caught my eye. It read, "Busy cardiologist looking for nurse practitioner." I called and talked with Dr. Eli Simon, who had a heavy New York accent. I agreed to send him my résumé. He called back, asking me to meet him on Saturday morning at a large hospital on the north side of the city. It was a beautiful facility on the big lake. It was the week between Christmas and New Year's. I showered and dressed in a very modern-style suit, a black blazer jacket with the sleeves pulled up, a white silk blouse with a fancy brooch at the neck, and a rust-colored skirt with a slit up the back. My curly black hair fell to my shoulders. It was a very cold day with lots of snow. I put on my mink coat and drove to the north end of the big city.

I went to the doctors' lounge where I was to meet Dr. Simon. I didn't know that so many doctors made rounds in a teaching hospital on a weekend. They looked me over and asked questions. Dr. Eli Simon was a small man, a typical Jewish doctor with salt-and-pepper curls. He was a few inches taller than me, suave and confident. "You must be Mary," he said, shaking my hand. He and the other doctors exchanged looks I didn't want to read. "I was very impressed with your résumé. I'm anxious to show you around."

"Thank you, I'd like that very much," I replied. We went from floor to floor, where many physicians greeted us. I noticed that things were not as advanced as at Our Lady of Light. I spent the whole day with Dr. Simon. We had lunch and talked a great deal about our backgrounds and experiences. When I learned that he was married and had three children, I felt a little more comfortable. I was just reading too much into that look he gave me earlier. When he walked me to my car later that afternoon, I was powerless over what happened.

"Look, Mary, I need you here with me. I'm really busy. I think I can work well with you. Please say you'll take the job."

"Okay, Dr. Simon, I think I can work with you," I replied.

"Please call me Eli. We'll be together almost every day," he said, standing very close to me.

"All right, Eli." Before I could finish what I was going to say, he took me in his arms and kissed me. I was stunned, flattered, shocked, and pleased all at once. The snow fell on my dark curls and mink coat. I saw my reflection in the window of my car. Snow caught the light, making me shimmer in a winter wonderland. I should have left, never to return, but I wanted that job.

The work wasn't hard. It was hard getting doctors to respect me and take me seriously, in the very male-dominated world of medicine. It wasn't my skill level or my knowledge about cardiology that raised objections. I was a woman and not even a doctor! I could do almost the same job. I thought my life was stressful, but it got even worse.

Mrs. Eli wasn't a kind, caring human being. She was selfish and self-centered, with little regard for her husband, his work, or the people in his care. She was a lot of things, but she wasn't blind or ignorant. She knew of our affair, but her husband wasn't going anywhere. She had more money than Eli and controlled his fortune as well as her own. She ordered him around like a pet dog, and he met her every demand. He wouldn't leave her and their millions; being a poor man wasn't his style. I didn't know why I became involved with him. I had avoided Jewish doctors when I was in school. When I told them I was Italian, they were disappointed but not deterred. I never accepted one dinner invitation. I was a Catholic, and being involved with a Jewish man was considered worthy of excommunication.

I already knew what it was like to have a husband who carried on with another woman. Now I knew, firsthand, what it was like to be that other woman. I didn't like it. It was demoralizing; my self-esteem crumbled. "I loved you the minute I laid eyes on you," he said. "I had to have you. I didn't care if you knew anything about cardiology. I figured it would be icing on the cake if you were knowledgeable. I have the best-looking nurse practitioner and the smartest. I can't believe my luck. I'm the envy of every doctor on the north side. I'm never letting you go."

Carrying on our relationship was easy. Hospitals had all kinds of places to hide. Drug companies were generous with overnight stays at five-star hotels for doctors who prescribed their drugs. As long as he did whatever Mrs. Eli wanted, she didn't care. The real reason she turned the other cheek was that I doubled Eli's income in a year. No laws governed how a nurse practitioner could practice. We were considered an extension of the physician. Eli was able to charge his fees for me to see the patients. It was twice the money for half the work. The good doctor and his wife remodeled their home. Eli bought three new luxury cars. I got my salary of fifty thousand a year, a small bonus at Christmas, and never a weekend or holiday off. The Simons took their family vacation over my holidays. I was good at my job! I won over doctors who were skeptical. The house staff of resident physicians loved me. I felt as if I had achieved what the dream girl had wanted, what she set out to do those many years ago. It seemed that she had arrived at last.

Pa became ill and was hospitalized in Freedom Falls; I left everything to go see him. I wasn't able to communicate with him and Mama without the interference of Carmella and Antonia. Pa had heart and kidney trouble. When they acted up, he became confused and disoriented. When I was still in the nurse practitioner program, he got ill. I wanted to take him to Our Lady of Light for care. I put Pa into my car. Henry Miller came out of the house and told me I couldn't take Pa anywhere. "If you don't get out of the way, Henry, I'll run over you with my car," I said. I wouldn't have done it, but he didn't know that, and he moved away. Pa had colon cancer and needed to have a colon resection. He was ninety-two. I had a hard time convincing a surgeon to operate on him. Being hospitalized caused lapses of memory. It was hard on Mama and him, but he recovered.

When I arrived at the hospital in Freedom Falls, he was in fulminating pulmonary edema. I called for Dr. Hemming. I told him what I wanted done for Pa. He did it, but he was very resentful. "You can't keep him alive forever, you know!" he yelled. Within an hour after all the meds were administered, he was awake and alert.

"You know, it is really awful when you can't breathe like that," he said.

"I know, Pa. You're all right now. I'll see you in a few weeks." He left the hospital and did fine for about five weeks. Another relapse sent me flying down to Freedom Falls, demanding he be saved. Dr. Hemming signed off his case. I spent that night at the hospital. Pa was doing better when I left the next afternoon. Sammy fed him lunch. His color was back, his breathing steady, and his oxygen level acceptable.

The next day at work, I received a phone call from the hospital saying that my pa had a cardiac arrest—actually, several. The nurses were upset because Mama wouldn't let them stop the resuscitation process. "He keeps arresting, and your mother won't give her consent to let him go. All your siblings are in agreement on stopping."

"My mother is in charge, and you just keep resuscitating him until she is ready to stop. I'm on my way," I said.

"You're damned nuts to keep that man alive. How stupid can you get?" the nurse said. I was stunned.

"Well, he's an old man. He has to die sometime. I don't want you to go," Eli said when I told him I had to leave on emergency. "I need you with me. You can't do anything for him anyway. You can't go. I won't allow it."

I got mad. "Oh, no? Well, just watch me!" With fire raging inside of me, I took off as if shot from a cannon.

Each time they resuscitated him, Pa came around and was alert and responsive to the voices around him, answering yes-or-no questions with some accuracy. "It's going to happen again, Mama," I said. "Do you want them to keep resuscitating him?"

With tears falling from her beautiful green eyes, Mama shook her head. Even in death, my pa's hands were outstretched, as if reaching for more life that was just beyond his fingertips. He always said he wanted to live to at least a hundred and ten, but he only made it to ninety-six. I had to hold myself together. Carmella was causing a scene. She hadn't seen Pa for some time. I guess she didn't realize he would die so soon. Antonia was there, giving everyone orders.

I hadn't slept; my mind was reeling with things for my pa's funeral. I drove to the hospital to tell Eli. I found him reading test results in the cardiology department. "I don't know why you people spend so much time on funerals. The person is dead," he said.

"Look, Eli, let me mourn in my own way. I don't criticize the way you do things. I'll meet up with you Friday after the funeral." I drove to Strawberry Fields. Everyone gathered to discuss funeral arrangements. Enzo wanted Pa's grandsons as pallbearers. I gave my niece money and told her to go to Fienberg's and frame Pa's large picture in his military uniform and frame his medals from the Italian army.

Mama picked out a beautiful bronze casket. Enzo raised an eyebrow at the price tag. "It's her money," I said sternly, cutting off any further discussion. We made arrangement for flowers to come from Enzo's store. I was the only one left at the funeral home when the newspaper man came to get a story about Pa. I told him my father came to America so many years ago, searching for a better life. Half an hour later I was ending with, "And did you know he was known as the Strawberry King?" I loved the article in the paper the next day. The headline read, "The End of an Era: Strawberry King Dies at the Age of Ninety-Six."

The wake was held for two nights, to accommodate the many mourners. The picture and the medals looked great. The large photo stood on an easel next to his coffin, and his medals were resting with him. A large wreath in the shape of a ripe, red strawberry was at the foot of his coffin. He looked so good, but his hands wouldn't stay folded. They kept coming apart, reaching up.

Carmella looked awful: old and ill. Her dear Norman had lost his battle with cancer a year ago. I had seen her last at his funeral. She always had been small, but now she was frail. She seemed a little out of touch with reality as she leaned on Antonia for support. Before it was all over, at least one thousand people passed by Pa's coffin. Christ the King Church was full on Friday morning. I felt terrible, but I couldn't cry. I had to be strong for everyone else. I had to make sure the whole affair went well. My friend David, who sang opera, filled the church with his beautiful baritone voice, singing the *Our Father* for the Mass. A large wreath was placed on the mailbox at the top of the drive at Strawberry Fields Farm. Ribbons of black and purple waved in the spring breeze. I insisted that the funeral procession take my pa past his beloved farm one last time. We were all packed into two black stretch limos. After it was over, I left the girls at home and drove to the north side to find Eli. I should have stayed to mourn with my daughters. Eli didn't really need me; he just wanted my attention, like a spoiled child. I tried visiting the farm more often, but Mama said little. Pa's chair sat empty in front of the TV, as if waiting for its master to return. My footsteps echoed as I walked back and forth.

Soon after Pa died, Nina fell ill and was hospitalized for a blood clot in her leg. I visited her and urged her to stop smoking and to follow the doctor's orders. "Did you know Carmella's here?" she asked. "Why don't you see what's wrong with her?"

Carmella looked so tiny lying in that bed that I almost didn't recognize her. "What's going on with you?" I asked.

"I have diabetes and a bad infection in my leg. I can't walk. They're going to keep me here and send me to rehab once the infection is gone. No one comes to see me. They leave me here, just like a dog," she said, crying. The nurse in me took over. I started to ask questions and helped her understand her condition. I bathed her and washed her hair. When I was done, she looked better. She even thanked me. I visited her several times, bringing her food and medications. But once she was better, she resumed her campaign against me.

My affair with Eli had reached a point of no return. I couldn't live with or without him. He treated me as his wife. He yelled and ordered me around, criticizing how I spent my money and raised my children. Since I spent so much time away from her, I purchased a car for Jenna-Lisa so she wouldn't have to ride the bus to school. She had been mugged twice since starting high school. .Eli thought it a waste of money but I needed a way to ensure her safety.

I had purchased one for Sarah-Jane the summer after her first year at college. She stayed in Omaha until she finished school. I was letting her make her own decisions. When it came to my older daughter, I had no judgment. I had little control of her since the day she was born. Once, when she was twelve, we went to Strawberry Fields for a visit. She was very cross with me. She wasn't happy. "You can't even drive. I can do a better job of it than you," she snapped.

"Oh, you think so, do you?" I asked. I threw the car keys at her. She caught them and got in behind the wheel. I was amazed—she could handle the car like an adult! I worried that we might get caught. She was relaxed and competent. I was always driving on no sleep. I gave in to her demands. She took the car most evenings, and I walked to Our Lady of Light for my night shift. I tried to put the fear of God in her every time she did it, telling her that if she was caught, I would go to jail and lose our house, and they would wind up in the Audie Home. She drove from that day on without an incident. I had no plan for raising my girls. I wasn't a good mother. I didn't know how to be a good parent; I had little parenting growing up. I used threats of the Audie Home, a place for troubled children. I don't really know who raised my kids. I was always at work. God raised them and watched over them. Every time I left the house, I asked His help. I'm sure He heard me.

I didn't have a chance to mourn my father. I had no time to cry. The hardest thing for me was seeing that empty overstuffed rocking chair. Every time I saw it, I would think that Pa was outside in the barn or in the field. Then it came to me that he was gone. The following year, Sammy closed up the downstairs kitchen and moved the TV up to the living room. He got rid of the old chair. It must have bothered him too.

In November of the year after Pa died, when my basement flooded for no apparent reason, I found a large lump in my left breast. I couldn't ignore my health any longer. I would see Dr. Castro after Christmas. Eli left the country, promising to spend New Year's Day with me when he returned. I ran the practice by consulting with another cardiologist. That New Year's Day Eve, I stared at the brightly wrapped package I had for Eli. His words rang sharply in my ear: "I'm just too tired. I'm not going anywhere tonight. I'll see you at the office on Monday." I had the day off from Our Lady of Light. We always spent New Year's Day together. It wasn't the first time Eli had broken a promise, but it didn't hurt. Garrison was the only one who could ever make me hurt; no other person had that power. You only have one true love in your life. I took Jenna-Lisa out to a nice restaurant, just us. We laughed and talked, enjoying each other's company.

I returned to work and presented Eli with a full report on all the patients. I finished at seven-thirty, surprising him by leaving early. "I'll be late tomorrow. I have a doctor's appointment," I said.

That January day I wasn't expecting my world to be turned upside down. The previous year in January I was almost taken from my home and sent to the Persian Gulf to fight a war that took us all by surprise. I was spared because my general liked me. "Your name was the first," my chief nurse said to me. "He wants you here! It's by the grace of God and the general you're not going." I was ready. I had made my will; I had my bags packed by the door. ER trauma experience and a cardiology background put me high on the list. Many were anxious to go. The Gulf War had more volunteers than places for them. I did my weekend at Fort Sherman, working for the general. I could hear trains being loaded with supplies to be shipped overseas. Supplies buried in large underground bunkers were dug up and loaded on waiting boxcars. The sounds of the soldiers preparing for war chilled the very souls of us who lay awake.

Eli cried real tears when I told him I wasn't going. "You have no idea how relieved I am. I just couldn't go on without you." I knew what he meant: it would be very inconvenient for him to have to replace me. I felt a little guilty that I missed that war.

When they told me that the lump was highly abnormal, the floor moved under me. I called Enzo, but he didn't know what to say. I hung up, promising him a visit. I called Marco. He was out of town on a business trip. By then, he was a wealthy man. "I think you need to look into unconventional treatments," he said. "I know they work. Medical doctors don't want people to know—they make money off cancer victims." I couldn't listen to him.

I was in Eli's arms for the last time, I knew. He did not. Cancer was about to take my left breast; my firm, slender body; my gorgeous, wavy black hair; and what little self-esteem I possessed. I ended the relationship. He was devastated, but I was too wrapped up in myself and my fight for life to notice. He resented that I was sick.

All humans are created equal; some are more equal than others. Nothing makes us more equal than illness. It doesn't matter—tall or small, rich or poor, everyone ill or injured is equal.

≈20≈

No Longer Young and No Longer Beautiful

CANCER CAME IN THE middle of the night, taking everything I had always taken for granted—my good health, my strength, my stamina, and my ability to stand up to any situation. I felt weak and vulnerable; the fire seemed to have gone. I feared for my life but told no one. I didn't want the girls to become afraid. I didn't want anything to interfere with their well-being and their goals in life.

Mama became ill and was hospitalized at Freedom Falls. Sarah-Jane returned to university life in Omaha. Jenna-Lisa was left home alone. "When will you be back, Mommy?" she cried.

"As soon as I make sure Grandma's okay," I said. "Are you sure you don't want to come along?" She shook her head. With my head as bare as the palm of my hand, I donned a wig and chose an outfit that hid the many black-and-blue marks and bulges that had appeared out of nowhere since starting treatment.

"So is that your real hair?" Carmella asked, staring at me up close. She and Antonia were practically gloating at my awful appearance.

"No," I said and moved to Mama's bedside.

She looked at me with sad green eyes. "I don't understand how you get cancer when you are supposed to be so smart and a nurse. How you let yourself get this?" she asked coldly. I was both saddened and shocked. She didn't seem sympathetic, only angry.

"Mama, just because one is a nurse or a doctor in the medical field, it doesn't automatically guarantee immunity to illness," I replied. But I don't think she understood my point. She seemed distant. I tried to make her comfortable and see that she had the best of care. I was uncertain that I would be able to return to see her, as I grew more ill with every chemo.

In early spring, Eli raved on about my illness, saying that I wasn't carrying my share of the workload. I realized that I couldn't tolerate him or the workload. Something deep within made me see that I might not survive. When there was a pause in his raving and our eyes met, I said, "May twenty-second."

"What about it?" he asked.

"Johnny Carson and I will be gone from our jobs for good. You'll have it in writing." I handed in my resignation the next day.

I was alone, sick and dying, and without a job. I thought the hours of the holiday weekend would pass slowly. Sarah-Jane was back at school. Jenna-Lisa was working at the mall. I was trying to prepare myself mentally, when there was a knock on the door, and my nephew Buddy came in. "I'm here to spend the day with you. Let's go do something fun," he said. We had a great day together. We ate barbecued ribs and talked for hours about our childhoods, our lives, and our kids.

All summer my friends took me to many gatherings and events. I wasn't alone, but I was frightened. I needed a job or to go on public assistance, something I had always feared. My hair started growing back. I lost the puffiness from my body and face. I desperately looked for another job. My friend told me that a group of cardiologists at the hospital in South Heights was seeking a nurse practitioner. I contacted them and sent in my résumé. My friend was certain that they intended to hire me. I was almost out of money, but with time on my hands I hadn't had in many years, I walked everywhere. My looks were so altered that most people around South Side didn't recognize me. Some pretended they didn't so they wouldn't have to talk to me. Everyone knew I had cancer, and wild rumors flew around that it was terminal. If I had breakfast or lunch in a local diner alone, no one spoke to me. My meal was always paid for, but I never knew who did it.

Buddy was divorced from his second wife. I volunteered to keep Little Buddy for a week while he worked a second job. We were playing ball in the front yard when a car pulled up. It was a city car. I didn't look up until Steve called out, "Mary, I'm glad to see you up and around. Are you feeling better? What on earth did you do to your hair?" Steve was a young local guy. We had a secret affair, on and off. I was surprised he had stopped by. He never wanted anyone to know about us. Our time together was spent sneaking around in the middle of the night. I hadn't seen him in some time.

"Almost bald, see?" I said as I put my head through the open window and pulled off my wig. "Cancer treatments are a bitch." He was a man who only saw my body. Good sex was the only thing we had in common. I knew that seeing me bald would scare him away forever. That river of men stopped flowing. If they looked at me, I looked away. Brian pulled up next to me at a stop sign one day. He tried getting my attention, but I refused to look at him. When I was diagnosed, I had called to tell him. His calls stopped coming. Until that day at the stop sign, I hadn't seen him. I had many acquaintances, but true friends are hard to find, and even harder when you have cancer.

One day I encountered my old friend and working partner from Our Lady of Light. Lupe and I were good friends when I started at Our Lady of Light. I saw her in the backyard as I walked over the bridge in her neighborhood. She said I should come back to work. I went back to the ICU part-time. A bedside nurse is never out of work. I prayed hard every day on those walks. I asked God to restore my good health and the career I had worked so hard to achieve. I begged His mercy, asking Him to shine His light upon me.

The chemotherapy and radiation treatments left me weak and tired. Unlike Don McLean, who sang with certainty about the Father, Son and the Holy Ghost taking that last train for the coast, I knew They hadn't left me. They carried me through that fire of hell. My strength began to return, and my weight dropped to normal. My dark, curly hair grew back in, darker and curlier.

I went back to work at the same mad pace. I worked seven days a week for cardiologists who treated me only a little better than Eli had. I was still working for my congressman until the end of the year. He lost his district in the redistricting process that year. I didn't return to the army reserve; I could no longer fit into the uniform. I wasn't strong enough to handle fieldwork or the demanding level of physical fitness. I left at the rank of captain.

Life was crazier than ever. I was a better nurse after my illness. I was much closer to the Father. I learned nothing about control and balance in life. I was still determined to achieve all of my goals, at any cost. I begged God for five more years to get my girls through college and see that they were self-sufficient.

I walked the halls of the hospital, attracting many glances. I wasn't looking back. My oncologist was worried that my cancer was returning. "I don't like this, Mary," he said at every visit. "You are too thin too fast, but your numbers look good."

"Well, stop worrying. I told you I lost the weight on purpose. I have an image to uphold," I said, smiling. "Besides, you told me you would put me on medication to prevent the cancer from coming back." He knew about my fast-paced life, with little sleep, lots of coffee, and too much stress. After I started the medication, I was swollen up again and short of breath within weeks. My feet hurt; I had trouble walking. I was good at ignoring my own health. It didn't dawn on me that I had a problem with the medication.

Now that I had my old life back, I wanted my old body back too. I went to see a plastic surgeon. Stripped to the waist, with a hospital gown opened in front, I faced an arrogant surgeon. He asked what I was looking for in the way of breast reconstruction. "Do you just want to look okay in your clothes, or do you want to be able to run naked on the beach without the slightest hint of a reconstructed breast?" he asked. He lifted my one remaining breast with a gloved hand and then let it fall from his fingers as if it were a water balloon. I guess I missed the irony in his question. I replied that I wanted the latter. Two other nurses had reconstruction done by him, with marvelous results. What I didn't take into account was that they were younger and smaller-breasted.

"I think you have unrealistic expectations of plastic surgery. I feel you're a little mentally unstable and may require some psychiatric help," he said. I was stunned! I didn't like him. He thought he knew everything about me after a consultation of less than two minutes. I canceled the surgery and went to another plastic surgeon.

Before surgery I had many tests. I was focused on the end result, not on surgical complications and recovery. One of the tests showed that my heart wasn't functioning well. I had trouble breathing. My oncologist did a bone scan that read abnormal. "We may be looking at a bone marrow transplant at some point," he said calmly. "Do you have anyone willing to be tested, in case you need a donor?" I called Marco. He called my sisters and asked them to stand by to be tested as possible donors. They both refused.

"They will be tested, even if I have to drag both of them there!" exclaimed Marco. He referred to them as the Merry Widows. They said I had too many good breaks in my life and I had a few bad ones coming. I had so much, and they had so little.

After an episode of shortness of breath that almost put me in the hospital, Dr. Pedro took me off the cancer-preventing medication. The symptoms decreased, and within a week I felt so much better. Other experts were consulted on the bone scan findings. It was severe arthritis. No cancer was found.

The autograft reconstruction surgery didn't go well. I was in surgery for twelve hours, under anesthesia, with my arms outstretched. The surgeon attempted to use my internal mammary artery to supply blood to the graft taken from my lower abdomen. The graft failed and began to rot away immediately. The artery was diseased and unable to give an adequate blood supply. My arms didn't work after too long in one position. I lost a lot of blood; I required six units. In my craziness, I refused any type of pain medication. I was in the hospital for over a month, in a private room. Every employee was trying to read my chart. The failed graft left a large hole in my chest, eleven inches long, five inches wide, and three inches deep. I refused further surgery and demanded that I be released. Many doctors and friends begged me to let someone try to close the wound. I refused and went home with home health nurses. Most were of little or no help. I fired them. I went to physical therapy every other day. My dressings were done there by my very capable therapist. My nurse friends came to my house and tended to the wound. I had to eat about twenty-five hundred calories a day in order to provide enough nourishment to close the wound. It was hard to stop eating after the six months it took to heal completely. I realized the great healing, comforting power of food.

Sarah-Jane graduated from college. Jenna-Lisa was attending a prestigious university in the big city. She was thriving and enjoying her studies. I began to review my list of goals. I was fifty years old. God had granted me many gifts. He held me from the jaws of death by cancer. I was grateful, but I wanted more. I wanted a new home for my family. I wanted weekends off, something I had not had in many years. I wanted a doctoral degree.

In the spring I put the house on Sunny Side Avenue on the market. To my surprise I had a buyer within two months. The neighborhood was changing. It was crime-ridden. Our cars were stolen more than a few times. Around nine o'clock one night, I opened my door to a black man and woman with three boys. "Mrs. Michael? My name's Artie Smith. I been here almost every evening, trying to get in touch with you. I was afraid to leave a message on your answering machine. I thought if you heard a black man's voice, you wouldn't call me back," he said. "I really want to buy your house."

"Well, please come in, and let's talk," I replied. "What kind of work do you do, Mr. Smith?" I inquired.

"I'm self-employed," he said, and my heart sank. "I own a junkyard. I'm a scavenger and do pretty well. Look, I already got approved for a loan at the bank in town. I need this big house for my family. We're living in a trailer on the other side of town. I like this place and this neighborhood. Won't you please sell me this house?" He was anxious to have the house, and I was anxious to be gone from it. Sarah-Jane remained in Omaha after her graduation. Jenna-Lisa was living on campus. My lovely next-door neighbors the Jays were the only friends on my block, but Mrs. Jay had died a year ago. The neighbor on the other side for the last twenty years was a mean old lady. She never was kind to me or my girls, no matter how nice we were to her. It was very ironic that she died the same day I moved out. I moved from Sunny Side on the exact day that I had moved in twenty years before.

I looked for a townhouse. I had little time for looking, but when I found one, Enzo looked at it with me. He gave me his expert opinion on whether it was a good buy. We looked at so many that I was able to spot problems on my own without him. I finished rounds early for my three cardiologists and went house hunting. I ventured into a town I couldn't afford. I looked at single-family homes I didn't want. I came to a beautiful place with a Jaguar in the driveway. A well-dressed man was seated on the porch, reading the paper. By now I had a low opinion of good looking, well-dressed men.

"Hi, the name's Paul," he said, extending his hand. "Paul Newman," he continued, shaking my hand firmly. "Are you interested in buying a home today? I'm a realtor, and I'm having an open house. Would you like to look?" he asked. There was no one but the two of us. He pleasantly pointed out lovely features as we walked from room to room. "So, Mary, is it?" I nodded. "What do you think of this one?"

"I'm thinking I don't know what the hell I'm doing here. I've wandered into territory that's beyond my ability to buy. It's a townhouse I'm looking for. I've seen a ton of them, but I can't bring myself to buy one. I looked at another single-family home not far from here.

It's nice, but I'm not sure about it. The builder said it was in this same neighborhood, but I don't think it is. I don't trust anyone who isn't truthful."

"Well, listen, Mary, I know the house and that man. It's not this same zip code. Here is my card. My wife is going to call you on Monday. Please give me your number," he said. I gave him the number, but I don't know why. He was nice but strange. He looked like Paul Newman, and his name was Paul Newman, but I knew he couldn't be *the* Paul Newman! Why was he going to have his wife call me?

Jenna-Lisa was off school the next day, and we were going to look at houses. The phone rang just as we were about to leave. "Mary Michael, please."

"Speaking," I replied.

"My name is Joanne Newman. My husband asked me to call you. Would you like to look at houses today?" she asked. This was just too weird.

"Well, okay," I replied.

"Good!" she exclaimed. "Meet me at the office." It was a realtor's office with a sign that read "Newmans' Own Real Estate, Inc." Mr. and Mrs. Newman were the nicest people one could ever know. They helped me with the sale of my own house, and they found the perfect brand-new house for me and my little family.

It was raining hard the day of the move and very warm for December. It was December 4, the exact day I had moved into the house on Sunny Side twenty years ago. I was crawling around in the grass on the front lawn, trying to locate the spot where I had buried my statue of St. Joseph when I decided I needed help selling the place. "Auntie, please get up. What kind of statue is it? I'll go and buy you another one. Just get up, come in, and get dried off. I'm afraid you'll get sick." Gilbert was Sally's second husband. He had come to help with the move. Moving a houseful of things accumulated over twenty years was no picnic. Everyone was tired and wanted this day to end. I just had to have my statue to put in a prominent place in my new house. I had followed all the instructions, and it had worked to help sell the house and find a new one.

"What kind of coordinates did you use when you buried it?" John asked. He was a great kid who had helped Sarah-Jane move her things from Omaha. I was glad for John. He was essential in getting things done right that day.

"I lined the hole up with the banister at the bottom of the steps," I said to John as he helped me to my feet. He stood by the banister and took a few paces away from it. He tossed a screwdriver to the ground, landing it point down in the grass. He started digging. In five minutes he pulled St. Joseph from his burial place, still in the plastic bag, clean and dry. The move was complete. It was strange that first week after I cleaned the house on Sunny Side and turned the keys over to the new owners. I kept feeling like I needed to go home to the old house. I loved the new house. I was happy and grateful. It took some getting used to after living in one place for so many years. Having Christmas dinner in my new home, with my whole family and cancer-free, was pure joy.

"She's real sick. I just thought I'd better tell you in case you didn't know," Marco said on the phone. He was away on another business trip that evening in the middle of January.

"What do you mean she's sick?" I asked. "What is it?" Marco was calling about Antonia.

"She has kidney cancer. They say nothing can be done for her. She hasn't got long," he replied. I sank to my knees at the side of my bed. I knew from my many years of experience in the health care field that the survival rate for people with the disease was about 3 percent. If it was as advanced in Antonia as Marco said, she wasn't in that small percentage of survivors. I couldn't sleep for days. At night I wondered why God had spared my life and why he was about to end Antonia's. Survivor's guilt invaded my mind. I knew better than to question God about anything. I had been given so much.

I knew I had to do the right thing. I just needed the courage to do it. I called Enzo. "Did you know about this?" I asked.

"Yah, I heard something about it. But she doesn't talk to any of us, and she has caused nothing but trouble in our family for so long." It was true, but I also knew that it was family Antonia needed.

"Marco, I know the right thing I must do. I need to go see her and find out what I can do to help. Will you come with me?" I asked. Marco was reasonable; he would go with me. "If she won't see me, then I'll know I tried to make it better between us."

A distraught Antonia poured her heart out when we visited. "They can do nothing for me. All they have are these shots I'm to take three times a week. I don't even know who will give them to me. I take my own insulin, but I can't do this. I just don't know how." She had no health insurance and no real savings either. She was at the mercy of the big research center in the state capital. They supplied the medication free. She clearly needed help. I taught Dean Martin how to give his mother the shots. I had a long talk with Enzo about forgiveness and regrets after she was gone. He, Carmella, and Sammy came to her aid. I was pleased that they saw the healing power and peace of forgiveness.

Antonia had custody of her granddaughter. I encouraged her to sign over the child and her home to someone responsible. I wanted Taylor to have a home to grow up in and a good education. "It's easy for you to say. You always had everything," she replied. It was useless to argue. Trying to reason with her wasn't going to work. Her son told me that the cancer had metastasized to her liver, lungs, and brain. It was a matter of time. It was impossible to have any legal papers drawn up. Although she quit smoking without help, it didn't happen in time. "If I had known it was that easy, I would have done it long ago."

She was home alone on the weekends. I decided to bring her and her granddaughter to my new home for a few days. Reluctantly she agreed. She walked around the house and went into the big kitchen, the dining room, and the living room. "I just don't get it," she said.

"Get what?" I asked.

"What I don't understand is how you have all this. What it is you really do, anyway?" she asked.

"Antonia, I'm a nurse practitioner. I earn a good living. I work every single day. That's why Sarah-Jane will be with you when I'm at work. My friends and neighbors will be calling to make sure you and Taylor are all right," I said. When we returned from church the next morning, I found Antonia standing in the master bathroom, staring at the tub. "What is it, Antonia? Are you sick? Do you need help?" I asked, alarmed.

"I want to take a bath in that tub. I don't have a tub like this at home, but I don't think I can do it myself," she replied. I ran the water and added some bubble bath. I got her undressed, and I lowered her into the warm, fragrant bubbles.

"You know, I think that this is the first time in our lives that I outweigh you," I said, marveling at how easy it was to lift her in and out of the tub.

"I wish I was two hundred pounds again, like I used to be," she said. I thanked God for being overweight.

Since that visit went well, I decided to have Easter dinner for the whole family. I invited Carmella and her new boyfriend. The day before Easter, Antonia became very ill and entered the hospital. She was gravely ill, but I didn't think her time had come. I went to the hospital in Freedom Falls to see her. She was very pale. "I'm sorry I ruined your dinner plans for tomorrow," she said.

"You didn't ruin it. We'll have dinner and then come here," I said. There were about twenty-five of us at the table. Sammy stayed home with Mama; she only left the farm to go to the doctor. Antonia didn't want anyone to tell Mama she was sick. I felt it was a bad idea to keep her in the dark, but it was Antonia's wish that she not be told. Sarah-Jane played the guitar and sang for a little entertainment. I was tired after everyone left. I called Antonia to say I would come in the morning to see her. She was in good spirits and joked about having cherry-flavored gelatin for Easter dinner.

When the phone rang at five in the morning, I knew it couldn't be good news. I felt so guilty for not having gone to see her. My nurse's brain knew that those who are dying choose to do it alone. I took her death hard. I became depressed and gained weight. When I looked into the mirror, it was Antonia's face, how she looked before her illness, her full, smooth face smiling with black and copper-red hair in curls.

A strange windstorm continued for days after her death. When I tried to sleep that night, it seemed to bring Antonia into my room. I woke to see her standing by the bed. On the third night I woke to a mournful-sounding wind and a dull light glowing in my bedroom. I turned on my side, away from the big mirror. I hardly slept on my left side; the scars were painful. I looked up at the wall, and I saw her picture. It was the one she had taken at Fienberg's when she became engaged to Redmond. I reached for the bedside lamp switch. Light flooded the room. I sat up and blinked several times as I stared at the blank wall. I hadn't hung any pictures yet. I knew that photo of Antonia was not even in my possession. It was at the house at Strawberry Fields Farm, sitting on the sideboard table with the others. But before I lit the lamp, I had seen every detail of it! Looking in the mirror was always hard. Since having the mastectomy and the failed reconstruction, I avoided it. But when I looked at my face, I saw Antonia's. I felt that I had failed her somehow. I should have done more for her.

Mama took Antonia's death very hard. Over the last ten years, they had been close. Mama had depended on her a great deal. I tried to fill in, but it wasn't easy, since Mama didn't seem to know me. Every time I visited, I had to tell her who I was. Carmella wouldn't go to the farm without me. Sammy still lived there. He did the shopping and cooking, if you could call what he made food. His ability to keep the place clean was nonexistent. Growing up, Mama had always waited on him hand and foot. I think she was still running his bathwater and doing his laundry. He smoked so much that Mama's clothes smelled of it. I did her laundry. I hated the state of her clothes. She had money and could afford to dress better. I bought her nice things and dressed her. "Where are we going, all dressed up like this?" she would ask.

"Nowhere, Mama. I just want you to look nice," I would answer her. I was no hairstylist like Antonia. She had done Mama's hair. I prayed each time I picked up the scissors. Somehow it seemed to turn out all right. Once or twice a week I bathed her and washed her hair, soaked her feet, and trimmed her toenails. She asked who I was and what I was doing in her house. I would answer, "It's me, Mama, Evalina. I'm here to take good care of you."

"You not Evalina! You fat!" she would exclaim, sending Carmella and me into fits of laughter. She would sometimes ask me how much the outfits I bought for her cost. I wouldn't tell her the real price. I bought her a beautiful black suit with a white blouse and black patent leather dress shoes for Antonia's memorial service. When I told her I spent one hundred and forty dollars for the suit, thirty-two on the blouse, and another forty on shoes, she put them all back in their packages, telling me to return them, because they cost too much money. I finally convinced her that they were a gift from me.

In 1997 I went back to work at Liberty Hospital. The pay was great and the hours good, although it was still a very bad place to work. The patient care was substandard. With shorter hours and more money, I worked with my nurse practitioner organization, getting laws passed to govern our practice. We were granted the best terms of any state, and it only took two years! Because of this, I was able to open my own practice in 1999. That year, my daughters got married. It was a year full of joy, emotional turmoil, and financial extremes. Jenna-Lisa became engaged the year she graduated from the university. Sarah-Jane became engaged to a man six years older than she was. They decided to marry that same year. Every waking moment was filled with wedding planning. I have always maintained that I couldn't have better sons-in-law if I had picked them myself. The weddings were spectacular.

By the new millennium, I was walking on air. I thought there was nothing I couldn't do in life. No mountain seemed too high. My life would finally have balance. But it wasn't meant to happen. Mama's health began to fail. Some days she just moaned, unable to tell anyone what was wrong. At the beginning of March, she suffered a massive heart attack. Four years earlier, when she fractured her hip, Sammy had changed her primary care provider. She had been under the care of Dr. Hemming's son; he was a chip off the old block, with a worse bedside manner than his father. Dr. Haines, the new provider, was no improvement. He was droll and never spoke to me when I went with Mama for her appointments. I would ask for test results and other types of health maintenance care. "I'm the doctor. I'll decide what she needs," he replied.

Dr. Haines had been there earlier and told everyone there was no hope for Mama; she was dying. Mama lay there moaning and calling out for deceased members of her family. She called out for Pa, her mother, and her brother. "Please, can't you give her something for pain?" I asked the nurse.

"Well, the doctor ordered a milligram or two of morphine if she needs it. But we can't give her too much. Her blood pressure is too low."

"Could you please page Dr. Haines, so I might have a word with him?" I asked. Sammy let out a big sigh and left, saying he wanted to get some sleep. Carmella followed him.

Enzo paced the room, then came to Mama's bedside and looked at her. "Call me when it's over." He left the room. I tried to talk to Mama, but she didn't hear me.

"Please, Dr. Haines, couldn't you order a nitro IV and a Dobutamine IV for my mother?" I begged him. "Her pressure could be maintained, and the nitro will ease her pain, and she will rest comfortably. The morphine isn't doing her any good."

"Just what do you hope to accomplish by giving such meds? They're a waste of time and money. Don't you understand they won't save her?" he replied. Of course I knew! I had given this combination many times in my long career. While it didn't prevent anyone from dying, it helped keep them comfortable. "She will die a lot quicker without it," he said and hung up the phone. I found her thrashing about the bed, covers all undone, and she was perspiring. I went back out to the station and asked for some clean linen to change her bed. I wanted to reposition her, make her more comfortable. A nurse and an aide followed me. "You can leave. We'll take care of this." The nurse's name tag said Amy.

"I'd like to stay and help make my mother comfortable," I replied.

"No!" she said, rather too firmly. "We'll do this and call you when we're done. Go and wait in the visitors' lounge." I knew they could call security and have me removed. I went to the lounge.

No one called me. After about half an hour I returned to the room and sat with Mama as she lay dying. She called out for everyone that had gone before her. She called for my father. "Nino! Nino!" she called. Then she started to call for Antonia, her mother, and her brother. At some point she called for Sammy. I tried to calm her, telling her that Sammy would return in the morning. Her eyes were wide open, in spite of morphine every two hours. She appeared to see things and people as she picked at the air.

At four-thirty in the morning, she fell silent, breathing her last. At five she was gone. I sat quietly, feeling empty and alone. "She's gone, you know," the nurse said when she entered the room.

"Yes, I know," I replied, wanting in the worst way to say something mean. But it would dishonor my mother, who was a kind and gentle woman.

"Well, the nursing supervisor will come to pronounce her, and then we're going to take her to the morgue. You'll have to leave!" she said.

"I'll phone other family members. They can say their final goodbye. The funeral home will come for her. I intend to stay with her," I said firmly, not moving from the chair. During the night, the priest came and gave her the last rites. He said a very formal prayer or two over her and left. I felt helpless. I hadn't wanted her to die, and I hadn't wanted to watch her suffer, but I couldn't leave her to die alone. One by one, my siblings came to Mama's room and cried. I wondered if they really had heard what they had been told last evening. They seemed shocked that she was gone.

Although we were never close, losing Mama was hard. It was many years since she had recognized me as her youngest child. I cried and mourned for her and everyone I had lost. In her eulogy, I spoke of her as she had been when I was young. She was quiet, kind, and caring, tending her gardens and her animals. She listened with infinite patience when we visited her. Once we became of age, she never judged us or corrected us. Who would listen, now that she was gone?

Carmella called me several times a week, asking me to meet her at Strawberry Fields to go through Mama's clothes and things. I just couldn't do it. "It's too soon, Carmella. I can't go. I don't care about her clothes," I told her.

"Well, you bought them. Don't you want to take them back?" she asked.

"No! What would I do with them? I guess you can have them." Carmella was tiny like Mama. "I have a few of her old dresses from the 1950s, when she went back to Italy, and the first dress I bought her with my first paycheck," I replied. The day we went, no one was there. We packed her clothes into Carmella's Lincoln. The only thing I took was the necklace Mama wore when she had that photo taken with her mother-in-law. It has little value, but it is a piece of family history. One week later Enzo called a family meeting at the farm. He demanded to know who had been in Mama's room and taken all of her belongings. "Well, it was Carmella and me," I replied.

"Everything here belongs to me now!" he yelled. "You don't come here and take anything without my approval." He was executor of her will, but I didn't think everything had been left to him. She had no jewelry, only her wedding band and a watch I had purchased. I never kept an account of what I'd spent. It was a total surprise when Sammy pulled out a notebook detailing every penny he had spent for household supplies, heating fuel, food, and many other items. I thought it petty, since he had lived there for sixty years rent-free. After he finished yelling at Carmella and me, I left. I never went back. For most of my life I had wished, hoped, and prayed to be taken from Strawberry Fields forever. The place haunted my dreams. As hard as it was to take care of Mama those last five years, it was harder living without her. I saw her in my dreams. She was standing by the stove, cooking, or she was walking up the hill with a quart of strawberries in each hand and smiling.

I was devastated one short year later when Carmella died of a sudden heart attack. She was sixty-nine and didn't look a day over forty-five. The whole town of New Moon came to a complete halt. She was such a vital part of that community. Hundreds came to mourn her. Police officers and firefighters from several towns had to assist with the crowds and traffic. Whenever the name Carmella was heard, everyone knew her. She was one of those rare people who needed only one name. I saw her in my dreams, as if she were in the same room. The image in the mirror was now Carmella. Her dark hair, olive skin, and shining black eyes were always present in my peripheral vision when I lay down to sleep or as I woke.

"I think you're alive in spite of my care, not because of it," my oncologist ranted as he held up a sheet of lab reports. "Didn't you have any symptoms of diabetes?" I neglected my own health, but this time I wasn't entirely to blame.

"I had many! I told you I was developing type two diabetes. You insisted I wasn't," I replied. I consulted an internist for high blood pressure and diabetes. Everything was going along just fine until I began to have lapses in memory and difficulty seeing and walking.

"I think you're having a stroke!" Dr. Sahib exclaimed when I reported these symptoms. I refused hospitalization but had outpatient testing. Dr. DeJohn did an angiogram of my carotid arteries. He had been my mentor in school. He taught me many things over the years. The test showed that one vessel was twisted and had minimal disease.

"I think these are transient," Dr. DeJohn said. "Make sure you take a coated aspirin every day and lower your stress level." I stumbled around for a few more weeks. After a few more falls, I went to rehab. Dealing with stress, however, proved to be much harder.

The atmosphere at Our Lady of Light had grown so toxic that I took a medical leave of absence. I always kept my job there, part time, in fear of being without income as well as needing extra money. I had many sick days and other paid days off. I received a check every payday for the next year and four months. "But don't you want to come back and work for a few months before you retire, so you will have completed a full thirty-six years here in our employ?" a human resources worker asked.

"No! I just want to retire," I replied. Even as I began to collect my pension, I was receiving sick benefits. My business thrived, and I was happy to be my own boss. I went back to school, hoping I could finally get that doctorate. School taught mostly false and outdated things. I dropped out after a semester. I tried to teach at the junior college level. I found that most who took my course in community health just wanted the credits. They weren't there to learn about helping others. I left after a year.

Sarah-Jane gave birth to a daughter, and two years later Jenna-Lisa had a son. I was thrilled to be a grandmother. I was busier than ever when Sarah-Jane gave birth to her second child, a beautiful boy. Life was moving fast, but I was happy living alone in my big house.

Follow-up tests every year were tedious. I became lax in doing them. I had a mammogram late that summer after Sarah-Jane had little Johnny. I wasn't alarmed when I was called back in for more films. Then I was called back again for an ultrasound. A third call asked for more tests. I was quite irritated. "Why do you keep asking for more tests? I've had every test known to mankind on this one breast. I don't have time for it." As I raved, the radiologist came into the room with many films and mounted them on the viewing box.

"Here's what I'm concerned about, Mrs. Michael, right in the upper outer right breast. It's suspicious for another malignancy," she said with confidence. The room was spinning as tears fell from my eyes. I needed at least a biopsy soon. It was another miracle. I could see that immediately. If I'd had the mammogram in January that year as scheduled, the tumor might not have been detectable. It might have been another year before the mass was detected, putting me at risk.

Dr. Murray had performed my left modified radical mastectomy. He was no longer doing surgery. He promised to assist if I chose one of his former partners. Dr. Hall didn't want to do a mastectomy. He felt that it was throwing away good tissue. "I can take off half your breast where that little tumor was removed," he said. "I'm really surprised to see this pathology report. I was certain it wouldn't be malignant."

"Then tell me something, Dr. Hall. Why would I spend the rest of my life worrying about half a breast? What purpose would it serve, other than causing distress and running up medical bills testing it every year?" I asked.

After surgery a line of doctors made their way to my private hospital room. Two oncologists, two surgeons, and two internists begged me to take chemotherapy. I refused. "You are strong, Mary. You can do it. Don't take a chance on losing your life," they pleaded. I was sick with another post-op infection. After five days, I begged to be discharged. I threatened to leave against medical advice. I went home.

When I had the first cancer, Eli had insisted that I see a specialist at the university. The specialist remembered me after more than eleven years. "Who told you that you needed to have more chemo? I want every one of their names, because I taught most of the oncologists. I will give them a piece of my mind. It isn't chemo you need. A preventative oral medication for the next five years will be enough. You will be fine, Mrs. Michael. You don't have any breast cancer or breasts to worry about. Take care of yourself. Stay well," she advised. I went home to live another day and enjoy my precious grandchildren. How many gifts, how many chances did one person get in life?

≋21≋

Still Looking for Jimmy

Mirror, mirror on the wall,
The face I see is not mine at all.
Whose face is it on the wall, if it is not your face at all?
It is not the one that it should be, the one that looks back at
     me.
This old woman that I see has come to stay for all eternity.

I STILL DON'T SEE my own face in the mirror. I see many faces; sometimes it's Carmella or Antonia, and sometimes it's Mama's face. The ugly child is gone. I can't match my face to the ones in pictures. This no longer frightens me. After all I've been through, fear is the real enemy. Fear can make or break a life. You can live with it but never without it.

Ask anyone if they want to trade their life and their problems for someone else's. The answer will almost always be the same. No one wants the troubles of another. How many chances do we get in life to make things right? The answer is as many as it takes.

I had a chance to learn how life had treated my childhood friends. When an invitation came in the mail for my high school class reunion, I almost didn't go. I was talked into it by a man I didn't remember knowing. He is a religious man with a kind heart. His kindness to me was worth the trip back in time. Some people hadn't changed in looks or behavior; others changed a great deal. Danny Manning thought I was Antonia. I had to explain that she had died. He had no memory of me. A couple was standing near me. I overheard the woman say, "Honey, show me someone you had a crush on when you were in school." The man walked up to me and took my hand.

"Here she is, right here!" he said. We had been together in those slow-to-learn classes. He was on the afternoon shift at the Ford plant. He told me that he retired. He and his lovely wife were moving south to live out their golden years. "The Ford Motor Company has been good to me," he said with a big smile.

Rodney hadn't changed since high school. He was very popular then. I don't think he said a word to me in school. He talked to me as if we were old friends! I sat with him at dinner; we talked about our families and how life had treated us. Some of those jock guys snickered as I walked by. Even after fifty years, they hadn't changed.

The bonds of friendship in childhood could be strong and lasting, no matter what paths we followed. One of the boys who was very popular in school was saying how hard it had been in our class for him and for others who were gay. I hadn't known that anyone like him had a hard time. I think I surprised them. "Well, I had no idea any of you more popular people were treated as outsiders," I said, looking around the table. "I don't believe in any type of discrimination. I didn't know anyone in our class who was gay. If I had, it wouldn't have mattered then or now."

Waldo came to the reunion. He still lived on the family farm with his wife. He hadn't changed. I think it was a very good thing. He was still so down to earth. Nothing was more important to him than family and the farm.

Graham Wilson didn't attend the reunion, and he faded into obscurity. Betty Sue refused to make eye contact with me. Grace Cain must have had plastic surgery done. I didn't recognize her. I said hello when she called me by name, but I just couldn't place her. She had divorced Eddie many years ago; then he died in a drowning accident.

Big Margaret wasn't at the reunion. I would have enjoyed talking to her. We had a lot in common. We both had loved Lucy Cavetti, had become nurses, and had two daughters.

Sarah and Nathan Miller still lived in New Moon. They had two grown sons and a few grandchildren. Since our families go way back, we enjoyed talking about our mothers and old times in Miss Wilhelm's classes. Some of my classmates wanted to know if I still sang Patsy Cline songs. "The only place I sing now is in the church choir," I told them. "It is one of the best things I do. I even sing for weddings and funerals." Singing for the Lord is a great healer.

After the reunion, I spoke to Janet Ray by phone. It was the first time we had talked in more than fifty years. I wanted her to know that I was writing about her and Bobby Ray in my memoirs. She's still married and very much in love with her high school sweetheart. They have two grown sons. She wrote songs and even tried to make it in Nashville. She's happy to be living in Henderson. Bobby Ray (his name was Bobby Ray Ray) is still married to Lila Peace, and they raised four children. I was pleased to hear that good things happened to good people.

When the conversation turned to Garrison, she had a lot to say. "You introduced us, Janet, remember?" I asked. She said she was sorry for it and sorry that I never remarried. "You need not be sorry. Garrison Michael was the love of my life, although he betrayed me and never kept his wedding vows. Marrying him was a lapse in judgment on my part. I was older and should have known he couldn't commit." I have two beautiful human beings from that relationship. I could never say that marrying him was a mistake.

In the end Garrison has gotten just what he wanted. He married a woman who worships him and will stay with him. If he is unfaithful, she won't leave him. If he is aloof and uncaring, she will stay. Carol gives him unconditional love. She is a good provider and has never left him on his own. She has cared for him as if he had special needs. She worked from home and dropped whatever she was doing to go with him everywhere. She will do anything he asks. Garrison was cared for by women all his life. He knew no other way to be but forever the youngest child, never leading, but always ready to follow. He will be with her forever, as long as he is the center of her world.

Over the years I made many attempts to renew my friendship with Lucy. Many years have passed since we were last in touch. I used to visit Gladys when she was living on the farm. A few years ago, I found another family living there. The man told me that he'd bought the place from Gladys. Her son, whose name he couldn't recall, handled the sale. He didn't know where she was living. She always kept me up to date with Lucy's life. Lucy and Big Randy lived all over the world because of his job. They had a full and exciting life together. The last time I saw Lucy was at Howie's funeral. It was after my first bout with cancer. We promised to get together and talk of old times, but it never happened. I tried unsuccessful Internet searches many times. My memories of her were happy ones. I hoped to see my friend again someday. I wanted to relive those innocent times we shared.

I went to Henderson for a birthday party for my great-grand-nephew. I have many grand-relations in Henderson and New Moon. I am invited to many gatherings and introduced as the grand matri-arch of the family. "Do you have a phone book you can spare?" I asked my niece. "I want to look up old friends." Looking through that book was like a walk down Old Sherman Acres Road! Among its pages I found many friends.

Gladys Cavetti still had the same phone number! When I called it, I discovered that she was hard of hearing and much too senile to talk on the phone. I asked about Lucy, and her answer was very strange. "Oh, I never see her anymore," she replied.

"Well, I'll come and visit you soon," I said before hanging up.

At the earliest opportunity, I went to Henderson to find Gladys.

I was sure she would remember me once we were face-to-face. I assumed that a woman in her nineties would be at home with her caregiver on a Sunday afternoon, so I didn't try calling. It wasn't easy finding her new home. So many different subdivisions were all over the area. I rang the bell, but no one was home. I returned to my car, hoping to find a number for Rocky or Mariano. There was none. As I ran my finger down the page, my eyes landed on a listing for Gavin Cavetti. I knew that he was one of Lucy's nephews. I called and got his voicemail. I left a message with my name and phone number, stating that I was trying to locate Lucy.

A soft breeze was blowing as I watched the sun set from my balcony. It was a perfect evening. I dreamed of the early days at Strawberry Fields Farm. I must have drifted off into a light sleep, and the phone rang. I knew that masculine voice belonged to Gavin Cavetti. "Mrs. Michael, my name is Gavin Cavetti. I am returning your call," he said politely. "I wish I could help you in your quest, but I'm afraid I cannot. You see, my aunt Lucy lost her battle with breast cancer two years ago." I was stunned. I made my apologies for having bothered him and offered my condolences. I inquired after his grandmother's health. I was informed that she was indeed quite senile and ill.

For many days after that call, I walked around in shock and disbelief. Why had I survived breast cancer twice, when Lucy had succumbed to it? She was younger, happier, and much stronger than I was. Why did she die and I live? I just had to pray and trust in God. He would reveal all in His own way. "Be prepared, for we know not the hour or reason we are called." The passage ran through my brain for days. Did she suffer? Did she know she was dying? Was Big Randy with her and their children? I wanted answers. Alice was much closer to her than I was over the last forty years, so I called her. I was amazed that she knew me right away. She told me that Lucy had known she was dying. She suffered a long, painful illness and death. Randy, her son, and her daughter were with her through it. "Did you know she wrote beautiful poems about life? She shared them with me. She made me promise not to publish them. I hope you will come and see me. I would like for us to read them together." It was out of fear of cancer and loss, and my inability to deal with my grief, that I didn't go. We e-mailed back and forth for a while. There were messages about Gladys and her health, news of Rocky and Mariano. Part of surviving is choosing only to remember Lucy happy and dancing in the sunlight. Someday I will sit with Alice and read Lucy's writings, but not just yet.

Mary Jean Tewlain lived out her destiny as her brother predicted. She went away to university and met and married the son of a Wall Street banker. She had two children and lived happily ever after in a world that was meant for her.

Unlike Lucy, Jimmy Tewlain was very easy to find. I entered his name and Henderson County into Google search. His address and the very same phone number he had when we were kids appeared. It's longer now, like all numbers these days, but the last four digits are still the same. True to his word and to the wonderful, honest person he always was, Jimmy still lives in the woods with his beautiful wife, Guinevere, and his kind and thoughtful mother, June. Jimmy got everything in life he wanted and deserved. His wife, who gave him unconditional love, has stayed in the woods with him since the day they wed.

I finally know what the author meant when he said, "You can't go home again." Longing not for my past but for the friends I had left behind, I traveled to Henderson County again. I visited all the places in my memory. Seeing it with adult eyes is quite different. The house at Strawberry Fields still stands, but it looks empty, stark, and lonely. The fields no longer contain the beautiful, fragrant strawberry rows that once brought fame to the Rosario family and my pa, the

Strawberry King. I closed my eyes. I took a deep breath. I caught a fleeting whiff of the blossoms that haunt my dreams. When I opened my eyes, it was gone. I looked around and saw old, dead grass on the hills.

Traveling north on Sherman Acres Road, I couldn't resist going to the woods. I didn't want to see Jimmy or interfere in his life. The cabin is gone, but the path is still there. I drove around the corner. The large black gates with the big golden *T* on each wing are gone. I went down the long driveway, stunned at how many trees were lost. The thin woods isn't the quiet, cool sanctuary I remember. The golden stone house isn't the grand home of my memories. I guess in its day it must have been so. The barn is gone, and in place of the meadow there's a large pond; the fence around it is no longer white. I felt like an intruder as I turned my big car around in the drive and slowly left. No one was about the place. I saw Jimmy's old Jaguar parked in the three-car garage. I knew in my heart it would be there. In my mind he's still that beautiful, sentimental boy. He is frozen in time in my memory, where I will keep him.

The Stayton pond is a dark, muddy hole in the middle of those woods. I felt pain deep in my heart as I stood by the water. No little pier remains. I walked to the meadow and sat under the big oak tree. "Where did the magic go?" I asked aloud, hearing no answer. Then the answer came to my lips from deep in my heart. I know that the magic of this place was in us and in the love we had for one another. All those times were magic, because we made them so. We were in paradise. Jimmy knew it. I couldn't see it then, but I saw it clearly with old eyes. It made me smile, inside and out. I'm a woman alone, growing old and weak with the passing of time. But I'm stronger in ways I've never known. It is ironic that the tiny dream girl with the big breasts doesn't exist anymore, and it makes me happy. She's been replaced by a wiser, older woman, humble and grateful for a life well lived.

Remarrying was never for me. I knew I would marry the same man again. It's strange—things you once dearly loved about another

never really die, no matter what happens to the two of you. I can still hear Garrison's beautiful voice in my head. I see him sitting by the fire in the house on Sunny Side Avenue, quietly reading a book as his long fingers turn the pages. I see him look up at me and keep looking. "Why do you look at me?" I asked.

"I'm just looking," replied that striking, tall, dark man of my dreams. I saw the man in him, not the boy. I always knew it wasn't Garrison I looked for in all those other men, too numerous to recall. I wasn't looking for a husband or for love. It was always Jimmy I wanted back in my life. It was really Jimmy I missed. He was the real man in my life. I made a choice those many years ago. As badly as I needed his unconditional love, I left it on the dance floor at Henderson High that night in 1963. I was blinded by my own view of life and what I wanted from it. It wasn't *happily ever after* that I wanted. What I prize most is my freedom, my own personal freedom—my right to choose. I didn't know it would come at such a high price. I was selfish and wanted my dreams. I hated compromise. In my mind it was defeat, and I couldn't admit defeat. I never could have loved Jimmy the way he loved me. The right to choose is my true love. I have paid dearly for it and my freedom, which has made me very happy.

The worst things in my life were never the obvious ones— two bouts with cancer, the two babies I lost, diabetes, and strokes. Although the failure of my marriage devastated me, I survived it. The loss of my family members is painful, but I know I will see them again. The two worst things in the entire world to me are ignorance and poverty. Somehow this poor, ignorant farm girl, the daughter of immigrant parents, left home and made it in the big city. I became what I always wanted to become. I didn't do it alone. I'm grateful to all those people in my life who helped me. Ignorance and poverty breed more of the same. It takes having the right tools in your toolbox to make it in the world. Integrity, honesty, perseverance, and a strong

will are just a few of those important tools. The poor, the disenfran-
chised, and those without a good guide in life never get the chance to
put enough tools in their box, but I got that chance. Hope is the most
vital tool. I've heard it said that hope is the best of things. I think
hope is everything; without it, I would have nothing.

A Note from the Author

THE NAMES AND PLACES in this memoir are made up. The stories, events, and times are true. I hope you have enjoyed hearing about them as I have enjoyed the emotional roller-coaster ride taken to write them.

I want to thank my family and friends for always standing by my side through this process. I couldn't have done it without your support and love. Thank you, Mrs. Alice Hopper, for all your help on this project. I could not have done this without you. Thank you, Debrah Williams, for your words of constant encouragement. My best friend, Toni Anderson, lived through the writing of this book with me. I'm so grateful to her for all her help.

Thank you, Judy Armstrong Brown, for your friendship all these years. Thanks for the memories.

Please feel free to comment and tell me your story. You can reach me by e-mail at maryemgibson@gmail.com. I can also be found on Facebook and Twitter. I'm looking forward to hearing from you.

CPSIA information can be obtained at www.ICGtesting.com
Printed in the USA
BVOW05s0311090115

382553BV00012B/425/P